FIRST EDITION

Remembering the Old Dominion

Readings on Virginia History

EDITED BY MATTHEW WHITLOCK

OLD DOMINION UNIVERSITY

cognella® ACADEMIC PUBLISHING

Bassim Hamadeh, CEO and Publisher

Kassie Graves, Director of Acquisitions

Jamie Giganti, Senior Managing Editor

Jess Estrella, Senior Graphic Designer

Mieka Portier, Acquisitions Editor

Sean Adams, Project Editor

Luiz Ferriera, Licensing Coordinator/Specialist

Cover image copyright © 2015 iStockphoto LP/zrfphoto.

Printed in the United States of America

ISBN: 978-1-5165-0689-7 (pbk) / 978-1-5165-0690-3 (br)

CONTENTS

Acknowledgments

T he creation of this important collection of Virginia texts would not be possible without the larger audience interested in Virginia and its relationship to American history. The editor wishes to acknowledge the following individuals and groups for their help in making this collection: Sean Adams, Mieka Portier, and the entire group from Cognella Publishing for being a great group of people to work with for this publication, my wife Hayley for allowing the long evenings of research, the history faculty at Old Dominion University and the University of Alabama who influenced my interest in Virginia history, my parents who always (and still) support me in everything I do, the authors in this volume for their excellent academic work, and each student who attended my class each week, visited during office hours, and emailed me at 2:00 am with that burning question about someone or something in history for their final exam. I propose holding off on the emails until at least 3:00 am.

Ronald Heinemann, John G. Kolp, Anthony S. Parent Jr., and William G. Shade. "Before Virginia." In *Old Dominion, New Commonwealth: A History of Virginia, 1607–2007*. 1–17. Charlottesville: University of Virginia Press, 2007.

Brent Tarter. "For the Glory of God and the Good of the Plantation." In *The Grandees of Government: The Origins and Persistence of Undemocratic Politics in Virginia*. 10–32. Charlottesville: University of Virginia Press, 2013.

April Lee Hatfield. "English Atlantic Networks and Religion in Virginia" In *Atlantic Virginia: Intercolonial Relations in the Seventeenth Century.* 110–136. Philadelphia: University of Pennsylvania Press, 2004.

John R. Maass. "'We Wage War Like Gentlemen': Two Battles and the Path to Yorktown." In *The Road to Yorktown: Jefferson, Lafayette and the British Invasion of Virginia.* 131–147. Charleston: The History Press, 2015.

Kevin T. Barksdale. "Our Rebellious Neighbors: Virginia's Border Counties during Pennsylvania's Whiskey Rebellion." *The Virginia Magazine of History and Biography* 111, no. 1 (2003). 5–32.

Anthony E. Kaye. "Neighborhoods and Nat Turner: The Making of a Slave Rebel and the Unmaking of a Slave Rebellion." *Journal of the Early Republic* 27, no. 4 (Winter 2007). 705–720.

Virgil Carrington Jones. "Libby Prison Break." *Civil War History* 4 no.2 (June 1958). 93–104.

James L. McDonough. "John Schofield as Military Director of Reconstruction in Virginia." *Civil War History* 15, no. 3 (Sept. 1969). 237–256.

Robert H. Gudmestad. "Baseball, the Lost Cause, and the New South in Richmond, Virginia, 1883-1890." *The Virginia Magazine of History and Biography* 106, no. 3 (Summer 1998). 267–300.

Sara Hunter Graham. "Woman Suffrage in Virginia: The Equal Suffrage League and Pressure-Group Politics, 1909–1920." *The Virginia Magazine of History and Biography* 101, no. 2 (April 1993). 227–250.

Charles W. Johnson. "V is for Virginia: The Commonwealth Goes to War." *The Virginia Magazine of History and Biography* 100, no.3 (July 1992). 365–398.

Matthew Mace Barbee. "Civil Rights and Memory, 1948-1970." In *Race and Masculinity in Southern Memory: History of Richmond, Virginia's Monument Avenue, 1948–1996.* 41–71. Lantham: Lexington Books, 2014.

Introduction

I t is human nature to acknowledge certain people, places, or events in history based on popular stories, engaging conversations, historical sites, or even a good book. While some history becomes fantasized or altered to alleviate some of the negative connotations, history is in fact relevant in everyday life. Virginia provides an excellent example of living history. No matter where you travel within our state, it is inevitable that something historical is lurking around every corner. Civil and Revolutionary War battlefields are plentiful while one of the earliest European settlements, Jamestown and one of the earlier capitals, Williamsburg are within a twenty-minute car ride of each other.

Do you remember the first time you visited a museum or historical site? Your parents might have proposed it for educational purposes or for their pleasure. Perhaps your school system forced you to attend. Maybe you attempted to come up with an illness but nothing worked. In the Tidewater region of Virginia, most fourth grade students travel to Jamestown to experience the establishment of England's first permanent settlement in North America. As students step off of the bus, their first thought is "bathroom!" Once the restroom break ends, students venture into the Native American village, British fort, and replicas of the *Susan Constant*, *Godspeed*, and *Discovery* along the James River. By the end of their trip, students leave happy and realize that history is not the worst thing in the world.

Prior to European colonization at Jamestown, French, Spanish, and British explorers ventured along the eastern seaboard of North America and the Gulf of Mexico. Unbeknownst to many of them, Natives inhabited the coastlines in numerous tribes. The area of focus at the beginning of this collection is the Outer Banks of North Carolina, a chain of barrier islands that separate the Atlantic from mainland North Carolina. Presently known as one of the best family beaches on the east coast, the Outer Banks caters to millions of tourists each year. The sun, sand, and surf beckon families to the beach daily and they return to their quaint cottages in the late afternoon and evening. While this seems pleasant to many, European explorers looked upon this land like they would a desert island in the 1500s. In the first chapter titled "The New World," a group of historians examine the landscape and culture of pre-European Virginia. Their research then leads to present-day North Carolina, where Spanish, French, and finally British explorers searched for fame, fortune, and a westward passage to the Pacific Ocean. The Spanish explored the area twice while the French explored only once. Fast forward to the 1580s and Sir Walter Raleigh sends three expeditions to the Outer Banks. After what he believes to be a successful endeavor with the return of the first expedition, Raleigh names the region "Virginia" to honor the virgin queen Elizabeth. The third expedition remains a mystery as the colonists vanished from their location. Archaeologists and historians are currently researching possible areas that may soon explain what happened to the "Lost Colony."

In 1607, 104 men settled at Jamestown with minimal knowledge of colonization. The first leaders utilized the colony as an enterprise rather than a settlement and nearly crippled everything within the first year. The rise of Captain John Smith as the leader in 1608 spared the colony from utter destruction but things would rapidly change in 1609 with the starving time. July 30, 1619 was the inaugural meeting of the first assembly at Jamestown and the proceedings and procedures were in place shortly after their initial meetings. Brent Tarter's first chapter "For the Glory of God and the God of the Plantation" in *The Grandees of Government* fixates on the early settlers' mandates for a healthy colony. The management of the early colony and a representative government was crucial to its survival.

As Jamestown and the surrounding colonies flourished in the mid-seventeenth century, the Virginia Company and Crown established trade networks through the use of an Anglican parish system. April Lee Hatfield's chapter "English Atlantic Networks and Religion in Virginia" in *Atlantic Virginia: Intercolonial Relations in the Seventeenth Century* analyzes the influence of Puritans and Quakers on Virginia's growing tobacco economy. Puritans provided a large number of settlers to the Tidewater and Eastern Shore regions early in Virginia's history. While some Puritans migrated from Virginia to the New England colonies, they maintained their shipping patterns and religious structure. Quakers also followed a similar pattern as the Puritans, establishing shipping routes along the Atlantic while expanding their communities. These religious and economic policies continued throughout Virginia and the other colonies until the beginning of the American Revolution.

Virginians played a pivotal role in the American Revolution. Most Virginians acknowledge the Battle of Yorktown as one of the final decisive victories for George Washington and the Continental Army. John R. Maass assesses France's Marquis de Lafayette and his military tactics on and off the battlefield against Britain's knowledgeable General Charles Cornwallis in June and July of 1781, approximately three months prior to the Battle of Yorktown. In *The Road to Yorktown: Jefferson, Lafayette and the British Invasion of Virginia*, Maass provides the movements of Lafayette and Cornwallis from the skirmish at Spencer's Ordinary in Williamsburg through the Battle of Green Spring near Jamestown. By October, Lafayette and Washington's armies squared off in Yorktown against Cornwallis' British and German armies. With the aid of the French fleet, Cornwallis surrendered within days but the Revolution continued until 1783.

The establishment of the Constitution generated a myriad of issues within each state. Alexander Hamilton's 1791 proposal of an excise tax on whiskey would disrupt Western Virginia's way of life. Pennsylvanians bordering Virginia reacted to the new tax with an insurrection, known as the Whiskey Rebellion. Although the insurrection remained within the state's borders, Kevin T. Barksdale suggests that the Virginia's border counties felt the effects of the tax and insurrection. Barksdale focuses on the counties of Ohio, Harrison, and Monongalia and their relationship to Pennsylvania post-Revolution in "Our Rebellious Neighbors: Virginia's Border Counties during Pennsylvania's Whiskey Rebellion." Both Pennsylvanians and Western Virginians struggled to ascertain the requirements imposed by the tax, leading to the Whiskey Rebellion in 1794.

Nat Turner was born into a Southampton County slave family in 1800. Turner grew up like many slaves in the area but he had the rare ability as a slave to read. Approximately thirty years later, Nat Turner led a group of runaway slaves in an uprising, moving from plantation to plantation. Regarded as one of the largest slave rebellions in American history, Nat Turner's Rebellion altered state laws throughout the South. While many historians look at *The Confessions of Nat Turner: The Leader of the Late Insurrection in Southampton County, Virginia*, Anthony Kaye approaches the history through the use of neighborhoods. The closest neighbor could be over one mile away but there existed a common connection between slaves at each plantation. As the visible figurehead to many slaves in Southampton County, Nat Turner established a bond within the neighborhoods, leading to the uprising. The aftermath of the rebellion rang through Southern states and invoked fear throughout each community.

Rather than approaching the Civil War with the typical summary of five years, I decided to focus on a unique event during the War: the Libby Prison Break. Many Confederate and Union prisons during the Civil War were overcrowded with deplorable living conditions. At Libby Prison in Richmond, Confederates housed Union army officers, many of which died due to malnutrition or disease. In 1864, Colonel Thomas Ellwood Rose of the Seventy-seventh Pennsylvania Volunteer Infantry resolved to escape from the prison. The story illustrated by Virgil Carrington Jones in "Libby Prison Break" details the daring escape of Union officers and their near-misses with Confederate officers while digging tunnels within feet of the surface. What happened to Rose and company? Did they escape? Keep reading!

Reconstruction was cruel to Virginians as the state struggled to gain recognition by the Union after the Civil War. Congress enacted a Reconstruction Bill in 1867 that forced all states but Tennessee to select military district commanders to delegate military law within their respective states. The First Military District in Virginia fell to John M. Schofield. Unlike other districts in the South, Schofield displayed some kindness towards Virginians by preserving peace and reviving voting rights to all men. As James L. McDonough explains in "John Schofield as Military Director of Reconstruction in Virginia," the best method of resolving issues within the South during Reconstruction was moderation.

The end of Reconstruction and the beginning of the 1880s marked a unique time in Virginia's history. Many former Confederates lamented the past but searched for something better in the future. In Richmond, the Virginia Base-Ball Association consisted of numerous former Confederate soldiers with the Civil War fresh on their minds. Robert H. Gudmestad posited the Virginia Base-Ball Association served as a tension reliever in the city due to the popularity of the new sport. How much did these games cost? Twenty-five cents! The Association failed to calculate the costs of running a professional sporting team and the cost per ticket required for a profit. To alleviate the problem, the Association created promotional games, brought in "big name" baseball teams, and finally joined a baseball league. The Association constructed a stadium to allow more fans to watch each game and increase revenue. The profit played a pivotal role in the structure of the Association, but Gudmestad's article "Baseball, the Lost Cause, and the New South" continually discusses the importance of Confederate veterans keeping the memory of the Civil War alive.

With numerous laws established following Reconstruction, voting rights remained out of reach for women. Out of forty-five states in 1920, only nine refused to acknowledge suffrage for women including Virginia. Sara Hunter Graham discusses the role of the Equal Suffrage League of Virginia in "Woman Suffrage in Virginia: The Equal Suffrage League and Pressure-Group Politics, 1909–1920." Established in 1909, the League initially struggled to maintain interest in suffrage within the state. The League reached out to the community but met opposition from antisuffrage leagues within and outside of the state. Utilizing methods from national suffrage organizations, the Equal Suffrage League's membership increased into the tens of thousands by 1920, proving the acceptance of the organization within the state.

Virginians started to worry about world powers by the 1930s with the rise of Adolf Hitler in Germany. The state dispatched a minimal amount of Virginians to Europe during World War I. At the onset of World War II, Virginians were hesitant to fight another global war. Military installations throughout the state were modified or reassigned, such as Langley Field in Hampton changing from a blimp station to a Submarine Warfare Wing. Charles Johnson analyzes the significance of Virginians and their role during World War II in "V for Virginia: The Commonwealth Goes to War." The state created the Virginia Protective Force to defend the state and the shoreline. Military installations boomed with soldiers and sailors while shipyards constructed battleships and aircraft carriers in record time. Virginians pitched in wherever necessary to help America win the war.

The civil rights movement ramped up in Virginia following the war through the 1970s. White elitists attempted to retain control of all political aspects of the state through legal and often illegal means. The creation of associations and councils led to a larger influx of franchising and voter registration. Matthew Mace Barbee addresses the significance of voter registration and the rise of African American organizations that demanded more rights for a segregated state. Unfortunately deep rooted hatred and the memory of the Civil War, including the one-hundredth anniversary of its end caused a larger struggle than expected at times in his chapter, "Civil Rights and Memory, 1948–1970." Finally in 1978 the African American community gained more political power than before within the state and in 1989, L. Douglas Wilder accepted the position as state governor.

The purpose of this collection is to create an interdisciplinary approach at understanding numerous variables within Virginia's history. The selected book chapters and essays are a culmination of recommendations from colleagues, emails from students who enjoyed reading required materials from my Virginia history courses, and a few personal favorites. The following eleven chapters focus on experiences Virginia and its inhabitants faced throughout the state's over-four hundred year timespan and its impacts on American history.

1

Before Virgina

By Ronald Heinemann, John G. Kolp, Anthony S. Parent Jr.,
and William G. Shade

O n the morning of 26 April 1607, three small ships carrying 143 Englishmen arrived off the Virginia coast of North America, having spent four months at sea. The men had come to advance the interests of England in its quest for New World wealth against other European competitors. They intended to build a colonial outpost— a military fort and a commercial trading post—like those that Spain and France had tried to establish along the southeastern coast of North America. These Englishmen had heard tales of the ill-fated Roanoke settlement two decades earlier and knew they would encounter native peoples, but they were confident that their superior English culture and technology would easily win the day over the "heathen savages." All hoped for financial success and perhaps a little adventure; as it turned out, their tiny settlement eventually would evolve from colony into a prominent state in an entirely new nation.

The region they colonized featured a variety of land forms, from coastal plain, to rolling hills, to valleys and mountains. Millions of years before, a massive meteor convulsed the Atlantic coastal plain below the Appalachian Mountains near where the Englishmen first made landfall, creating the largest impact crater in what is now the United States. During the last glacial period, beginning about 18,000 years ago, the ice melt running down the mountains began mixing with the rising seawater below, slowly filling the crater and swelling it into a great bay. As the temperatures warmed, a 3,000-year melt (11,000–8,000 BCE) elevated the water level, submerging sixty miles of coastline and filling in not only the bay but also the river channels. The coastal basin became a giant estuary, the largest on the continent. The freshwater running down from the mountains, which had formed millions of years before the bay, mingled with the saltwater, forming tidal estuaries that widened with the glacial thaw. The Algonquian speakers called this tidal motion *rappahannock*, and one of the four great rivers in Virginia still carries this name. It and the Potomac, the York, and the James all drain into the bay in a parallel southeasterly direction, creating peninsulas or "necks." Waterfalls and rapids punctuate these rivers at the fall line, separating Tidewater from Piedmont. The soils of the alluvial floodplain are sandy and silt loam, but clay and gravel are found along the streams. From the wet Tidewater soils grow huckleberries, cranberries, and chinquapins. Poplars, pines, cedars, and cypresses rise together with sweet gums, hollies, sweet myrtles, and live oaks.

In the Piedmont above the fall line, where the land rises gently upward to the mountain ridges, the soils are more diverse, ranging from rich black loam to a reddish-brown mixture of dirt and clay. A canopy of deciduous trees graces the Piedmont where twenty species of oaks reign. In their shadows sycamores, silver maples, box elders, and green ashes tussle with black and sweet gums and hickory and beech trees. In their shade wild strawberries and blueberries blossom and bear fruit.

To the west lie the mountain chains of the Appalachians: the Blue Ridge and the Alleghenies divided by the Great Valley of Virginia, which runs northeast to southwest for 360 miles. Its limestone-based soils are among the most fertile in the state. Running northward down the upper half of the Valley is the Shenandoah River, its name an Indian word for "beautiful daughter of the stars." Rivers on the far side of the Alleghenies run westward to the Ohio and Tennessee River basins. The mountain slopes are covered with deciduous and evergreen trees, whose hydrocarbon emissions give the ridges their distinctive blue haze. Throughout Virginia the climate is temperate, ranging from the cooler mountain elevations to the warmer, more humid areas of the Tidewater, with an average rainfall of forty inches a year.

Paleo-Indians entered the region about 12,000 years ago as hunters, fishers, and foragers. With the great melt creating new coastal estuaries and new sources of food, these seminomads of the Archaic Period migrated to the marshlands near the Dismal Swamp. Knowing where to set their weirs in the streams and rivers, the Indians caught herring, striped bass, and sturgeon. They continued to hunt white-tailed deer, as former game like elk and caribou migrated northward in search of a colder climate. About 4,500 years ago as the estuaries began to table off, mixtures of salt and fresh water combined with sea grasses to produce reefs where fish and shellfish became abundant. These reefs became ideal incubators for oysters, which the Indians began harvesting along with clams and mussels. The aboriginal Algonquians called the bay *k'tchisipik* (Chesapeake), the "great shellfish bay."

The Virginia Algonquians of the Early Woodland Period, beginning about 5,000 years ago, comfortably exploited this ecosystem for food and freshwater, which was essential when living alongside the brackish estuaries. Like their ancestors, they were hunters, foragers, and fishers, who knew the best sources and seasons for procuring food. They tracked smaller animals than their ancestors had—beavers, possums, rabbits, raccoons, and squirrels—and trapped turtles and snakes and shot migrating turkeys and ducks with bow and arrow. They harvested shellfish and fished creeks, streams, and rivers for catfish, gar, golden shiner, yellow bullhead, and pumpkinseed.

Unlike their ancestors, they eventually became farmers about a millennium ago by cultivating wild grains, amaranth, gourds, and sunflowers. By 900 CE or so, they had applied their experience with domesticating wild plants to the cultivation of corn, beans, squash, and tobacco. The seed corn apparently came from Mexico, providing convincing evidence of long-distance contact with other aboriginals. By the Late Woodland Period (900–1500 CE), the Virginia Algonquians had founded towns on the alluvial soil of the Tidewater. Because corn depletes the soil of nitrogen, they periodically shifted their farms up or down Virginia's major rivers. After 1400 they increased their supply of oysters, roasting and drying them for later use, adding one more ingredient to their relatively stable subsistence economy.

Indian cultures also developed in the mountains and valleys of western Virginia. The Mississippian people migrated to Virginia from the Tennessee River area around 700 CE, while Ohio Valley groups migrated up the New River. From about 950 CE until the European settlers arrived, a group known as the Earthen Mound Burial Culture lived in the Shenandoah Valley and the northern Piedmont region of Virginia. Their mounds were sacred places where they buried their ancestors. The English may have encountered two tribes that were members of this culture: the Mannahoacs, near the upper Rappahannock River, and the Monacans at the falls of the James River, both of whom spoke a Siouan language, rather than the Iroquoian languages of the Indians living south of the James River or the Algonquian languages of the coastal tribes. By the time the settlers moved into the Piedmont and the Shenandoah Valley, disease had severely reduced the population of these inland tribes.

The need for farmers, foragers, and hunters led to both seasonal and gendered divisions of labor. The Virginia Algonquians divided their year into five seasons: *popanow* (winter), *cattapeuk* (early spring), *cohattayonough* (late spring), *nepinough* (summer), and *taquitock* (fall). During the cold months of popanow, men hunted migrating fowl and women gathered dry reeds and fibrous plants for matting used for building houses. During the spring months of cattapeuk and cohattayonough, men set their traps and weirs for spawning fish. Women gathered sapling and bark suitable for mat making. As men went off to hunt after the spring harvest and during taquitock, the time of the falling leaf, women foraged. Women also took on the responsibility for the crops on fields that men had cleared with slash-and-burn techniques. Women cultivated the corn, harvesting green corn, the year's first crop, during cohattayonough and mature maize during nepinough. Because the corn required a four-month growing season with adequate rainfall, drought brought dire consequences for their main dietary staple.

To supplement the corn crop during these uncertain times, women foraged for tuckahoes, starchy edible tubers, in freshwater marshes during the cattapeuk and cohattayonough seasons. During the late fall taquitock season, the men hunted white-tailed deer, which women dressed. All prized its venison, both fresh and dried, for sustenance, its hide for clothing, and its bones for tools. Indians used their environment; they did not abuse it, knowing that their survival as well as their relationships with nature depended upon its preservation.

The Virginia Algonquians occupied 6,000 square miles of coastal plain that they called Tsenacommacah. Their land was bounded by the bay in the east, the fall line in the west, the Potomac River in the north, and the James River basin in the south. Hemmed in by the Appalachian Mountains and by Siouan and Iroquoian enemies and without access to a major artery feeding into the Mississippi or the St. Lawrence River valleys, the Virginia Algonquians began to develop an insular, cohesive culture. This culture can be discerned in religious beliefs, pottery styles, political organization, marriage patterns, burial rites, and housing and palisade construction.

The Virginia Algonquians believed in *mantoac*, a cosmology of deities with a diversity of powers over a sacred universe. Priests engaged in divination, appealing to animistic powers for protection in a natural world fraught with danger. Their propitiations to these deities were ritualized in ceremonies devoted to the harvest, the hunt, and war. At powwows they entreated rain deities to favor farmers, forest deities to shield hunters from harm, and river deities to protect travelers. Warriors girded themselves for battle amid chants for victory. Priests aided in judicial procedures, determining truth by reading minds. They also prophesied important events and conjured up natural phenomena to deal with invaders. Only priests and chiefs could enter temples, which were mortuaries for the relics of chiefs, caches of treasures, armories for weapons, and stores of healing herbs. The holiest site in Tsenacommacah was the temple at Uttamussak on the Pamunkey River.

If men could serve as priests, assuming the mantle of spiritual power, women celebrated material culture by crafting ceramics. During the Late Woodland Period, women artisans shaped, coiled, and decorated pots tempered by shells that they used for everyday household chores. After 1550, however, a shift in ceramic styles suggests a growing cultural and economic integration of the entire Chesapeake region. While pottery glazed with crushed quartz or tempered sand now became the norm, innovators in specific locations developed at least three distinct styles that can be identified by archaeologists today: Potomac Creek, Gaston-Cashie, and Roanoke.

Pottery trade and marriages between Indian groups in the region added to the cultural exchanges and helped cement diplomatic and political alliances that became critical to the development of a large coalition on the eve of English colonization. It was not the presence of European explorers or depopulation from European disease that influenced the move toward consolidation. The Virginia Algonquians combined into a paramount chiefdom—the Powhatans—after 1570 in response to the threats posed by Siouans in the west and Iroquoians in the north. The Massawomecks, an Iroquoian-speaking people, raided Algonquian villages along the Potomac River in their swift birch canoes. Iroquoian Susquehannocks harassed Algonquians living on the northern banks of the Potomac. Siouan Monacans and Mannahoacs regularly raided Algonquian villages in the summer or fall for wives and slaves.

To ward off these hostile attacks, the Powhatans constructed and fortified towns. Using stone hatchets, they shaped and set poles to build palisades, which were closely latticed with branches and small saplings to shield dwellers from both visibility and arrows. The strategic location of these towns, overlooking the river networks for trading and defensive purposes, gives evidence of the consolidation into chiefdoms. Most towns accommodated fewer than one hundred people; but larger sites included Powhatan near the James River falls, Patawomeck near the bend in the Potomac River, and Werowocomoco on the York River.

Powhatan consolidation was also designed to control trade routes that would bring them high-status goods. From their home bases at the fall line of the James River, they guarded traffic on rivers and roads and controlled the copper, puccoon, and shell trades within Tsenacommacah. Indicative of high status, copper was esteemed by Virginia Algonquians. They treasured the reddish-colored metal imported from the Great Lakes and the Appalachians through Siouan-speaking Mannahoacs and Monacans to the west or the Iroquoian-speaking Tuscaroras to the southeast. Monacans had been the chief suppliers of copper to the Powhatans; but when relations soured between them, the Powhatans turned to the Tuscaroras for copper. Jewelers fashioned tubular beads and flat sheets of copper into necklaces, pendants, bracelets, chokers, earrings, and chimes or "tinklers."

Virginia Algonquians also esteemed the mulberry-colored dyes extracted from the puccoon root. They imported puccoon from the Iroquoian-speaking Nottoways and Tuscaroras to the south. The chiefs' wives ceremonially painted their necks and faces with puccoon dye, vaunting their elevated position in society. Women provided to very important visitors readied themselves for their assignations with the reddish dye.

Mollusks were also important trade goods, serving Algonquian society not only as a food source but also as ornaments and currency. Powhatans valued the freshwater pearls harvested in the James River at Weyanoke Point and exchanged *rawranoke* (roanoke) shells as money. Harvesters dredged seacoasts for the tubular conch shells and white and dark blue disks of hard clams, prizing the rarer blue. Artisans crafted these shells into pendants, necklaces, and burial masks. Regular, uninterrupted access to copper, puccoon, and mollusks remained an important impetus for political confederation.

The development of the paramount chiefdom was the key political development in the Late Woodland Period. A kinship-based society, Algonquian groups organized themselves into chiefdoms governed by a *weroance* (male) or by a *weroansqua* (female) under the umbrella of the paramount chief or *mamanatowic*. In a matrilineal society where descent is passed down on the mother's side of the family, Powhatan women enjoyed higher status than did their counterparts in English society. Men were, however, allowed more than one wife. The weroances were assisted in their governance by a council of elders. Each weroance in turn pledged loyalty and offered counsel to the mamanatowic. Contrary to the usual tributary order, the mamanatowic gave gifts to the weroances for their allegiance. But the weroances and mamanatowic also received tribute from their subjects in the form of foodstuffs, skins, and luxury goods and held these in common storehouses for use by their own families and for religious ceremonies and other communal activities.

Wahunsonacock, born about 1540, inherited three districts on the James River and three districts on the Pamunkey River. Becoming the mamanatowic about 1572, he took the name Powhatan from his ancestral home near present-day Richmond on the James River. By the time the English arrived in 1607, he had expanded his hegemony to include thirty districts covering 6,000 square miles and 14,000 of the 20,000 Algonquian speakers in the eastern Tidewater. Only the Chickahominies to the south and the Patawomecks to the north managed to maintain their autonomy. The Chickahominies shielded the Powhatans from the Monacans, their traditional enemy; and the Patawomecks buffered Tsenacommacah from the Iroquoian-speaking Susquehannocks. The Patawomecks also controlled an antimony mine which produced a widely traded silver-white substance used like puccoon as decorative body and facial paint that the Powhatans highly valued. (See map on p. 9.)

The Chesapeakes, who inhabited what are now Virginia Beach and the Elizabeth River sites of Norfolk and Portsmouth, were the last to fall to Powhatan expansion. Covetous of the coastal shell trade, Wahunsonacock or Powhatan pressed them to join the paramount chiefdom; but they refused, causing bad feeling between the two groups. Although Algonquian, they were more closely related to the Roanokes in North Carolina than to the Powhatans. Indeed, in an effort to shore up their defense in the face of the Powhatan menace, the Roanokes may have loaned them the remnants of the "Lost Colony." Enmity intensified with a prophecy that Powhatan received from the oracles of Uttamussak that a nation from the Chesapeake Bay would emerge and destroy the Powhatan paramount chiefdom. Partly because of this prophecy and partly because of their economic significance, Powhatan destroyed the Chesapeakes early in 1607, perhaps terminating the last link to the Roanoke colony. Meanwhile, the English had arrived in the Chesapeake Bay, fulfilling the prophetic warning.

Years before the English arrived, the Spanish had claimed the Chesapeake Bay as part of a large North American territory they called La Florida. Their claim was recognized by the papal bulls issued by Pope Alexander VI from 1493 to 1495 and the Treaty of Tordesillas with Portugal. Lucas Vasquez de Ayllón, a Spanish administrator in Santo Domingo, first fired European enthusiasm about the Chesapeake Bay with his tales of the "Land of Chicora," a vision of a Mediterranean-like climate similar to Andalucia in southern Spain where grapes and olives could be fruitfully grown. Ayllón also promoted Chicora as the location of a Pacific passage to the China trade. Bolstering his claim, he ventured that the Indians there could easily be subjected by the Spaniards and could supply them with gems and pearls.

Searching for a new Andalucia and a westward passage to the Pacific, Ayllón sent expeditions under the command of Pedro de Quejo to the Chesapeake Bay in 1521 and again in 1525.

Quejo explored the Outer Banks, the barrier islands that run from southern Virginia to North Carolina. He found neither the westward passage to China nor Chicora. Instead, he determined that the barrier islands' sandy soil and the absence of an exploitable Indian population made the area unsuitable for colonization. From the Outer Banks, Quejo explored the southernmost inlet of the Chesapeake Bay, arriving there on 2 July, the feast day of Mary, the mother of Jesus. For this reason he called his sighting the Bahía de Santa Maria. After the last Ayllón voyage in 1526, Spain ignored the Chesapeake for a generation, realizing that both Chicora and a western passage were myths. During the 1540s and 1550s Spain regarded the Outer Banks and its environs as a desert island, not a new Andalucia.

The Spaniards' indifference did not dampen French desires for American colonies. Giovanni da Verrazano, a Florentine, sponsored by King Francis I of France, voyaged in 1523–24 toward the Chesapeake Bay. Looking across the Outer Banks at the Albemarle and Pamlico sounds, he presumed this body of water to be a passage to the Pacific. Promoting his discovery as a western passage, he christened the land Francesca after King Francis. However, France instead chose to explore a northwest passage, encouraged by reports from cod fishermen in the North Atlantic of a great river on the continent there. In 1534 Francis I sponsored Jacques Cartier's voyage to the St. Lawrence River.

For the remainder of the century, the two European powers continued to sail into the South Atlantic region, largely to keep an eye on possible colonization by the other. Small garrisons were established in the Florida and South Carolina areas. To counter a French outpost, the Spanish established St. Au gustine in 1565, the first permanent European settlement in the future United States. When their activity attracted the interest of England, the Spanish renewed efforts to colonize their northern frontier. After hearing the description of Tsenacommacah from two Powhatans picked up by an expedition which had taken refuge from a storm in the Chesapeake Bay in 1561, they believed that this colonization could best be accomplished from the Bahía de Santa Maria. One of the Indians, Paquiquineo, was renamed Don Luis de Velasco, after the viceroy of Mexico.

Lucas Vasquez de Ayllón the younger and Pedro Menéndez de Avilés now planned expeditions to the Chesapeake. Ayllón revived interest in his father's Chicora, but his failure to satisfy his investors ended in his disgrace. Menéndez was more successful. Encouraged by what he learned of the Chesapeake Bay from the Indian informants, Menéndez requested that Don Luis and his companion accompany his expedition. After one unsuccessful attempt, a disappointed Don Luis returned to Seville where he was schooled by the Jesuits. In return for his education, he promised to aid them in establishing a mission in Virginia.

With support from Menéndez for another expedition, the missionaries arrived at Bahía de Santa María on 10 September 1570, disembarking along the James River not far from the later Jamestown site. From there they crossed the peninsula to where Kings Creek feeds the York River. Don Luis and other Indians assisted them in building their base camp, which came to be called Ajacán. However, the Jesuit-trained Algonquian soon abandoned his Christian colleagues and returned to his people. By January 1571 the mission, reduced to privation, sought assistance from Don Luis and the Powhatans, but their request resulted in martyrdom; he had the entire group massacred except for one boy, who was spared by the local weroance. The grisly failure of the mission led Spain to abandon the Chesapeake, leaving an opening for the English.

England's penetration of the New World had been delayed by internal disputes high-lighted by Henry VIII's breach with the Catholic Church in Rome and the religious strife under his children, Edward VI and Mary I. The ascendancy of Elizabeth I to the throne in 1558 brought relative calm to the realm, but the growing animosity toward Spain encouraged English interests in a variety of maritime activities. Added to this was a certain envy of the successful and expanding long-distance trade of Holland. Finally, new social and economic pressures caused by a booming rural population and the agricultural enclosure movement that forced migration to crowded cities demanded release. Excited by the stories of discovery, the English looked westward.

Those promoting English exploration and settlement of North America had to convince investors and the queen that these expeditions would return a profit and redound to the glory of England. They emphasized the gold and silver that had made Spain into a world power. They pointed to lessons learned from European exploration literature and experiences in Ireland about how to colonize indigenous peoples and establish trading centers and networks. They painted Spanish political, military, and religious activity in the New World in the worst possible light and offered, instead, a positive alternative of English civility and Protestant Christianity: an English empire.

But for the lure of precious metals, these were precisely the arguments advanced by the Hakluyt cousins. The elder Richard Hakluyt, a lawyer resident at London's Middle Temple, encouraged the English to abandon the model of Roman conquest employed in Ireland; he wrote in 1578 that successful colonization could be achieved with peaceful overtures to the Indians. The colonists should treat them humanely and convert them; then they could count them as dutiful subjects. When confronted with a plurality of Indians in the same place, care-fully crafted alliances should be made.

Richard Hakluyt the younger received not only his name from his guardian cousin but also his passion for English colonization. He advocated a systematic approach to naviga-tion, exploration, and settlement. Trained as a minister, Hakluyt promoted Christianity as the primary motive for colonization. He pointed to the abuses in Spanish colonization and projected the English as American liberators who would offer civility and true religion to benighted Indians. Once converted, they would become cooperative, and settlement, trade, and an enduring peace would follow suit. If they resisted, they would be conquered. Hakluyt accepted Allyón's Chicora myth of a new Andalucia: the middle latitudes of North America could provide olive oil, wine, silks, and other semitropical products such as rice and sugar that England now procured from Spain. He recognized America's potential as a refuge for the English poor, a post for attacking Spanish shipping, and a supplier of raw materials. Hakluyt's major work, *The Principal Navigations, Voyages, Traffiques, and Discoveries of the English Nation*

(1589), chronicled English activity abroad, introducing the English public to the recent expeditions of Frobisher, Gilbert, and Ralegh.

Searching for a northwest passage, Martin Frobisher's Cathay Company made three voyages from 1576 to 1578. His first voyage established a colony at Baffin Bay in the first English effort at American colonization. He encountered Inuits and kidnapped a family of three who died shortly after arrival in England. He was convinced that a successful settlement could be sustained by gold mining, but when the local ore proved to be fool's gold, the settlement collapsed.

Like Frobisher, Sir Humphrey Gilbert looked for a passage to China, but he also sought a place suitable for a farming settlement where Eng-land's poor could be suitably employed for their own good and that of the nation. Yet his violent experience in the Irish war of the 1560s tempered his perspective on colonization. As a military man he understood that the logistics in America differed from those in Ireland. The long-distance supply lines and the numerical superiority of the Indians made peaceful overtures to the natives a prudent strategy. Although he received royal patent rights in 1578 to discover lands, his personal efforts came to nothing when he was lost at sea in 1583 on a return voyage from North America.

Walter Ralegh inherited his half brother Gilbert's patent to explore and exploit the North American coast. One of the most notable of the Elizabethans, Ralegh was a Renaissance man with interests in politics, the arts, history, and adventure, who was to die on the chopping block for suspected treason. But he is best remembered for his association with the Lost Colony. Sensitive to the loss of Gilbert, Queen Elizabeth denied Ralegh permission to command the expedition. Instead, Ralegh sent Philip Amadas and Arthur Barlowe to the Outer Banks of the North Carolina coast in 1584.

The Indians encountered on Roanoke Island were the Carolina Algonquians, who, like the Virginia Algonquians, hunted, fished, and foraged under the authority of weroances while living in farming towns along the riverbanks. They grew corn, beans, squash, and tobacco and celebrated both corn and tobacco in their festivals. At first, relations between the Roanokes and the explorers were cordial. Led by Granganimeo, brother of Roanoke weroance Wingina, the Roanokes welcomed the English, perhaps seeing them as useful allies against sporadic Spanish encroachment. As a sign of friendship, two Indians, Manteo of Croatoan and Wanchese of Roanoke, returned to England with the expedition.

Ralegh's delight in the success of the voyage prompted him to name the new land Virginia after his "virgin queen"; Elizabeth returned the favor by granting him a knighthood. With knowledge gained from the 1584 reconnaissance, Ralegh planned a Virginia colony based upon his experiences in Ireland. Believing that the entry to the Chesapeake Bay lay along the Outer Banks, he began to promote English claims to the region north of 36° and the possibility of a westward passage there. Ralegh selected Richard Grenville to command the expedition and Ralph Lane to govern the settlement. Principal among the explorers were the mathematician Thomas Hariot and the painter John White, both of whom may have been on the first voyage. What we know of the people and the land can be found in White's "Map of Virginia" (1585) and Hariot's *A Brief and True Report of the New Found Land of Virginia* (1588). Elizabeth endorsed the second voyage not only in spirit but materially as well, loaning Ralegh her ship *Tiger*, which along with six other ships set sail 9 April 1585 with 600 passengers. One-half were soldiers and sailors, most with military experience in Ireland or the Netherlands. Their efforts were hamstrung at their arrival when the *Tiger* wrecked on the shoals and nearly sank, ruining most of the colonists' food supply.

In early July, Grenville established the Roanoke colony at the north end of the island near Wingina's town; however, it soon became apparent that this would not be a good site for a future port because of shallow waters. Grenville soon departed for England, leaving Lane and 107 men to live off the munificence of the Indians. They built a palisade to serve as a refuge for settlers in case of attack from sea and to secure livestock at night. They began brick making but dug no wells, relying instead on rainfall or assistance from the natives in locating freshwater. The English also made no preparations for their subsistence and continually made demands on the Roanokes to supply them with corn. Under normal conditions the Indians might have complied, but their surpluses were limited because the area was experiencing one of the worst droughts in nearly 800 years. Despite their growing dependency on the Roanokes, Lane and his colleagues treated them as inferiors, not equals, and overreacted when an English silver cup disappeared. Finding the home village of the alleged thieves abandoned, the English retaliated by burning another village and spoiling their corn. This was not the approach to indigenous peoples that Gilbert and others had recommended, but it fit well with the experiences and attitudes of men like Ralegh.

In search of a better harbor with deeper water, Lane sent out scouting expeditions that ventured into the Pamlico and Albemarle sounds and the Chesapeake Bay. Lane personally explored the Chowan and Roanoke rivers. Amadas, Hariot, and White reached the Chesapeake Bay and wintered in what is now Norfolk. Their survey of the bay was covered up on their return to England, so as not to alert the French or Spanish, whose interest in the region was renewed by fears of the English establishing a base for piracy. The New World had become a potential battleground in Spain's quest for European domination.

Initially, the Carolina Algonquians viewed the newcomers as an especially powerful foreign tribe who could bring good or evil to their society. The English possessed large supplies of precious copper that might be obtained through friendly trading. And the strange men from across the sea had ships and weapons that might be useful against the Roanokes' traditional enemies. But the Algonquians also had no immunity from European diseases; and within days of Englishmen visiting their towns, the Indians began dying at a very high rate. Indians and English both believed that the power of the English god had been demonstrated in this mysterious killing of people without weapons. Making death and supplying copper demonstrated the power of the English mantoac. But if the Roanokes were at first awestruck by the English presence, they quickly became disenchanted with the newcomers, put off by their demands for gold and corn and by their heavy-handed tactics in the reaction to the stolen chalice.

When the friendly Granganimeo died, Wingina changed his name to Pemisapan, meaning "one who watches over his people," signaling a change of attitude toward the English. Now believing that death and drought were brought on by the English presence, Pemisapan decided to separate his Roanoke people from them. Using the wealth generated from his control of the copper trade, Pemisapan began making allies to drive out the English, but in a skirmish he was killed and beheaded. Shortly afterward, ships of Sir Francis Drake, who had been raiding Spanish ships and harbors, arrived at Roanoke. Seeing the plight of the settlement, Drake provided provisions and offered passage home, an offer that Governor Lane and the demoralized colonists readily accepted.

Ralegh's third expedition in 1587 differed from the earlier ventures in that this group included ninety-four colonists organized in fourteen families. It had the goal of establishing a colony separate from Roanoke in the Chesapeake Bay, an area the new governor, John White, had reconnoitered two years earlier. The vessels left London in March and arrived at Roanoke in July 1587 where the Spanish captain refused to go any farther. What they found disheartened them. The fort erected by Lane had been abandoned and was in disrepair. The fifteen soldiers left to safeguard it were not to be found, save for a single skeleton found on the settlement grounds. If the skeleton served as a bad omen, the birth of the first English child born in America, on 18 August 1587, augured a fortuitous outcome for this new venture. White's grandchild was christened Virginia Dare, her name expressing the hope that a colony of that name would become a reality. Manteo's Croatoans warily offered friendship but cautioned the English that they had no corn to supply them, at which point White returned to England to lobby for further support. War with Spain, however, deterred any immediate efforts at resupply; and White did not return until 1590, only to discover a deserted settlement and the word "Croatoan" carved into a tree.

SOURCES CONSULTED

Philip Curtin, Grace S. Brush, and George W. Fisher, eds. *Discovering the Chesapeake: History of an Ecosystem* (2001); Keith Egloff and Deborah Woodward, *First People: The Early Indians of Virginia* (1992); Frederic Gleach, *Powhatan's World and Colonial Virginia* (1997); Paul Hoff man, *A New Andalucia and a Way to the Orient: The American Southeast during the Sixteenth Century* (1990); Hoff man, *Spain and the Roanoke Voyages* (1987); James Horn, *A Land as God Made It: Jamestown and the Birth of America* (2005); Harry Kelsey, *Sir Francis Drake, the Queen's Pirate* (1998); Karen Ordahl Kupperman, *Roanoke: The Abandoned Colony* (1984); Eugene Lyon, *The Enterprise of Florida: Pedro Menéndez de Avilés and the Spanish Conquest of 1565–1568* (1979); Peter Mancall, ed., *Envisioning America: English Plans for the Colonization of North America, 1580–1640* (1995); Debra Meyers and Melanie Perreault, eds., *Colonial Chesapeake: New Perspectives* (2005); Lee Miller, *Roanoke: Solving the Mystery of England's Lost Colony* (2000); Michael Oberg, *Dominion and Civility: English Im-perialism and Native*

America, 1585–1685 (1999); David B. Quinn, *North America from the Earliest Discovery to First Settlements: The Norse Voyages to 1612* (1977); Helen C.

Rountree, *Pocahontas, Powhatan, Opechancanough: Three Indian Lives Changed by Jamestown* (2005); Rountree, *Powhatan Foreign Relations, 1500–1722* (1993); Rountree, *The Powhatan Indians of Virginia: Their Traditional Culture* (1989); Helen C. Rountree and E. Randolph Turner, *Before and after Jamestown: Virginia's Powhatans and Their Predecessors* (2002); Camilla Townsend, *Pocahontas and the Powhatan Dilemma* (2004); Peter H. Wood, Gregory A. Waselkov, and M. Thomas Hatley, eds., *Powhatan's Mantle: Indians in the Colonial Southeast* (1989).

2

For the Glory of God and the Good of the Plantation

By Brent Tarter

This late nineteenth-century etching by Margaret M. Taylor (courtesy of the Library of Virginia) for Historic Churches of America: Their Romance and Their History *(Philadelphia, ca. 1891–94) depicts the ruin of the church at Jamestown. In a smaller church that once stood near the site of the 1640 tower, the first General Assembly of Virginia met from 30 July through*

Brent Tarter, "For the Glory of God and the Good of the Plantation," *The Grandees of Government: The Origins and Persistence of Undemocratic Politics in Virginia*, pp. 10-32. Copyright © 2013 by University of Virginia Press. Reprinted with permission.

4 August 1619. Nearly two centuries after James-town ceased to be the capital of Virginia, portions of the town site reverted to a state not unlike what the first settlers encountered in 1607. The lasting importance of what took place in Jamestown during the seventeenth century made the island a popular tourist destination and, as the title of the illustrated volumes for which the image was produced suggests, generated romanticized interpretations of the past, to which this image in turn contributed. The reality of what the members of the first assembly did is fundamentally important for understanding Virginia's history and political culture.

T he church and the storehouse in Jamestown were the most substantial buildings that the English settlers erected during their first years in Virginia. From the beginning they served both God and Mammon. On Friday, 30 July 1619, something new and important happened in the church. The governor, the members of his advisory council, the treasurer, the secretary of the colony, and twenty-two other men gathered there to make some regulations for the better management of the colony. They acted under an authorization of the Virginia Company of Lon-don, which had just received from the king the new Charter of 1618, soon to be known as the Great Charter, in part because of what began in the church that day. It was the little colony's second change of administration. The dysfunctional council of 1607, of which Captain John Smith had once been president, gave way in 1610 to a military government that imposed order on the English outpost. By the time King James I granted the Great Charter, the English-speaking residents of Virginia had made themselves more or less self-sufficient. They had imported cattle and swine, planted grain, and made good use of the fruits and the game and fish that the land and water provided in abundance after fresh rains resumed and ended a long and severe drought midway through the military regime. In 1619 they began again.[1]

That the colony had survived the first dreadful years was almost miraculous. Virtually everything that could have gone wrong in the beginning had gone wrong. Drought had reduced the Indians' harvest on which the first settlers planned to rely, and the men of 1607, following the company's instructions, carefully selected a particularly poor site for settlement in a time of drought, although they did not know that one of the worst dry spells in all of Virginia's history had just begun. By drinking water from the river or from the well that they dug a few paces from the riverbank, they may have contracted an enervating low-grade salt poisoning. Jamestown was also adjacent to a marsh that exhaled a foul-smelling breath, but it was not the marsh gases, it was the malaria that the marsh's mosquitoes carried that made people sick or die. The resident Indians were sometimes helpful, sometimes harmful. Until Captain John Smith took charge in 1608, the colony's leaders had squabbled among themselves and the enterprise looked doomed, but he took command and ordered that men who did not work would not eat. After Smith left in 1609, the people hid themselves in the little fort at Jamestown and during the following winter, which soon was called the starving time, died miserably of disease and hunger, reduced to eating rats and snakes, even the corpses of other men and women.

During the first years of military government, the acting governor, Sir Thomas Dale, made Captain John Smith look like a softie. Dale enforced to the letter the brutal Laws Divine, Moral, and Martial. He executed men who blasphemed, shirked their responsibilities, or refused to obey. When a man stole food from the common stock, Dale had him tied to a tree and left him there to starve to death in plain sight, for the encouragement of the others, as the French would later say. But Dale made the colony succeed. He ordered men to plant grain, raided Indian towns for food, destroyed other Indian towns, erected palisades to protect the little settlements, and created a new town upriver on a high, easily defended bluff. He called it Henricus after the king's son. Dale also allowed men to farm small tracts of land for themselves rather than work communally on company land. By the time he returned to England in the spring of 1616, having been in charge for more than half of the colony's short history, the future prospects for Virginia had begun to look bright. He took with him one of the first large crops of Virginia tobacco and also its grower, John Rolfe, and also Rolfe's wife, Rebecca, or Pocahontas, or Matoaka.

On the same ship with Dale, the Rolfes, and the tobacco was an Indian man, Uttamatomakkin, or Tomocomo. He was a principal adviser of Wahunsenacawh, also known as Powhatan, the paramount chief who thirty or forty years earlier had assembled an affiliation of Indian tribes into the most impressive alliance on the mid-Atlantic coast. His chiefdom, called Tsenacomoco, covered the same part of the earth as the English company's colony, called Virginia, and he was worried. During his long life he had seen Spaniards and Englishmen come into the great bay of Chesapeake in their ships and then leave. Some tarried a few days or weeks, but they all soon left except one group of Spanish Jesuits who in 1570 established a mission on the banks of the York River, but the Indians wiped it out a few months later. The English who arrived in 1607 showed signs of staying, but they did a poor job of surviving until after the drought broke and Dale brought over cattle, hogs, and heavily armed soldiers in 1611. By 1616 they had remained far longer than any other Europeans, and Wahunsenacawh sent Uttamatomakkin to England and directed him to count the men and the trees there in order to learn how many more Englishmen might come and whether they merely came for trees to build more of their ships. It is not certain whether Wahunsenacawh, who died in 1618, ever received a report of Uttamatomakkin's observations. In fact, so numerous were the men and trees in England that he gave up trying to count them; the stick on which he notched his tally was too short. If Wahunsenacawh did not learn, he probably suspected that the population of England and its technological resources were so superior to those of his people that the future prospects for Tsenacomoco no longer looked bright.

By the summer of 1619 the English settlers numbered several hundred and lived in four little towns and worked on several company-owned farms, called particular plantations or hundreds, along the James River. They had erected a large church building in Jamestown, probably the only European-style building in the colony large enough that all of the members of the assembly could meet in one room without having to shift casks of tobacco, supplies, and trade goods out of the way. The settlement on the island had been "reduced into a hansome forme, and hath in it two faire rowes of howses, all of framed Timber, two stories, and an upper Garret, or Corne loft high, besides three large, and substantial Storehowses, joined togeather in length some hundred and twenty foot, and in breadth forty." Adjacent to the original town site were "some very pleasant, and beutiful howses," two blockhouses, "and certain other farme howses."[2]

Governor Sir George Yeardley, the council members, Treasurer Edwin Sandys, Secretary John Pory, and the other men who assembled in the church in Jamestown on that 30 July 1619 had all, so far as can be determined, arrived in Virginia after the starving time winter of 1609–10. The colony that the Virginia Company had planted in the New World was a mere twelve years old, but it was already by far the longest-lasting English settlement in the Western Hemisphere.

Beginning that Friday in July 1619, those men completed the formation of a new local government. They still operated under the general superintendence of the governing council— the board of directors, as it were—of the Virginia Company back in London, and they still functioned within limits that the king's charter imposed on them; but the new charter empowered a governor and a Council of State to govern the colony, and the governor's instructions authorized him to summon a second council, called the General Assembly, to make the laws. What they did and how they did it influenced the whole future of Virginia's history and the history of the United States. The political history and culture of both began with what the company's officers and employees did that day in the church in Jamestown.

When the men met in the church that morning, it was probably not the first time that day that they had been to the church. From the very first landing of English-speaking people in Virginia, the company's instructions had required all of the settlers to attend the morning and evening services of the Church of England and the two services and sermons on Sundays. It is likely that many or most of the men summoned to meet as a General Assembly had probably attended the morning service that day and watched and listened as Richard Bucke, the minister, read from his copies of the Bible and the Book of Common Prayer. Precisely which words he read and the men and women assembled in the church heard is unclear. The Latin, Greek, and Hebrew texts had been translated by then into several English-language editions of the Bible, each with subtle and sometimes significant differences in tone and meaning. Bucke probably had a copy of what was called the Geneva Bible, which was likely the English version most widely used at the beginning of the seventeenth century and the edition that the church's reformers, known as Puritans, preferred. The Virginia Company's shareholders and officers included many Puritans, and several of the colony's early clergymen, including Bucke, were sympathetic to the Puritans. Bucke might possibly have had a copy of the new translation of the Bible, the one that King James had commissioned not long before he issued the first charter to the Virginia Company in 1606 and that was published in 1611, not long after Bucke first stepped ashore in Virginia and walked among the starving men in Jamestown.

Directions printed in Bucke's copy of the Book of Common Prayer required that he read the service and the words of Scripture distinctly and with a loud voice that the people might hear, that none by virtue of being unlettered remain ignorant of the word of God. The words that he read would have been familiar to the people in the church. The services of the church were so arranged that the same significant texts were read aloud once each year and the psalms once in every month, "that the people (by daily hearing of holy scripture read in the Churche)," according to the explanatory preface in the 1559 Elizabethan Book of Common Prayer, "shoulde continually profite more and more in the knowledge of God, & be the more enflamed with the love of his true religion."[3]

If Bucke conducted the full morning service for the thirtieth of July, the first of the three psalms for the day was Psalm 144, which began, in the words of the Geneva Bible, "Blessed *be* the Lord my strength, wc teacheth mine hands to fight, & my fingers to battel. *He is* my goodness & my fortres, my tower & my deliverer, my shield, and in him I trust, which subdueth my people under me."[4] Those words may have carried a special significance that morning to the men who gathered in the church in that little town on the bank of a great river on the edge of a vast continent that contained no more than a few hundred Protestant Christians. They needed all the earthly help and divine aid that they could get. The psalm concluded with the prayer "That our corners *may* be ful, and abunding with divers sortes, *and* that our shepe may bring forthe thousands, and tens thousands in our stretes: That our oxen may be strong to labour: that their be none invasion, nor going out, nor no crying in our stretes. Blessed *are* the people, that be so, *yea*, blessed *are* the people, whose God is the Lord."

Those words of the psalmist must have resonated in the souls of the men in the church that day. They needed moral and spiritual support to make a reality of their dreams of peace, full storehouses, and plentiful flocks. One wonders what Richard Bucke thought about those words. He had been shipwrecked en route to Virginia in 1609 (in the storm that suggested to William Shakespeare the plot for the *Tempest*) and had been in the first ship to reach Jamestown in May 1610 at the end of the starving winter. His wife died. It is possible that he married a second time and that his second wife died, also. He named his children Mara (meaning bitter), Gershon (expulsion), Peleg (division), and Benoni (sorrow), and Benoni was feeble-minded.[5] Bucke's life in Virginia was hard, but that was one of his bonds with every other man and woman who entered the church then or any other day.

Bucke then read the two passages from Scripture prescribed for that day. From chapter 8 of the book of Jeremiah, he read about how the kings and people of Judah had sinned and ignored God's warnings and how as a consequence their bones were taken out of their tombs and spread "as dung upon the earth." In the third verse were the words of warning that would have made any one who recalled or knew about the starving time in Virginia shudder: "And death shalbe desired rather then life of all the residue that remaineth of this wicked familie, which remaine in all the places where I have scatred them, saith the Lord of hostes." Bucke then read from chapter 18 of the book of John about the arrest of Jesus in the garden, how Peter thrice denied him, how Jesus denied that he was a mere earthly king, and how Pilate prepared to hand Jesus over to the Jews for trial and execution.

The lessons that day, for both the lettered and the unlettered, reminded men and women of their duty to obey God and to avoid sin, to recognize Jesus as a greater king than an earthly king, and that even earthly kings were subject to the word of God through the words of Jesus. To the people in the church in Jamestown that day, the words in the psalm about subduing "my people under me" meant not only the unchristianized and possibly dangerous Indians, they also meant all of the men and women, all of the people who were free and those who were bonded by indenture to labor for other people or for the company. Except the king, every soul was under some other person's temporal and spiritual authority.

Later that morning Bucke met in the church with the governor, councilors, company officers, and other men when they assembled as the first General Assembly of Virginia. The report of the meeting records that "forasmuche as mens affaires doe little prosper where Gods service is neglected," Bucke offered a prayer "that it would please God to guide & sanctifie all our proceedings, to his owne glory, and the good of this plantation."[6] The assembly members conducted their secular business as if with God's eyes watching over their shoulders.

The eyes of the king and the officers of the Virginia Company were also looking over their shoulders. Perhaps, too, residents of the town peered in at the church windows or stood inside or sat on the benches in the church to watch and listen. The official report of the proceedings of that and the succeeding four days does not mention Jamestown's residents. The eyes of God, king, and company were doubtless of much more concern to the members of the assembly than the eyes and ears of the people. If the men and women who lived in Jamestown were watching and listening and not busy working in their tobacco or corn fields, tending their cattle, fishing in the river, cooking, or looking after children and supervising servants, they would have seen and heard that the men in the church acted in the combined contexts of obedience to God and to the king: proper service and obedience to either was proper service and obedience to the other.

The assembly first met sometime in the morning of Friday, 30 July 1619. The members resumed their work later in the day after dinner, and they met again all day on Saturday. The members did not meet on Sunday. They no doubt attended the morning and evening church services, but on that day one of the members, Walter Shelley, from Smith's Hundred, died,[7] and the weather probably being hot, they may have buried him that same day. On Monday and Tuesday the members again met for most of the day, but the weather was so very hot on Wednesday that they hastened to conclude their business that afternoon rather than continue one or more additional days as originally planned.

In several very important ways, but not in all, their proceedings resembled meetings of Parliament, even though the participants were not officers of a government in the modern sense but merely members and employees of the Virginia Company of London meeting to regulate the company's local business. The governor's instructions for convening the assembly are lost, but when the company appointed Sir Francis Wyatt governor in 1621, officials probably copied Yeardley's instructions for Wyatt's use as they did on several later occasions. Wyatt's required him to convene the assembly annually but no oftener unless an emergency arose. The company specified that burgesses from the principal settlements be "Chosen by the inhabitants" and their decisions in the assembly be made "by the greater part of the voyces then present, Reserveing alwaies to the Governor a negative voyce," or veto. The governor named Secretary John Pory to be Speaker and appointed a clerk to assist him. He also named a sergeant at arms, and Bucke acted as chaplain. The assembly's officers had the same titles as the officers of the House of Commons. The company's instructions to the governor required that the assembly's laws be consistent with England's laws, and the company reserved the right to disapprove them; but the instructions also required the assembly to approve new company policies before they went into effect in the colony.[8] Neither king nor Parliament had any role in the creation or enforcement of what the company's assembly called laws.

The similarities between the assembly's procedures and Parliament's were important, but so were the differences. In its structure the assembly more nearly resembled a royal court or a very early version of Parliament, with the monarch—in this instance, the governor—attended by his assistants and functionaries. All of the members met in unicameral consultation, including the governor, council members, and burgesses, and they not only considered laws and regulations for the colony, they also received and passed along or ruled on complaints, petitions, and charges of misbehavior, more like a medieval princely court than like a modern legislature. Pory had the title of Speaker, but the governor presided. Pory acted as secretary, organized the business of the five days, and prepared the copies of the "reporte of the manner of proceeding in the General assembly" for each of the jurisdictions represented in the assembly and for the officers of the Virginia Company of London.[9] The copy that he prepared for the company is the only one that survives and the only account of the proceedings.

Pory was a remarkable linguist and translator, a graduate and former tutor in Greek at Cambridge, and he was the only member of the assembly who had once been a member of the House of Commons. It is possible that he more than any other one person was responsible for the resemblances between the assembly's proceedings and those of Parliament.[10] Before the assembly members met, the governor, perhaps with the advice of the council members, Treasurer Sandys, and Secretary Pory, prepared an agenda, which Pory presented after Bucke said his prayer and the members were sworn and took their seats.

The preliminaries were important and deserve some attention. Pory's report did not indicate how the twenty-two burgesses from the towns, hundreds, and particular plantations were elected and who elected them. The governor's instructions stated that they were to be especially "Chosen by the inhabitants" but not how. Pory's report indicates only that the governor "having sente his summons all over the Country" for "the election of Burgesses," two men from each of the eleven settlements appeared in Jamestown.[11] The words *election* and *chosen* meant and mean essentially the same thing and did not imply the method of selection or indicate whether all inhabitants of each settlement participated in the selection or only adult men who were not in any way dependent on, or subservient to, anyone else. The idea that women or servants might participate in the selection of representatives probably would have been regarded in Virginia in 1619 as absurd, and in England only men who owned certain classes of property were permitted to vote for members of the House of Commons. The scant surviving documents do not indicate who chose the first Virginia burgesses. The assembly's own records and the regulations that it adopted routinely distinguished between commanders and masters and free men on the one hand and servants on the other, and the two were not equal in the eyes of the assemblymen. The word *burgess* back in England signified a free man entitled to exercise certain civic responsibilities in a city or borough; in Virginia the word may have been employed to signify a free man thought to be correspondingly respectable enough in his community for this new role in the management of the company's colony. Those twenty-two men were certainly responsible men in their towns or plantations, and the commanders no doubt approved their selection. Two of the men, Christopher Lawne and John Warde, were actually the commanders of their plantations.

After Bucke's prayer, Pory called the names of the twenty-two burgesses and administered to them the oath of supremacy, which required them to swear that the king was supreme over the pope. That should have exposed and disqualified any Catholics. Pory noted with satisfaction in his report, "(none staggering at it)."[12] When he reached the name of Captain John Warde, Pory stopped and explained that Warde had settled on Captain John Martin's portion of the company land without the company's permission and might therefore be regarded not as his own man representing his own plantation but as a mere "limb or member" of Martin's settlement. Pory put the question whether Warde and his fellow burgess, John Gibbes, as men in some ways dependent on Martin and in the same ways independent of the company, should be allowed to participate in the company's assembly. The two men withdrew. "After muche debate" and Warde's agreeing to seek the company's approbation for his plantation, the members voted to admit Warde and Gibbes, explaining that Warde had expended a great deal of his own money to establish his plantation and that he had imported a valuable cargo of fish. Moreover, as the commander of a plantation, Warde had received a summons from the governor, and therefore he and Gibbes were entitled to seats in the assembly.[13]

Governor Yeardley then interrupted and produced and read from a copy of the company's commission to John Martin, which allowed his plantation, Martin's Brandon, a unique exemption from obedience to the decisions of the assembly. The members voted to summon Martin and ask him to forgo that portion of his commission and on behalf of his settlement submit in advance to the regulations that the assembly adopted before they seated the two burgesses from Martin's Brandon. Otherwise, Pory wrote in his account of the decision about Martin's burgesses, "they wer utterly to be excluded, as being spies, rather than loyal Burgesses; because they had offered themselves to be assisting at the making of lawes, wch both themselves, and those whom they represented might chuse whether they would obey or not."[14] Martin appeared on Monday and refused to relinquish that privilege in his commission. The members of the assembly then refused to allow his two burgesses to take their seats,[15] so Martin's Brandon and its inhabitants were not represented in the first General Assembly of Virginia and did not participate in making its laws and were therefore not bound to obey them.

After voting on that first morning to ask Martin to relinquish that one privilege in his commission, the members of the assembly also heard a complaint about the behavior of some of the men of Martin's Brandon, which perhaps influenced the decision that they made on Monday about the burgesses. Some of Martin's employees (including Thomas Davis, one of the men selected as a burgess) had risked the fragile peace with the Indians by seizing a canoe and its corn after the Indians refused to sell the corn. Opechancanough (Wahunsenacawh's brother and successor as paramount chief) complained to the governor. Keeping the peace with the Indians was a matter of such importance to the whole colony that the governor presented the issue to the assembly. When, on Monday, Martin appeared before the assembly, he agreed that for the future he would pledge that when he sent his men into the bay to trade, he would guarantee the "good behaviour of his people towardes the Indians."[16]

Even before making any laws for the better management of the colony, the assembly members had made a rule and established a precedent, rooted in parliamentary law and practice, asserting their own exclusive right to judge who was qualified to take part in the assembly and requiring that those who took part and the people at the settlements they represented adhere to the decisions of its members. Regardless of whether commanders of towns and plantations allowed democratic means to select the members, the assembly in effect treated the individual burgesses as representatives in a modern sense, with the understanding that the commanders and residents of the towns and plantations would obey what their representatives agreed to as members of the assembly. That was the essence of, and the beginning of, representative government in Virginia.

The qualified members being sworn in, Pory read the company's commission and instructions for holding the assembly and then informed the members about the agenda, which he—or perhaps the governor—had divided into business of four kinds. The first was to examine the charter, laws, and privileges of the colony to ascertain whether the assembly should request the company's board to make modifications of provisions "not perfectly squaring wth the state of this Colony, or any lawe wch did presse or binde too harde ... especially because this great charter is to binde us and our heyers for ever." The second was to inquire into which provisions of the company's instructions to the governors since 1610 should be enacted into law in the colony. The third was to consist of all private matters that members might bring before the assembly, and the fourth was to determine what petitions on behalf of the colony the assembly should send to the company in England.[17]

Pory appointed two eight-member committees of burgesses to look into the first of the "bookes" of business and report back to the full assembly. Then after dinner the governor, councilors, and "Non Committies" took up consideration of the second of the four subjects and discussed it for three hours, until the two committees reported. It being late in the day by then, the assembly adjourned until the next morning.[18] The appointment of committees to investigate or consult and then report to the whole assembly was in imitation of recent innovations in the procedures of the House of Commons, another of Pory's important contributions to American parliamentary practice. Moreover, most of the recommendations from committees or from the floor were read out loud to the members for their assent at least twice, normally three times, also in imitation of parliamentary practice.

The orders that the assembly began adopting on Saturday contain much useful evidence for evaluating the condition of affairs in the colony; and just as important, they also indicate what subjects were most important to the men in charge.

The two committees brought in six requests, which the whole membership considered and adopted. The first subject in the sequence and perhaps the first in importance involved landownership. During the military regime the governors beginning with Dale had granted portions of land to men who had been in the colony since the early days—later records refer to them as ancient planters—but the assembly members were uncertain whether the company had fully authorized the governors to make those grants. The assembly requested the company to explain the land-granting authority with which it had invested the military governors. The members wanted assurances that the land "might not nowe, after so muche labour and coste, and so many yeares habitation be taken from them."[19] Private landowner-ship had only recently been introduced into Virginia, but it remained for centuries the single most important concern and after 1670 also the basis for participation in public affairs.

The second request to the company was in two parts, the first that it send out more men to work the land at the "fower Incorporations"—James City, Charles City, Kicoughtan, and Henricus—to provide better for the maintenance of members of the new Council of State, "who are nowe to their extream hinderance often drawen far from their private busines" to attend council meetings. The second part was that the company also send men to the four settlements as tenants for the ministers to cultivate "theire gleab to the intente that the allow-ance they have allotted them of 200£ a yeare may the more easily be raised."[20] The ministers' glebes were tracts of land with a house that the company provided for their residence and support. With proper tenants working the glebe lands, the ministers' salaries could be raised on the property set aside for that purpose. Glebes provided at public expense and taxes that parish vestries later levied on the inhabitants supported the ministers of the Church of England in Virginia, who were vitally important members of the community in many ways, for 157 more years. All of the expenses of the government and the church—each was a part of the other—were paid by the people whose lives were to be governed and whose souls were to be saved.

The assembly's third request of the company was that all men who had settled in Virginia "upon their owne chardges" since the departure of Dale in 1616—men like John Warde, presumably—should have equal shares of land with the men the company had sent out and supported. The assembly also requested that the company "alowe to the male children of them and of all others begotten in Virginia, being the onely hope of a Posterity, a single share a piece, and shares for their wives as for themselves; because that in a newe plantation it is not knowen, whether man or woman be the more necessary."[21] That recommendation indicates that the assembly members clearly intended that the settlement become a permanent colony, that it should be populated with families rather than with male soldiers and explorers, and that private landownership and the ability to acquire and bequeath land to descendants would be, as in England, the foundation of the society.

Company officers in London were beginning at that very time to consider measures to increase the number of women who could be enticed to settle in Virginia and convert the commercial and military outpost into an agricultural society. The company's officers stated part of the problem two years later: too many men in Virginia were "enflamed wth a desire to returne for England only through the wants of the Comforts of Marriage without wch God saw that Man could not live contentedlie noe not in Paradize." The men in the colony, "upon esteeminge Virginia, not as a place of habitation butt only of a short sojourninge: have applied themselves and their labours wholly to the raysinge of present profitt, and utterly neglected not onlie the Staple Commodities, but even the verie necessities of Mans liffe."[22]

The fourth petition was that the company send out a subtreasurer with authority to receive rent in the colony rather than in London and in kind rather than "to exacte mony of us (wherof we have none at all, as we have no minte) but the true value of the rente in comodity."[23] Among themselves in their private transactions, the settlers probably engaged in day-to-day exchanges of goods and foodstuffs by barter because money—coins—was in very short supply. At an early stage some of the merchants and other men in the colony began using account books that allowed them to make a permanent written record of who owed how much to whom and when and how it was paid so that honest business could be done when there was no money to change hands, rather as modern credit card accounts and electronic funds transfers allow business transactions without any actual money changing hands. In practice it was to be the merchants, commanders, planters, and ship captains who kept the account books, not the ordinary farmers and laborers; and until the mid-1640s account book entries were evidently treated in court as conclusive evidence of a debt, giving the keepers of account books a distinct advantage over all other people.[24]

It is also very likely that from the early days those accounts expressed the value of goods and services not only in English pounds or even Spanish coins, which circulated in the American colonies, but in pounds of tobacco. Tobacco, or notes promising payment in tobacco, or book accounts expressed in pounds of tobacco, became the currency of the Virginia economy and remained so for nearly two hundred years. That fact indicates how thoroughly the production of tobacco influenced the society throughout the colonial period. The colony's surviving archival records show that the colonial government, too, used pounds of tobacco to express the value of many things, to assess taxes, to set rates of payment, and to specify the value of land, slaves, ships, and other goods. In fact, one of the last things the first assembly did, on Wednesday, 4 August 1619, was to assess every person in the colony one pound of tobacco to compensate the Speaker, clerk, and sergeant at arms for their time and services.[25]

The fifth recommendation from the committees was that the company build the college that had been proposed for the colony and send over "workmen of all sortes fitt for that purpose."[26] The college intended for the inland settlement at Henricus was to provide education for both English and Indian children in the rudiments of Protestant Christianity and in reading, writing, and arithmetic, so that they could read their Bibles and perhaps even keep their own accounts. It remained a plan only, because the community at that place was almost completely wiped out in the spring of 1622 when Opechancanough launched coordinated raids on several of the outlying English settlements. That the company and its colonial residents planned an institution of the kind was another indication that they expected the colony to be permanent and to resemble England and also that they hoped to convert Indians to the Christianity of the Church of England. Colonists and English men and women largely abandoned that latter objective following the king's revocation of the company's charter in 1624, which left no organization with the authority or the ability to command and marshal resources for the conversion of the Indians of Virginia.

"The sixte and laste" of the committee recommendations that the assembly approved that Saturday was to request that the company "wilbe pleased to change the savage name of Kicowtan and to give that Incorporation a newe name."[27] That may not seem like nearly so important a recommendation to the company's English directors as the first five, but it is interesting and instructive, nonetheless. In the first place, it probably came from the elected burgesses, perhaps from one or both of the members from that town, William Capps and William Tucker. From the day back in the spring of 1607 when Captain Christopher Newport first entered Chesapeake Bay with three little ships, 104 men and boys, and plans to explore and settle North America, English-speaking men had been imposing English names on the landscape of Tsenacomoco—beginning by giving Cape Henry, Cape Charles, James City, and James River the names of the king and of his two sons—taking possession of the land in that subtle but significant manner. What the Indians thought about that act, if they knew about it or understood it, is not clear; but to English settlers far from home, giving English names to their new places in their new colony was no doubt a matter of importance. The council in England agreed to this request and later named Kicoughtan after the king's daughter, Elizabeth City. Within a few years maps of Virginia sported dozens of English names: York River, Elizabeth River, and Warwick River (and later a Warwick County) and counties named for English places including Northampton, Southampton, Isle of Wight, Norfolk, and many more.

Before concluding its business on Saturday, the assembly members adopted one of the orders that the governor and council members and the burgesses who were not on committee duty had prepared on Friday afternoon. It had its origin in the company's instructions to the governor. With the consent of Abraham Peirsey, the cape merchant who was in charge of the colony's stores and its trade, the assembly ordered that all tobacco planters sell their crops to the cape merchant for transportation to the company in England, the best quality of tobacco at a rate of three shillings per pound and inferior tobacco at half that rate, one shilling six pence.[28] All of the other items that the assembly had discussed on Friday afternoon were then referred to the two committees, which reported back on Monday.[29]

On Sunday the members of the assembly attended the morning and after-noon services in the church and perhaps attended the funeral of Walter Shelley, who had been a member of the first of the two committees. The seven surviving members of the first committee and the eight members of the second probably worked that day to present on Monday a draft of "lawes drawen out of the Instructions" to the colony's governors since 1610.[30]

"By this present generall Assembly be it enacted," Pory wrote in his report about Monday's work, "that no injury, or oppression be wrought by the Englishe against the Indians, wherby the present peace might be disturbed and antient quarrells might be revived."[31] Another law adopted later in the day specified how Indians working for colonists in "places well peopled" were to be treated, protected, housed, and guarded, "for generally (though some amongst many may proove good)," Pory explained in the official report, "they are a most trecherous people, and quickly gone when they have done a villany."[32] A law "for laying a surer foundation of the conversion of the Indians to Christian Religion" required each town and settlement to admit "a certaine number of the natives children" for education "in true religion and a civile course of life." A few of the most promising boys were to be taught "the firste Elements of litterature so to be fitted for the Colledge intended for them; that from thence they may be sente to that worke of conversion."[33]

In "detestation of Idlenes" the assembly directed that the commanders of towns and plantations have power to appoint a master for any person, even a free man, "founde to live as an Idler or runagate," the idler to work "til he shewe apparant signes of amendment" in his behavior.[34] It required people convicted of "gaming at dice & Cardes" to forfeit their winnings and fined all winners and losers ten shillings. Perhaps to encourage vigilance against the vice of gambling, but also in keeping with English laws at the time, the person who disclosed the gambling was entitled to receive ten shillings by way of reward.[35]

The law "Against drunkenes" discriminated according to the rank of the person. It empowered the minister quietly to reprove a "private person" for the first offense and publicly for a second offense, but for a third offense the person was to be sentenced to lie in irons for twelve hours in custody of the provost marshal and pay the fee that the provost marshal imposed, "and if he still continue in that vice, to undergo suche severe punishment, as the Governor and Counsell of Estate shall thinke fitt to be inflicted on him." A company officer, however, if convicted of drunkenness, would be reproved by the governor for a first offense, openly by the minister in church for a second offense, and for a third would be stripped of his office, although the governor retained the right to restore a man to office.[36]

Men who violated standards of proper apparel for their stations in life—standards that the assembly's law did not specify—were to be assessed a penalty in support of the church according to his station or "if he be married, according to his owne and his wives, or either of their apparell."[37] That simple but vague law, together with the gradations of punishment in the law against drunkenness, suggest two important things about the culture of Virginia in 1619 and the values of the men who made the laws. All men were not equal, and they were not to appear dressed in such a manner as to give a false appearance about their rank in the society. Everyone had a place in the society and a specific role to play, and as with modern military insignia, each person's rank and role should always be visible for the maintenance of order and discipline and for the preservation of the social structure. It is not clear how many visible gradations of social status there were between the governor at the top and the lowest serving girl or Indian laborer at the bottom, but the vague wording of the law indicates that there were several and that they were so well recognized that the assembly members did not think they needed to enumerate them.

The laws included several regulations designed to guard against food shortages and to promote agricultural diversification. One law required that every household have on hand for every inhabitant one spare barrel of corn.[38] (In seventeenth-century English the word *corn* meant any small grain such as wheat or oats or barley; when Virginians of that time meant what twenty-first-century Americans call corn, they specified maize or Indian corn.) The law required every household to plant or purchase more grain than the head of the household anticipated needing for the current year, much as Joseph had advised the Egyptians to store extra grain after his dream of famine. Another law required that every man who worked his own land plant and tend at least six mulberry trees each year for seven consecutive years, cultivate "silke-flaxe" and hemp, and plant and tend ten grapevines each year.[39] Repeatedly throughout the seventeenth century the company's officers and royal officials tried to stimulate production of silk, cloth, cordage, and wine in Virginia, at which some of the planters were fairly successful during the middle decades of the century.

The assembly decreed that "necessary tradesmen"—smiths, coopers, cobblers, and other craftsmen—should be paid "according to the quality of his trade and worke, to be estimated, if he shall not be contented, by the Governor and officers of the place where he worketh."[40] The terms of all contracts made in England between employers and servants, between the company and its employees, were to be enforced, and the assembly ordered that no person employ any "crafty" or "advantagious meanes" to entice away another person's servants or laborers.[41] Management of laborers and control of the behavior of laborers were of fundamental importance to the members of the first General Assembly and became increasingly so later, as the surviving records of the colony's courts and future General Assemblies demonstrate.

The assembly endorsed a company order allowing the cape merchant, as manager of the colony's principal storehouse, called the magazine, to keep as his allowance 25 percent of the value of the merchandise and the tobacco, sassafras, and other crops that passed through it or were grown for sale in En-gland. The law repeated the requirement that all planters sell their tobacco to the cape merchant, but it allowed managers of particular plantations established with the company's approval to trade on their own account, and if any private ships arrived in Virginia with goods that colonists wished to purchase, they could ship tobacco to England on those ships rather than through the magazine.[42] The assembly's final regulation about tobacco specified that leaf tobacco in such bad condition that it could not be sold even at one shilling six pence was to be "burnt before the owners face,"[43] a measure intended to keep the worst leaf from depressing the price that the planters and the company hoped to receive for the better and the best.

On Tuesday morning the assembly referred to the committees the subjects that individual members submitted for consideration and again read and again approved the acts that it had approved on Monday.[44] While the committees worked, the governor, council members, and other burgesses received and considered a complaint from Captain William Powell, a burgess for James City. Powell charged that one of his employees neglected his work, engaged in lewd behavior with Powell's widowed servant, and also made false charges to the governor that Powell was guilty of drunkenness and theft, which charges might cost Powell his captaincy. The assembly ordered that the servant stand four consecutive days with his ears nailed to the pillory and be whipped each day.

The records of the first decades of the colony are replete with instances of courts routinely ordering severe corporal and even capital punishment for both major and minor misdeeds. As the records of the first General Assembly indicate, misdeeds of servants were often punished differently than those of gentlemen or freemen. The lower classes were more often the object of physical punishment, the upper classes of degradation from their military or social ranks. The latter was probably regarded as a severe disgrace among the commanders and planters, who relied on their social standing and official positions for their leadership roles. Physical punishment of a man of status was the most degrading punishment of all. For both masters and servants, shaming, such as forcing an offender to stand in the stocks or cutting his ears off, was a punishment, but the threat of it might have been regarded as a deterrent, and the experience of it might have been perceived as an occasion for a miscreant to repent of misdeeds and resolve to do better in future. The assembly members allowed the governor and council to determine "what satisfaction" Powell's servant was to be required to make to his master for neglecting his work.[45] The power of masters over servants was expansive, as long as the master did not grossly violate the explicit contractual provisions of the indenture that bound the laborer to him.

During Tuesday afternoon the committees reported and the assembly spent most of the remainder of the day discussing "the third sorte of lawes," but John Rolfe also submitted a petition against John Martin. He alleged that Martin had criticized Rolfe and also the "present government," probably meaning Sir George Yeardley's administration.[46] Pory's report indicates that the assembly referred Rolfe's complaint to the governor's council, but the text leaves it unclear whether it was Rolfe's opinion, Pory's opinion, or the collective opinion of the assembly members that the "present government" was "the most temperate and juste that ever was in this country, too milde indeed for many of this Colony, whom unwoonted liberty hath made insolent, and not to knowe themselves."[47] The men in charge clearly believed that they needed a strong controlling hand to maintain social order, economic prosperity, and their own superior status.

Wednesday, 4 August, began hot, and the members agreed to conclude their business. Even though the Speaker had been ill, he read, "as he was required by the Assembly," all the laws and orders that had already passed, "to give the same yett one reviewe more and to see, whether there were any thing to be amended, or that might be excepted against."[48] The members then adopted the laws.

The assembly allowed all men, "servants onely excepted," to trade with the Indians but prohibited selling Indians "any Englishe dog of quality." It ordered that no person sell firearms, shot, or powder to Indians "upon paine of being helde a Traytour to the Colony, and of being hanged, so soon as the facte is prooved, wthout all Redemption" or any opportunity for pardon or reprieve. Men had to obtain permission to visit an Indian town or to go more than twenty miles from their dwelling places.[49] Later in the day the assembly also required that any person traveling by water either from above or below James-town was to stop there and register with the governor, and it required people trading in sailing vessels in the bay to obtain a license from the governor.[50]

Another act required the commander of every settlement to provide the secretary of the colony with a correct list of all people residing there, the details of their commissions and land grants, and the terms of service remaining for each of the servants.[51] And another law required the ministers to provide the secretary annually with lists of all the people they had christened, married, and buried. In settlements without ministers, the law required commanders to send in these lists.[52]

The assembly also forbade the killing of "any Neattcattle whatsoever."[53] Draft animals were more valued for their work cultivating fields and perhaps producing milk, butter, and cheese than for their meat. The assembly specified penalties for stealing boats, oars, and canoes. Stealing from English-speaking owners would be proceeded against as a felony; stealing from Indians was to be punished by making restitution and a fine of £5 if committed by a free man or a fine of £2 and a whipping if by a servant.[54]

At different times during that final day the assembly adopted several laws concerning religion, all evidently at the suggestion of the members of the assembly. One required ministers to "read divine service, and exercise their Ministerial function, according to the Ecclesiasticall lawes and orders of the churche of England, and every Sunday in the afternoon shall Catechize suche as are not yet ripe" to take Communion.[55] Another required the ministers and churchwardens to present to the court evidence of "all ungodly disorders" and "skandalous offenses, as suspicions of whordomes, dishonest Company-keeping with woemen, and suche like."[56] Yet another specified punishments, including excommunication from the church, if "any person, after two warnings doe not amende his or her life, in point of evident suspicion of Incontinency"—sexual misbehavior generally—"or of the commission of any other enormous sinnes."[57] A law "For reformation of swearing" levied a fine of five shillings on every free man guilty of swearing and decreed that servants who swore would be whipped and their owners would be fined five shillings.[58]

The first of the final two laws concerning religion directed that "All persons whatsoever upon the Sabaoth daye shall frequente divine service and sermons both forenoon and afternoon; and all suche as beare armes, shall bring their pieces, swordes, poulder, and shotte."[59] That some people were entitled to bear arms indicates that others were not, and those others probably included not only women and children but some or all of the colony's indentured servants. The other law directed that "No maide or woman servant" marry without the consent of her parents or of her master or mistress "or of the Magistrat and Minister of the place both together."[60] The law imposed no corresponding restriction on male servants, which suggests that masters and mistresses were determined to keep serving women from the child-bearing that would interfere with the performance of their work, or even might well kill them. Fornication and begetting or giving birth to an illegitimate child were already illegal under English law, and both men and women were subjected to specific punishments for those offenses; forbidding serving women from marrying in Virginia might have been regarded as an attempt to reduce the loss of work that masters and mistresses might expect to get out of their female servants.

Before writing "Here ende the lawes," Pory entered the final act of the assembly, directing that any person who contracted to work for a man in Virginia but stealthily remained in England and sold his services to another man had to serve the full terms of both contracts consecutively.[61]

Completing the adoption of the laws did not conclude the assembly's business that hot Wednesday. Captain Henry Spellman, one of the young men who early in the colony's history had been sent to live with the Indians to learn the language and act as an interpreter, was "called to the Barre" and examined on charges that he had defamed the government "in Opochancanos courte" and as a consequence put "the whole Colony in danger of their slippery designes." Spellman admitted some details in the charge against him, but when the assembly moved to strip him of his title of captain and sentence him to seven years of service to the company, Pory wrote that "hee as one that had in him more of the Savage then of the Christian, muttered certain wordes to himselfe, neither shewing any remorse for his offences, nor yet any thankfulness to the Assembly for their so favourable censure."[62] Pory may have believed that Spellman should have been grateful for not being hanged. More likely, Spellman was not destitute of notions of civilization; he did not fail to grasp the seriousness of being reduced in rank from a valued interpreter with the rank of captain to a mere servant facing seven years of service to the company.

The residents of nearby Paspeheigh (also called Argall's Town and Martin's Hundred) then petitioned to be relieved of paying bonds that they had once posted for the acquisition of land there. The assembly requested that the company cancel the bonds because the company had since set aside that land as a plantation to provide income to support the governor of the colony.[63]

"The last acte of the Generall assembly was a Contribution to gratifie their officers," which required every person older than sixteen to contribute one pound of the best quality tobacco to be delivered to Speaker John Pory, who would divide it among himself, the clerk, and the sergeant at arms "according to their degrees and rankes."[64]

The assembly adopted resolves apologizing to the company for adjourning the proceedings so soon, as a consequence of the heat, and authorizing Pory to make and authenticate copies of the proceedings for all of the settlements represented in the assembly and for the company's council in England.[65] The assembly begged the company not to reject the whole body of laws if it adjudged any part defective but to allow "these lawes wch we have nowe brought to light, do passe currant & be of force" pending the company's final determination.

"Otherwise," Pory wrote, "this people (who nowe at lengthe have gotte the raines for former servitude into their owne swindge) would in shorte time growe so insolent, as they would shake off all government, and there would be no living among them."[66] Pory's condescension toward and apprehensions about his social inferiors were typical for an English gentleman of his standing, and Virginia's planters and public officials exhibited the same attitudes for many decades thereafter.

The assembly repeated its plea that the company allow it to pass on the propriety of rules that the company proposed just as the king "hath given them power to allowe or to reject our lawes," and the governor then adjourned the assembly until the first day of March.[67]

That was the beginning of representative government in Virginia. It was also to a large extent the beginning of the political culture that nourished the ideas and beliefs that informed Virginia's subsequent political history. What the assembly members did and how they did it were both important, and the nature and details of the laws that they adopted indicate what was most important to them. The men who met in Jamestown and adopted those laws made certain that they sustained their authority, defended their people against sins and enemies, regulated the economy in what they believed was their best interest, imposed regulations on servants and laborers, and more or less formally established the Church of England as the official church of the colony investing it with important responsibilities in keeping good order, peace, and civility in the colony. All governments then and all governments before and after them shared or share most of those same concerns. All governments at that time also were intimately involved in prescribing and proscribing religious beliefs and practices. From that beginning in Jamestown, the church and the state were part of each other, and neither, from the perspectives of the governors or the governed, was likely to be perceived as possible without the other. The symbolism of the company's officers doing secular business in a sacred place may not have been something that the people in Jamestown that week needed to have pointed out to them.

Perhaps the members of the assembly who resided in Jamestown or nearby remained in town that hot Wednesday afternoon for the evening service at the church. When Richard Bucke read the prayers and passages of Scripture, the second of the two psalms for the day was the twenty-third. Appropriately enough, it offered a kind of benediction on the secular business that the governor and the other company officers and the burgesses had done in that sacred place. Listen to it in the accents of the Geneva Bible:

> The Lord *is* my shepherd, I shal not want.
> He maketh me to rest in grene pasture, & leadeth me by the stil waters.
> He restoreth my soule, & leadeth me in the paths of righteousnes for his
> Names sake.
> Yea, thogh I shulde walke through the valley of the shadow of death, I wil feare no evil: for thou art with me: thy rod and thy staffe, they comfort me.

Thou doest prepare a table before me in the sight of mine adversaries: thou doest anoint mine head with oyle, *and* my cup runneth over.

Doubtles kindenes, & mercie shal follow me all the dayes of my life, and I shal remaine a long season in the house of the Lord.

Those blessings intended for the deserving godly were in sharp contrast to the punishments intended for the undeserving ungodly. The first lesson from Scripture that day was chapter 19 of the book of Jeremiah, from which Bucke read the dire warning that the prophet pronounced to the wicked people of Tophet, concluding with the fifteenth and final verse: "Thus saith the Lord of hostes, the God of Israél, Beholde, I wil bring upon this citie, and upon all her townes, all the plagues that I have pronounced against it, because they have hardened their neckes, and wolde not heare my wordes." And from chapter 7 of Paul's letter to the Hebrews, Bucke read how Jesus offered people who believed in him a better covenant with the Lord, in the words of the twenty-fifth verse: "Wherefore, he is able also perfitely to save them that come unto God by him, seing he ever liveth, to make intercession for them."

About three weeks later, long before Pory's report could have reached London, probably even before he had an opportunity to put it on board a ship to send back to his employers in the capital of the emerging English empire, a ship that belonged to the company arrived at Point Comfort, near Kicoughtan, which still had its "savage" name. On board, in the words of John Rolfe, were "20. and odd Negroes, wch the Governor and Cape Marchant bought."[68] Those recent captives from the west coast of Africa may or may not have been the first Africans to arrive in Virginia. It is possible that a few had arrived earlier, and more certainly arrived not long afterward.[69] The men who made the first laws and established representative government in Virginia also took the first steps toward creating a system of slavery. Unlike the indentured servants and employees of the company about whom the laws of 1619 had much to say, the Africans came without indentures, without any legal protections or status at all, falling through the cracks in English statute and common law and adding to the small population of the colony a new group of laborers who by the middle of the century were degraded far below the most contemptible servant or Indian.

To purchase the labor or bodies of a few captive Africans was a small step for the men in Jamestown who had already purchased the labor of indentured servants and written laws to control them, but it was a step with large consequences, much as with the first legislative steps that they also took. It added one new lower level to the social ranks, and it ultimately augmented the authority of heads of households, who ruled their African laborers free of some of the restraints of law and contracts that governed how they ruled their indentured servants. Later General Assembly members had to create a whole new body of law that permitted masters to rule their new laboring force more violently than their indentured servants, not a contractual law of master and servant but a brutal law of master and slave.

In Jamestown in 1619 a small number of influential men took the first steps in creating two antithetical social systems, republican government and slavery. In 1624 King James I revoked the company's charter, and in 1625 King Charles I made Virginia the English Crown's first royal colony. During the subsequent decades the institutions and practices that the first General Assembly created and the political economy based on slavery that had its beginnings at the same time and place developed along lines that the planters and government officials of Virginia directed without much royal or any parliamentary interference. Republican government and slavery dwelled together in the colony and commonwealth of Virginia for nearly two hundred and fifty more years.

Representative government got off to a promising beginning in 1619. Slavery got off to an ominous beginning. Less than five years after the first assembly met, William Capps, a prominent company officer and a burgess, asked for "3 or 4 score slaves to work about a ffort or for servile work." He was well aware of the troubles that owners or masters could have with involuntary workers, but he knew exactly what to do if they tried to run away. He also knew that he need not worry about other owners or company officials interfering with him when he disciplined or terrorized his workmen into obedience. And he knew that nothing in English law as it was being administered in Virginia would hinder him in doing what he believed he needed to do to control his workers. "I will make them sing new Toes, old Toes, no Toes at all," Capps wrote, "because they shall not outrun me."[70]

3

English Atlantic Networks and Religion in Virginia

By April Lee Hatfield

Puritan, Quaker, and Dutch Reformed merchants predominated intercolonial American trade during the seventeenth century. The transatlantic and intercolonial trade and migration routes that shaped Virginia's economy and its settlement patterns also influenced the colony's religious map. The Church of England was strongest in the Peninsula and Middle Peninsula counties that grew the best tobacco and therefore maintained the closest connections to England. Puritans and Quakers, who made up a significant proportion of Virginia's population in several counties during the middle decades of the seventeenth century, concentrated south of the James River and on the Eastern Shore, the areas most involved in intercolonial trade, and constituted a disproportionate percentage of Virginia's intercolonial merchants. Seventeenth-century Puritans and Quakers constituted Adantic communities that included England and the Netherlands and multiple colonies. These nonconformists in Virginia depended on intercolonial networks of family and trade. Intercolonial religious and economic networks thus overlapped and reinforced one another.

The Virginia Company established an Anglican parish system that lasted through the end of the colonial period. That parish system divided the colony geographically into parishes that, like English parishes, encompassed all English residents. The parishes were intended to collect tithes, oversee poor relief, enforce church attendance, and provide discipline for some ethical transgressions. Because Anglican clergy required theological training and ordination by a bishop, and because neither was available in the colonies, Virginia's Anglican church necessarily depended on transatlantic ties. The Anglican clergy who traveled to Virginia not surprisingly chose (or were chosen by) wealthier parishes in counties with the best access to England and the highest quality tobacco (important not only because it created better transatlantic contacts but also because clergy salaries were paid in tobacco). Their English educations, their relationships with former classmates and other clergy in England, and their subordination to English episcopal hierarchy all served to reinforce for Virginia parishioners their membership in a religious world cen-tered in England.[1]

However, the number of Anglican clergy in Virginia was always insufficient to supply the population, and for most of the century most English residents had no access to regular Anglican worship. Between the 1640s and 1670, as the colonial population of Virginia increased from about eight thousand to about thirty thousand and spread throughout the coastal plain, there were seldom more than five to ten ministers resident in the colony at any one time.[2] Even by the end of the century, the average parish encompassed about 270 square miles, and many of those parishes often went without clergy many Sundays.[3] Those parishes that were active in seventeenth-century Virginia did not conform to a particular vision for the Church of England but, rather, represented a wide range of theological and liturgical preference that only became controversial at midcentury. When Virginia was planned and established at the beginning of the century, the church of Elizabeth and James I encompassed a spectrum of practice from Puritan to very high church. During the late 1620s and 1630s, Charles I and his archbishop William Laud worked to enforce a more narrow definition of the Church of England and ultimately created sharp distinctions that forced many Puritans within the church to choose between a more elaborate worship form (and the theology that such liturgy represented) and separation from the church. The Great Migration to New England in the 1630s stemmed from pressure on Puritans to conform to Laud's vision of Anglicanism.[4] Into the 1640s, transatlantic and intercolonial interactions alike supported both Puritans and non-Puritans within Virginia's Anglican church. However, the Eastern Shore and Southside counties with closer ties to New England already began to encourage the emergence of the regional religious pattern in which nonconformist tendencies followed immersion in intercolonial trade. By the mid-1640s, Virginia was no longer able to persist in earlier more locally flexible parish system. The English Civil War that began in 1642 spread religious conflict throughout the English Atlantic, and royalist Governor Sir William Berkeley, who arrived in Virginia that year, came with a perspective on the church derived from Laud's England in the 1630s and a conviction (as the Civil War began) that Puritans represented a serious threat to the English world, and he intended to enforce his Laudian view of the Church of England in Virginia. Thus, by the 1640s the English Atlantic imposed on Virginia a clear distinction dividing Puritans from Anglicans.[5] Thereafter, the links joining strong intercolonial connections and nonconformity, on the one hand, and relatively stronger transatlantic connections and Anglicanism, on the other, grew more pronounced.[6] As Quakers emerged in the 1650s, they too depended on transadantic and intercolonial communication, but even those Quaker evangelists who came to the colonies from England relied on intercolonial networks once they had crossed the Atlantic, so in Virginia they arrived via other colonies along intercolonial shipping (or overland) trade routes.

Commercial and familial intercolonial webs such as those maintained by the Emperors, the Gookins, and the Varletts, helped foster the development of dissenting religious communities in seventeenth-century Virginia and strengthen Virginia's dissenting communities that already existed. The development of long-distance ties between American nonconformists occurred through written correspondence, intercolonial migration, and the intercolonial travel of ministers. Puritans and Quakers, like Anglicans, perceived themselves as members of Atlantic communities, which they actively and consciously fostered. Their intercolonial movements, like almost all colonial migrations, followed patterns established by coastal trade routes.

In addition to larger migrations, ministers sometimes moved between colonies especially to serve religious needs or to build connections between dispersed congregations. In the case of Quakers, building such ties involved a well-established practice, in which traveling ministers (Public Friends) left their homes in England or one of its colonies to travel for months or years at a time, visiting Quaker meetings to proselytize, serve religious needs, or build connections between dispersed Friends. Unlike many other migrations, Quaker ministers' travels followed Indian overland paths in addition to shipping routes. The migrations of Puritans and Puritan ministers between colonies and the intercolonial and overseas traveling by Quaker men and women ministers indicate the permeability of colonial boundaries and served to break down those boundaries further. Quaker traveling ministers not only preached but also visited, sometimes setded, and invariably brought news of family, friends, and events elsewhere.

The porosity of intercolonial boundaries, especially pronounced for those merchant families involved in coastal trade, allowed intercolonial travel and migration for religious reasons, strengthening nonconformist communities within Virginia. Many of the most important intercolonial traders in Virginia were nonconformists who lived in the parts of Virginia (the Eastern Shore and the Southside of the James) most heavily dependent on intercolonial trade. By the middle of the seventeenth century, Puritans and Quakers constituted a significant presence in Lower Norfolk, Nansemond, Isle of Wight, Accomack, and Northampton Counties, all counties with substantial trade to other American colonies. Religious and commercial links reinforced one another, and commerce was a part (perhaps both as means and as end) of the nonconformists' attempts to build intercolonial communities.[7]

Puritan, Quaker, and Dutch Reformed conversions and intermarriages created families that included a variety of nonconformists and involved multiple Adantic world markets and locales. A few connected individuals clearly Illustrate this aspect of intercolonial networks.

Isaac Allerton, his son (also Isaac Allerton), and their associates exemplify the ways that several intercolonial trade, migration, and communication routes overlapped to form a Complex intercolonial web and a broadly colonial world with Puritan and Dutch connections central to its maintenance.[8] Isaac Allerton, Sr., born in London between 1583 and 1585, moved to Leiden in 1609. He, his wife Mary, and three of their children traveled on the *Mayflower* to Plymouth as part of the Puritan migration there in 1620. Allerton, a merchant and the wealthiest of the migrants to New England, owned several trading vessels and played an instrumental role establishing intercolonial coastal trade and the New England fishing industry. He disagreed with the New England religious leadership on issues of tolerance and moved to New Amsterdam around 1636. For the next ten years he lived mostly in New Amsterdam, where he was involved in intercolonial trade and tobacco reexport and owned a warehouse. While living in New Amsterdam, he traveled to Virginia, the Caribbean, and New England. He helped Massachusetts ministers get to Virginia when they wrecked on Long Island.[9] He did business with Govert Loockermans of New Amsterdam who traded with the Chesapeake and later moved to Maryland where he became naturalized.[10] In 1643 Allerton became one of eight assistants to New Nether-land Governor Willem Kieft, obviously having earned a place of high status in the Dutch colony. In 1646 he moved to New Haven, where he lived the rest of his life, continuing to travel and trade to New Amsterdam, Massachusetts, and Virginia.[11] He died in early 1659.

His son Isaac Allerton, Jr., followed his father's footsteps as an intercolonial trader. Born in Plymouth in 1630 to his father and second wife Fear Brewster, he graduated from Harvard in 1650, just before the arrival of Virginian Nathaniel Utie, stepson of future governor Richard Bennett.[12] Allerton, Jr., accompanied his father on trading voyages between Plymouth, New Haven, New Amsterdam, and Virginia, and gradually became a partner with his father in intercolonial trade. By the 1650s he managed much of his father's business.[13] When his father died, Isaac, Jr., away from New Haven at the time, returned to settle the estate, which included debts in Barbados, Delaware Bay, Virginia, and New Netherlands.[14]

Isaac, Jr., purchased his father's New Haven house from creditors for his mother to live in.[15] In the 1650s, Isaac, Jr., and his wife Elizabeth lived in New Haven and had three children there. By 1655, however, he had purchased land in Virginia, at Wicomico in Northumberland County. He moved to Virginia after his first wife died (around 1660) and became close friends with Thomas Willoughby of Elizabeth City. Willoughby was the only son of Barbadian trader and immigrant Captain Thomas Willoughby of Elizabeth River in Lower Norfolk County, who had delivered Lower Norfolk's 1654 request (written by Francis Emperor) to find a minister in New England. Allerton married Elizabeth Willoughby, daughter of his friend, granddaughter of the immigrant, and widow of Dutch Eastern Shore merchant Simon Overzee (who had traded Ann Toft's goods in his ship and entertained Augustine Herman on a 1659–60 official voyage to Maryland for New Netherland). Isaac and Elizabeth Allerton named their son Willoughby Allerton.[16] Isaac Allerton became justice of Northumberland County in 1663, and a member of the "Committee of the Association of Northumberland, Westmoreland, and Stafford Counties" in 1667. In September 1675 he and Barbadian-connected immigrant Colonel John Washington led the Virginia forces that pursued Doeg Indians across the Potomac river (after the Doegs killed Barbadian immigrant Thomas Matthew's servant) and thereby helped precipitate the Virginia-Susquehannock War and Bacon's Rebellion. The Northern Neck (and southern bank of Rappahannock River) was another Chesapeake region that attracted intercolonial immigrants, and those immigrants seem to have disproportionately participated in precipitous events of the mid-1670s there.[17] Such involvement apparently did not hurt Allerton's political career. By February 1677 he was a member of the House of Burgesses.[18] Throughout his life, he maintained the nonconformist beliefs of his parents (and probably his wife).[19] Isaac's and his second wife Elizabeth's son Willoughby furthered and strengthened family involvement with other nonconformist traders by marrying Hannah Keene, widow of intercolonial trader John Bushrod, whose father was a Quaker merchant.[20]

The strong link between nonconformist religion and intercolonial trade emerges clearly in the lives of seventeenth-century Virginians: moreover, the Puritans in Virginia played a greater role than many historians have supposed, requiring that we rethink not only the Chesapeake's religious history but its economic and geographic history as well. The regions most deeply enmeshed in intercolonial trade—the Eastern Shore, the Southside Counties, and to a lesser degree the Northern Neck-Rappahannock area—also had the largest Puritan and Quaker populations. The connections that residents of those regions maintained in other colonies placed them firmly in an intercolonial world. Their trade contacts facilitated a development of religious communities transcending colonial boundaries. As well, their long-distance interaction webs put these individuals at the forefront of the economic, social, and political negotiations and transfers that provided the context for the development of Chesapeake slavery and that grew into the larger intercolonial networks of officials who worked to regularize colonial administration and fight the emergent creole identities that became so forceful in eighteenth-century Virginia.

While Anglican officials in Virginia supported the exchange networks intercolonial traders created, they opposed the strengthening of nonconformist intercolonial communities that accompanied the growth in trade. They realized that freedom of movement between colonies bolstered the position of religious minorities within Virginia. In response, Anglican officials attempted to prevent nonconformists from using intercolonial trade networks to build intercolonial religious communities. Though never able to keep Puritans and Quakers out of Virginia, by trying to enforce Virginia's political borders as effective cultural (though not economic) boundaries, officials did succeed in adding a perceived cultural meaning to Virginia's political borders. In doing so, they helped define Virginia as an Anglican colony.

Puritans formed an important part of Virginia's population from the outset of its colonization. English Puritans had gone to the Netherlands, mostly to areas near Middleburg and Amsterdam, during the late sixteenth and early seventeenth centuries to escape persecution in England. Some of the largest Puritan settlements in Virginia came from these English congregations in Holland As well, the Virginia Company included several Puritans with broadly American plans and aspirations involving two or more colonies. For example, the Puritan Robert Rich (second earl of Warwick) was a prominent member of the Virginia Company, sat on the Virginia Council, and was involved as well in the New England, Somers Island, and Providence Island Companies and in the colonization of Guiana, Newfoundland, and Barbados. His cousin Nathaniel Rich, also a Puritan, was a member of the Virginia Company as well, in addition to the Somers and Providence Island Companies.[21] The Virginia Company planned that Puritan minister Patrick Copland would be rector of the college they hoped to establish at Henrico in Virginia.[22]

Puritans settled and converted in the largest numbers on the Southside of the James River and on the Eastern Shore. These areas contained Virginia's clearly Puritan congregations, as well as the largest number of Anglican parishes with Puritan leanings.[23] As in England, many nominally Anglican parishes in early seventeenth-century Virginia had nonconformist tendencies. In the 1620s and 1630s several hundred Puritans settled in Nansemond and Isle of Wight Counties, many of them adjacent to one another. Puritans Christopher Lawne, Nathaniel Bosse, and Edward Bennett patented adjoining landholdings in Isle of Wight County, Bosse and Bennett receiving their patents within three days of one another in 1621.[24] Bennett, formerly an elder of Johnson's ancient church in Amsterdam, established the largest Puritan settlement south of the James. More than three hundred settlers came to Bennett's plantation by early 1622, fifty-three of them killed in the March 22 Indian attack. Bennett survived and continued to recruit settlers, bringing as many as six hundred Puritans to Virginia from the Netherlands and England. He used his own ships to transport colonists and to trade. His nephew Richard Bennett became leader of those Puritans, and later friend of Daniel Gookin, governor of Virginia, and father and stepfather to Harvard students Richard Bennett, Jr., and Nathaniel Utie.[25]

As the Civil War began and Berkeley arrived in Virginia as governor, theological differences among Virginians grew much more visible and became political. Virginia's Puritans, beginning to feel threatened, looked to New England as a source of guidance and clergy. In May 1642 seventy-one Virginians from Nansemond, including Richard Bennett and Daniel Gookin, sent a letter (hand delivered by Philip Bennett) to the "Pastors and Elders of Christ Church in New-England and the Rest of the Faithfull" explaining "their sad condition for the want of salvation" and requesting that ministers be sent to them from New England.[26] The writers described themselves as "the Inhabitants of the County of the upper Norfolke [Nansemond] in Virginia," rather than as a particular group from the county. As the tithables in Nansemond County in 1637 numbered about five hundred, the seventy-one men who signed the letter constituted a substantial minority of the county's population.[27] They wrote so "that the word of God might be planted amongst us by Faithfull Pastors and Teachers."[28] Their actions and words indicate that Puritans in Virginia and Massachusetts considered themselves part of a spiritual community that transcended space and linked people with one another across both political boundaries and physical distances. When Philip Bennett delivered the letter, he explained the needs of the Virginia Puritans to the elders, who according to Edward Johnson of Massachusetts, hoped "to take all opportunities for inlarging the kingdome of Christ."[29] Because English reformed thought held that both understanding the Bible and achieving salvation depended on "the work and preaching of upright clergymen," the lack of ministers in Virginia (particularly of ministers that Virginia Puritans could consider "upright") potentially prevented salvation for the colonists there and thus intensified the need to recruit clergy.[30]

Shortly after the Nansemond parishioners requested ministers, Norfolk County Puritan William Durand wrote to John Davenport, pastor of Christ Church in New Haven, sharing his fear that the unworthy Anglican priests in Virginia would doom Virginia Puritans: "If we continue under these wreched and blind Idoll shepards the very bane of this land we are like to perish."[31] Durand painted a picture for Davenport of the ways in which Puritans in Virginia belonged to the same community as Davenport and other New England Puritans, connected by spiritual links reaching across geographical boundaries. Though the two men had never met, Durand trusted that Davenport would concern itself in a matter as important as "the Enlargement of christs king-dome and the good of many poore soules in Virginia." Durand wrote that he (and others in Virginia) had benefitted from hearing Davenport preach in London, which to Durand indicated that they were already spiritually linked to one another. Those of the Virginia faithful who had not heard Davenport in London were nonetheless joined with him in their mutual love of Christ, which "doth even bind the hearts of all Christians," and further connected with one another through prayer. Durand believed that the growth of Puritanism in Virginia answered prayers he knew Davenport had offered "for the conversion of such as abide in the shadowes of death, and chaynes of darkenesse."[32] Durand's belief that spiritual links overcame physical space enabled him to initiate a more tangible connection with the New Haven minister. In other words, Puritans' belief in their spiritual unity encouraged them to form relationships that would involve migration and strengthen trade connections.

In response to the request of Lower Norfolk Puritans, the elders of Christ Church in Boston decided to dispatch William Tompson from Braintree and John Knowles from Watertown.[33] Massachusetts Governor John Winthrop later wrote that the court and the congregations sending ministers to Virginia welcomed the chance to contribute to the growth of Virginia Puritanism. According to Winthrop, they considered the men sent "as seed sown, which would bring us in a plentiful harvest, and we accounted it no small honor that God had put upon his poor churches here, that other parts of the world should seek to us for help in this kind."[34] Puritans in colonies other than Virginia also looked to New England for religious leadership. Winthrop noted that at about the same time as the Virginia request, two trading vessels brought letters from Barbados and other Caribbean islands asking for New England ministers.[35]

Tompson and Knowles sailed for Virginia in October 1642, along with a third minister, Thomas James of New Haven, but were shipwrecked near Manhattan.[36] The Dutch director-general apparendy did little to help them, but Isaac Allerton, Sr., a Puritan merchant and Massachusetts-New Nether-land-New Haven migrant whose son Isaac Allerton, Jr., moved to Virginia, took care of them in New Amsterdam and got them a pinnace and enough supplies to continue to Virginia. They arrived in mid-December, eleven weeks after leaving New England.[37]

In Virginia, according to Winthrop, the three ministers were well received in several places. The Virginia Assembly initially approved of their arrival. Governor William Berkeley, however, did not welcome them, despite their letter of introduction from Winthrop. In March 1643 the Virginia Assembly ordered the ministers out of the colony. In June John Knowles returned to Massachusetts from Virginia, bringing letters from his congregation and from other Virginians to the Christ Church elders. The letters, read in Boston at an open lecture, indicated that, despite the Assembly's order, the Puritans' ministry had succeeded in "inflaming" the hearts of some Virginians, who organized services in private houses once the parish churches were off limits.[38] A year later, the Powhatans' 1644 uprising against Virginia colonists demanded the attention of Virginia officials and prevented them from fully implementing their directive to suppress Puritanism in Virginia. In Massachusetts, Winthrop wrote in his journal that God had obviously sent the attack to express displeasure at the Virginia Assembly's persecution of Puritans.[39] Edward Johnson, in his *Wonder-working Providence of Sion's Saviour in New England* (1653), similarly saw in the Powhatans' attack "the hand of God against this people, after the rejection of these Ministers of Christ." Johnson also pointed out that the attack stopped jnst short of the Puritan settlements in Lower Norfolk and Nansemond. When it neared "that place where Christ had placed his little flock, it was discovered and prevented from further proceeding." To Johnson, this development proved that "the Lord pittied the little number of his people among this crooked generation."[40] Winthrop claimed that the Indian attack forced Virginia Anglicans to acknowledge that God had punished them for expelling the New England ministers.[41] New Englanders clearly regarded their beleaguered fellow Puritans in Virginia as part of their religious community, mandating communication between the colonies to ensure that members of "the kingdome of Christ" could look out for one another.

After the Assembly's order and the 1644 Anglo-Powhatan war, several Virginia Puritans left the Chesapeake for New England. In the mid-seventeenth century, persecutions by the Virginia government sparked further communication that encouraged Puritan leaders in other colonies to continue attention and concern for Virginia Puritans.[42] Berkeley's attempts to suppress Puritans and define Virginia as an Anglican colony within its political boundaries did succeed in encouraging emigration and decreased the visibility of Puritans who remained. However, Anglican hostility strengthened Virginia Puritans' ties to New England, binding them more fully into the intercolonial Puritan network on which these Chesapeake nonconformists depended.

Most Puritans who left Virginia in response to official persecution went to Maryland or New England. In the early 1640s, Richard Bennett, Daniel Gookin, and William Durand considered establishing a Puritan settlement on the Rappahannock, farther from the reach of Virginia officials. They decided on Maryland instead, but the setdement in Rappahannock of intercolonial traders and migrants such as Puritan Isaac Allerton, Jr., suggest the region remained attractive for some Puritans.[43] Gookin himself moved to Boston, where he and his wife quickly joined the Roxbury congregation.

During the English Civil War, Lord Baltimore, Catholic proprietor of Maryland, needed to ensure continued religious toleration for Maryland Catholics and so actively courted Puritans. He welcomed Virginia Puritans and also in 1643 sent an agent to New England to recruit New England Puritans who might prefer a warmer climate. Baltimore continued such attempts to ensure toleration for Catholics in his colony during the Interregnum. In a move designed to position himself favorably vis-à-vis Puritan England, he appointed William Stone, a Puritan from Virginia's Eastern Shore and brother of deceased ship captain (De Vries's acquaintance) John Stone, as governor. In choosing his new governor, Baltimore perceived an intercolonial talent pool, rather than one encompassing only Maryland and England. Baltimore stipulated that when Stone came to Maryland as the new governor (in 1648), he bring five hundred colonists. In 1649 about three hundred nonconformists migrated from Virginia (mostly from southeastern Virginia) to the Severn River in Maryland, though by 1649 English laws guaranteed Puritans religious freedom in Virginia as well.[44]

Despite these migrations, the Southside Puritan community persisted. Its members maintained connections to New England, strengthened by migrations and shared projects early in the decade. Thomas Harrison, Puritan minister to Elizabeth River Parish in Lower Norfolk county in the 1640s, also saw New England as a source of guidance and corresponded with John Winthrop, though he himself did not possess prior ties to New England or English Puritan networks but rather had come to Virginia as Berkeley's Anglican chaplain.[45] In April 1645 the Elizabeth River church wardens brought charges against him for not reading the Book of Common Prayer, not catechizing on Sunday afternoons, and not administering baptism correcdy. He and his followers considered migrating to New England and were "in a posture of removing" by 1646, but when they consulted Winthrop about the move, he suggested they stay in Virginia.[46] In November 1646 Harrison wrote that Win-throp's arguments carried "weight and worth and force enough in them to have stakd us down againe."[47] So his congregation of Virginia Puritans stayed in the Southside counties and Harrison soon reported to Winthrop that his church was growing.[48] The Massachusetts elders clearly enjoyed respect as leaders of Puritanism in America not only from their own parishioners but from those in Virginia as well, who looked to them for decisions about their own church. That they could carry on such a correspondence depended on intercolonial traders such as Edward Gibbons (Eastern Shore merchant Edmund Scarborough's trading partner), who carried at least one letter from Harrison to Winthrop.[49]

During the English Civil War, New England leaders saw the distinct possibility that Puritanism might increasingly define the English Atlantic world, including Virginia. Harrison, however, knew that such a development did not seem imminent to those on the ground in Virginia. He told the Massachusetts elders that he needed to consider other options. One possibility involved William Sayle's plans to settle Eleutheria in the Bahamas. Sayle had drawn up a covenant for all potential participants providing for liberty of conscience, "wherein ... the civil magistrate should not have any cognizance of any matter which concerned religion, but every man might enjoy his own opinion or religion, without control or question." When Sayle, in Virginia seeking provisions for his project, discovered that the Virginia government had oppressed Puritans. tans and threatened them with expulsion, he tried to persuade them to move to Eleutheria. Interested, but, according to Winthrop, "very orthodox and zealous for the truth," they would not decide before receiving advice from New England, which Harrison asked for when in New England. Winthrop and other New England religious leaders sent aid to Eleutheria but returned letters to Virginia dissuading Harrison and his congregants from joining under the terms of Sayle's commission.[50] Sayle's project ultimately failed and the Committee for Trade and Plantations sent instructions to Jamaica to rescue any English left on Eleutheria. The involvement of Puritans from at least three other colonies and the expectation that Puritans in various colonies would migrate between colonies in order to further Puritanism in the Americas nevertheless illustrates the sense among Puritans that their religious ties transcended political boundaries. Their understanding of these ties as spiritual forged their "kingdome in Christ" unbound by physical or political geography. Two years later, however, because Harrison had disobeyed Berkeley's orders to conform to Anglicanism, the Lower Norfolk county officials in May 1648 followed the governor's and assembly's orders and commanded the inhabitants of Elizabeth River to stop their illegal meetings. Justices of the Peace Cornelius Lloyd and Edward Lloyd and several other county residents refused to obey, and instead helped William Durand, in trouble for lay preaching, avoid arrest. In response, Berkeley banished Durand and Harrison.[51] Durand later helped move former neighbors and parishioners to the Severn River in Maryland.[52]

Other New England Puritans besides John Winthrop followed these events in Virginia. Humphrey Atherton wrote to John Winthrop, Jr., in August 1648 that "the Church in verginy is in sum truble there minster is cam to boston: I thinke hee is bannished."[53] Two days latter Adam Winthrop wrote also to (his brother) John, Jr., at Pequot that "Mr Harrison the paster of the church at verjenya being banished from thence is arrived heer to consult about some place to settle him selfe and his church some thinke that youer plantation [Connecticut] will be the fittst place for him, but I suppose you have heard more amply before this."[54] Puritans in both Virginia and New England considered themselves enough a part of an intercolonial Puritan world that such a group migration from one colony to the other neither antagonized nor surprised them.

In New England, Harrison reported that his church in Virginia had grown to 118 people "and many more looking towards it."[55] He asked the Massachusetts magistrates and elders "whether their church ought not to remove" because of Anglican prosecution, and, if so, where they should go. The New Englanders answered "that seeing God had carried on his work so graciously hitherto, etc., and that there was so great hope of a far more plentiful harvest at hand, (many of the council being well inclined, etc., and one thousand of the people by conjecture,) they should not be hasty to remove, as long as they could stay upon any tolerable terms." Harrison, however, moved on. Following his expulsion, he stayed in Boston long enough to marry Governor Win-throp's niece, Dorothy Simonds.[56] He returned to Virginia briefly during the winter of 1649 before going to England and then serving as Cromwell's chaplain in Ireland. The Nansemond vestry and parishioners petitioned the Council of State in England to have him reinstated, but to no avail.[57] Continued strong ties to New England (or possibly an attraction to intense spiritual experience that encouraged their support of both Puritanism and Quakerism) may have contributed to Lower Norfolk's being the only region of Virginia to experience significant witchcraft accusations during the seventeenth century. However, the county officials' greater immersion in an Atlantic world in which rationalism was overtaking belief in the supernatural may in part explain why Lower Norfolk officials reacted so differendy than New Englanders. Instead of investigating such claims, the Lower Norfolk court imposed a fine of one thousand pounds of tobacco on persons who, by their "divers dangerous & scandalous speeches," had accused "severall women in this Countie" of being witches, thereby ruining "theire reputacons."[58]

After the Puritan leaders' expulsion, Lower Norfolk lacked a minister, though Puritans did enjoy reduced persecution after 1649 English law guaranteed them religious freedom and the 1652 "reduction" of the colony by an English fleet defeated Anglican royalist holdouts and installed Puritan governor Richard Bennett. In 1655 the Lower Norfolk county court, including Francis Emperor, asked Barbadian ship captain (and later father-in-law of Isaac Allerton, Jr.) Thomas Willoughby to try to "p[r]ovide a Minister of Gods word for us" as he traveled to England, presumably to trade. The following year they asked minister John Moore, part of the New England settlement on New Netherland's Long Island. Both attempts apparently failed.[59]

Even during the Interregnum, some hoped to find a more supportive community in New England and migrations to New England for religious reasons continued. In July 1657 Mrs. Rebecca Burrows told the Roxbury church that she had moved there from Virginia in order to "enjoy God in his Ordin, in N. E."[60] However, many Virginia Puritans who had remained in the colony throughout the repression of the 1640s found the 1650s a much better decade. Some nonconformist intercolonial traders, such as Francis Emperor and Isaac Allerton, Jr., appeared for the first time in the Chesapeake during the 1650s. Many Puritans gained political offices in Virginia during the Interregnum. After Richard Bennett helped organize the 1649 migration to Maryland, he stayed for several months in the new setdement on the Severn, but kept his property in Virginia, returned there to live, and became governor of Virginia. Edward Major and Colonel Thomas Dewes, both Speakers of the Assembly under the Commonwealth, were Puritans from Nansemond. John Hill, who had signed the 1642 petition to New England for ministers, stayed in Isle of Wight and in the 1660s, as sheriff, prosecuted Quakers. Edward Lloyd went to Maryland, but his brother Cornelius stayed in Virginia and was a burgess for Lower Norfolk County in the 1652–53 session.[61] The decade of Puritan government provided opportunities for nonconformists to establish and strengthen intertwined economic and religious networks, which remained strong enough to persist after the 1660 Restoration. Some, like Allerton, continued to hold office and retain prominent political as well as economic positions beyond 1660.

Before 1676 nonconformists on the Eastern Shore encountered less oppression than did those elsewhere in Virginia.[62] Nevertheless, a number migrated up the peninsula to Maryland. Visible by 1637, the movement peaked in 1649, the year after William Stone moved to become governor.[63] Stone's move from the Virginia Eastern Shore to Maryland and his recruitment of Southside Virginia Puritans to join him reflected and reinforced ties joining Eastern Shore and Southside Virginia Puritans. At least three ministers served both Southside and Eastern Shore churches.[64] Their presence surely helped attract New England Puritans such as Nathaniel Eaton and Francis Doughty, discussed in Chapter 4. The presence of Dutch Reformed Calvinists on the Eastern Shore and English Puritans who had lived in the Netherlands, and ties between New England Puritans on Long Island and in New Netherland and the Dutch Reformed Church complicated the Puritan leanings of Eastern Shore Virginians. In 1653 when New Netherland Governor Peter Stuyvesant sent Dutch Reformed Dominie Samuel Drisius from New Amsterdam to the Easten Shore to try to encourage the resumption of intercolonial trade after the 1652 Anglo-Dutch War, Drisius preached at Hungar's parish in Northampton County, where New England Puritan Francis Doughty served as minister.

A prominence in intercolonial trade of individuals who had both Puritan and Dutch ties may have originated in the communities of English Puritan exiles in the Netherlands and been further strengthened by their common Calvinisrn. Moreover, the strong positions of New England and New Netherland in intercolonial trade may have given Puritan and Dutch Virginians an advantage in intercolonial trade. The connections between religious and economic ties surface in Stuyvesant's sending a Calvinist minister (whom he could reasonably hope would be well received by Puritan Governor Bennett) to address his concerns about trade relations between the colonies.[65] Ultimately, it was Anglican Governor Berkeley rather than Puritan Governor Bennett who approved the proposed trade agreement, illustrating that while religious and economic networks overlapped for many, some Anglicans such as Berkeley hoped to promote intercolonial economic networks while severing them from their frequent connections to religious networks.

Puritans used intercolonial shipping patterns to communicate with one another and build religious networks spanning the English and Dutch Atlantic world. Intercolonial traders from other colonies who spent time in Virginia (such as John Stone, David Peterson De Vries, Edward Gibbons, Isaac Allerton, Jr., and Augustine Herman), were likely to be Puritans or members of the Dutch Reformed Church. In Virginia, Puritans lived in the regions best connected to New England and New Netherland commercially. The migration of intercolonial merchants such as Edward Gibbons, Isaac Allerton, Jr., and Augustine Herman further increased the Calvinist presence in those Chesapeake regions most immersed in intercolonial trade. Local Puritan leaders in Virginia, such as Cornelius and Edward Lloyd, William Stone, Daniel Gookin, Thomas Willoughby, Francis Emperor, and Isaac Allerton, Jr., numbered among the most prominent intercolonial traders.

After the 1650s, webs of Quaker interaction patterns overlapped with those of Puritans in Virginia. Although Quaker reliance on overland trade routes made them less dependent than Puritans on intercolonial shipping, their success in converting Virginia Puritans, their involvement in Atlantic trade, and their focus on creating an intercolonial American community ensured that their presence too would be strongest in the Southside and Eastern Shore intercolonial trading regions.

Quakers very consciously attempted to build a transatlantic and intercolonial religious community. In Virginia, Quakers best succeeded in areas with strong nonconformist traditions because the strength of trade with other colonies provided transportation that put residents in contact with coreligionists elsewhere. In addition, the regions that produced more intercolonial goods and less tobacco had inferior connections to England, less economic success, and therefore appealed less to Anglican ministers, whose scarcity gave them some choice about where they went in the Chesapeake. Quaker belief that every person possessed an inner light (a divine spark whose presence precluded the need for sacraments or ordained clergy to mediate between laity and God) also held special appeal to regions plagued throughout the seventeenth century by a lack of clergy, necessary for full worship in Anglican and Puritan religion.[66]

The first traveling ministers brought Quakerism to Virginia in the 1650s. Conversions happened both when these Public Friends held meetings, and on a more local level, through the activities of family and friends. Between 1652 and 1702 almost 150 Quaker ministers visited America from England. Many of these included Virginia in their travels.[67] They made converts and established Quaker meetings in several counties. Most came from England by way of Barbados and Jamaica, and some had spent time in New England before traveling to the Chesapeake. The first Public Friend whose voyage to Virginia is recorded, Elizabeth Harris of London, arrived in Virginia in 1656 and stayed for about a year. When she returned to England she wrote letters and sent books to those she had converted (or who were Quakers before her arrival).[68] The next Public Friends to go to Virginia, Josias Coale and Thomas Thurston, came in late 1657 and stayed until the following summer.[69] Their activity prompted an order from the General Court to leave Virginia by the first ship available. Virginia officials at first imprisoned Coale and Thurston without pen and ink until a ship arrived but during the winter released them and allowed them to go to Maryland.[70] During the same year, William Robinson, Christopher Holder, and Robert Hodgen arrived. They went first to the Eastern Shore, where they held meetings in private houses. They spent over a year in Virginia, traveling throughout the colony. Robinson spent at least six months in jail there. After their work in Virginia, Robinson continued to New England, where his ministering got him hanged.[71]

In 1661 at least five ministers included Virginia in their trips: Josias Coale (on his second trip), George Wilson, George Rose, Elizabeth Hooten, and Joan Brocksoppe. The end of 1662 found Joseph Nichelson, John Liddal, Jane Millard, and John Perrot in the colony. In 1663 ministers Mary Tompkins, Alice Ambrose, and Wenlock Christison all went to Virginia. John Burnyeat made two trips, in 1665 and 1671. In the latter year, Daniel Gould from Rhode Island also came; William Edmundson came in 1672 and 1676.[72] In 1672, Quaker founder George Fox visited Virginia with Robert Widders, Joseph Lancaster, and George Patteson. In 1677 William Gallway of Scotland died preaching in Nansemond. In 1678 John Bowater visited most of the settled meetings. Thomas Story, Thomas Chalkley, and William Ellis also visited Virginia.[73]

Quakers elicited a stronger reaction from Anglican authorities in Virginia than did Puritans, in part because their belief in a universal inner light posed potential challenges to the social order. Moreover, officials perceived Quaker intercolonial networks, when combined with Quaker pacifism, as a unique threat to the colony that went beyond cultural concerns to impinge on military considerations. Quakers consequently faced imprisonment, fines, whipping, or expulsion. A 1660 act ordered a £100 fine on shipmasters transporting Quakers into the colony, reflecting the Assembly's recognition of shipping's importance to the Atlantic Quaker community that nourished its Virginia members.[74] That officials correctly gauged the importance of shipping can be seen in a 1663 incident in which later the Lower Norfolk County sheriff broke up a meeting "aboard the Shipp Blessinge rideing at anchor in the southern branch of Elizabeth River."[75] George Fox described a 1673 meeting on the Eastern Shore of Maryland at which "there was 4 new England men masters of shipps and marchants: the truth spreads blesed bee the lord."[76] Both incidents illustrate the role of intercolonial shipping in the spread of nonconformity. Because Mew England officials persecuted Quakers so vigilandy, the New England ship masters and merchants present at the Maryland meeting may have depended wholly on their intercolonial travels to express their Quaker sympathies. William Chichester, the Salem, Massachusetts, master of the *Hopewell,* who deserted his wife in Salem and relocated to Lower Norfolk (the county whose court had heard his 1654 lawsuits with Joseph Huffey and William Selby), later appeared as a Quaker and householder.[77]

Virginia officials quickly noted the intercolonial aspect of Quaker communities. The preamble to a 1663 anti-Quaker statute stated that the Quakers, by assembling in great numbers in different parts of the colony under the pretense of religious worship, spread terror among the people and endangered the public peace; moreover, they kept up a constant and secret correspondence with each other, separated themselves from the rest of the king's subjects, and avoided regular congregations. The Assembly further noted the importance of coastal trade in advancing the development of the intercolonial Quaker networks that strengthened Quaker communities within Virginia. The law instructed shipmasters who brought Quakers to

Virginia to keep them on the ship while in the colony, prevent them from communicating with colonists, and carry them out of the colony when the ship left.[78] Virginia officials punished Quaker outsiders much more harshly than those resident in Virginia. Virginians who converted apparently never suffered worse punishment than a fine, but those who came into the colony from England or other colonies faced harsher penalties such as whipping and imprisonment.[79]

The fact that travel to more tolerant Maryland legitimately took ships through Virginia's portion of the Chesapeake Bay provided cover for Quakes illegally traveling into Virginia, the shipmasters who brought them, and the colonists who hosted them. Ambrose Dixon, a prominent citizen of North-ampton County, having already given bond that he would not entertain the Quaker minister William Robinson, continued to violate the statute forbidding the importation of Quakers. Under pretense of transporting them up the Chesapeake Bay to Patuxent, he landed them at Nassawaddox on the Virginia Eastern Shore, where there was a Quaker meeting house, and where Living Denwood (one of Augustine Herman's business associates) welcomed them.[80]

Despite the oppression, some Quakers managed to obtain or maintain important positions in their counties or in the colony. For example, the Quakers John Porter, Sr., and his son John Porter, Jr., were both Lower Norfolk justices of the peace in 1665. John Porter, Jr., was sheriff in 1660 and a burgess in 1663. He married the daughter of another justice and burgess, Colonel John Sidney. William Robinson was a justice of the peace in 1660. Mary Emperor, a Quaker, married Puritan Barbadian immigrant Francis Emperor, a justice and sheriff of Lower Norfolk and Princess Anne Counties and a surveyor of Virginia. All of these relatively prominent Quakers lived along or near the Elizabeth River, an area with strong Puritan traditions.[81]

By the 1670s, Quakers permeated all parts of Virginia. Most numerous on the Eastern Shore and south of the James, they also lived on the Rappahannock and Potomac Rivers and in York County, and included many justices and some burgesses.[82] In 1672 William Edmundson converted the Puritans Richard Bennett and Thomas Dewes, who had been governor and speaker of the Assembly, respectively, during the Interregnum.

The pattern of travel for Quaker missionaries resembled that of other travelers from England to Virginia, following trade routes that commonly dictated a first stop in Barbados. Friends considered Barbados the center of American Quakerism before the 1682 establishment of Pennsylvania. In 1661 one Quaker called Barbados "the nursury of the Truth." English Quakers who wrote circular epistles to multiple colonies often named Barbadian Quakers first in their lists of intended audiences.[83] Because ministers so often came to Virginia directly from Barbados and before traveling elsewhere, Virginians usually heard most about Quakers in Barbados (after England) and about Barbados in general from these traveling public friends. Because of the prevalent trade patterns, Quakers coming to the Chesapeake from Barbados were more likely to find passage to the Lower Norfolk area than to any other part of Virginia.

From Virginia the ministers went either overland or by sea to other colonies. Ministers traveled overland and by canoe more frequently than other travelers because they wanted to stop at all meetings and potential meetings to try to convert colonists and Indians along the way, and perhaps because Virginia officials' efforts to prevent shipmasters from bringing Quakers into Virginia hindered their maritime access to the colony. Their overland travels therefore fore depended on precontact Indian trade routes and on guidance from Indians who knew them. Whether maritime or overland, religious travel ultimatey relied on networks whose primary purpose was trade.

Apparently these ministers did not plan ahead, instead trusting divine "leadings" and "drawings" to tell them where to go.[84] The continuing missionary tradition fostered a sense of an intercolonial and transatlantic community of Quakers.[85] They relayed more than religious news. In 1697 a friend asked traveling minister William Ellis to look for a family member of this in West jersey "and take account from them of their welfare, both as to the things of this life and to the Truth."[86] Ministers fostered community by discussing Quakers' experiences in England and other colonies as well as by establishing meetings on the English pattern in the different places they went. George Fox was particularly concerned with establishing a common organization.[87] In August 1671 Fox and several other Quaker ministers left England for its colonies. In October they arrived in Barbados, where Fox met with Deputy Governor Christopher Codrington. The Quaker ministers held several meetings with white and black Barbadians.[88] From there they dispersed, with some remaining in Barbados while others went to Jamaica and from there to various mainland colonies. During the next two years described in Fox's journal, the ministers who had parted ways in Barbados crossed paths several times in their respective travels throughout the English colonies. Fox himself went from Jamaica to Maryland, from Maryland to Rhode Island and through New England, back overland to Maryland, and first arrived in Virginia in 1672.

When Public Friends dispersed in their travels, they planned to reunite at appointed places. They clearly conceived their sphere of operation to include all the English world, and they knew well of the existing commercial, familial, and social networks that allowed them to include all colonies in their travels.[89] George Fox, coming to Maryland from Virginia, reported arriving at John Mayor's house "where wee mett with some from New England which before wee had left behind there, & glad wee were to see each other after our longe traveils." Those arriving from New England informed Fox that Quakers had left New England for Jamaica, Ireland, Barbados, the Leeward Islands, New Jersey, and "the New Countries" to visit Friends.[90] Though Public Friends claimed to follow divine leanings as they felt them, they clearly made some prior arrangements and relied on the intercolonial movement of letters and word of mouth information to know the whereabouts of sympathizers and Quaker settlements. Maryland, perhaps both because of its central location and its policy of tolerance, was a common rendezvous point for Quaker traveling ministers in America. Fox describes going in Maryland to Quaker William Stephens' house, which he described as a place "where frinds mete that hade bee[ne] abrode."[91]

The Quaker traveling ministers stayed with whoever would have them. Their reputation and news of their imminent arrival often preceded them. In Nansemond County, Virginia, when Fox and other Quaker ministers arrived, "there came an old man a Justice to a friend, and saide that Geo ffox was a very famous man." In his journal Fox repeatedly reported his fame and the desire of Quakers and non-Quakers to meet him or to attend meetings. He reported that non-Quakers beyond Somertowne in North Carolina ("their was no friends in those parts") "had heard of mee, & had beene at ye house where wee lay, & had a great desire to heare & see us but miss'd us: The truth sounds abroad everyway."[92] Fox expressed confidence in intercolonial information networks. Several times after describing meeting Quakers in his travels, especially where missionaries had not traveled, he ended his story with the words "the truth spreadeth," noting that information and interest had preceded the arrival of the ministers themselves.[93] Both Friends and "people of the world" welcomed the arrival of Quaker ministers, who had meetings whenever they could, stayed with colonists in settled areas, and, while traveling overland, camped or stayed with Indians. They tried to convert everyone with whom they came into contact.[94]

The Quaker meetings that visiting ministers attended were popular in Virginia. Thomas Jordan wrote to George Fox from Virginia in 1687 that many colonists went to meetings when visiting Friends appeared there "but few will com & sett & waight wth us then they are gon." If more visitors came to Virginia, wrote Jordan, Quakerism there would benefit, clearly suggesting that intercolonial and transatlantic travel strengthened Quaker communities in Virginia.[95]

Quaker ministers' journals enable us to explore how Quakers created an intercolonial community and describe in more detail than many other sources the logistics of overland and coastal travel. They also allow us to consider the overlapping of Indian and colonial geographies on the mainland. Ministers stayed for weeks at a time in each colony and for days at each location. Their practice of traveling overland as well as by sea partly stemmed from their interest in converting Indians, but it also allowed them to avoid officials and reach areas Europeans had sparsely settled, that lacked clergy, and perhaps felt most open to Quaker teachings.

Fox's journal contains several references to passing through "Indians Countryes," often hiring Indian guides to take them part way or canoes to cross rivers.[96] As they traveled, they slept sometimes "in the woods by a fire and sometimes in the Indian Cabbins" until they "came at last & lay at one Indian Kings house and hee & his queen received mee lovingly and his attendants allsoe and laid me a mat to lie upon." At the next Indian town, the chief, who could speak some English, greeted Fox "very lovingly." Fox "spake to him much and his people" and procured from him a second guide who took them from New Casde to Middle Towne in New Jersey.[97] When they returned from New England they again traveled overland on a "longe Journey through the woods toward Mary Land, & soe hired Indians, for it was upon me to passe thorrow ye woods" on the other side of the Delaware Bay. They again passed through many Indian towns and over rivers and bogs, several times hiring Indian guides.[98] Precontact Indian travel routes, then, allowed Quaker ministers (like European traders) to travel overland across colonial boundaries, bypassing the more usual method of travel for colonists. Such association with Indians aided their travels, but could not have endeared them to Anglican officials who already regarded Quakers as subversive, secretive, and dangerous.

Indians served as guides, not just between colonies, but in them. They commonly came to Quaker meetings, sometimes as expressly invited guests, sometimes on their own initiative. Quaker teachings or other aspects of Quaker meetings appealed to some Indians. Their frequent appearance without active Quaker recruiting and their seemingly easy attendance at meetings imply frequent interaction between colonists and Indians. Sometimes interpreters at the meetings were Indians, sometimes colonists.[99] In Maryland, Fox referred to an "Established and seded" meeting at a Friend's house on the Eastern Shore. The "Judge of that Couenty," his wife, three other justices, the high sheriff and his wife, the "Indian Emperour & an Indian King & there speaker" all attended, "& all was very loving." Shortly after that meeting, Fox and his party went by water about ten miles to the Indian town where the tayac lived. Fox had sent him a message ahead of time so that he could ask the "Kings & there Counsell [to come] togeather" for a Quaker meeting. Two justices and some other English Quakers accompanied Fox as interpreters and attendees.[100]

Such meetings indicate Quaker belief in potential for a religious community that not only transcended political borders between English colonies using shipping routes, as Puritans did, but also political/cultural borders between Indians and Europeans using overland routes discussed in Chapter 1. George Fox's explicit belief that Indians could be Quakers gave Anglican officials further cause for concern. After meeting a werowance "a pretty sober man" in Carolina, Fox argued in the presence of "the Governor & ye people" that "the Light & the spiritt" were present in everyone. As proof, he asked an Indian whether "when he did wronge, was not there somethinge in him, that did ... reproove him." The Indian confirmed that he did in fact possess such a conscience, which according to Fox, provided proof that Indians possessed inner light just as Europeans did.[101] Many Indians saw great distinctions separating Quakers from other English colonists. Indeed, Jaspar Dankaerts reported in 1679 that "The Indians ... say [the Quakers] are not Englishmen, always distinguishing them from other Englishmen. ... The Indians say 'they are not Christians, they are like ourselves.' "[102] Such an identification with Quakers may have resulted both from Quaker theology and from Quaker travel patterns.

The combination of Quakers' challenges to such cultural boundaries and their disregard for political borders was what caused such concern among Anglican officials. Thomas Thurston, a Public Friend who traveled in several colonies, often stayed with Indians from whom he received "the most Courteous Entertainment." When Virginia officials jailed Thurston in 1657, some Susquehannocks with whom he had stayed came to visit him in prison.[103] Susquehannocks lived in Maryland, Delaware, New York, and what became Pennsylvania, so in this instance Quaker travel encouraged Indian intercolonial travel, facilitating cultural and political boundary crossing, not a situation calculated to improve Quaker standing with Virginia officials. Just as the Quaker combined use of overland and coastal travel depended on both Indian and European (and increasingly overlapping) trade routes, Quakers' belief in the possibility of a spiritual community including Europeans and Indians depended on the existence of already overlapping and interacting physical worlds. Sometimes Indians they met spoke English. The journals make it obvious that Indians interacted with English colonists in a variety of ways on a casual or daily basis, particularly in areas less central to the English.

The travels of English Friends in American colonies facilitated the intercolonial travel of American Quakers. While George Fox and other Quaker ministers were in Barbados, John Jay, described by Quaker John Stubbs as "a pretty rich planter in Barbados," decided to accompany the ministers to New England, New Jersey, Long Island, Delaware, Maryland, Virginia, and Carolina. After his travels through the mainland colonies, Jay returned to his wife, plantation, and family in Barbados, taking news about the mainland colonies that would contribute to American Quakers' sense that they belonged to a shared world.[104] Other American Quakers also used English traveling Friends' journeys to facilitate their own intercolonial travel. While in Elizabeth River, Lower Norfolk County, Fox reported that "wee passed about 6 miles by land and water to take in freinds for Maryland" before leaving Virginia.[105]

After returning to England, Fox and others wrote letters encouraging American Quakers to visit other colonies. In a 1684 circular letter, Fox urged Friends to visit Virginia and Carolina.[106] In 1699 James Dickinson encouraged Friends to "visit remote parts that want help; as Virginia, Carolina, New England, Barbados, Jamaica, Antigua, Nevis."[107] Fox suggested that Public Friends in Pennsylvania and New Jersey, where there were more in ministry, "divide [themselves] to other meetings, and two and two to visit friends" in New England, Maryland, Virginia, and Carolina.[108]

Fox's writing also reveals his expectation that Quakers would continue to travel between colonies beyond his explicit recommendations. Quakers sometimes in fact traveled across intercolonial boundaries not to proselytize but simply to attend meetings. In a 1673 letter from the Worcester jail to Quakers in Virginia, Fox wrote that if they went "over again to Carolina," they should ask Captain Nathaniel Batts, "the Old Governor," about a paper Fox had left with him to read to "the Emperor and his Thirty Kings under him of the Tusrowres, who were to come to Treat for Peace with the People of Carolina."[109]

Persecution itself could encourage communication, travel, and migration between American Quakers. Fox reported a meeting at the Clifts in Maryland "and there Came a Justice from potomake in Virginia a prety man & had beene under persecution & threatned by the preeste & others hee & his man came 40 milles on fote hee hath a greate love to the truth."[110] John Copeland, a Quaker who had his ears clipped in Massachusetts, later moved to southern Virginia, possibly hoping to escape persecution.[111] George Wilson, persecuted in New England in 1661, went to Virginia but fared worse there and died in jail in Jamestown.[112] Quaker minister William Edmundson reported that, having visited in North Carolina in 1672, he met Henry Phelps. Edmundson wrote that "Henry Phillips and his wife had been convinc'd of the Truth in New-England, and came there to live (1665), who having not seen a Friends for Seven Years before they wept for Joy to see us."[113]

Fox and other ministers clearly tried to foster conformity and a sense of unity among Quakers throughout the English Atlantic world. In Rhode Island daring the summer of 1672, Fox reported that he and those accompanying him came from New England to Rhode Island for a general meeting, which they had encouraged and helped organize. Planned to last ten days, "by the Continued comeing of people in sloopes from divers other Collonies & Jurisdictions it Continued longer." Fox planned the 1672 Rhode Island General meeting as the first of many that would supplement annual meetings within each colony.[114] During his visit, Maryland may have held a general meeting as well. For several days after the 1672 Rhode Island General Meeting many of the Quakers stayed and had more large gatherings. At one of them "A Marriage for Example sake," which Quakers and non-Quakers attended, took place at the house of the Quaker and former Deputy Governor William Coddington to serve as "an Example to all the rest of the Jurisdictions, some [people] out of many places was there."[115] Unity in ceremony would foster the Quakers' sense of belonging to an Atlantic community of Friends.

Quakers also sent circular letters to meetings, which read them publicly and sent them on.[116] These epistles and those sent from one American meeting to another had the potential to produce mutual shared assumptions on a variety of subjects. Those who carried the letters formed further contacts between meetings, carrying news and experiences from one place to another. In the summer of 1672, Fox, still in Rhode Island, gave a public lecture recounting his travels in Jamaica, Virginia, and through "the Indian Countrey" to New England. He sent a copy of the narrative to Thomas Rouse in Barbados to be read in meetings there. He intended that it also be read at the London meetings and copies of it distributed throughout Quaker meetings in England.[117] In addition to organizing meetings to conform to a common model, Fox and other ministers hoped to encourage American Quakers to continue communicating with one another and maintain their intercolonial and transatlantic community. He continued in his writings to encourage them to travel and hold a yearly North American meeting. He also wanted them to send minutes and episodes with religious and other advice from meeting to meeting.[118]

With its founding in 1682, Pennsylvania became a new center for Quakerism in America. The large-scale migrations of Quakers to the new colony and the political power of Quakers within that colony made Pennsylvania a de facto, though not official, influence on other Quakers and also made it a primary line of communication between American Quakers and the London meeting. Some Pennsylvanians adopted a sense of responsibility for Quakerism in America.[119] In 1683 William Penn suggested "a general meeting of friends from New England to Carolina." In 1684, representatives from Maryland and Rhode Island held a yearly meeting where they made plans for another yearly meeting and asked meetings in the colonies to "send two or three for each province to our Yearly Meeting here being a center or middle part that so communion and blessed union may be preserved among all."[120] These general meetings were not to include Quakers from Caribbean colonies, perhaps reflecting that the importance of overland travel for Quakers on the mainland and the presence of possible

Indian converts created a distinction between island and mainland colonies just beginning among other English colonists. Their overland travels perhaps led them to an early perception that as Restoration colonies filled in the once vast spaces between England's mainland colonies, they were less "islands" of English settlement, like the Caribbean, but began to form a contiguous whole that did not include the Caribbean.

Tracing the spread of one Quaker heterodoxy and the effort to prevent the spread of another shows the facility with which ideas spread within the Quaker intercolonial network. "Perrot's heresy," which involved a denial of all outward signs of worship (including removing one's hat as a sign of respect to God when another Friend prayed), began in England in 1661. John Perrot carried his doctrine to the Caribbean and thence to Virginia and Maryland. It spread eventually to New York and Rotterdam.[121] In a similar case thirty years later Pennsylvania Friend George Keith attacked the Quaker belief that the inward Christ alone saved, with or without faith in a historic Christ or in biblical scriptures. In 1692 the Philadelphia Yearly Meeting disowned as many as one quarter of the Quakers in Pennsylvania and New Jersey for ascribing to Keith's heresy. Soon afterward, Quakers in Barbados, Virginia, Maryland, New Jersey, Long Island, and Rhode Island censored him, indicating both that the news had spread and that Quakers considered it useful to voice opinions across the distances their community spanned.[122]

Because Quakerism combined an intercolonial community with significant challenges to the social order, with a greater acceptance of Indians as potential spiritual equals, and with pacifism, officials perceived them as posing a unique threat that rested on intercolonial communication and strengthened other kinds of intercolonial dangers, particularly those posed by Indians' traveling. Officials responded with increased attempts to prevent Quaker travel, thereby attempting to make their political borders serve as religious boundaries as well. Though James II's "Declaration for Liberty of Conscience and Indulgence in Religious Matters" assured toleration for nonconformists, and the Glorious Revolution in 1688 assured its continuance, Quakers in Virginia remained subject to suspicion.[123] The strength they derived from their intercolonial community, combined with the challenges they presented to social order, created a threat, especially with regard to fears about Indians crossing political and cultural boundaries. As a result, persecution of Quakers continued and officials increased their attempts to create firm religious boundaries along their political borders.

In 1691 when France and England were at war, Virginia Governor Francis Nicholson and his Council heard that the Quakers of Pennsylvania had declared that if the French and Indians came to their settlements armed with rifles, tomahawks, and torches, Pennsylvania would offer no resistance. On hearing this report, Virginia councilors worried that if French colonists and their Indian allies invaded the Chesapeake they would obtain provisions in Pennsylvania and that the pacifism of Penn's colony would provide them with a safe retreat after raiding Maryland and Virginia. The Virginia Assembly noted that recently many Quaker meetings in Virginia had assembled without informing the local authorities, as the Toleration Act required. The Council worried that if the French and their Indian allies took Pennsylvania, they would learn Virginia's strengths and weaknesses through the frequent communication between Virginia and Pennsylvania Quakers and through the Quaker practice of welcoming Indians into their midst. The French and their allies could thereby discover the best way to attack the Chesapeake.

Nicholson and his Council issued a proclamation warning Virginia Quakers not to "come together" in a general assembly unless they had informed officials of their meetings. Most importantly, Quakers must send a message immediately to the nearest "magistrate" if a Pennsylvania Quaker came with a message from the Pennsylvania government. Magistrates were to summon any traveling Quakers instantly and question them closely, finding out where they came from, why, and their destination. If the replies seemed suspicious, the magistrate was to send the travelers to Jamestown.[124]

Meanwhile the Church of England increased its presence in Virginia. Henry Compton, bishop of London (with authority over the colonial church) for the final decade of Charles II's reign and again under William and Mary, took much greater interest in the colonial church than had his predecessors. In 1677 he initiated an investigation into the quality of Virginia clergy, and in 1680 required that colonial governors ensure that parish clergy possessed certificates issued by Compton himself. He sent clergy to Virginia and for the first time appointed a commissary (bishop's agent) to oversee church governance in the colony.[125] James Blair, commissary during the 1690s, used increased transatlantic flow of clergy and money to strengthen Anglicanism in the colony. He failed in some attempts to assert the Church's authority, as in his effort to reestablish church courts to discipline clergy and laity for their moral failings. Nicholson, as governor of Virginia, supported the effort as part of an overall desire to bring England's colonies into greater conformity with one another and more firmly under England's control, and backed plans to establish the College of William and Mary, which would serve in part as a training ground for Anglican clergy. The decade also saw renewed support for the appointing of an American bishop, and in 1701 the establishing of the Society for the Propagation of the Gospel in Foreign Parts, an Anglican missionary society that devoted much of its attention to England's unchurched colonists in America.[126]

Anglican church officials, in their criticisms of Quakers, detailed the ways in which Quakers created and maintained their intercolonial networks. In November 1702 the Anglican (and former Quaker) George Keith and a committee of six others were charged with investigating the state of the Church of England in America. Their report included twenty-four headings on the ways in which Quakers supported their meetings and schools, including "organization, uniformity of discipline, circulation of literature, ... active missionary enterprise," and collections of a common fund with which they financed printing and meeting house buildings. Keith also noted that Quakers strengthened their position in the colonies "By keeping there Trade within themselves and maintaining a strict Correspondence and Intelligence over all parts where they are" and "By suffering none of themselves to marry but with those of their own profession."[127] Documenting the scope and efficiency of the Quaker network, the Anglican Reverend John Talbot, in a 1703 letter to the secretary of the

Society for the Propagation of the Gospel, expressed his concern that "The Quakers compass sea and land to make proselytes; they send out yearly a parcel of vagabond Fellows that ought to be taken up and put in Bedlam. ... Their preaching is of cursing and Lyes, poysening the souls of the people with damnable errors and heresies, and not content with this in their own Territories or Pennsylvania, but they travel with mischief over all parts as far as they can goe, over Virginia and Maryland, and again through Jersey and New York as far as New England."[128]

Keith and his fellow committee members recognized clearly the links between intercolonial religious networks, the marriages that formed longdistance family ties, and the colonial shipping that shaped seventeenth-century intercolonial networks and held them together. His comments on Quaker endogamy and trade would have held for Puritans in the seventeenth-century Atlantic world as well. Quaker and Puritan bonds functioned for some like family ties in providing a basis of trust on which to form commercial linkages.[129] Enough Puritans (including merchants) converted to Quakerism to procure similar and overlapping networks. The movements of ministers, the best documented, provide the geographical outlines for more general migration patterns. Ministers' movements both created and reflected the sense among nonconformists that they belonged to communities not bounded by political colonial borders. The fact that these networks mirrored almost exactly the intercolonial trade routes (encompassing most fully those regions of Virginia that traded most extensively with other colonies) substantiates the high degree to which the religious, family, and economic networks intertwined.

The Church of England changed by the end of the century, exhibiting greater toleration that accompanied the growing influence of latitudinarian beliefs in rational religion. Religious dissent increased in England after 1660.[130] The Toleration Act of 1688 assured non-Anglican protestants the right to worship and hold office, so Anglican officials' victories in confirming Virginia's official status as Anglican did not limit Virginians' options as it might have had Berkeley succeeded in suppressing them in the 1640s. In 1699 the House of Burgesses reduced Virginians' church attendance requirement to once every other month, recognizing that Virginia's geography and demography and history limited the colony's ability to impose a more meaningful Anglicanism on unwilling inhabitants.[131] Puritans' and Quakers' persistence to that time had depended on intercolonial ties that allowed them to survive until Virginia allowed greater toleration. Those intercolonial ties did not end with toleration, but continued into the eighteenth century, existing alongside the elaborated transatlantic ties to England that accounted for the growth of the Anglican Church, and ensured that Virginians' religious lives, while lived largely in local parishes and meeting houses, kept them firmly ensconced within the British Atlantic.[132]

Because Anglican officials realized the dependency of nonconformists in Virginia on their links to other American colonies and to England, they attempted to limit the religious travel of Quakers and Puritans across colonial borders. While all colonists recognized the necessity of economic links between colonies, in the case of religious intercolonial networks of nonconformists, authorities contested the fluidity of colonial boundaries. Virginia Anglicans attempted to strengthen and add cultural meaning to intercolonial political boundaries in response to the intercolonial religious networks described in this chapter. The interaction between nonconformists and Anglican officials in Virginia embodied a contest over the fluidity of boundaries and over the cultural definition of Virginia. Easy movement between colonies strengthened Quaker and Puritan communities south of the James River and on the Eastern Shore. As long as other colonies remained only partially Anglican, fluid boundaries allowed some degree of religious diversity in Virginia, despite periods of persecution at the hands of Anglican officials. In response to nonconformists' reliance on porous intercolonial borders, Virginia officials tried to seal those boundaries, at least against Quakers and Puritans. By the end of the seventeenth century, when Virginia officials, impelled by their colonists' frequent intercolonial interactions, succeeded in defining Virginia as an Anglican place theoretically, its history of religious diversity was fully established and facilitated the successes of future nonconformist proselytizers. We must, therefore, reconceive Virginia as a place where intercolonial trade and travel altered colonists' religious choices and allowed them to contest officials' attempts to make Virginia an exclusively Anglican colony.

NOTES

1. Joan R. Gunderson, "The Search for Good Men: Recruiting Ministers in Colo-nial Virginia," *Historical Magazine of the Protestant Episcopal Church* 48 (1979): 453–64. Vestry independence in Virginia mitigated ties to England during the seventeenth century. Warren M. Billings, *Virginia's Viceroy: Their Majesties' Governor General: Francis Howard, Baron Howard of Effingham* (Fairfax, Va., 1991), 81; Edward L. Bond, *Damned Souls in a Tobacco Colony: Religion in Seventeenth-Century Virginia* (Macon, Ga., 2000), 211–14; Gunderson, "The Myth of the Independent Virginia Vestry," *Historical Magazine of the Protestant Episcopal Church* 44 (1975): 133–41.

2. James Horn, *Adapting to a New World,* 385.

3. Bond, *Damned Souls,* 240.

4. Peter G. Lake, "Calvinism and the English Church, 1570–1635," *Past and Present* 114 (1987): 32–76; Lake," The Laudian Style:Order, Conformity and the Pursuit of Holiness in the 1630s," in Kenneth Fincham, ed., *The Early Stuart Church* (Stanford, Calif., 1993), 161–85; Lake, "A Charitable Christian Hatred: the Godly and their Enemies in the 1630s," in C. Durston and J. Eales, eds., *The Culture of English Puritanism, 1560–1700* (New York,1996), 145–83. See also Anthony Milton, "The Church of England, Rome and the True Church: The Demise of a Jacobean Consensus," in Fincham, ed., *The Early Stuart Church,* 187–210; Peter Collinson, *The Religion of Protestants: The Church in English Society, 1559–1624* (Oxford, 1982); Lake, "Defining Puritanism-Again?" in F. Bremer, ed., *Puritanism: Transatlantic Perspectives on a Seventeenth-Century Anglo-American Faith* (Boston, 1993), 3–29; Judith Maltby, "'By this book': Parishioners, the Prayer Book and the Established Church," in Fincham, ed., *The Early Stuart Church,* 115–37;

John Morrill, "The Religious Context of the English Civil War," in Richard Cust and Ann Hughes, eds., *The English Civil War* (London and New York, 1997), 159–80; Nicholas Tyacke, "Puritanism, Arminianism and Counter-Revolution," in Cust and Hughes, eds., *The English Civil War*, 136–58.

5. Bond, *Damned Souls*, 140–45. Bond suggests that the presence of Indians may have mitigated differences between Puritans and Anglicans, but the absence of clergy seems a more likely explanation.

6. James Horn argues that "England's religious heterogeneity was transferred to the Chesapeake: Nonconformity in Virginia and Maryland was not an aberration." *Adapting to a New World*, 410–11. This chapter will argue that as the century progressed, intercolonial ties as well as transatlantic ones nurtured nonconformity in Virginia, while officials used their links to England to enforce Angicanism on the colony.

7. Indeed, Frederick Tolles found that most of Philadelphia's "early Quaker merchants" came "from the other American colonies, where for a period of years they had had an opportunity to exercise their talents in mercantile pursuits." *Meeting House and Counting House: The Quaker Merchants of Colonial Philadelphia, 1682–1763* (Chapel Hill, N.C., 1948), 43. J. F. Bosher finds similar connection between religious and commercial networks for French Huguenot merchants in the last two decades of the seventeenth century, arguing that the Huguenot merchants formed part of a larger Protestant international merchant community based on both commerce and common religion. He claims that the "overseas business of Huguenot merchants flourished in the atmosphere of personal trust based on a common religion and carefully fostered relations of scattered families." Doing business with others of the same religion produced a sense of common purpose and responsibility that reduced the risk of fraud. See J. F. Bosher "Huguenot Merchants and the Protestant International in the Seventeenth Century," *WMQ* 3rd ser., 52 (1995): 77–102, quote, 78.

8. See Cynthia Jean Van Zandt, "Negotiating Settlement: Colonialism, Cultural Exchange, and Conflict in Early Colonial Atlantic North America, 1580–1660" (Ph.D. diss., University of Connecticut, 1998), 187–225. See also Van Zandt, "The Dutch Connection: Isaac Allerton and the Dynamics of English Cultural Anxiety in the *Gouden EEUW*" in Rosemarijn Hoefte and Johanna C. Kardux, eds., *Connecting Cultures: The Netherlands in Five Centuries of Transatlantic Exchange* (Amsterdam, 1994), 51–76

9. Walter S. Allerton, *A History of the Allerton Family in the United States, 1585–1883, and A Genealogy of the Descendants of Isaac Allerton* (New York, 1888), revised by Samuel Waters Allerton (Chicago, 1900), 13, 21–23.

10. For Loockerman's Chesapeake–New Netherland trade, see Dennis J. Maika, "Commerce and Community: Manhattan Merchants in the Seventeenth Century" (Ph. D. diss., New York University, 1995). On January 20, 1642, Allerton sold his yacht Hope to Loockermans and in 1643 Allerton and Loockermans received a grant in New Amsterdam for two lots on the Great Highway. Isaac J. Greenwood, "Allertons of New England and Virginia," *New England Historical and Genealogical Register* 44 (1890): 290–96. For his naturalization, see Wyand and Wyand, *Colonial Maryland Naturalizations*, 7.

11. On September 27, 1654, New Haven Governor John Davenport wrote that Mr. Allerton was then on a voyage to Virginia. Allerton, *History of the Allerton Family*, 24–25.

12. Greenwood, "Allertons," 292.

13. Allerton, *History of the Allerton Family*, 26.

14. Greenwood, "Allertons," 291; Allerton, *History of the Allerton Family*, 27. The will referred to specific debts (including one determined by arbitration of Augustine Herman) owed by and to Allerton, and general reference to "all my debts in Delaware Bay and Virginia ... and in Barbadoes."

15. Allerton, *History of the Allerton Family*, 31.

16. Greenwood, "Allertons," 292.

17. The island in the Potomac between Washington, D.C., and Arlington, Virginia, now the National Park Service's Theodore Roosevelt Island, was called Barbados Island in the mid-seventeenth century, perhaps so named by an immigrant from the Caribbean.

18. Allerton, *History of the Allerton Family*, 32, citing *VMHB* 1 (1893), 199; Northumberland and Westmoreland records; Hening, *Statutes*, 2:257. Allerton was a Westmoreland County justice of the peace in 1677.

19. On June 10, 1691, Governor Francis Nicholson reported to London that Richard Lee, Isaac Allerton, and John Armistead, out of scruple of conscience, refused to take the oath and were left out of the Council. Allerton, *History of the Allerton Family*, 33.

20. Isaac and his first wife Elizabeth had three children. Their son Isaac, after accompanying his father to Virginia as a child, returned to New Haven as an adult. Allerton, *History of the Allerton Family*, 34.

21. Babette M Levy, "Early Puritanism in the Southern and Island Colonies," *American Antiquarian Society Proceedings* 70 (1960): 81–85. See also Kevin Butterfield, "Puritans and Religious Strife in the Early Chesapeake," *VMHB* 109 (2001): 5–36.

22. John Frederick Fausz, "The Powhatan Uprising of 1622: A Historical Study of Ethnocentrism and Cultural Conflict" (Ph.D. diss., The College of William and Mary, 1977), 296. The 1622 Indian attack ended the plans for the college at Henrico. Copland went instead to Bermuda, where in 1635 he was organizing a school. Copland wanted to build a missionary college from which men could be sent to convert Virginia Indians. See *Winthrop Papers* (Boston, 1929), 3:84–85; 5:96–97, 182–85; and Levy, "Early Puritanism," 175. Levy cites Edward D. Neill, *Memoir of Reverend Patrick Copland* (New York, 1871).

23. Levy, "Early Puritanism," 109–10.

24. Bosse moved from Virginia to New England in 1631. Kingsbury, ed., *Records of the Virginia Company of London*, 3:414. See also Levy, "Early Puritanism," 107.

25. Levy, "Early Puritanism," 108–9.

26. The letter, dated May 24, 1642, is reprinted in Jon Butler, "Two 1642 Letters from Virginia Puritans," *Massachusetts Historical Society Proceedings* 84 (1972): 99–109, quotes, 105–6.

27. Edmund Morgan, *American Slavery, American Freedom*, 412.

28. Nansemond Puritans to Christ Church Elders, May 24, 1642, in Butler, "Two 1642 Letters," 105.

29. Butler, "Two 1642 Letters," 105–9.

30. Butler, "Two 1642 Letters," 106, citing William Haller, *The Rise of Puritanism* (New York, 1938), and Christopher Hill, *Society and Puritanism in Pre-Revolutionary England* (New York, 1964), for examples.

31. Butler, "Two 1642 Letters," 108.

32. William Durand to John Davenport, July 15, 1642, in Butler, "Two 1642 Letters," 107. Durand and the other Virginia Puritans who had written to New England believed that prayer connected the Virginians not only to Davenport but to New England Puritans in general. Durand explained to Davenport that the letter the parishioners had sent had been addressed generally rather than to any specific person "because the worke is great and of deepe consequence, wherein the more are interested, the more prayers and better successe is hoped for."

33. John Winthrop, *The History of New England from 1630 to 1649*, ed. James Savage (Boston, 1853), 2:94. Winthrop wrote of Bennett's arrival in a small pinnace and stated that the letters were openly read in Boston on a lecture day. The General Court approved of the elders' choice and "ordered that the governour should commend them to the governour and council of Virginia, which was done accordingly."

34. Winthrop, *History*, 2:94.

35. New England churches also sent material help to other colonies. On July 29, 1666, the Roxbury Church reported that "Divers strangers that came from Christopher's Island being in that necessitie & distress by sicknes lamenesse &c besides the prvision made for them by the Generall Court, the severall Churches contributed towards their relief." Boston Records Commission, Report 6, *A Report of the Record Commissioners, containing the Roxbury Land and Church Records* (Boston, 1881), 204.

36. Winthrop, *History*, 2:73, 74, 94, 95.

37. Winthrop, *History*, 2:115–16.

38. Winthrop, *History*, 2:115–16. This Puritan worship in private houses may have set the stage for Quaker popularity in the same areas.

39. John Winthrop, *Journal*, ed. James Kendall Hosmer, *Original Narratives of Early American History* (New York, 1908), 2:167–68; cited in Wilcomb E. Washburn, "Governor Berkeley and King Philip's War," *New England Quarterly* 30 (1957): 363–77, quote 363–64. For the Virginia Assembly's order that the ministers leave the colony, see Hening, *Statutes*, 1:277.

40. Edward Johnson, *The Wonder-Working Providence of Sion's Saviour in New England*, ed. J. Franklin Jameson, *Original Narratives of Early American History* (New York, 1910), book 3, 265–67; cited in Washburn, "Governor Berkeley," 365.

41. Winthrop, *Journal*, 2:168, cited in Washburn "Governor Berkeley," 364.

42. Levy, "Early Puritanism," 89.

43. Horn, *Adapting to a New World*, 399.

44. Levy, "Early Puritanism," 132–33; Daniel R. Randall, *A Puritan Colony in Maryland* (Baltimore, 1886), 17. Puritans in Nansemond County later said that they had been "invited and encouraged" by Stone to move to Maryland and that he had promised they would find religious liberty there. "Virginia & Maryland, or, the Lord Baltimore's Printed Case 1655," in Force, ed., *Tracts and Other Papers*, 2:28–29.

45. Harrison arrived in Elizabeth River in 1640. Horn, *Adapting to a New World*, 389.

46. *Winthrop Papers*, 5:434–40. See also Levy, "Early Puritanism," 126–27, citing Lower Norfolk County Orders, May 25, 1640.

47. Thomas Harrison to John Winthrop, November 2, 1646, in *Winthrop Papers*, 5:116–17.

48. Levy, "Early Puritanism," 127; Winthrop, *History*, 2:334; Johnson, *Wonder-Working Providence*, 351–53. American Puritans relied on one another and on their growing intercolonial networks for religious news from England as well as for prayers. Both kinds of connections strengthened the bonds that tied Virginia Puritans to New Englanders. In another letter to Winthrop in the winter of 1648, this time from Nansemond, Harrison discusses with Winthrop news that had reached Virginia of toleration in England, reporting that "Parliament proceeds to settle the affaires of the Kingdome: That golden apple The ordinance for toleration, is now fairly fallen into the lap of the Saints"

49. *Winthrop Papers*, 5:212–13.

50. Sayle had received a grant from Parliament for the project. Longtime Puritan Atlantic world resident Patrick Copland, originally part of early Virginia Company plans, and now elder of the Puritan church in Bermuda, was among the group of seventy Bermudian migrants to Eleutheria. Winthrop, *History*, 2:407–9.

51. Durand may have preached using notes he had taken from sermons he had heard Davenport give in London. Horn, *Adapting to a New World*, 391; Levy, "Early Puritanism," 237; Philip Alexander Bruce, *Institutional History of Virginia in the Seventeenth Century* (New York, 1910), 1:257.

52. Levy, "Early Puritanism," 130.

53. Atherton to Winthrop, Jr., August 30, 1648 (received November 9), in *Winthrop Papers*, 5:273.

54. Adam Winthrop to John Winthrop, Jr., September 1, 1648, in *Winthrop Papers*, 5:277.

55. Winthrop, *History*, 2:334.

56. Lucy Downing to John Winthrop, Jr., at Pequot, Salem, December 17, [1648]. In *Winthrop Papers*, 5:290–91. In the fall of 1649 New Englanders still referred to Harrison as the minister of the Church at Virginia. Boston Record Commission, Report 9, *Boston Births, Baptisms, Marriages, and Deaths, 1630–1699* (Boston, 1883).

57. Levy, "Early Puritanism," 128–29, citing Edward D. Neill, "A Chapter in American Church History," *New Englander* (1879).

58. Norfolk County Reel 44 Wills & Deeds C 1651–56, 157a; Richard Beale Davis, "The Devil in Virginia in the Seventeenth Century," *VMHB* 65 (1957): 131–49; McIl-waine, *Minutes of the Council and General Court of Colonial Virginia*, 111–14; Bruce, *Institutional History*, 1:278–88.

59. Horn, *Adapting to a New World*, 393–94, citing Edward Papenfuse, *A Biographical Dictionary of the Maryland Legislature* (Baltimore, 1979), 1:290; 2:534, 574–75, 593–94, Lower Norfolk

County, Wills & Deeds B, 1646–51, f. 88, 115, 129, 209, C (1651–55), f. 113–14, 117, 158, D (1656–66), f. 29. See also Levy, "Early Puritanism," 135.

60. Boston Records Commission, Report 6, *A Report of the Record Commissioners, containing the Roxhury Land and Church Records* (Boston, 1881), 87.

61. Levy, "Early Puritanism," 134.

62. In 1676, when William Berkeley fled to the Eastern Shore during Bacon's rebellion and realized the extent of nonconformity there, Anglican officials responded with attempts to enforce Anglican conformity.

63. Levy, "Early Puritanism," 140–41.

64. John Rosier, who served Bennett's Plantation in the early 1630s, was in Nansemond during the late 1630s, in York county in 1640, on the Eastern Shore in 1641, and in Northumberland County in 1650. Francis Bolton preached on the Eastern Shore before moving to Bennett's Plantation in 1623. Levy, "Early Puritanism," 140.

65. His preaching was noted as a memorable event in Eastern Shore court records. For example, in May 1654, Sara Hinman, testifying to the Northampton County Court in a case completely unrelated to Drisius' presence in the region, noted time by referring to "The last Sabbath that Mr Drissius preached here." Northampton County Court Order Books, 1654–61, typescript by Susie May Ames, Virginia Historical Society Mss 3N8125a, fol. 1, 36–37. For a discussion of Drisius's Dutch contacts, see Levy, "Early Puritanism," 144.

66. Horn, *Adaptitig to a New World*, 398; Michael Graham, "Meetinghouse and Chapel: Religion and Community in Seventeenth-Century Maryland," in Carr et al., *Colonial Chesapeake Society*, 260.

67. For a discussion of Quaker travel in England's American colonies, see Frederick B. Tolies, *Quakers and the Atlantic Culture* (1947) (New York, 1960). For numbers, see ibid., 14.

68. Kenneth L. Carrol, "Elizabeth Harris, the Founder of American Quakerism," *Quaker History* 57 (1968): 96–111; Bruce, *Institutional History*, 1:225–26. According to Bruce, the Quaker sect was first heard of in England about 1647. See also Kenneth L. Carroll, "Quakerism on the Eastern Shore of Virginia," *VMHB* 74 (1966): 170–89.

69. Levy, "Early Puritanism," 150–51. Tolies provides examples of a typical trip, that of Christopher Holder who went to New England in 1656 and stayed until 1657 when he went to the Caribbean. He returned by Bermuda to Rhode Island and Massachusetts. He went from there to Virginia, returning in 1659 to Rhode Island and Massachusetts. In 1660 he returned to England. After that he made several more trips to America. An atypical trip was that of Mary Fisher, who went to Barbados in 1655, from there to Massachusetts in 1656, to England in 1657, to Nevis in 1658, to Constantinople in 1660, ending in Charleston, South Carolina. Tolies, *Quakers*, 26–27.

70. Bruce, *Institutional History*, 1:226. The legislature reacted quickly to Quaker missionary activities and in 1658 banned Quakers from Virginia. Hening, *Statutes*, 1:532–33.

71. Bruce, *Institutional History*, 1:226–27.

72. In 1683 he went from England to the Caribbean. Tolies, *Quakers*, 27.

73. Levy, "Early Puritanism," 150–51.

74. Governor Berkeley ordered county sheriffs to suppress Quaker meetings. During the mid- and late-1670S Henrico and Nansemond county officials persecuted Quakers. Levy, "Early Puritanism," 154–55.

75. Quoted in Horn, *Adapting to a New World*, 395, citing Lower Norfolk County, Wills and Deeds D (1656–66), f. 360–74, 380, 392, 396; John Bennett Boddie, *Seventeenth Century Isle of Wight County, Virginia* (Chicago, 1938), 113–14.

76. George Fox, *The Journal of George Fox*, ed. Norman Penney (Cambridge, England, 1911), 2:242.

77. Horn, *Adapting to a New World*, 396.

78. Hening, *Statutes*, 2:181–83; Bruce, *Institutional History*, 1:239.

79. In 1663, magistrates sentenced Mary Thompkins and Alice Ambrose to receive thirty-two lashes each and to be drawn to the pillory with a noose around their necks. Bruce, *Institutional History*, 1:240.

80. Bruce, *Institutional History*, 1:232, citing Northampton County Records, 1657–64. 82, 84.

81. Horn, *Adapting to a New World*, 396–97; Bruce, *Institutional History*, 1:240; Levy, "Early Puritanism," 396. There were limits to these Quakers' ability to hold their offices, however. In 1663 the Virginia Assembly accused the Lower Norfolk County Burgess John Porter of being "loving to the Quakers" and expelled him from the House of Burgesses for refusing to take the burgess's oath, showing that not all those nonconformists who gained political influence during the Interregnum were able to maintain it after the Restoration. Horn, *Adapting to a New World*, 395.

82. Fox, *Journal* 2:240, for descriptions of meetings in Potomac and Rappahan-nock.

83. Letter of George Rofe to Stephen Crisp. The letter is summarized in C. F. Smith, *Stephen Crisp and his Correspondents*, which is cited in Henry J. Cadbury "Inter-colonial Solidarity of American Quakerism," *Pennsylvania Magazine of History and Biography* 60 (1936): 362–74; quote, 363.

84. Tolies, *Quakers*, 26.

85. Many of the Quaker ministers' journals are rich in narrative information about a variety of subjects, in particular the interactions between Indians and Europeans in Virginia and Maryland. Though several of them have been published, they have been underused, especially considering the dearth of this kind of detailed description for the seventeenth-century Chesapeake.

86. John Tompkins to William Ellis and Aaron Atkinson, December 1, 1697, in James Backhouse, *The Life and Correspondence of William and Allice Ellis* (London, 1849), 40–41.

87. See Fox's *Journal* and Epistles. For a discussion of Fox's concern with organization, see Cadbury, "Intercolonial Solidarity," 364.

88. Their meetings with slaves provoked serious concern among Barbadian elites. George Fox, *To the Ministers, Teachers, and Priests, (So called, and so Stileing your Selves) in Barbadoes* ([London], 1672).

89. John Stubbs, writing to England from Newport, Rhode Island, in August 1672, reported to George Fox's wife Margaret that her husband had gone to Maine and that "wee are not likely to see thy husband, till wee see him in Virginia." In the same letter, Stubbs told Margaret Fox that she could direct a letter to him "to Edward Man for Conveyance to us in Puttuxan River

in Maryland, to James Preston there." Letter of John Stubbs to M. Fox, from Newport, Rhode Island June 14, 1672 in Fox, *Journal* 2:217.

90. Fox, *Journal*, 2:240–41.

91. Fox, *Journal*, 2:244.

92. Fox, *Journal*, 2:233–34 .

93. See for example Fox, *Journal*, 2:235.

94. Meetings with public friends were attractive in part because they were different. Not only was Fox famous throughout the English colonial world, the meetings themselves were out of the ordinary and seem to have attracted many besides Quakers, though it is difficult to tell in what capacity non-Quakers came to the meetings. Fox reports all attendants as converts, but some were surely observers.

95. Tolies, *Quakers*, 26, quotes Thomas Jordan to George Fox, November 18, 1687, in *Journal of the Friends Historical Society* 33 (1936): 57.

96. For example, see the letter from John Stubbs to Margaret Fox, written from Rhode Island, April 19, 1672, printed in Fox, *Journal* 2:205; and the letter of George Fox to Friends in London, written from Rhode Island the same day, in Fox, *Journal* 2:210–11. See also *The Second part (or an Addittion to the Journall of G ffs Travailes in America in the year* 1672 and "Fox's Epistles and Queryes," in Fox, *Journal*, 2:224–29, 235–37, 240, 244, 245n, 246.

97. Fox to Friends in London, Rhode Island, April 19, 1672, in Fox, *Journal* 2:211.

98. Fox, *Journal*, 2:224–28.

99. See Fox, *Journal*, passim.

100. Fox, *Journal*, 2:240, 244.

101. Fox, *Journal*, 2:235.

102. Dankaerts, *Journal*, 156.

103. Fox, *Journal*, 2:245n, citing George Bishop, *New England Judged by the Spirit of the Lord* (London, 1703), 29 for quote.

104. Letter of John Stubbs to Margaret Fox, from Newport, Rhode Island, January 29, 1672, printed in Fox, *Journal*, 2:216–17. Jay was also Gay.

105. Fox, *Journal*, 2:239.

106. Cadbury, "Intercolonial Solidarity," 366, citing only MS at Swarthmore College.

107. Cadbury, "Intercolonial Solidarity," 366.

108. Tolies, *Quakers*, 26, quoting circular letter, "To ministering Friends" May 1685, printed in *Pennsylvania Magazine of History and Biography* 29 (1905): 105–6.

109. He also asked to be remembered to Richard Bennett and Thomas Dewes, Virginians he had converted from Puritanism. Fox, *Journal*, 2:234n.

110. Fox, *Journal*, 2:246.

111. Levy, "Early Puritanism," 156, citing Lower Virginia Monthly Meeting Minutes.

112. While imprisoned in Virginia, he wrote letters, now in the Friends Library in London, to New England clergy. Fox, *Journal*, 2:231.

113. Fox, *Journal*, 2:235, citing William Edmundson, *A Journal of the Life, Travels, Sufferings, and Labour of Love ... of ... William Edmundson* (London, 1715), 59.

114. Fox, *Journal*, 2:223.

115. Fox, *Journal*, 2:221–22.

116. In 1657 George Fox wrote an epistie to "Friends beyond sea, that have Blacks and Indian Slaves." He and other Quakers sent circular letters to the American colonies. See for example, "The Books & Divine Epistles of Josiah Coale" (London, 1671), discussed in Tolies, *Quakers*, 32.

117. Stubbs to Fox, June 19, 1672, printed in Fox, *Journal* 2:202–6.

118. Cadbury, "Intercolonial Solidarity," 367. Fox wrote an open letter at Elizabeth River in Lower Norfolk County which sixteen Lower Norfolk residents signed before sending it on to the Nansemond meeting. Levy, "Early Puritanism," 156.

119. Cadbury, "Intercolonial Solidarity," 363.

120. Cadbury, "Intercolonial Solidarity," 364, citing R. M. Jones, ed., *The Quakers in the American Colonies* (1911) (New York, 1962), 434. The plan was never realized.

121. Tolies, *Quakers*, 34.

122. Tolies, *Quakers*, 34.

123. Bruce, *Institutional History*, 2:244–45, provides examples of Quakers' establishing meeting houses during the following years. The Act of Toleration required that every Protestant sect which had seceded from Church of England present regular statements about where they held their services.

124. Bruce, *Institutional History*, 2:247–49, citing Henrico County Records, 1688–192–93. The same proclamation is recorded in York County Records, 1690–94, 27.

125. Bond, *Damned Souls*, 215–20; Jon Butler, *Awashin a Sea of Fith: Christianizing the American People* (Cambridge, Mass., 1990), 42–43.

126. Bond, *Damned Souls*, 204–6, 231, 234.

127. *Collections of the Protestant Episcopal HistoricalSociet* (New York, 18 51:53), 1:xix, cited and quoted in Cadbury," Intercolonial Solidarity" 368–69.

128. September 1, 1703. *Collections of the Protestan Episcopal Historical Society*, 1:xl-xli, quoted in Tolles, *Quakers and the Atlantic Culture*, 25.

129. Notwithstanding considerable evidenceto the contrary, including Keith's report, Tolles argues that the development of family-bsed intercolonial commercial networks did not occur on any significant scale until the eighteenth century. Tolles, *Quakers*, 31. Hall, *Contestd Boundaries*, offers an assessment similar to Tolles.

130. According to James Horn, "Neitherin England nor in the colonies was the ideal of one church and one nation achieved. Increasingly after the Restoraton, the Anglican church was one church among many." *Adapting to a New Wold*, 406.

131. Bond, *Damned Souls*, 238; Hening, *Statutes*, 3:170–71.

132. Quaker merchant networks flourished in the eighteenth century, using strengthened and increasingly integrated transatlantic and intercolonial trade connections.

4

"We Wage War Like Gentlemen"

TWO BATTLES AND THE PATH TO YORKTOWN

By John R. Maass

Of dry top'd oaks they seem'd two forests thick,
So did each host with spears and pikes abound:
Bent were their bows, in rest their lances stick,
Their hands shook swords, their slings held cobles round.
— *"A Face-off in the Crusades," Torquato Tasso, sixteenth century*

Having followed the British closely since the middle of June, part of Lafayette's army finally caught up with an enemy detachment six miles west of Williamsburg. Cornwallis had sent Simcoe with the Queen's Rangers and some Hessian jaegers to forage and destroy additional supplies and vessels along the Chickahominy River. The marquis learned of Simcoe's expedition and planned to cut off the young dragoon colonel as his small force retired to Williamsburg. For this operation, he employed Colonel Buder's Pennsylvania Regiment, two companies of riflemen, and over fifty cavalrymen under Major William McPherson, all commanded by Buder. These troops moved quickly dirough the night of June 25 "in full speed" and, on the way, encountered a "negro man with the small pox lying on the road side," left there by Simcoe "to prevent die Virginia

71

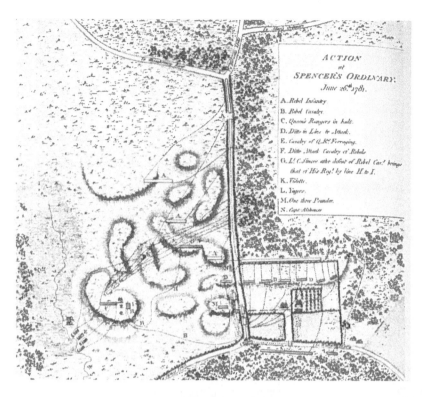

FIGURE 4-1 Plan of the June skirmish at Spencer's Ordinary. *Colonial Williamsburg Foundation.*

militia from pursuing them, which the enemy frequently did." On the next morning, these American troops encountered Simcoe's force halted at Spencer's Ordinary, along the Williamsburg Road near its intersection with the Jamestown Road, near what was called Hot Water Plantation by many Virginia militiamen.[1]

McPherson attacked with about fifty of his dragoons and fifty mounted New Jersey light infantrymen and quickly drove in Simcoe's pickets. Simcoe counterattacked on the American right flank, and in the "severe skirmish," McPherson was thrown from his mount, although he managed to escape while the rest of his horsemen were scattered. Simcoe claimed that McPherson "crept into a swamp, lay there unperceived during the action, and when it was over got off." From captives taken on the field, Simcoe learned that more Patriot troops were nearby, so he called to Cornwallis for reinforcements.[2]

Soon the Virginia rifle companies arrived at the scene and engaged in a hot, confusing firefight with the Queen's Rangers, who gradually pushed them back to the lines of Butler's Pennsylvanians. Wayne, meanwhile, sent more of his Pennsylvania troops forward to support Butler's attack. Sensing his predicament, Simcoe deployed his force to make it appear larger and then withdrew, leaving his wounded on the field and by the tavern after two hours of fighting. Butler's men fell back on Wayne's Continentals around Byrd's Ordinary and then to Lafayette's camp at Tyree's Plantation, where the American forces stayed until July 5, on the west side of Diascund Creek. Some of the American wounded were brought to a military hospital at New Kent Court House.[3]

Lafayette reported on the action to Governor Nelson two days later:

> *Colonel Simcoe was so lucky as to avoid a part of the stroke; but altho' the whole of the* [American] *light corps could not arrive in time, some of them did. Majr. MacPherson having taken up fifty light infantry, behind fifty dragoons overtook Simcoe, and regardless,* [illegible] *of numbers made an immediate charge. He was supported by the rifle-men who behaved most gallantly and did great execution. The alarm guns were fired at Williamsburg (only six miles distant from the field). A detachment just then going to Gloucester was recalled, and the whole British army came out to save Simcoe. They retired next morning when our army got within striking distance.*[4]

Cornwallis brought his troops west and met Simcoe, with whom he returned to secure the wounded and claim possession of the field. The marquis, who regarded the affair as a victory, reported his losses as nine killed, fourteen wounded and "one Lieut. [and] 12 privates whose fate is not known." He claimed sixty British were killed, "which must be attributed to the great skill of our rifle-men," but Cornwallis reported far fewer losses. Nevertheless, Lafayette noted that "his little success has given great satisfaction to the troops, and increased their ardor."[5]

In late June, Lafayette's command included 850 of his light infantry detachment, 600 Pennsylvania Continentals under Wayne, 400 Virginia Continental recruits and 120 dragoons. Shoes, medicine, "hard money," arms and cavalry equipment were sorely lacking within his army, however, and he still needed more horsemen. Although he expected to have almost 3,000 militiamen with him soon, many of these Virginians began to leave the ranks as their terms expired and as harvest time began to draw near.[6] By early July, the marquis found that "the three [militia] brigades are so amazingly reduced that to have them of a tolerable strength I have been obliged to put them into two," under Generals Lawson and Edward Stevens. Desertions were increasing, with many men saying "they were only engaged for six weeks and the harvest time recalls them home," even the western riflemen. "You might as well stop the flood tide as stop militia whose times are out," Lafayette complained. The Frenchman called on the governor to immediately muster dragoons and thousands more soldiers from the militia as "an absolute necessity," as well as a unit of black pioneers and wagoneers, who would "afford great services" to the army.[7]

In the beginning of July, Lafayette's four thousand troops were in several dispersed camps northwest of Williamsburg, where Cornwallis's redcoats retired after the skirmish at Spencer's Ordinary. "We never encamp in a body," Lafayette wrote to General Greene, taking precaution not to present an inviting target for Cornwallis to attack. He expected Morgan's

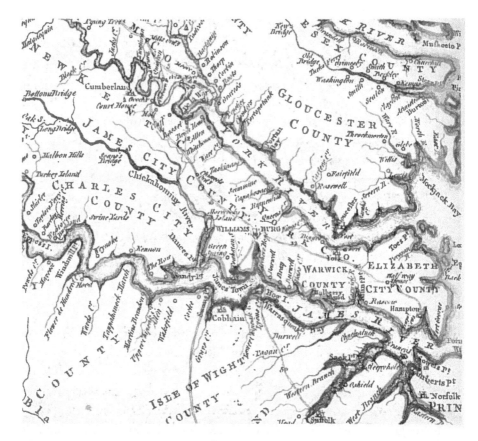

FIGURE 4-2 Map detail of the area between Bottom's Bridge and Norfolk, where both armies maneuvered in July and August 1781. *North Carolina Collection, University of North Carolina Chapel Hill.*

newly raised command to join him, though it was only four hundred men. "Our movements are offensive and we appear eager for action," he told Greene.[8]

By this time Cornwallis's operations had taken on a defensive quality compared to his destructive expedition in May and June. "The enemy are extremely cautious," Lafayette concluded on the fourth, suspecting that the British general would embark his troops and leave the state, except perhaps for a small garrison at Portsmouth. Lafayette intended to keep his distance from Williamsburg, watch his own flanks and prevent the enemy from making foraging detachments. Still, the young French general was frustrated. "I do what I can, but cannot do what I wish," he confided to Greene, concluding that "I manage matters for the best, try to correct abuses, get angry five or six times a day, and I hope you will be satisfied at least with my good intentions."[9]

Upon Cornwallis's arrival in Williamsburg on June 25, he received two June letters from Sir Henry Clinton in New York. Clinton was concerned that Washington and his French allies were preparing an assault on New York by land and sea, which could overwhelm its garrison of

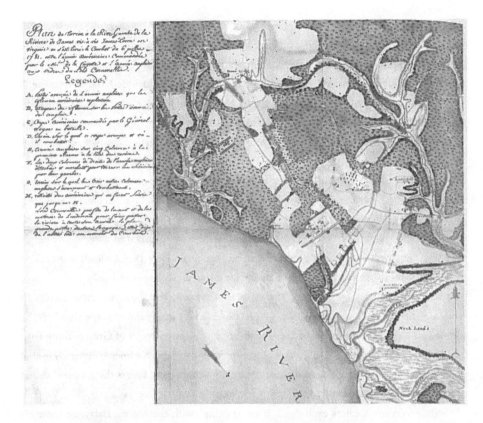

FIGURE 4-3 French map of the battle at Green Spring, fought near Jamestown on July 6, 1781. *Library of Congress.*

eleven thousand men. Clinton directed Cornwallis to secure a favorable port in the Chesapeake region to establish a defensive post and ordered him to send three thousand of his troops to New York, once active operations had concluded. Cornwallis quickly readied his troops to move eastward to Portsmouth, wary of Lafayette's army, which he suspected had "an intention of insulting our rearguard when we pass James River." His lordship planned to cross the river around James Town, first striking at the Americans if he saw "a favorable opportunity," but he also warned Clinton that he saw "little chance of being able to establish a post capable of giving effectual protection to ships of war" in Virginia's coastal area.[10]

On July 4, the British left Williamsburg and marched south to a camp at Humbler's (or Ambler's) Plantation near James Town Island in order to cross to the south side of die river. The Queen's Rangers crossed the James that night and moved to Cobham, a small town in Surry County at the mouth of Grays Creek that no longer exists. Cornwallis moved his baggage and stores across on the fifth and intended to move all his troops across the river on July 7.[11]

Lafayette learned that Cornwallis left Virginia's old capital on the fifth. The marquis moved his own troops to Byrd's Tavern and Norrell's Mill on Yarmouth Creek, just east of the Chickahominy River, and then occupied a position for a few days beginning July 6 at

Chickahominy Church, about ten miles west of Williamsburg. In an attempt to reconnoiter the location of Cornwallis's troops at the vulnerable position crossing the James, Lafayette ordered on the sixth an advance detachment numbering eight hundred men under General Wayne to scout the enemy near James Town. These troops included the Pennsylvania Continentals, militia riflemen and three guns. "Nothing but a forced march with the lightest & most advanced part of the troops could arrive in time to effect their rear," Wayne wrote. He found the enemy's camp pickets near Green Spring, a large plantation dating from the mid-seventeenth century, a few miles northwest of James Town. The old plantation still included the large brick house that had been the residence of Virginia governor William Berkeley in the 1670s and was described just after the Revolution as "a brick building of great solidity, but no attempt at grandeur."[12]

Cornwallis learned of Wayne's approach to the river and planned to surprise the rebels by concealing most of his army from the American general's view, thereby leading Wayne to believe that most of the British force had already crossed the James and only a token force remained near James Town Island. The three Pennsylvania battalions advanced in line to within eighty yards on the redcoats' posidon "under a very heavy fire of grape shot." As the sun began to set, Wayne attacked the British cavalry outposts south of Green Spring with his riflemen. Cornwallis allowed Wayne's troops to move near his lines., "concluding that [Wayne] would not bring a considerable force within our reach, unless they supposed that nothing was left but a rear guard."[13]

While Wayne's soldiers exchanged "a smart firing" with the enemy, Lafayette came on the field with additional Continentals and seems to have suspected that the British had more than a rear guard fighting Wayne's men.[14] "It was soon discovered," Wayne wrote, "that a very considerable part of their army yet remained on this side [of] the river [at Ambler's] which induced the General [Lafayette] to send for the remainder of the Continentals distant about Six miles." Wayne described the most significant engagement of the campaign in detail to General Washington two days later.

> At 2 OClock P.M. a large smoke was raised by the Enemy, probably as a signal to their parties to return to camp, & for all such as had crossed the river to repass it, at 3 OClock the rifle men supported by a few regulars began & kept up a galling fire upon the Enemy which continued until five in the Evening when the British began to move forward in five Columns[.] The Marquis anxious to view them near had proceeded rather far upon their left, it was then thought proper to Order Major [William] Galvan of the head of the advance guard to meet & attack their front who after a spirited tho' unequal contest retired upon our left[.] A Detachment of the Light Infantry under Major [John] Willis [Wyllys], having that moment arrived also commenced a severe fire upon the Enemies left but were obliged to fall back, which the enemy taking advantage of & beginning to turn our flanks, a _Manoeuvre_ in which had they persevered, they must inevitably penetrated between this Corps &

the Other part of the army; but being joined at this Crisis by Lieut Colo. [Josiah] Harmer & Major Edwards with two Detachments from the 2nd & 3rd Battalions of Penns [ylvani] ans under Colo. [Richard] Hampton, it was determined among a Choice of Difficulties to advance & Charge them[.] This was done with such vivacity as to produce the desired effect i.e. checking them in their advance & diverting them from their first maneuver.[15]

Wayne reported that "being enveloped by [superior] numbers [and] many brave & worthy Officers & soldiers killed or wounded, we found it expedient to fall back half a mile" to Green Spring plantation. Two of the Continental six-pounder field pieces that "were served with equal spirit & effect, until disabled by having Captain [Jesse] Crosby with many matrosses dangerously wounded & all the horses killed, at last fell into their hands." One of Wayne's officers wrote that "our artillery horses being nearly all killed or wounded we were obliged to abandon our two pieces of artillery which fell into the enemies hands." Wayne managed to retire safely with his wagons and ammunition, and after falling back one mile, his infantrymen managed to reform "and retired in good order."[16]

British officers, unsurprisingly, reported the affair somewhat differently. Tarleton recalled that the first cannon shot of the Americans was the forward dragoons' signal to withdraw and for the infantry to form and advance. Cornwallis reported that Lafayette "intended to attack our rear-guard, and luckily stumbled on our army." The British commander "put the troops under arms and ordered the army to advance in two lines. The attack was begun by the first line with great spirit." In his front line, the light infantry advanced on the right, and on his left, he sent forward Lieutenant Colonel Dundas's brigade, consisting of the Forty-third, Seventy-sixth and Eightieth Regiments, against Wayne's Continentals and two field guns. Soon, "a smart action ensued for some minutes," and Wayne's hard-pressed battalions began to get enveloped by the longer lines of redcoats coming against him. Upon perceiving that he was almost surrounded, Wayne ordered a bayonet charge against the enemy line in his front, which temporarily checked the British advance and gave time for Wayne's force to retreat to the lines of the American light troops, one half mile to the rear. Although Cornwallis's troops had forced the Americans back, they failed to deliver the telling blow his Lordship anticipated would destroy most of Lafayette's command. "The darkness of the evening prevented me from making use of the cavalry, or it is probable the Pennsylvania line would have been demolished," his lordship reported. British losses were eleven killed, sixty-six wounded and one missing.[17]

Most of Lafayette's troops returned to Chickahominy Church, while the militia at Byrd's Ordinary moved forward to support the regulars. The marquis reported losses of twenty-eight killed, ninety-nine wounded and twelve missing, including Colonel John Bowyer of the rifle battalion from Rockbridge County, taken prisoner during the action.[18] "The services rendered by the officers make me happy to think that although many were wounded, we lost none," wrote the marquis. He was proud that Wayne's command "attacked the whole British

Army, close to their encampment, and by this severe skirmish hastened their retreat." To Washington, he wrote that Cornwallis "seems to have given up the conquest of Virginia."[19]

Wayne's report to Washington was boastful and sought to put a positive face on events at Green Spring. He noted that

> our small reconnoitering party of Horse & foot who had the hardiness to engage Lord Cornwallis at the head of His Whole army with the Advantage of so Numerous a Cavalry on their own ground & in their own Camp, is more to be envied than pitied—as it not only disconcerted the British General & effectually aroused him from his premeditated maneuver, but precipitated his retreat to James Island the same night to avoid a Genl action in the morning which the pointed attack he experienced in the Evening might be the sanguinary prelude to.

The Pennsylvania general also noted that Lafayette lost two horses during the battle, in which the marquis was exposed to enemy musketry at the front of his men. "He was frequently requested to keep at a greater Distance," Wayne reported, but "his Native bravery rendered him deaf to the Admonition."[20]

From the batdefield, where Lafayette moved the majority of his command by July 8, he congratulated Wayne's command for their bravery against the "total of the British Army" in "a warm and close action."[21] Although Cornwallis moved all of his troops across the James on July 7, Lafayette knew better than to think the British commander was retreating. In a letter to the Vicomte de Noailles, another French officer serving in America, he wrote candidly about his wily opponent. "This devil Cornwallis is much wiser than the other generals with whom I have dealt," wrote the marquis, "he inspires me with a sincere fear, and his name has gready troubled my sleep. This campaign is a good school for me. God grant that the public does not pay for my lessons."[22]

In fact, the American public did *not* pay for Lafayette's military education. When the British moved to the south bank of the James, the marquis withdrew his forces west from Green Spring back toward Bottoms Bridge and Richmond and did not pursue the redcoats on their march to Suffolk. The sharp contest at Green Spring, the only significant engagement between the forces of Cornwallis and Lafayette during their 1781 maneuvers in the Tidewater and Piedmont of Virginia, marked the end of the two generals' cat-and-mouse game. To be sure, the campaign was not over—Cornwallis and his powerful host still threatened the state from Portsmouth. Lafayette too remained in Virginia, close enough to the enemy to keep a watchful eye on British operations while securing as much of the Old Dominion as possible with his smaller forces. Meanwhile, far to the north at Washington's headquarters at Newburgh, New York, and in French camps in Rhode Island and Connecticut, plans were being made to bring thousands of troops and ships to Virginia to capture the king's forces along the wide rivers of coastal Virginia.

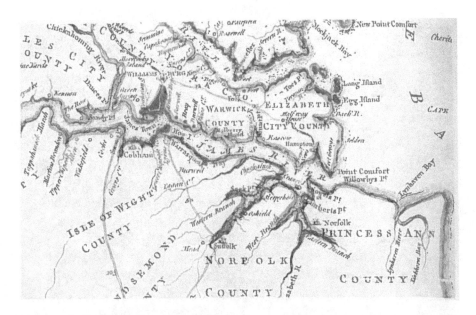

FIGURE 4-4 Lower James River region around Norfolk, Suffolk and Yorktown. *North Carolina Collection, University of North Carolina—Chapel Hill.*

After the battle at Green Spring, the British troops crossed James River on July 7 with "great labor and difficulty," and Cornwallis moved soudieast to Suffolk by July 12. With General Leslie's assistance, he began preparing to send back part of his command from Portsmouth to New York, per Clinton's repeated orders, which Cornwallis finally received upon his arrival at Suffolk.[23]

Soon, however, the British commander in New York changed his mind. Clinton sought to establish a station in the Chesapeake region for ships of the line, which the current British post at Portsmouth could not accommodate, and he favored Hampton Roads. After consulting with Rear Admiral Thomas Graves, who replaced Arbuthnot as commander of the North American Squadron in May, Clinton told Cornwallis in July not to abandon Virginia, but to remain on the defensive, and to consider Yorktown or Old Point Comfort (Hampton) as a possible deep-water port for British warships. Specifically, in a July 11 letter, he ordered Cornwallis not to send the troops he previously requested to New York.[24]

If Virginians thought they no longer had to fear the destructiveness of British arms as Cornwallis moved to the coast, they were mistaken. On July 8, Cornwallis ordered Tarleton to strike out from Cobham for "an excursion" along the south side of the James River, with his dragoons and the light company of the Royal Welch Fusiliers.[25] Cornwallis concluded that since most of the Continental and Virginia forces were on the lower James with little opportunity to cross the river due to their lack of boats, "I thought it a good opportunity to endeavor to destroy the magazines between James River and the Dan," which were being gathered for the use of Greene's army in South Carolina. Tarleton was to aim for the depots at Prince Edward Court House and New London, the latter in far-off Bedford County.

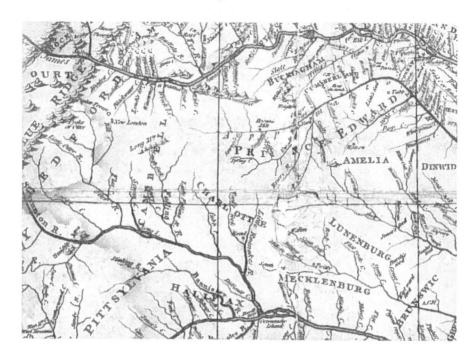

FIGURE 4-5 Key sites of Tarleton's Southside raid are depicted in this colonial period map, including New London, Amelia and Jefferson's Poplar Forest. *Library of Congress.*

"All persons of consequence, civil or military," were to be brought to Cornwallis's headquarters "before they are paroled." To Tarleton, he wrote that while on this raid "you will be in no haste to return but do everything in your power to destroy the supplies destined for the rebel army." At the same time, Cornwallis sent part of the Eightieth Regiment under Colonel Dundas south to destroy rebel supplies at South Quay, in Southampton County on the Blackwater River, and "if possible I shall send a detachment to Edenton [North Carolina] for the same purpose before I fall back to Portsmouth."[26]

Tarleton and his expeditionary force passed through Petersburg on their way west to Amelia. He "proceeded by long movements in the morni and evening," in order to avoid the heat of the summer and give his troops "refreshment and repose." At Benjamin Ward's Tavern along West Creek in southern Amelia County, several of his troopers skirmished with Peter Francisco, a rebel veteran of several previous battles during the war and known for his great size and courage. Francisco wrote a dramatic account of the affair in the third person decades after the war:

> He fell in accidently, at the house of Benjamin Ward, in Amelia comfy, Va., with a
> plundering party of British detached from the main body of Tarleton's command,
> who came to Ward's for plunder, he [Francisco] being at Ward's when they came,
> and not having time to escape. One of the British demanded his watch and some
> other jewelry that he owned, and also at the same time placed his sword under his

FIGURE 4-6 Peter Francisco fought off a detachment of Tarleton's dragoons in Amelia County in July 1781. *Library of Congress.*

> *right arm, whilst disposing of the other property. He stepped back one pace in the rear, seized his sword by the hilt, cut off a large portion of his skull and killed him. He had then neither sword nor pistol of his own, but fought with his adversary's own weapons, which he took from him. He wounded and drove off the others, and took eight horses, with their trappings, out of nine; the ninth man escape[d] with a large cut on his back. They all joined Tarleton, who was about a mile off, except the slain man. This was the last favor I ever did the British.*

Francisco made his escape from the tavern on one of the enemy's mounts, driving the others before him.[27]

After riding through Amelia County, the dragoons traveled south by way of Jenning's Ordinary and Burke's Tavern (Burkeville). They next went to Prince Edward Court House, site of a gunpowder manufactory, and Charlotte Court House and then to the supply depot at New London. With an arsenal, a prison and three hundred inhabitants, the town was also the site of the first courthouse of Bedford County, beginning in 1761. Coincidently, Thomas Jefferson was then residing at his Poplar Forest estate only seven miles to the north of New London, but Tarleton did not capture him.[28]

At Prince Edward Court House and New London the British were disappointed to find that most of the military stores thought to be located at these depots had been previously sent to Greene's army. Throughout the raid, Tarleton discovered that "the stores destroyed, either of a public or private nature, were not in quantity or value equivalent to the damage sustained in the skirmishes en route, and the loss of men and horses by the excessive heat of the climate."[29] The dragoons returned east toward Cornwallis's position by a different route and, along the way, burned Reverend James Craig's mill, a supply depot and a "public magazine" on Flat Rock Creek in Lunenburg County. Tradition holds that Tarleton forced Reverend Craig, "though in poor health," to help slaughter pigs for the British soldiers' provisions and took off most of his slaves. Craig and many of his neighbors "were gready injured in their property," according to a petition they sent to Governor Nelson soon after the enemy had departed, "and compelled" to sign paroles "when taken from their own homes."[30]

Tarleton's column, "almost destitute of necessities and accoutrements," rode east across Virginia's Southside to the Nottaway River at Walker's Mill in Brunswick County and then trotted along on the Boydton Road through Dinwiddie Court House, "with many unfavorable circumstances to the corps." The British dragoon colonel must have been aware that some of Lafayette's troops under Wayne had moved to western Chesterfield County and tried to avoid them. Even so, the British sustained casualties in several skirmishes with militia forces on their return route. After halting at Prince George Court House, Tarleton brought his troops along the James River to meet Cornwallis's main body at Suffolk, about seventy miles southeast probably by way of Surrey Court House and Smithfield. Tarleton's command had been gone fifteen days and ridden over four hundred miles. Once Tarleton united with Cornwallis on July 24, his lordship marched his men to Portsmouth.[31]

North of the James, Lafayette repositioned his troops. After the contest at Green Spring, Lafayette moved his wounded to New Kent and marched west from Williamsburg to Holt's Forge and Long Bridge along the Chickahominy River, reaching Richmond by July 15. A few days before this, he ordered General Wayne to reinforce General Greene in the Carolinas with his five hundred Pennsylvania Continentals and the three hundred recruits von Steuben had raised in June. The marquis decided to detach this "much reduced" force because of his belief that Cornwallis would soon send most or all of his forces to New York or South Carolina.[32]

Lafayette also learned of Tarleton's mounted expedition south of the James and worried about supply caches all over the southern Piedmont. "From the best intelligence I can get the enemy's cavalry are gone very high up the country," he informed Wayne. Lafayette authorized "a stroke at Colonel Tarleton" if "found practicable" by Wayne, whom he expected to join General Morgan's troops at Goode's Bridge, a crossing of the Appomattox River between Chesterfield and Amelia Counties. He suggested that Governor Nelson call out enough militia to "render their return a very hazardous maneuver" south of City Point, but this was not realized.[33] Wayne's command crossed the James River at Woodson's Ferry on July 16 and then marched to Ware Bottom Church at Bermuda Hundred in Chesterfield County. Three days later, the troops arrived at Goode's Bridge, where they joined Morgan's riflemen and some Maryland cavalry troopers. Because the British had not embarked their forces at Portsmouth as Lafayette expected, Wayne's troops remained here until July 30, when they, fatigued by very hot weather, crossed the Appomattox into Amelia County.[34]

At Malvern Hill east of Richmond, Lafayette's remaining militia troops were encamped and resting in a healthy position. His most reliable troops were still the light infantry, "the best troops that ever took the field … far superior to any British troops." Lafayette boasted that these Continentals "saved this state, and indeed the southern part of the Continent." Additionally, some militia companies were at Williamsburg, and the Gloucester County militiamen were "in their own County." Some three hundred militia units remained on the south of the James River as well, ordered by the marquis "to keep clear of danger from an attack."[35] Despite being in no imminent danger from Cornwallis, still at Portsmouth, Lafayette continued to trouble state and Continental authorities to collect well-equipped cavalry for his host. "Upon my word," he wrote in late July, "unless we have a cavalry the defense of this state wholly depends upon the mistakes of our enemy."[36]

Lafayette was still trying to discern what the enemy's intentions were. Some of the redcoats had boarded transport ships and were off Hampton Roads but had yet to sail. The marquis considered that their intended destination was New York or Charles Town but could not rule out an expedition up the Potomac or to Baltimore. Cornwallis was observed inspecting Old Point Comfort by local spies, surely an indication he was considering fortifying that point. Baffled, the marquis ordered Wayne to move his troops back toward the James River opposite Manakin (in eastern Goochland County) in early August.[37]

In the lower Chesapeake, meanwhile, the British were active in late July. Cornwallis found Old Point Comfort unacceptable as a port for large ships. Accordingly, he decided to abandon Portsmouth and, instead, fortify Yorktown and the small peninsula opposite the town, Gloucester Point, obeying what he considered to be Clinton's orders. British forces arrived

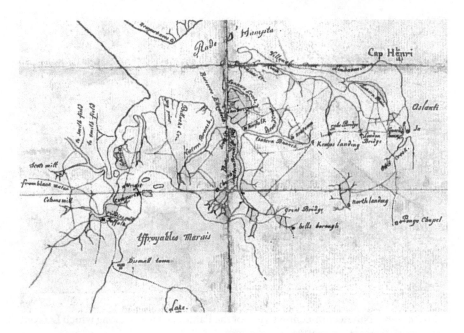

FIGURE 4-7 Hampton Roads and Norfolk map detail. *Library of Congress.*

on the York River and occupied both Yorktown and Gloucester Point during the first two days of August and completed the evacuation of their defeneses at Portsmouth on August 18. The British took a large number of runaway slaves with them, but "a number of Negroes" were "left dead and dying with the small pox." Redcoats, Hessians and former slaves began the laborious construction of defenses at both Yorktown and Gloucester Point, where they would remain until disaster struck in mid-October at the hands of a combined American and French army.[38]

Lafayette received prompt reports of the British movement and began to shift his own forces accordingly. He moved his command from Malvern Hill to Brook's Bridge, north of the capital, and then to Newcastle on the Pamunkey River by August 4, which allowed him to guard against a possible enemy thrust against Fredericksburg. General Wayne marched north, crossed the James River with his troops on August 5 at Westham and marched through Richmond to a position near Bottoms Bridge on the ninth. By August 11, Lafayette had moved his force over die Pamunkey at Ruffin's Ferry and then went on to Colonel Bernard Moore's Romancoke Plantation between the Pamunkey and Mattaponi Rivers in eastern King William County near West Point, where fodder and provisions were more plentiful. Lafayette also collected there numerous boats for transporting supplies to his camp and for anticipated troop movements. He remained until August 30, frustrated at the lack of mounted troops and militia sent to his headquarters and still wary of Cornwalhs, despite his adversary's inactivity. "The two sides pretend to be sleeping," he wrote to his cousin the Prince de Poix, a young French officer serving in the Continental Army, "but from a cursory glance I think they will

FIGURE 4-8   Nineteenth-century view of the Pamunkey River, along which Lafayette's army encamped in August 1781. *Library of Congress.*

soon awaken." Lafayette "would rather be rid of Cornwallis than a third of his army," he wrote to the Chevalier de La Luzerne, adding that although "we wage war like gendemen ... after all this, in the end he will give me a thrashing."[39]

In his letter from King William County to La Luzerne in mid-August, he wrote plaintively of the military situation he faced in Virginia. "If the French army could all of a sudden arrive in Virginia and be supported by a [naval] squadron," Lafayette opined, "we could do some very good things." Perhaps Lafayette would have been more confident in the course of events to come—and in avoiding a thrashing—had he known that his wishes were soon to be fulfilled.[40]

NOTES

1. Johnston, *Yorktown Campaign*, 56; Ward, *War of the Revolution*, 2:875; Feltman, *Journal*, 6; Egle, "Journal of Lieut. William McDowell," 300.

2. Simcoe *Military Journal*, 229; Johnston, *Yorktown Campaign*, 56; Feltman, *Journal*, 6; Egle, "Journal of Lieut. William McDowell," 300.

3. Johnston, *Yorktown Campaign*, 56; Simcoe, *Military Journal*, 229–36; McAllister, *Virginia Militia*, 86, 111. Tyree's Plantation was near today's Lanexa, north of U.S. Route 60.

4. Lafayette to Thomas Nelson, June 28, 1781, Rockefeller Library.

5. Ibid.; Morrissey, *Yorktown 1781*, 25, 39, 43; Lafayette to Greene, Idzerda, *Lafayette*, 4:216.

6. Tower, *La Fayette*, 2:351.

7. Lafayette to Thomas Nelson Jr., July 1, 1781, Idzerda, *Lafayette*, 4:228–31.

8. Tower, *La Fayette*, 2:354–55; Lafayette to Greene, July 4, 1781, Idzerda, *Lafayette*, 4:231.

9. Lafayette to Greene, July 4, 1781, Idzerda, *Lafayette*, 4:234.

10. Tower, *La Fayette*, 2:355–56; Cornwallis to Clinton, Ross, *Correspondence of Cornwallis*, 1:103–6.

11. Tower, *La Fayette*, 2:356.

12. Ibid., 356–57, 361; Anthony Wayne to George Washington, July 8, 1781, Founders Online; quote regarding Green Spring house is of the architect Benjamin Latrobe, given at the National Park Service's "Green Spring Plantation" webpage, http://www.nps.gov/jame/historyculture/green-spring-plantation.htm.

13. Tower, *La Fayette*, 360.

14. Ibid., 361; Shepard, *Marchingto Victoiy*, 13; Ward, *War of the Revolution*, 2:876.

15. Wayne to Washington, July 8, 1781, Founders Online.

16. Ibid.; Shepard, *Marching to Victory*, 13; Egle, "Journal of Lieut. William McDowell," 301.

17. Tower, *La Fayette*, 362–64; Cornwallis to Clinton, July 8, 1781, Ross, *Correspondence of Cornwallis*, 1:106; Ward, *War of the Revolution*, 2:477; Idzerda, *Lafayette*, 4:238n; Cornwallis to Nesbit Balfour, July 16, 1781, Saberton, *Cornwallis Papers*, 5:285.

18. Shepard, *Marching to Victory*, 13; Tower, *La Fayette*, 366.

19. Lafayette to Greene, July 8, 1781, Idzerda, *Lafayette*, 4:238, 239.

20. Wayne to Washington, July 8, 1781, Founders Online.

21. Lafayette, General Orders, July 8, 1781, Idzerda, *Lafayette*, 4:240; Lafayette to Allen Jones, July 10, 1781, ibid., 4:241.

22. Lafeyette, *Memoirs*, 1:420; Lafayette to the Vicomte de Noailles, July 10, 1781, Idzerda, *Lafayette*, 4:241.

23. Cornwallis to Clinton, July 8, 1781, Saberton, *Cornwallis Papers*, 5:117.

24. Clinton to Cornwallis, July 8, 1781, Saberton, *Cornwallis Papers*, 5:141; Clinton to Cornwallis, July 11, 1781, ibid., 5:139, 142–43.

25. Cornwallis to Clinton, July 17, 1781, Saberton, *Cornwallis Papers*, 5:137.

26. Ibid., 5:138; Cornwallis to Tarleton, July 8, 1781, ibid., 5:228.

27. "Peter Francisco, American Soldier."

28. Mapp, *Thomas Jefferson*, 160; Tarleton, *Campaigns*, 369; Hendricks, *Backcountry Towns*, 74–76. New London was just south of the current city limits of Lynchburg, along U.S. Route 460 at Route 811, New London Road.

29. Tarleton, *Campaigns*, 369.

30. Bell, *Cumberland Parish*, 105–8; Craig's Mill was located two miles south of modern Kenbridge, on Route 637.

31. Tarleton, *Campaigns*, 369–70; Morrissey, *Yorktown 1781*, 43; *Virginia Gazette*, March 23 1775, 4; Lafayette to Morgan, July 17, 1781, Idzerda, *Lafayette*, 4:253; Lafayette to Wayne, July 25, 1781, Idzerda, *Lafayette*, 4:278.

32. Lafayette to Nelson, July 13, 1781, Idzerda, *Lafayette*, 4:244–45; Wayne to Washington, July 16, 1781, Founders Online; Lafayette to Washington July 20, 1781, Idzerda, *Lafayette*, 4:255–56.

33. Lafayette to Wayne, July 15,1781, Idzerda, *Lafayette*, 4:248–49; Lafayette to Morgan, July 16, 1781, ibid., 4:251. Goode's Bridge is where U.S. 360 passes over the Appomattox River in western Chesterfield County.

34. Shepard, *Marching to Victory*, 14–16.

35. Lafayette to Washington, July 20, 1781, Idzerda, *Lafayette*, 4:255–57; Lafayette to Greene, July 23, 1781, ibid., 4:269–70.

36. Lafayette to William Davies, July 27, 1781, Idzerda, *Lafayette*, 4:279.

37. Lafayette to Washington, July 30, 1781, Idzerda, *Lafayette*, 4:86–87; Shepard, *Marching to Victory*, 15; Idzerda, *Lafayette*, 504.

38. Cornwallis to Clinton, July 24, 1781, Saberton, *Cornwallis Papas*, 6:11–13, 27–28; Josiah Parker to Lafayette, August 19, 1781, Idzerda, *Lafayette*, 4:334.

39. Lafayette to Wayne, August 4, 1781, Idzerda, *Lafayette*, 4:294; Feltman, Journal, 9; Wayne to Lafayette, August 9, 1781, Idzerda, *Lafayette*, 4:307; Lafayette to Greene, August 12, 1781, Idzerda, *Lafayette*, 4:315–17; Morrissey, *Yorktown 1781*, 36; Lafayette to the Prince e Poix, August 24, 1781, Idzerda, *Lafayette*, 4:346–47; Lafayette to La Luzerne, August 14, 1781, Idzerda, *Lafayette*, 4:321–22. Lafayette's Continentals were encamped during this period along Sweet Hall Road, south of King William Road (Route 30).

40. Lafayette to La Luzerne, August 14, 1781, Idzerda, *Lafayette*, 4:321–22.

5

Our Rebellious Neighbors

VIRGINIA'S BORDER COUNTIES DURING PENNSYLVANIA'S WHISKEY
REBELLION

By Kevin T. Barksdale

Western Pennsylvania's 1794 Whiskey Rebellion has achieved almost mythic status. Across the rolling hills of western Pennsylvania, the infamous insurrection remains a celebrated event, with local parades, festivals, and reenactments occurring annually to mark the occasion's anniversary. Symbolically, the event has come to represent a plethora of nostalgic and patriotic notions in the nation's collective memory. Participants in so-called "Whiskey Rebellion Festivals" are often drawn to the recreations of frontier life, the celebration of America's tradition of resistance against governmental tyranny, and above all else, the opportunity to assert vigorously their pride in being Pennsylvanians. Western Pennsylvanians have clearly embraced their rebellious forbears and the historical moment that occurred in the region.

The Whiskey Insurrection has continued to capture the attention of scholars, inspiring a remarkable amount of historical analysis. Several monographs, dozens of articles, and countless local studies have chronicled the events and analyzed the importance of this moment in time. Almost all of this historical scrutiny focuses on the epicenter of the rebellion, the "four western Pennsylvania counties in a state of rebellion." These counties were Washington, Fayette, Allegheny, and Westmoreland.[1] Indisputably, the vast majority of incidents related to the passionate resistance to the 1791 excise tax on distilled spirits were concentrated in this section of western Pennsylvania, but the Whiskey Rebellion did not occur in a vacuum. Pennsylvanians were not the sole participants in the historical drama, nor did the effects, sentiments, and resistance sparked by Alexander Hamilton's whiskey tax remain contained within Pennsylvania's borders. The events surrounding the Whiskey Rebellion had a dramatic effect on the emerging United States as a whole. Nowhere outside western Pennsylvania was the backlash against the whiskey excise felt more strongly than in the Virginia counties that bordered Pennsylvania. Residents of Virginia's border counties, principally Ohio, Harrison, and Monongalia, became embroiled in Pennsylvania's Whiskey Insurrection, and in the process they faced many of the same social, political, economic, and personal consequences experienced by Pennsylvania's western settlers.

Before the publication of Thomas P. Slaughter's *The Whiskey Rebellion: Frontier Epilogue to the American Revolution* and Steven Boyd's *The Whiskey Rebellion: Past and Present Perspectives*, the Whiskey Rebellion had long been viewed as an isolated occurrence on Pennsylvania's western frontier. Slaughter devotes part one of his work to the development and synthesis of a broad national backdrop against which post-Revolutionary frontier unrest might be understood. The local and regional tensions surrounding North and South Carolina's Regulators, North Carolina and Virginia's Frank-linites, and eighteenth-century statehood movements in Vermont and Maine demonstrated many of the same historical characteristics, stemmed from similar economic, political, and social motivations, and resulted in strikingly similar outcomes to those of western Pennsylvania's Whiskey Rebels. Additionally, essays by historians Mary K. Bonsteel Tachau and Roland M. Baumann, collected in Steven Boyd's edited work, illustrate the extensive nature of anti-excise sentiment in post-Revolutionary America. These works "expand the geographic perimeters" of the rebellion, illustrating that resistance to the excise tax also occurred in Kentucky, Maryland, and the Carolinas.[2] The efforts of these historians to expand their historical scope beyond the confines of western Pennsylvania provide much of the inspiration for this essay.

The response to the excise tax and the effects of western Pennsylvania's Whiskey Rebellion were particularly dramatic in the Virginia border counties of Ohio, Harrison, and Monongalia. Virginia's portion of the Monon-gahela Valley during the years surrounding the Whiskey Insurrection bore a remarkable resemblance to the tumultuous communities in western Pennsylvania. The Virginia border counties were unquestionably entangled in the events surrounding the resistance to the excise tax on numerous fronts, and the resulting insurrection altered the social, economic, and political landscape of Virginia's Appalachian frontier.

To understand the relationship between the western Pennsylvania Whiskey Insurrection and the Virginia border counties, it is necessary to be aware of the frontier dynamics occurring in Appalachian Virginia after the American Revolution. Two principal concerns dominated the lives of the mountaineers: the Native American "menace" and the material concerns that were associated with frontier existence. Despite years of constant frontier conflict between Native

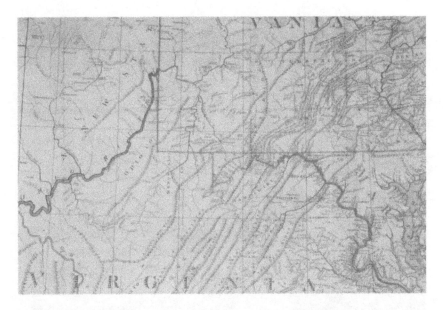

FIGURE 5-1 The Virginia counties of Ohio, Harrison, and Monongalia were the most affected by the Whiskey Rebellion in neighboring Pennsylvania. Ohio and Monongalia appear at the southwest corner of Pennsylvania on this map engraved for Thomas Jefferson's *Notes on Virginia* (1787). The map does not show Harrison County, which was created out of Monongalia. (*Virginia Historical Society*)

Americans and whites, many historians agree that these Indian wars reached their most brutal and vicious peak after the American Revolution. Virgil A. Lewis states, "The barbarian warfare which devastated the settlements west of the Alleghenies, after the close of the Revolution, was merciless in the extreme."[3] Several factors led to the escalation of antebellum frontier violence. The British, in an effort to maintain their western trading posts and perhaps eventually reclaim their territories and authority in North America, launched a campaign aimed at inciting the tribes occupying the Monongahela Valley and central Appalachia against Americans. Western Virginia's residents realized their immediate peril from the British-backed Indians, asserting that "they were in greater danger than ever before."[4]

As the Native American tribes of the Northwest struggled to maintain their presence in the Appalachian region and preserve their ancient traditions, the newly formed United States and its land-hungry citizens were equally as determined to expand frontier settlements to the western borders established by the treaty of Paris of 1783. Land speculation remained one of the most lucrative business ventures in the Virginia mountains, and the principal impediment to the expansion of the Upper Monongahela Valley frontier settlements was the indigenous population. The volatile mixture of greedy land speculators, ambitious white settlers, and determined Native American tribes ultimately led to a protracted period of frontier violence. Throughout the eighteenth century, Native Americans clashed with whites, resulting in tremendous bloodshed and loss of life. The French and Indian War, the American Revolution, and the numerous expeditions and campaigns launched by England, France,

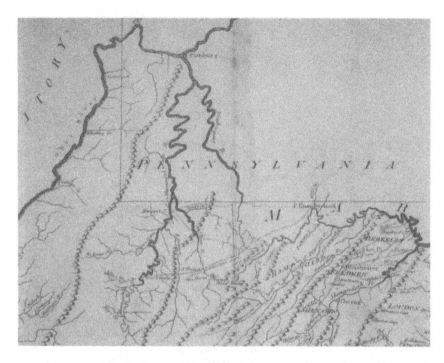

FIGURE 5-2 By the end of the eighteenth century, Native Americans had effectively been subdued along the western borders of Virginia and Pennsylvania, shown here in a 1796 map entitled *The State of Virginia from the Best Authorities*. But the memory of a century of frontier violence was the context in which the Whiskey Rebellion took place. (*Virginia Historical Society*)

and the United States escalated frontier violence.[5] As western Virginia's frontier settlements matured into stable communities, the Native American threat cast a perilous shadow in the mountains. Western Virginians turned to both the state and federal governments for protection, ultimately demanding the systematic annihilation of the regional tribes. During the late eighteenth century several government-backed military expeditions were launched to control and destroy the tribes that threatened the Virginia and Pennsylvania frontiers. Expeditions led by Josiah Harmar in 1790, Arthur St. Clair in 1791, and Gen. Anthony Wayne in 1794 attempted to extinguish the Indian threat.[6] By the end of 1795, the natives were effectively subdued, but the memory of a hundred years of frontier violence played a critical role in the events that surrounded what became the Whiskey Rebellion.

It was into this unsettled atmosphere on the frontier that Secretary of the Treasury Alexander Hamilton introduced his 1791 excise tax on distilled spirits. In an effort to bolster the power of the new federal government and alleviate financial pressures brought on by the American Revolution and by constant Indian warfare, Hamilton enacted his unpopular tax of four cents per gallon on whiskey. He established an extensive network of revenue officers, taxation districts, and government agencies to administer and collect the new tax.[7]

For mountain residents, the taxation of distilled spirits caused enormous financial hardships. Farmers in the mountainous western portions of Virginia and Pennsylvania had little choice but to distill much of their surplus grain. Inadequate transportation and the potential income offered by whiskey because of its popularity led to the expansion of distilling operations and profits throughout the frontier period. A farmer who distilled his grain into whiskey could transport the resulting product to both local and regional markets with greater ease and for a far higher profit than he could the raw material. With the regional popularity of western Virginia's principal whiskey, Monongalia rye, Virginia distillers stood to suffer greatly from the imposition of the federal tax. The combination of these financial burdens, back-country localism, and the perceived advantages the excise provided to larger distillers led to immediate public outrage among mountaineers.[8] Over the next

FIGURE 5-3 Secretary of the Treasury Alexander Hamilton (1755–1804) proposed the 1791 tax on distilled spirits to strengthen the power of the federal government as well as raise revenue. Hamilton's four-cent-per-gal-lon levy provoked an immediate and angry response from frontier farmers. (*Virginia Historical Society*)

four years, opposition to the whiskey tax spawned rhetoric rivaling the patriotic fervor that preceded the American Revolution. As mountain distillers braced for an economic crisis, regional and state newspapers published the first detailed reports of the impending internal taxation.[9]

Between the passage of the whiskey excise tax and 1793, the state of Virginia scrambled to comply with the new federal regulations. During the first few months that followed the passage of the excise in Congress, Hamilton dispatched federal surveyors into northwestern Virginia and western Pennsylvania. These men were directed to establish revenue districts with a single, county-appointed revenue officer in charge. At least two districts were established in northwestern Virginia, one encompassing Monongalia County and the other in Ohio County.[10] Ohio County appointed Zachariah Biggs as "Revenue Officer of the United States," and Monongalia County named Col. William McCleery its "collector of internal revenue," to be stationed in Morgantown. With the districts surveyed and revenue officers in place, all that remained was the implementation of Hamilton's tax."[11] This would prove to be easier said than done.

FIGURE 5-4 Ease of transporting their product as well as the lure of higher profits enticed many western Virginia and Pennsylvania farmers to convert their surplus grain into alcohol. This whiskey still is from the Oliver Miller Homestead, in what is now Allegheny County, Pennsylvania, where the first violence of the Whiskey Rebellion occurred. (*Colonial Williamsburg Foundation*)

FIGURE 5-5 Men who accepted commissions to collect the new excise duty of 1791 soon discovered they were the targets of angry protest. Robert Johnson, an excise officer for Washington and Allegheny counties, Pennsylvania, was "tarred and feathered and his hair cut off, and required to promise not to show his face again west of the mountains." This conjectural drawing by an anonymous artist shows irate Whiskey Rebels tarring and feathering an excise officer. (*ART145364, ©Art Resource, NY*)

FIGURE 5-6 Though the epicenter of the Whiskey Rebellion lay in four western Pennsylvania counties, the uprising also embroiled residents of Virginia's border counties. The most important community in the center of the disturbed region was Pittsburgh, built at the point where the Allegheny and Monongahela rivers flow together to form the Ohio. Louis Brantz, a Philadelphia merchant, sketched Pittsburgh in 1790, and Seth Eastman redrew the original for Henry R. Schoolcraft's *Information Respecting the History; Conditions, and Prospects of the Indian Tribes of the United States ...* (1851–57). (*Virginia Historical Society*)

The passage of the excise tax in March of 1791 brought immediate protests from Pennsylvanians. Local political and community leaders organized petitions, protests, and meetings to demonstrate their opposition to "Mr. Hamilton's excise." Several meetings on the issue were held throughout western Pennsylvania in the summer and fall of 1791, and the first signs of the impending violent backlash emerged in a fiery anti-excise meeting held in Washington County, Pennsylvania, on 27 July 1791.[12]

Following the assembly in Washington County, anti-excise delegates held a series of organizational meetings aimed at formulating a concise resolution, garnering public support, and coordinating local leadership. Surprisingly, no Virginians were involved in the anti-excise conventions held in Pittsburgh (7 September 1791 and 31 July 1794) and Mingo Creek (23 July 1794). It was not until the largest such gathering took place at Parkinson's Ferry, Pennsylvania, in the summer of 1794 that the first formal participation by Virginians occurred. After months of planning, on 14 August 1794 three delegates from Ohio County, Virginia, met with western Pennsylvania's anti-excise leadership.[13] There appear to be no definitive reasons explaining why only Ohio County sent delegates to the meeting nine miles east of Pittsburgh, but historian Leland Baldwin asserts that, "In Ohio County, Virginia,

Pittsburgh, July 20, 1794.

FINDING the opposition to the revenue law more violent than I expected, regreting the mischief that has been done, and may from the continuation of measures, seeing the opposition changed from disguised rabble to a respectable party, think it my duty and do resign my commission.

ROBERT JOHNSON.

Mr. Scull,
I am under the necessity of requesting you to put the following in your next paper.—It was found pasted on a tree near my distillery.
JOHN REED,
July 23, 1794.

ADVERTISEMENT.

IN taking a survey of the troops under my direction in the late expedition against that insolent exciseman John Neill, I find there were a great many delinquents, even among those who carry on distilling; it will therefore be observed that, I Tom the Tinker, will not suffer any certain class or set of men to be excluded the service of this my district, when not fit to attend on any expedition carried on in order to obstruct the execution of the excise law, and obtain a repeal thereof.

And I do declare on my solemn word, that if such delinquents do not come forth on the next alarm, with equipments, and give their assistance as much as in them lies, in opposing the execution and obtaining a repeal of the excise law, he or they will be deemed as enemies, and stand upon virtuous principles of republican liberty, and shall receive punishment according to the nature of the offence.

And whereas a certain John Reed, now resident in Washington, and being at his place near Pittsburgh, called Reedsburgh, and having a set of stills employed at said Reedsburgh, entered on the excise docket, contrary to the will and good pleasure of his fellow citizens, and came not forth to assist in the suppression of the execution of said law by aiding and assisting in the late expedition, have, by delinquency manifested his approbation to the execution of the aforesaid law, is hereby charged forthwith to cause the contents of this paper, without adding or diminishing, to be published in the Pittsburgh Gazette, the ensuing week, under the no less penalty than the consumation of his distillery.
Given under my hand this 19th day of July, 1794.

Tom the Tinker.
P. S.

the opposition [to the Whiskey tax] followed the lead of the rioters of adjacent Washington County, Pennsylvania." The willingness of Ohio County residents to align themselves with what was arguably Pennsylvania's most vocal antiexcise opposition possibly explains their initial participation. Additionally, Pennsylvania's anti-excise leadership issued a formal invitation, written by Maj. Gen. David Bradford of Washington County, to "the inhabitants of Monongahela, Virginia" to attend the meeting at Parkinson's Ferry.[14] The circular implored Virginians to "come forward and join us in our deliberations," and "hear our reasons influencing our conduct." Bradford's invitation, combined with Ohio County's sympathy for Pennsylvania's Whiskey Rebels, prompted the attendance of Robert Stephenson, William McKinley, and William Sutherland.[15] The meeting at Parkinson's Ferry was the most important one regarding the excise to that point.

In conjunction with this early phase of relatively peaceful organization, Pennsylvania's Whiskey Rebels engaged in a series of violent acts. Antiexcise supporters, under the guises of "Tom the Tinker's Boys," "Whiskey Boys," and the "Black-faced Boys," engaged in guerrilla tactics to demonstrate their opposition to the tax. Across western Pennsylvania, the newly appointed excise officers and supporters of the excise were subject to verbal threats, physical intimidation, and ultimately assaults on their persons and property. On 6 September 1791, Robert Johnson, excise officer for Washington

FIGURE 5-7 At the top of this 1794 clipping from the *Pittsburgh Gazette* is the resignation letter of the tarred and feathered excise collector, Robert Johnson. At the bottom is a warning left near John Reed's still by "Tom the Tinker," a leader of the Whiskey Rebels.

FIGURE 5-8 This watercolor by Benjamin Latrobe (1764–1820), *View on the Ohio River*, suggests why the river and its watershed became a magnet for migration in the late eighteenth century. Broad and navigable, the river is formed by the confluence of the Allegheny and Monongahela rivers at Pittsburgh and runs for almost a thousand miles before emptying into the Mississippi. Settlers on the Ohio or its tributaries were thus afforded a vital connection to U.S. and world markets that many backcountry dwellers did not enjoy. (*Courtesy of the Maryland Historical Society, Baltimore, Maryland*)

and Allegheny counties was "tarred and feathered and his hair cut off, and required to promise not to show his face again west of the mountains."[16] The assault on Johnson was followed by several incidents, including the 22 November 1793 burning of the home of Fayette County excise officer Benjamin Wells, the June 1794 burning of the home of Westmoreland County excise officer John Wells, the destruction of the still and grist-mill of excise supporter William Conghbran, and the notorious assault on "Chief Inspector of the Revenue" Gen. John Neville's home in mid-July 1794.[17] Soon, excise officers and many local law enforcement officials found themselves powerless to enforce the law in western Pennsylvania.

The violence and intimidation occurring in western Pennsylvania eventually spread into Virginia's western reaches. According to contemporary accounts, the first attacks on Virginia excise officers occurred in the spring of 1794. In Ohio County on 8 August 1794, in an effort to increase public support among Virginians for their scheduled 14 August anti-excise meeting at Parkinson's Ferry, a determined group of Pennsylvanians and Virginians launched a campaign of terror against local revenue officer Zachariah Biggs. A group of approximately fifty men approached Biggs and demanded that he "ignore the [excise] law."[18] The men then proceeded to remove "certain bonds" from the officer. Several Virginia men, including Alexander Campbell, William Laidley, William Sutherland, and John Edie, were subse-quently indicted in Ohio County District Court for the "robbery against Zachariah Biggs."[19] The next day, a large group of approximately thirty men entered Monongalia County to continue their assault on Virginia's excise officers. Several local citizens joined this mob, which immediately targeted the excise office in Morgantown.[20] Several accounts of this event are in existence. A contributor to the *Pittsburgh Gazette* stated

> The insurgents have been quite outrageous, and done much mischief. Here [in Morgantown] we have been quiet until a few days ago, when about 30 men, blacked, came in the night of the 9th instant, and surrounded the house of the collector of this county [William McCleery], but the man escaping, and advertising that he had resigned his office, they went off peaceably.[21]

Before the Morgantown incident, Monongalia County excise officer William McCleery received a letter stating, "if he did not resign he would be forced to give up his commission and his property would be destroyed."[22] McCleery offers this account of the warning:

> I am threatened from all quarters in my own country, and the Pennsylvanians came into our Town and ordered me to give up my papers, as they would come and destroy them with all my property; in the meantime no collection can go on, as our distillers will not pay 'till they see the event.[23]

McCleery ignored the warning, and his decision ultimately forced him to disguise himself as a slave as he "fled from his home, swam the river and escape[d]." As historian Earl Core states, "[McCleery] had no desire to come to blows with the party that had come to Morgantown on August 9." "A considerable party" of anti-excise men did pursue McCleery, but upon hearing of his resignation, they did not destroy his property.[24] After the aborted assault on McCleery, the band of Whiskey Rebels settled down for a prolonged siege of Morgantown's excise supporters.

For the next three days, the anti-excise men recruited local citizens and terrorized the inhabitants of Morgantown. A heightened sense of fear settled upon the county of Monongalia, as Morgantown briefly became the national center of anti-excise activity. An excise officer from the Virginia counties of Hampshire and Hardy, Edward Smith, refused to travel to Morgantown. In correspondence to Virginia governor Henry "Light-Horse Harry" Lee, Smith recounted a letter he had recently received from a Morgantown tax "Collector," identified only as Weaver. He wrote that his "intended visit was well known, and that he is confident that I would be in the hands of the Pennsylvanians in a short time after my arrival at Morgan Town. Under the circumstances, I deemed it needless to proceed."[25]

The effects of the Morgantown siege were not isolated to Monongalia County. There was growing alarm among Governor Lee and various Virginia excise officials that additional western counties might be influenced by the incidents in Morgantown. Edward Smith stated,

"Some of the Distillers in Hampshire and Hardy counties, which join the boundaries of Monongalia express their doubts of longer paying the duties, and would embrace the earliest opportunity of non-compliance [to the excise tax] if they could calculate on protection in their opposition." Concern also emerged that distillers in Harrison and Randolph counties would be unwilling to comply with the excise law.[26] The efforts of the Whiskey Rebels in Virginia seemed to be paying large dividends, and the siege of Morgantown had not yet ended.

On 12 August, two days before the meeting at Parkinson's Ferry, the antiexcise men launched another attack on Morgantown's excise supporters. A letter in the *Pittsburgh Gazette* detailed the event: "Three days after [the initial raid on Biggs], at our court, a number of men, mostly from Pennsylvania, came to Morgantown, and in the evening, began to beat up for proselytes, but they were in a few minutes driven out of town." The citizens of Morgantown had banded together to "clear the town of trouble makers."[27] It is difficult to gauge the level of support or opposition regarding the Whiskey Insurrection using this isolated incident, but Monongalia County residents were clearly divided on the subject. Morgantown's position as the center of northwestern Virginia's tax collection network and its connections to the state capital at Richmond undoubtedly helped lead to the repulsion of the Whiskey Rebels. What is apparent is that the Whiskey Insurrection transcended the borders of Pennsylvania and forced Governor Lee to confront anti-excise resistance in his home state.

Amidst the violence and turmoil that had ravaged the western Virginia and Pennsylvania frontiers, anti-excise delegates rallied at Parkinson's Ferry, Pennsylvania. On 14 and 15 August, 223 delegates from across western Pennsylvania, and the three Ohio County, Virginia, delegates, assembled in an "open field on the banks of the [Monongahela] river, with fallen timber and stumps, with a few shade trees, instead of buildings for accommodation of this important assembly." The gathering, which was dominated by prominent western Pennsylvanians such as Albert Gallatin, Edward Cook, and Hugh Henry Brackenridge, had two principal objectives: the organization of the excise resistance and the drafting of a definitive anti-tax declaration. After erecting a large liberty pole emblazoned with the inscription "Liberty and no Excise! No Asylum for Traitors and Cowards!" heated debates began among the attendees. The ultimate result of the two-day event was the formation of three committees: a standing committee of safety of sixty delegates, a committee of conference composed of twelve members, and a smaller sub-committee of three leading delegates. The meeting also resulted in the drafting of a series of five resolutions that would be presented to President Washington and Congress.[28] The resolutions covered a broad range of issues, including establishing the illegality of "taking citizens of the United States from their respective abodes ... for real or supposed offenses," creating a standing committee of safety in the western country, drafting "a remonstrance to Congress, praying the repeal of the excise law," establishing a committee to meet with President Washington, and finally, pledging their compliance to all United States laws, except the excise law.[29] The resolutions and activities of the Parkinson's Ferry delegates were widely published in regional newspapers and were immediately brought to the attention of President Washington, Governor Lee, and Governor Thomas Mifflin of Pennsylvania.

Despite their election to the committee of conference of twelve, the three Ohio County delegates did not participate in that body's deliberations, which occurred on 20 August in Pittsburgh.[30] Immediately following this meeting, however, the delegates from both western Pennsylvania and Ohio County met with a group of federal commissioners dispatched by President Washington and a smaller commission assembled by Mifflin to mediate a peaceful conclusion to the insurrection. These negotiations produced a tentative agreement, as the anti-excise delegates reluctantly agreed to "temporary submission" to the law, under the condition that the United States commissioners recommend to President Washington that he refrain from using the army to force compliance with the federal tax.[31] Presumably at Governor Lee's behest, the federal commissioners requested a separate meeting with the Ohio County delegates. On 23 August, Stephenson, Sutherland, and McKinney met with the government representatives. In a series of subsequent communications, the three Ohio County delegates stated why they were inclined to suspend formal negotiations.

> Gentl.:- Having Concidered your Letter of this Deate since the Departur of the speachel Comatie delegated from Westmoreland, Washington, Featt, & Aleganie countis, in Pensilvenea, & Considering our Selves a Justifyabel representation of those inhabtents of Ohio County, by whome we were Deligated, & a part of that speachell Comitiee to whom your proposals wear mead and Accepted yesterday, and the day posding and relying on the faith alr'dy pledged by you, and Acepted by the Speachell Comatee, we d'clin entering any further on this Bussens, untell we Consult our Constaituents & the Cometee of Safety. We are, Gentl., with esteem, your most Obed. Humble Serv't
>
> Robert Stephenson, William Sutherland, Wm. McKinley[32]

The series of negotiations produced few results, and the three delegates from Ohio County, who had also been elected to the sixty-member standing committee of safety, prepared to meet on 2 September at the Old Fort at Redstone (now Brownsville), Pennsylvania, to decide their next course of action.[33]

The escalation of frontier violence against federal excise officers, the resolutions passed at the meeting at Parkinson's Ferry, and the unsuccessful series of negotiations forced President Washington to confront the insurrectionists. On 7 August 1794, a week before the Parkinson's Ferry meeting, Washington had issued a proclamation that voiced his contempt for the "vindictive menaces" and demanded that those responsible for the assaults on the Pennsylvania excise officers be brought to justice. Washington's proclamation became the focus of anger among the Parkinson's Ferry delegates. Additionally, Washington issued an order to the governors of Pennsylvania, Virginia, New Jersey, and Maryland to call up thirteen thousand militiamen from their states to suppress the rebels, and he added, "I also require all officers and citizens to bring under the cognizance of the law all offenders in the premises."[34]

Washington was prepared to quell the insurrection by force. Lacking a strong regular army, however, he was forced to rely on local militias, citizens, and state governments for assistance.

In Richmond, Governor Lee was deeply concerned about the rebellious activities occurring on his western border. Lee's disdain for the "lawlessness" of the Whiskey Rebels, and the underlying conspiracy he attached to the insurrection, fed his antipathy for the rebels.[35] Lee's alarm increased when he learned that delegates from Ohio County participated in the Parkinson's Ferry convention, fearing "the prospect that the insurrection might find support in Virginia." Lee's concerns were warranted. In response to Washington's call to arms, and voicing his growing concern that "loyal" western Virginians might not be able to hold off the Whiskey Rebels, on 20 August 1794 Lee issued a defiant proclamation.[36] In it, he denounced the 9 August assault on the Morgantown excise offi-

FIGURE 5-9 Serving as governor of Virginia when the Whiskey Rebellion erupted, Henry Lee (1756–1818) was a natural choice to assume overall command of the military force assembled by President George Washington in August 1794 to quash the insurrection. Lee had served as one of Washington's most trusted and successful lieutenants during the Revolution, when he earned his nickname "Light-Horse Harry." Sadly, upon the completion of his gubernatorial term in 1794, Lee's fortunes, political and otherwise, deteriorated. He bequeathed a troubled legacy of debt and imprisonment to his family, including the fourth child of his second marriage, Robert Edward. (*Virginia Historical Society*)

cer, Biggs, demanded the "banditti" be brought to justice, and finally called "on all officers, civil and military, to exercise with zeal, diligence, and firmness, every legal power vested in them respectively for the purpose of detecting and bringing to trial every offender or offenders in the premises."[37] Soon after Washington's request for militiamen, Lee was appointed military commander of the yet-to-be-assembled multi-state militia force.[38] Lee would have his chance to suppress the Whiskey Insurrectionists and secure Virginia's western borders.

Assembling the thirteen thousand militiamen requested by President Washington became a far more challenging assignment than the actual suppression of the Whiskey Rebels. Across New Jersey, Maryland, Virginia, and Pennsylvania, men who opposed the government's economic policies and supported the rebel cause refused to enlist in the volunteer state militias. The lack of enthusiasm for enlistment prompted Washington to call for a military draft. Passionate resistance quickly emerged in all four states.[39]

Despite resistance to conscription in eastern Virginia, on 15 August, Governor Lee, commander-in-chief of the militia, commenced with Washington's orders and "issued a General Order stating that the President of the United States had called upon the Commonwealth [of Virginia] for three- thousand Infantry, and three hundred Cavalry for immediate service." Revolutionary War hero Gen. Daniel Morgan was placed in command of the two brigades that constituted the Virginia militia force.[40] General Morgan appeared extremely confident in Virginia's ability to recruit soldiers. He averred, "The State of Virginia seems to be unanimous and determined to suppress it [insurrection]: and it is my opinion that we shall in a very few days have men enough at this post to do that

FIGURE 5-10 To help suppress the Whiskey Rebellion, President Washington ordered Virginia to contribute three thousand infantry and three hundred cavalry. Gov. Henry Lee appointed Revolutionary War hero Gen. Daniel Morgan (1736–1802), pictured here, to command this Virginia force. When voluntary enlistment lagged, Washington called for a military draft. Despite resistance to conscription, Morgan expressed confidence in Virginia's ability to raise this force. (*Virginia Historical Society*)

business." Virginia's western brigade, commanded by William Drake of Berkeley County, consisted of militia regiments from Ohio, Randolph, Monongalia, Hardy, Hampshire, Berkeley, and Pendleton counties. Out of the eventual 4,800 soldiers taken from the state of Virginia, "fully twelve hundred were from Military Organizations then existing within the present limits of West Virginia."[41] Barring a peaceful resolution to the insurrection, militiamen from western Virginia would face their neighbors on the field of battle.

In the western Virginia border counties, as Morgan and Drake assembled local militiamen to "suppress the black hydra rising in the west," violence against excise supporters and officials subsided. By mid-September, under growing threat of military intervention, continued warnings, and the peril of federal prosecution, Virginia's anti-excise protesters appeared to have withdrawn from the rebellion.[42] Even one of Ohio County's leading whiskey rebels, William McKinley, altered his stance on the use of extra-legal violence. McKinley stated, "the more I think of the excise the more I hate it, but I have no Intention of opposing it, but in a

Constitutional way." West Virginia historian Otis K. Rice states that McKinley's ideological shift "undoubtedly reflected the thinking of the majority of the inhabitants of trans-Allegheny West Virginia."[43]

Despite the decline in violence within Virginia border counties, the ongoing military preparations and intense law enforcement scrutiny occurring there meant that the tension and fear lingered. In a letter dated 24 September 1794, Gen. Daniel Morgan described the situation in the Virginia mountains. He wrote,

> For my part, I wish I was at Morgantown at this time with 2,000 men, which would be as many as I could ask with what would join me at this place, to bring these people to order. They are very much alarmed at this time. This I have from the best intelligence.[44]

Meanwhile, western Virginia's local militia commanders scrambled to assemble the soldiers necessary to fulfill President Washington's demands. Brig. Gen. Benjamin Biggs, of Ohio County, spent the next few weeks coordinating the assembly of militiamen drawn from the northern panhandle of Virginia, and Morgan and William Drake did the same for Monongalia, Hardy, Hampshire, and Pendleton counties. By early October 1794, Morgan commanded a substantial number of "western men," and the military force was complete.[45]

In late October, Drake and Biggs marched their troops to Moorefield, Hardy County, where they rendezvoused with Morgan and the remainder of the Virginia troops. From Moorefield, General Morgan advanced the entire Virginia militia contingent to the designated meeting point at Cumberland, Maryland. Upon arriving in Cumberland, the entire force underwent inspection by President Washington and Governor Lee. The latter subsequently devised his strategy for the suppression of the Whiskey Rebels. He directed the Pennsylvania and New Jersey troops to serve as the right wing of the army, "to take position, with their left towards Bud's Ferry, and their right towards Greensburg."[46] He ordered the troops from Virginia and Maryland to serve as the left wing of the army, "to occupy a line between the Monongahela and Youghigany Rivers."[47] Lee's strategy aimed to surround the western Pennsylvania Whiskey Rebels and systematically sweep the counties of the insurgents and their leaders. As the army advanced across the Allegheny Mountains, Lee's troops arrested known rebels and imprisoned them at various locations throughout western Pennsylvania. By 16 November 1794, troops under the command of Daniel Morgan, with almost no resistance, had marched into Pittsburgh and effectively suppressed the rebels there. As one historian summarized the surprisingly quick end to the hostilities: "Thus happily terminated, without spilling a drop of blood or the firing of a hostile shot, the event in our national history popularly known as the whiskey insurrection."[48] The rebellion had been suppressed, but its effects on the western Virginia border counties would linger for years.

The communal concerns, social tensions, and alarm created during the Whiskey Insurrection remained after the rebels had been suppressed. In western Pennsylvania, General

By HENRY LEE, *Governor of the Commonwealth of Virginia, Major General therein, and Commander in Chief of the Militia Army in the Service of the United States,*

A PROCLAMATION.

BY virtue of the powers and authority in me vested, by the President of the United States, and in obedience to his benign intentions, therewith communicated, I do, by this my Proclamation, declare and make known to all concerned, that a full, free, and entire pardon, (excepting and providing as hereafter mentioned) is hereby granted to all persons resident within the counties of Washington, Allegheny, Westmoreland, and Fayette, in the State of Pennsylvania, and in the county of Ohio, in the State of Virginia, guilty of Treason, or Misprison of Treason against the United States, or otherwise directly or indirectly engaged in the wicked and unhappy tumults and disturbances lately existing in those counties; excepting nevertheless from the benefit and effect of this pardon all persons charged with the commission of offences against the United States, and now actually in custody, or held by recognizance to appear and answer for such offences at any judicial court or courts; excepting also all persons avoiding fair trial by abandonment of their homes; and excepting moreover the following persons, the attrocity of whose conduct renders it proper to mark them by name for the purpose of subjecting them, with all possible certainty, to the regular course of judicial proceedings, and whom all officers, civil and military, are required to endeavor to apprehend, or cause to be apprehended and brought to justice, to wit. BENJAMIN PARKINSON, ARTHUR GARDNER, JOHN HOLCROFT, DANIEL HAMILTON, THOMAS LAPSLEY, WILLIAM MILLER, EDWARD COOK, EDWARD WRIGHT, RICHARD HOLCROFT, DAVID BRADFORD, JOHN MITCHELL, ALEXANDER FULTON, THOMAS SPIERS, WILLIAM BRADFORD, GEORGE PARKER, WILLIAM HANNA, EDWARD MAGNER, Junior, THOMAS HUGHES, DAVID LOCK, EBENEZER GALLAGHER, PETER LYLE, JOHN SHIELDS, WILLIAM HAY, WILLIAM M'ELHENNY, THOMAS PATTON, PATRICK JACK, STEPHENSON JACK, and ANDREW HILANDS, of the State of Pennsylvania, and WILLIAM SUTHERLAND, ROBERT STEPHENSON, WILLIAM M'KINLEY, JOHN MOORE, and JOHN M'CORMICK, of Ohio county, in the State of Virginia.

Provided, That no person who shall hereafter wilfully obstruct, or attempt to obstruct the execution of any of the laws of the United States, or be in any wife aiding or abetting therein, shall be entitled to any benefit or advantage of the pardon herein before granted: And provided also, That nothing herein contained, shall extend, or be construed to extend to the remission or mitigation of any forfeiture of any penalty incurred by reason of infractions of, or obstructions to, the laws of the United States for collecting a revenue upon distilled Spirits and Stills.

GIVEN under my hand, at Head-Quarters, in Elizabeth Town, this twenty ninth day of November, 1794.

HENRY LEE.

FIGURE 5-11 At the conclusion of hostilities between federal forces and the Whiskey Rebels, Henry Lee issued this proclamation, nominally on behalf of President George Washington, to residents of Ohio County, Virginia, and four Pennsylvania counties. The document is intriguing for its audacious claim that those "guilty of treason" are hereby pardoned. This despite the fact that no one involved in the rebellion had been tried for that crime, much less convicted. The proclamation is also notable for the way it singles out by name a handful of Rebel ringleaders, "the attrocity of whose conduct" renders them outside the scope of the general pardon. These include Virginians William Sutherland, Robert Stephenson, William McKinley, John Moore, and John McCormick. (*Papers of James W. Singleton, Series V, Old Dominion University Libraries, Norfolk, Virginia*)

Morgan, on the orders of Governor Lee and President Washington, remained camped with 2,500 men a few miles outside Pittsburgh. Washington instructed Morgan to arrest the remaining insurgents. Morgan drew a number of his troops who remained in western Pennsylvania from Brigadier General Drake's western Virginia forces. Morgan ordered the other troops to return home, and the soldiers departed "by way of Morgantown to Winchester [Virginia]." Morgan was left the daunting task of "controlling and conciliating the people [of western Pennsylvania] over whose conduct he was left to guard."[49]

In the border counties of Virginia, local law enforcement carried out the arrest of known anti-excise activists. Those western Virginians arrested included William Sutherland, Robert Stephenson, William McKinley, John Moore, John McCormick, John Laughery, Alexander Campbell, John Edie, and William Laidley, all from Ohio County. Local law enforcement officials transferred these men to the jails at Greensburg and Uniontown, Pennsylvania, to await trial. Those arrested avoided prosecution after President Washington, in an effort to reconcile the lingering regional tensions, ordered Lee to issue a "full, free, and entire pardon" to most of the participants in the insurrection.[50] Out of the hundreds of rebels arrested, only twenty-eight Pennsylvanians and five Ohio County residents were excluded from Lee's 29 November 1794 pardon, which stated,

> I do declare and make known to all concerned that a full, free, and entire pardon is hereby granted to all persons residing within the counties of Washington, Allegheny, Westmoreland, and Fayette, in the State of Pennsylvania, and in the county of Ohio, in the State of Virginia, guilty of Treason or Misprison of Treason against the United States, or otherwise directly or indirectly engaged in the wicked and unhappy tumults and disturbances lately existing in those counties.

Though named as being outside the scope of the pardon, the Ohio County men managed to avoid federal convictions when the cases against them collapsed because of the unwillingness of witnesses to testify against their neighbors, jurisdictional conflicts, and the difficulties of transporting witnesses to district court.[51]

The Ohio County Whiskey Rebels escaped federal prosecution but ultimately faced their accusers in Ohio County District Court. In a series of cases continuing throughout 1795, local prosecutors indicted the men accused of assaulting excise officer Zachariah Biggs, but the plaintiffs ultimately had their cases dismissed in September 1795. As best as can be determined, no western Virginians were fined or imprisoned for their actions during the Whiskey Rebellion.[52]

Beyond the series of indictments and acquittals, the border counties of western Virginia experienced additional ramifications resulting from the Whiskey Rebellion. Counties across the western frontier had long maintained small volunteer militias, primarily for protection against Indians. In the years following the Whiskey Insurrection, militia captains bolstered their

FIGURE 5-12 In this crude caricature by an unknown artist, a federal exciseman is pursued by two farmers (at right) with designs on tarring and feathering him. The tax collector is met by a demon who, with a long barbed hook, pulls the man to a gallows upon which he is hanged and his body burned over a barrel of whiskey. Although political in nature, it is interesting to note the cartoon's religious subtext: the enforcer of an unpopular federal law is shown to be susceptible to, and perhaps thus in league with, the forces of darkness. (*Courtesy of the Atwater Kent Museum of Philadelphia*)

ranks to serve as both protection and a deterrent against further internal unrest. Throughout 1795, Brig. Gen. Benjamin Biggs sent correspondence to Governor Lee seeking the requisition of funds, supplies, ammunition, and additional troops for the "protection of the exposed part of Monongalia."[53] Clearly, in light of the success of Gen. Anthony Wayne's campaign against the Indians in 1794, western Virginia militia leaders retained their units' strength out of fear that white frontier settler violence would resume. This fear of insurrection loomed large over western Virginia for years.

What became of the Ohio County and western Virginia anti-excise leadership after the conclusion of the insurrection? The three most vocal and active Virginia Whiskey Rebels, Ohio County residents William McKinley, William Sutherland, and Robert Stephenson, were brought before the "old District Court held at Morgantown" on 5 May 1795, for "stirring up the inhabitants of Ohio County." At the next session of the court, in September, the deputy attorney general did not prosecute the three men. Afterwards, the three men returned to their positions in state and local government.[54] Politically, the Ohio County Whiskey Rebels seem to have suffered few ill effects from their activities during the insurrection, but the same cannot be said for George Jackson. Jackson, a Federalist from Clarksburg, Virginia, and a leader of the 1784 political movement that established Harrison County, utilized the partisan nature of the Whiskey Insurrection to advance his political influence in the region.[55]

His 1794 bid for election to Virginia's newly formed Third District in the United States House of Representatives suffered from his Hamiltonian views and support of the excise tax. After being defeated by Joseph Neville of Hardy County by just five or six votes, Jackson again sought election to the House in 1795. This time, Jackson shifted his political allegiance to the Republican Party and largely based his political platform on a conservative, anti-excise stance. While campaigning in the bitterly divided counties of Ohio and Monongalia, Jackson hoped to "make a bridge of the Excise Law upon which he would walk into the house of Congress."[56] The crafty politician realized that a moderate stance regarding the whiskey excise tax might be beneficial to his political ambitions. During the height of the insurrection, Jackson cautiously retreated from his vocal anti-excise views and declared his "neutrality." In an editorial published in the *Pittsburgh Gazette*, he stated,

> In the first place, I have ever been opposed to the law, and have often expressed my sentiments to that amount, and as far as words or remonstrances would go, I should still find a freedom to exert them, but upon the present occasion, as to the conduct of the Pennsylvanians, I wish to lay neutral, and my sincere wish is, that my country and fellow citizens may act upon the same principles.[57]

Despite a series of negative editorials published in the *Pittsburgh Gazette* throughout 1795 that derided his previous Federalist views, Jackson succeeded in securing a seat in Congress.[58] In much the same manner as successful western Pennsylvania politicians, such as Albert Gallatin, Hugh Henry Brackenridge, and William Findley, western Virginia's politicians utilized the Whiskey Rebellion as a catalyst to achieve or maintain positions of political power.[59]

Politics was not the only arena transformed by the rebellion. The insurrection and subsequent military occupation also had a dramatic effect on the economy of western Virginia. The presence of a large military force injected a large dose of needed specie. The soldiers' demand for supplies and propensity to consume large quantities of Virginia whiskey assured that money flowed into the burgeoning regional economy. One historian comments, "The army was the largest consumer of whiskey in the West."[60] One wonders if local merchants and distillers saw the irony in the fact that soldiers sent to enforce a hated tax on whiskey spurred such demand for the product that profits soared.

In addition to the economic changes sparked by the Whiskey Rebellion, the western Virginia border counties experienced a dramatic population increase following the rebellion. Settlement by a number of militiamen and the increased security after the suppression of the Whiskey Insurrectionists and Native Americans undoubtedly spurred this demographic trend.[61] Each of the three western Virginia border counties experienced considerable population growth. From 1790 to 1800, the population of Harrison County more than doubled from 2,080 to 4,848, Monongalia County grew from 4,768 to 8,540 inhabitants, and in the most rebelliously active county, Ohio, the population increased from 5,212 to 9,446.[62]

With the doubling of the regional population, western Virginia began to experience its first period of substantial economic growth. This period of development stimulated the improvement of regional trade and transportation arteries. As early as the mid-eighteenth century, residents of western Virginia's frontier had been demanding federally funded transportation improvements.[63] The Ohio County anti-excise delegates had even included demands for "free navigation of the Mississippi River," and the "opening up" of the lands surrounding the Ohio River in their negotiations with United States commissioners. Congress's passage of the 1803 act that allocated funds for the development of the nation's first federally funded road ensured that the western Virginia frontier was soon thereafter connected to eastern markets. Construction of the National Road commenced in 1811 and eventually crossed the insurrection counties to reach Wheeling, Virginia, in 1818.[64] The completion of the National Road was the culmination of the regional internal improvements that followed the Whiskey Rebellion. Though the majority of incidents relating to that period of unrest occurred in western Pennsylvania, residents of western Virginia border counties certainly experienced the aftermath of one of America's first internal insurrections. Frontier violence, communal tensions, and socioeconomic upheavals all left their marks on Appalachian Virginia.

At this point, one final question must be considered. Given that Virginia's distillers faced repercussions from the excise tax, why was the Whiskey Rebellion centered in western Pennsylvania and not western Virginia? A few historians have offered reasons for western Virginia's modest participation. Historian Otis K. Rice states that, "The importance West Virginians attached to efforts of the federal government to pacify the Indians, more than anything else, explains their failure to give general support to the Whiskey Rebellion."[65] This argument seems overly simplistic when one considers that western Pennsylvanians suffered from the same Native American threats. Other historians have argued that western Virginia's strong connection to the federal government, through the success of prominent Virginia politicians, waylaid any widespread frontier violence. This too fails to explain adequately western Virginian's reactions to the insurrection. Historian Steven Boyd argues that resistance to the excise tax was prevalent on much of America's frontier. He notes that "violent resistance marked attempted enforcement in Maryland, Kentucky, Virginia, North Carolina, South Carolina, and Georgia," and that "the four western Pennsylvania counties were not the heart of excise opposition until the officers of the federal government marked them as such."[66] A more precise and complex explanation as to why Virginia's mountaineers failed to embrace the rebellion fully must combine many elements. Regional concerns regarding the Indian threat, intense loyalty to the federal and state governments, strong Federalist leadership within the state and region, and the effective state control exerted by Governor Lee determined the course of action for many western Virginians during the Whiskey Rebellion. In the end, whether a Virginian participated in, supported, or opposed the Whiskey Rebellion was largely an individual choice. Political ambition, economic motivations, disaffection with the federal government, loyalty to neighbors or the federal government, kinship ties, and military obligation all served as factors in determining an individual's level of participation in the Whiskey Insurrection.

The motivations behind the actions of the residents of western Virginia's border counties during the Whiskey Rebellion of 1794 are difficult to discern. What is clear is that the Whiskey Rebellion dramatically affected Appalachian Virginia and its inhabitants. After all, "Strong art thou O Whiskey upon the Western mountains, and strong is thy brother Brandy in the vales below."[67]

NOTES

1. This number of Pennsylvania counties should be expanded to include Bedford as well. The terms "rebellion" and "insurrection" are used interchangeably in this article.

2. Thomas P. Slaughter, *The Whiskey Rebellion: Frontier Epilogue to the American Revolution* (New York, 1986), pp. 3–8; Steven R. Boyd, ed., *The Whiskey Rebellion: Past and Present Perspectives* (Westport, Conn., 1985), pp. 97–118, 135–64, 183–85. Slaughter's introduction offers a brief summary of the historical context within which the Whiskey Rebellion must be viewed. Mary K. Bonsteel Tachau's essay is entitled "A New Look at the Whiskey Rebellion," and Roland M. Baumann's essay is entitled "Philadelphia's Manufacturers and the Excise Tax of 1794: The Forging of the Jeffersonian Coalition." Both essays are contained in Boyd, ed., *Whiskey Rebellion*.

3. Otis K. Rice, *West Virginia: A History* (Lexington, Ky., 1985), p. 48; Virgil A. Lewis, *The Soldiery of West Virginia in the French and Indian War; Lord Dunmore's War; the Revolution; the Later Indian Wars; the Whiskey Insurrection; the Second War with England; the War with Mexico* (Baltimore, 1978), p. 119.

4. Rice, *West Virginia*, p. 48; Lewis, *Soldiery of West Virginia*, p. 119. The British refused to relin-quish their northwestern trading posts as agreed upon in the 1783 treaty of Paris. They continued to supply the Native Americans of the Monongahela Valley with guns, ammunition, knives, and logistical information.

5. Rice, *West Virginia*, pp. 15, 22–48; Joseph Doddridge, *Notes on the Settlement and Indian Wars: Of the Western Parts of Virginia and Pennsylvania from 1763 to 1783 Inclusive, Together with a Review of the State of Society and Manners of the First Settlers of the Western County* (Akron, 1824), pp. 26–28. Essentially the treaty of Paris provided the victorious Americans with all British lands east of the Mississippi River, excluding present-day Florida and a portion of Alabama and Mississippi. Land speculation existed in northwestern Virginia from as early as the 1760s. George Washington launched a much-heralded expedition into the Virginia mountains in 1754, and his efforts paved the way for much of the early settlement in the region. Several excellent monographs examine the eighteenth century "Indian Wars." Joseph Doddridge's *Notes on the Settlement and Indian Wars ...* (Wellsburgh, Va., 1824) is one of the earliest publications to chronicle these events. Additionally, Alexander Scott Withers, *Chronicles of Border Warfare ...* (Cincinnati, 1895) and Willis De Hass, *History of the Early Settlement and Indian Wars of Western*

Virginia ... (Wheeling, Va., 1851) offer interesting narrative accounts of the violence between Native Americans and whites in the Virginia mountains and the Upper Ohio River Valley.

6. Rice, *West Virginia*, pp. 48–49; Doddridge, *Notes on the Settlement*, p. 16. Both Harmar's and St. Clair's expeditions ultimately met with catastrophic consequences and failed to end the Indian conflict. Gen. "Mad" Anthony Wayne's expedition in August of 1794, about the same time the Whiskey Rebellion reached its pinnacle, succeeded in defeating the native tribes that threatened western Virginia and the entire Ohio River Valley. His victory in the battle of Fallen Timbers (1794), near present-day Toledo, Ohio, and the subsequent treaty of Greenville (1795) effectively ended any real threat to western Virginia.

7. *History of Monongalia County, West Virginia; From its First Settlement to the Present Time, with Numerous Biographical & Family Sketches* (Kingwood, W.Va., 1883), pp. 95–96; Leland D. Baldwin, *Whiskey Rebels: The Story of a Frontier Uprising* (Pittsburgh, 1967), pp. 67–69. Taxes on distilled spirits were nothing new to Americans. There had been a series of whiskey taxes beginning as early as 1764 aimed at generating revenue for the royal colonies and helping alleviate the financial burdens of the French and Indian War and the American Revolution. Before 1791, however, enforcement of such excises was nearly impossible.

8. Kevin T. Barksdale, "Whiskey Distillation in Antebellum Western North Carolina," *Tuckasegee Valley Historical Review* 5 (1999): 1–5; Baldwin, *Whiskey Rebels*, p. 70; Melba Pender Zinn, *Monongalia County, (West) Virginia: Records of the District, Superior, and County Courts, Volume 1: 1776–1799* (Bowie, Md., 1990), pp. 66–68; Slaughter, *Whiskey Rebellion*, pp. 4, 22–24. Slaughter uses the term "localism" to describe the anti-excise sentiment on the western frontier. According to him, backcountry localist sentiment, as it was applied to the Whiskey Rebellion, combined several "disparate issues," including concerns over representation, taxation, governmental frontier policies, and "the tensions between eastern mercantile and western agricultural regions."

9. James Morton Callahan, *History of the Making of Morgantown, West Virginia: A Type Study in Trans-Appalachian Local History* (Morgantown, W.Va., 1926), p. 71. John Alexander Williams notes "Monongahela Whiskey was famous in America long before the frontier reached Bourbon County, Kentucky" (*West Virginia: A Bicentennial History* [New York, 1976], pp. 102–3). Western Virginia did not have a newspaper at the time of the passage of the excise, but with the wide circulation of the *Pittsburgh Gazette* and several papers published in the Richmond area, Virginia's mountaineers were painfully aware of Hamilton's measures.

10. Baldwin, *Whiskey Rebels*, pp. 76–80; H. M. Brackenridge, *History of the Western Insurrection in Western Pennsylvania, Commonly Called the Whiskey Insurrection* (Pittsburgh, 1859), pp. 18–22; Callahan, *History of the Making of Morgantown, West Virginia*, pp. 71–72; Zinn, *Monongalia County, (West) Virginia*, pp. 81–83. Although not explicitly stated, Monongalia County court records (which include Ohio, Harrison, Randolph, and Monongalia counties) and additional sources make it clear that two districts existed, encompassing both the northern panhandle and the southern border of Pennsylvania with Virginia.

11. Baldwin, *Whiskey Rebels*, p. 206; Zinn, *Monongalia County, (West) Virginia*, pp. 82–83; Earl L. Core, *The Monongalia Story: A Bicentennial History* (5 vols.; Parsons, W.Va., 1976), 2:222–23. It must be noted that Ohio County revenue officer Zachariah Biggs was also known as Zacheus Biggs. "The excise provided for inspection districts, in each of which an inspector was appointed whose duty it was to examine all distilleries, the capacity of the stills, gauge their barrels, brand their casks, and note in his book the result, and to crown the most odious feature—the duty" (Alfred Creigh, *History of Washington County from its First Settlement to the Present Time, First Under Virginia as Yohogania, Ohio, or Augusta County until 1781, and Subsequently Under Pennsylvania* [Harrisburg, Pa., 1870], pp. 61–62).

12. Baldwin, *Whiskey Rebels*, pp. 56, 75–84; Bracken-ridge, *History of the Western Insurrection*, pp. 22–23. William Findley, John Smiley (Smilie), James Marshall, Albert Gallatin, and Edward Cook led the western Pennsylvania anti-excise meeting in Washington County.

13. Creigh, *History of Washington County*, pp. 67–72, 75; Baldwin, *Whiskey Rebels*, pp. 174–75; Core, *Monongalia Story*, 2:222–23. Creigh offers a detailed account of the resolutions, leadership, and activities of these meetings, which brought together dozens of local leaders to formulate plans for the resistance to the excise tax. The delegates chose Parkinson's Ferry (present-day Monongahela City) because of its central location with- in the region.

14. Baldwin, *Whiskey Rebels*, p. 267; Creigh, *History of Washington County*, pp. 69–73. Alfred Creigh states that anti-excise leader David Bradford was a lawyer "who had been a member of the legislature of Virginia, when Washington and Allegheny counties were considered as belonging to Virginia."

15. The complete letter from David Bradford to the "Inhabitants of Monongahela, Virginia," dated 6 August 1794, is contained in Creigh, *History of Washington County*, pp. 72–75, and in *Pennsylvania Archives* Second Series (19 vols.; Harrisburg, Pa., 1876), 4:95–96. Baldwin, *Whiskey Rebels*, pp. 173–76.

16. Creigh, *History of Washington County*, pp. 64–66; Jerry Clouse, "The Whiskey Boys Versus the Watermelon Army," *Pennsylvania Heritage* 17 (1991): 27–28. "Tom the Tinker" was the moni-ker taken by Washington County resident John Holcroft, one of the most vocal leaders of the rebels, and he often used this pseudonym when submitting editorials to the *Pittsburgh Gazette*.

17. Creigh, *History of Washington County*, pp. 65–67; Brackenridge, *History of the Western Insurrection*, pp. 46–49. Both Creigh and Brackenridge include detailed accounts of these events in their works.

18. Zinn, *Monongalia County, (West) Virginia*, pp. 67, 71, 78–79; *Calendar of Virginia State Papers and Other Manuscripts ...* (11 vols.; Richmond, 1875–93), 7:33–34; Rice, *West Virginia*, p. 50. It hardly seems a coincidence that the first publicized assaults on Virginia excise officers occurred during the month of August 1794. The summer of 1794 witnessed the issuance of the circular inviting the "Monongahela inhabitants" to Parkinson's Ferry, a thwarted assemblage of anti-excise men at Braddock's Field in Fayette County, Pennsylvania, in late July, and rising concern evinced by regional newspapers, state governments, and the federal government.

19. Baldwin, *Whiskey Rebels*, p. 206; Zinn, *Monongalia County, (West) Virginia*, pp. 67–79. Court records describe these "bonds" as official papers that included "an entry of William Griffith's stills and diverse other documents of his said office." Ohio County offered Campbell, Laidley, Sutherland, and Edie clemency, but the county's anti-excise delegates refused the deal.

20. Core, *Monongalia Story*, 2:223; *Bowen's Virginia Centinel & Gazette* (Winchester), 18 Aug. 1794 and 3 Sept. 1794; *History of Monongalia County, West Virginia*, p. 96. Accounts of the incidents occurring in Morgantown are contained in contemporary newspaper accounts. There is little information to indicate that any Monongalia County citizens joined the mob, comprising Pennsylvanians and Ohio County residents.

21. Core, *Monongalia Story*, 2:223; *History of Monongalia County, West Virginia*, p. 96.

22. Baldwin, *Whiskey Rebels*, p. 206.

23. *Calendar of Virginia State Papers*, 7:267–68.

24. Core, *Monongalia Story*, 2:223.

25. *Calendar of Virginia Stale Papers*, 7:267–68.

26. Ibid.; A. S. Bosworth, *A History of Randolph County, West Virginia: From its Earliest Exploration and Settlement to the Present Time* (Parsons, W.Va., 1961), p. 234. William McCleery, Monongalia County excise officer, wrote, "We are all in this, Harrison & Randolph counties in Peace & also Ohio with some exceptions; a state of neutrality is all we are able to support, and indeed we are in a town much threatened now for lying still by our Powerful neighbors."

27. *History of Monongalia County, West Virginia*, p. 96; Core, *Monongalia Story*, 2:223; Baldwin, *Whiskey Rebels*, p. 206.

28. Brackenridge, *History of the Western Insurrection*, pp. 152–55; Baldwin, *Whiskey Rebels*, pp. 174–79; Albert Gallatin, 14 Aug. 1794, Papers of Albert Gallatin, 1761–1849, New-York Historical Society (microfilm; Philadelphia, Pa.: Rhistoric Publications); Slaughter, *Whiskey Rebellion*, p. 207; Core, *Monongalia Story*, 2:225. Brackenridge offers a detailed account of the meeting at Parkinson's Ferry in chapter 7 of his book. Gallatin includes a partial list of delegates to the Parkinson's Ferry meeting. Gallatin served as secretary of the convention and Cook served as chairman.

29. Brackenridge, *History of the Western Insurrection*, pp. 156 (first quotation), 160 (second quotation); Baldwin, *Whiskey Rebels*, pp. 175–82; *Pittsburgh Gazette*, 6 Sept. 1794.

30. Brackenridge, *History of the Western Insurrection*, pp. 155–57; Creigh, *History of Washington County*, pp. 74–75; *Pennsylvania Archives*, Second Series, 4:155. The committee of conference of twelve comprised three delegates from each of the four Pennsylvania counties and three delegates from Virginia. The Virginia delegates did not participate in the deliberations, a fact reflected in the body's name.

31. Otis K. Rice, *The Allegheny Frontier: West Virginia Beginnings, 1730–1830* (Lexington, Ky., 1970), pp. 350–51; Baldwin, *Whiskey Rebels*, pp. 185–92. The federal commission consisted of William Bradford, James Ross, and Jasper Yeates; the Pennsylvania delegation included Thomas McKean and Gen. William Irvine.

32. Boyd Crumrine, ed., *History of Washington County; Pennsylvania, with many Biographical Sketches of many of its Pioneers and Prominent Men* (Philadelphia, 1882), p. 289; *Pennsylvania Archives* Second Series, 4:201–3. The complete letter, dated 23 August 1794, is contained in the published Pennsylvania Archives.

33. Crumrine, ed., *History of Washington County*, pp. 288–90; Gallatin Papers (microfilm), pp. 253–55. The Redstone meeting was moved to 29 August to comply with a request made by the United States commissioners. Led by Gallatin, the fifty-six delegates in attendance passed a series of resolutions that further demonstrated their resolve to resist the tax.

34. John C. Fitzpatrick, ed., *The Writings of George Washington from the Original Manuscript Sources, 1745–1799* (39 vols.; Washington, D.C., 1940), 33:457–61, 509; Baldwin, *Whiskey Rebels*, pp. 184–85, 225; Crumrine, ed., *History of Washington County*, p. 286. The complete proclamation is contained in Fitzpatrick's work. The governor of Maryland was Thomas S. Lee and that of New Jersey, Richard Howell. The initial troop estimates were to total 12,950, but the final number was probably closer to 15,000.

35. Boyd, ed., *Whiskey Rebellion*, pp. 124–25; Jeffrey A. Davis, "The Whiskey Rebellion and the Demise of the Democratic-Republican Societies of Pennsylvania," *Journal of the Liberal Arts* 45 (1994): 22–38. Charles Royster states, "although Lee later called the insurrection 'a comedy,' he took its warnings seriously" (*Light-Horse Harry Lee and the Legacy of the American Revolution* [New York, 1981], pp. 130–31). Washington, Hamilton, and Lee believed that the Whiskey Rebellion was part of a much larger scheme, enacted by political partisans, Democratic-Republican Societies, and subversives, to destroy Hamilton's financial policies and Washington's foreign policies. Historian James Roger Sharp, in an essay entitled "The Whiskey Rebellion and the Question of Representation" in Boyd, ed., *Whiskey Rebellion*, argues that, "while Washington and Hamilton undoubtedly exaggerated the extent of the connection between Democratic-Republican Societies and the Whiskey Rebellion, it is clear that western Pennsylvania rebels and members of the societies had a common purpose" (pp. 124–25).

36. Boyd, ed., *Whiskey Rebellion*, pp. 124–25; Henry Lee, proclamation of 20 Aug. 1794, Draper Manuscript Collection, State Historical Society of Wisconsin (microfilm; Chicago: University of Chicago); Lewis, *Soldiery of West Virginia*, pp. 136–37. Lee's alarm was made clear in a proclamation issued "To the Inhabitants of Certain Counties lying west of Laurel Hill, in the State of Pennsylvania, Friends, and Fellow Citizens." In it Lee offers "loyal citizens" the reassurance that military preparations are underway to ensure their safety and also issues a warning to the insurrectionists that they will be dealt with swiftly.

37. Lewis, *Soldiery of West Virginia*, pp. 136–37. Lee called upon Monongalia County residents to protect themselves and their government from the *Whiskey Rebels*, but Lee knew they would need additional assistance in their efforts. Lee's proclamation was published in the *Pittsburgh Gazette* and appears in his papers as well as those of George Washington and Albert Gallatin.

38. Noel B. Gerson, *Light-Horse Harry: A Biography of Washington's Great Cavalryman, General Henry Lee* (Garden City, N.Y., 1966), pp. 190–91; Baldwin, *Whiskey Rebels*, p. 192. Lee's

previous military experience, loyalty to Washington in the American Revolution, and intense contempt for the Whiskey Rebels made him the natural choice to command the militia force.

39. Baldwin, *Whiskey Rebels*, pp. 220–23.

40. Lewis, *Soldier of West Virginia*, pp. 140–41; Don Higginbotham, *Daniel Morgan: Revolutionary Rifleman* (Chapel Hill, 1961), pp. 188–89. Morgan's past military accomplishments made him a logical choice to command the Virginia units, despite the fact that he was in his late fifties and had recently been ill. The 3,300 Virginia troops formed a division commanded by Morgan, and the division was divided into two brigades. Brig. Gen. James Mathews of Norfolk commanded the eastern brigade (comprising men from the eastern part of the state), and Gen. William Drake of Berkeley County commanded the western brigade (comprising men from Ohio, Monongalia, Randolph, Hardy, Pendleton, Hampshire, and Berkeley counties).

41. James Graham, *The Life of General Daniel Morgan of the Virginia Line of the Army of the United States, with Portions of His Correspondence; Compiled from Authentic Sources* (New York, 1856), pp. 141, 427. Before the Whiskey Rebellion, Brig. Gen. Benjamin Biggs commanded Virginia's 10th Brigade (comprising the following regiments: 4th [Ohio County], 11th [Harrison County], 76th and 104th [Monongalia County], and 107th [Randolph County]. During the rebellion, Biggs's 10th Brigade became part of Drake's larger western brigade and, according to Virgil Lewis, Biggs assumed joint command of the 11th and 107th regiments (*Soldiery of West Virginia*, pp. 139–41).

42. Baldwin, *Whiskey Rebels*, p. 224. This assumption is based on the fact that after the scheduled 2 September 1794 meeting at Old Redstone Fort, there is no mention of the participation of Virginians in any anti-excise meetings, rallies, or assaults. Additionally, no accounts exist of violence occurring in the Virginia border counties after the 9 August assault on Morgantown's excise officer.

43. Rice, *Allegheny Frontier*, p. 350. Rice cites a letter dated 23 August 1794, from William McKinley to James Ross, Jasper Yates, and William Bradford (federal commissioners) to substantiate his claim (William McKinley to James Ross, Jasper Yeates, and William Bradford, 23 Aug. 1794, Jackson MSS, 1781–1832, Eli Lilly Library, Indiana University, Bloomington, Ind.)

44. Graham, *Life of General Daniel Morgan*, p. 427; Daniel Morgan to George Washington, 24 Sept. 1794, George Washington Papers, Library of Congress (Presidential Papers on Microfilm).

45. In a document written by Benjamin Biggs, the brigadier general states that the western Virginia regiments were commanded by Mores Chapline (Ohio County), William Lowther (Harrison and Randolph counties), Vincent Williams (Hardy County), Peter Hull (Pendleton County), Samuel Hanaway (Monongalia County), and Andrew Wodrow (Hampshire County). Biggs gives little indication that he had difficulty recruiting Ohio County volunteers into the militia (attachment by Benjamin Biggs, June 1794, Draper Manuscript Collection [microfilm]; Lewis, *Soldiery of West Virginia*, pp. 140–41).

46. Lewis, *Soldiery of West Virginia*, pp. 140–42; Graham, *Life of General Daniel Morgan*, pp. 429–31. This placed the Pennsylvania and New Jersey troops along a north-south line.

47. Lewis, *Soldiery of West Virginia*, pp. 140–41; Graham, *Life of General Daniel Morgan*, pp. 429–31. This placed the Virginia and Maryland troops along an east-west line.

48. Crumrine, *History of Washington County*, pp. 298–99; Creigh, *History of Washington County*, pp. 80–81; Graham, *Life of General Daniel Morgan*, pp. 430–31. The militiamen arrested the majority of the principal Whiskey Rebels in the early morning hours of Thursday, 13 November, an event that became know as "the terrible night," or "the dreadful night." Crumrine includes a firsthand account of the events of that "frosty night" in his work. Undoubtedly, troops from Morgan's Pittsburgh invasion force were from the western Virginia border counties, but this information is not available.

49. Lewis, *Soldiery of West Virginia*, p. 141; Graham, *Life of General Daniel Morgan*, pp. 432–35. Morgan was stationed near McFarlane's Ferry, on the Monongahela River.

50. Crumrine, *History of Washington County*, pp. 302–5; Zinn, *Monongalia County, (West) Virginia*, pp. 66–83, 108–9.

51. Henry Lee, proclamation, 29 Nov. 1794, Papers of James W. Singleton, Old Dominion University Libraries, Norfolk, Va; Baldwin, *Whiskey Rebels*, pp. 262–3; Crumrine, *History of Washington County*, pp. 302–4. The five Virginians excluded from the pardon were Sutherland, Stephenson, McKinley, John Moore, and John McCormick. According to Melba Zinn, Robert Stephenson and William McKinley were indicted in the District Court of Ohio County in May of 1795 "for inciting and stirring up the inhabitants of Ohio County in opposing the execution of the laws of the United States in the collection of the revenues on stills and distilled spirits." Both cases were dismissed in September 1795. William Sutherland was indicted for the robbery of excise officer Zachariah Biggs in May of 1795. The charges against Sutherland and three other men also accused of the robbery were ultimately dropped in September of 1795 after the attorney for the commonwealth declined to pros-ecute further. (*Monongalia County [West] Virginia*, pp. 71–72, 77–79).

52. Zinn, *Monongalia County, (West) Virginia*, pp. 66–83, 108–9. Reasons for the dismissals are not available in Zinn's book, and the original court records are missing. As in Virginia, very few in Pennsylvania received punishment for participating in the Whiskey Insurrection.

53. W. Brooke to Benjamin Biggs, 25 July 1795, Draper Manuscript Collection (microfilm).

54. Ohio County Order Book 3, 1792–94, pp. 170, 192, 219, 226, and 260–63; and Ohio County Order Book 4, 1794–1800, pp. 104, 121, 126, 149, 204, 207, and 220–21, West Virginia and Regional History Collection, Morgantown, W.Va.; *History of Monongalia County*, pp. 97–98; Rice, *Allegheny Frontier*, p. 352. William Sutherland, who had been appointed land assessor for Ohio County in 1790 and 1793 became county commissioner in 1794 and served as lieutenant (1790) and captain (1793) in the Ohio County militia. William McKinley was appointed justice of the peace for Ohio County in 1790 (he resigned in 1793) and second lieutenant (1792) and first lieutenant (1793) of the 10th Brigade of the Ohio County militia.

55. Dorothy Davis, *John George Jackson* (Parsons, W.Va., 1976), pp. 12–15; Stephen W. Brown, *Voice of the New West: John G Jackson, His Life and Times* (Macon, Ga., 1985), pp. 3–4. Jackson represented Harrison County in the Virginia House of Delegates from 1785 to 1788, 1789

to 1791, and in 1794. He also served on the 1788 Virginia Convention that ratified the U.S. Constitution.

56. Brown, *Voice of the New West*, pp. 3–4. Dorothy Davis states that Congress created the Third District in 1792 out of the "transmontane Virginia counties' (*John George Jackson*, pp. 23–27).

57. *Pittsburgh Gazette*, 21 Mar. 1795; James Veech Scrapbook, 1859, pp. 94–95, James Veech Papers, 1793–1879, Historical Society of Western Pennsylvania Archives, Senator John Heinz Pittsburgh Regional History Center, Pittsburgh. This letter, written 18 August 1794, was sent to Jackson's political opponent, Baldwin Weaver of Morgantown, and subsequently published to illustrate Jackson's new moderate stance. James Veech, a well-known western Pennsylvania author, politician, lawyer, and historian, assembled two scrapbooks that contain most of the contemporary articles published in the *Pittsburgh Gazette* concerning the Whiskey Insurrection.

58. Baldwin Weaver published two scathing editorials regarding Jackson's candidacy, describing the Clarksburg native as "a character exceedingly suspicious" (*Pittsburgh Gazette*, 14 Feb. 1795, 21 Mar. 1795). Rice, West Virginia, p. 51; James Veech Scrapbook, pp. 94–95.

59. Jerry A. Clouse, *The Whiskey Rebellion: Southwestern Pennsylvania s Frontier People Test the American Constitution* (Harrisburg, Pa., 1994), pp. 41–42. Clouse states that "most local leaders of the rebels stayed and became or continued as local officials and judges."

60. Helene Smith, *The Great Whiskey Rebellion: Rebels with a Cause* (Greensburg, Pa., 1994), p. 126.

61. Ibid., pp. 125–26.

62. First and Second Censuses of the United States, 1790 and 1800, Harrison, Monongalia, and Ohio counties, Virginia, schedules 1 and 2, available at the United States Historical Census Browser, http://fisher.lib.virginia.edu.census (accessed 5 Oct. 2001). The 1790 and 1800 censuses were destroyed during the War of 1812, and the population statistics were compiled by the Inter-university Consortium for Political and Social Research (ICPSR) using Virginia tax records. It is also worthy to note that Ohio County was divided to form Brooke County in 1797. The population figures for Ohio County take this fact into consideration.

63. Karl Raitz, ed., *A Guide to the National Road* (Baltimore, 1996), pp. 3–45; Beulah Boyd, "The National Road Comes to Wheeling" (Ph.D. diss., Columbia University, 1925), pp. 1–50.

64. *Pennsylvania Archives*, Second Series, 4:228–29; Smith, *Great Whiskey Rebellion*, p. 126; Raitz, *Guide to the National Road*, pp. 3–45. The Ohio County delegates' demands are contained in a series of resolves dated 18 September 1794. The navigation restrictions on the Mississippi River were removed in 1795 with the signing of Pinckney's treaty with Spain, which opened the markets of the Upper Ohio Valley and allowed Monongalia rye to be distributed throughout North America. Ironically, the National Road initially stretched from Cumberland, Maryland, to Wheeling, Virginia. The National Road's route crossed through the Pennsylvania counties most involved in the Whiskey Rebellion and terminated in Virginia's most active insurrection county, Ohio.

65. Rice, *West Virginia*, p. 50; Charles Henry Ambler, *Sectionalism in Virginia: From 1776 to 1861* (Chicago, 1910), pp. 64–65. Ambler argues that, "the inhabitants of the west sympathized

heartily with the efforts of the federal administration to defeat the Indians of the Northwest Territory."

66. In his afterword, Boyd also considers several different reasons why the excise resistance "escalated into a so-called rebellion in only" western Pennsylvania. Boyd argues, citing research by Dodee Fennell, that historians must consider the "inequity" of the financial burden the excise tax placed upon westerners and smaller distillers as a motivating factor in the rebellion. Additionally, the author asserts that the Scots-Irish origins of western Pennsylvanians and Appalachian settlers must be "considered when evaluating the causes of the rebellion" (Boyd, ed., Whiskey Rebellion, pp. 170–85). David Hackett Fischer considers the relationship between the mountaineers' Ulster origins and whiskey distillation and rebelliousness in his work *Albion's Seed: Four British Folkways in America* (New York, 1991).

67. *Pittsburgh Gazette*, 8 Aug. 1794. This quote is from a poem entitled "Eulogy on Whiskey" by Absalom Aimwell.

Neighborhoods and Nat Turner

THE MAKING OF A SLAVE REBEL AND THE UNMAKING OF
A SLAVE REBELLION

By Anthony E. Kaye

When Nat Turner looked back on the origins and progress of his revolt, he told the story from beginning to end as a neighborhood enterprise. Neighborhood was the place where he found confirmation of his childhood sense that he was intelligent beyond his years. When he was a boy, no one had taught Nat his letters. But when his family handed him a book to stop his crying, he spelled the objects pictured, "a source of wonder to all in the neighborhood." Turner never felt compelled to steal, but those who did relied on him to plan their exploits, for such was the store that "the negroes in the neighborhood" placed on his judgment. All his initial recruits were other slaves from his neighborhood. And the rebellion proceeded apace as long as it remained there. When the rebels left the neighborhood, divisions opened up in the ranks, and the revolt began to collapse.[1]

Neighborhoods like Turner's shaped the contours of slave society across the South. In the Natchez District of Mississippi, for example, neighborhoods were the place where slaves worked together, cultivated family ties, practiced Christianity, socialized, and struggled. This was a terrain of conflict as well as solidarity. Indeed, conflict between slaves was intrinsic to making neighborhoods the locus of solidarity in the first place. Neighborhood had little meaning apart from distinctions between people inside and outside the place.

Neighborhoods drew these distinctions most sharply with runaways. Slaves often captured fugitive strangers who ventured into their neighborhood, and runaways lay out in their own neighborhood because here they could expect to find allies. Slave narratives vividly describe slave neighborhoods in Maryland, North Carolina, Kentucky, Tennessee, along with Mississippi and Virginia. Turner's neighborhood in Southampton was by no means identical to neighborhoods in those states, but he was all too familiar with their dynamics as an arena of both solidarity and conflict.[2]

Neighborhoods posed the problem of rebellion sharply. Rebels had to unite slaves across neighborhood lines, yet slaves typically cultivated solidarity within those lines, and slave society was everywhere divided along them. Two generations of revisionist work have trained us to think of slave society as a single, unitary community. Slave society, however, was not monolithic but plural, comprised not of one community but many neighborhoods, each with its particular ties of family, work, sociability, and struggle. The challenge of slave rebellion was to build on neighborhood solidarities and break down the divisions between neighborhoods. Turner counted on the solidarities of neighborhood and ran up against its divisions at every turn. *The Confessions of Nat Turner* is one of the most widely read documents in the history of slavery in the United States, but scholars have yet to explore the discussion of neighborhood that runs throughout Turner's account.

Can we be certain, however, that all the talk of "neighborhood" in *The Confessions* was Nat Turner's talk? Fixing the geographic limits of the rebellion was one of many tasks of suppressing it, part and parcel of taking up rebels, putting the accused on trial, hanging perpetrators, expelling collaborators from Virginia, and, in the immediate aftermath, slaughtering black people indiscriminately. For a week after the insurrection, fears coursed through southern Virginia that rebels had coalesced in the hundreds from across the region. On the second day of the revolt, families in Brunswick County fled to the county seat as word spread that 300 to 400 rebels had crossed into Greenville County, adjoining Southampton. Three days later Southampton was quiet enough for militia to begin disbanding, yet three days after that commanders in two other adjoining counties, Surry and Nansemond, requested arms from the state to put down an anticipated insurrection.[3]

Meanwhile, authorities sought to contain the alarm by mapping the terrain of the uprising. The same day militia officers in Surry and Nansemond appealed for armaments, General Richard Eppes, appointed by the governor to command troops on the scene, assured a newspaper that "no great concert among the slaves" had prevailed and exonerated "all slaves in the counties around Southampton" of any prior knowledge about the revolt. Throughout the week after the rebellion, editors and correspondents discredited early reports as exaggerating its size. These newspaper accounts, estimating the rebels' maximum numbers between 100 and 400, hardly minimized the insurrection. Yet some correspondents who aimed to narrow the terrain of the revolt did so in terms of neighborhood.[4]

John Hampden Pleasants, editor of the Richmond *Constitutional Whig*, was explicit about the connections between quelling fears about the revolt, dispelling rumors about the rebels' vast numbers, and pinning down its geography on neighborhood grounds. "Here for the first time," Hampden reported on August 25 from Jerusalem, the county seat of Southampton, "we learnt the extent of the insurrection, and the mischief perpetrated. Rumor had infinitely exaggerated the first, swelling the numbers of the negroes to a thousand or 1200 men, and representing its ramifications as embracing several of the adjacent counties, particularly Isle of Wight and Greenville." Pleasants was quick to locate the origins of the rebellion southwest of town, "in the neighborhood of the Cross Keys." The following week, Pleasants disposed of questions about the immediate causes of the rebellion as relatively unimportant. "A more important inquiry remains—whether the conspiracy was circumscribed to the neighborhood in which it broke out, or had its ramifications through other counties." As this query suggests, the place of neighborhood in the rebellion persisted after the panic subsided as a subject of fraught debate.[5]

Thomas R. Gray, Turner's collaborator on *The Confessions*, was a participant in that debate. All documents are collaborations, and fortunately a good deal is known about Gray. He had recently fallen from the planter class, losing half his land and all his adult slaves by 1831 within a decade of inheriting them. At the time of the insurrection, Gray plied his trade as a lawyer. In fact, he represented five slaves tried as rebels, including one of Turner's neighbors, Hark Travis. As defense counsel, Gray served as an officer of the court and did his part to restore order in Southampton County. All five of his clients were found guilty and duly condemned to hang or exile from Virginia. Gray picked up fees as defense counsel, but they were not the main chance, as he saw it. *The Confessions* were. Gray's appointments by the court as defense attorney authorized him to conduct his own investigations during the ten weeks Turner was at large. Gray, like other responsible parties, aimed to map the geography of the rebellion. Even before his interviews with Turner, Gray had contributed a dispatch to Pleasants's newspaper describing the uprising in terms of "neighborhood." Fears of a wider conspiracy were evidently one of the "thousand idle, exaggerated and mischievous reports" that Gray condemned in his preface to *The Confessions*, which suggested Turner's revolt "was entirely local."[6]

The Confessions derived much of its immediacy and power, for contemporaries and historians, from its seemingly unmediated account of Turner's story, but some words attributed to Turner were Gray's. Many of these interventions are plainly marked, as queries Gray addressed to Turner, or with parentheses and brackets. Some of these expressed Gray's opinions of Turner, distilled in his parenthetical reference to "these barbarous villains." Other interventions come with no helpful markers of Gray's hand, but they have a pattern, and it dovetails with Gray's expressed opinions of Turner. Thus Turner is supposed to have referred to "our blood-stained track" and to a failure "to gratify our thirst for blood." These statements sound improbable coming from Turner, not least because the narrative reveals his evident distaste for bloodshed, as we shall see. Exact body counts of the dead at different farms, and the forces of whites rallying against the rebels are also more likely Gray's than Turner's estimate, which was bound to be imprecise in the welter of the revolt. In short, Gray put words in Turner's mouth. Some are more or less readily apparent, but others may not be.[7]

If *neighborhood* was one of those words, Gray did not invent the term but rather picked it up from the slaves he interviewed in the course of his investigation. Gray had learned much about the revolt by the time he interviewed Turner and had already described the origins of the revolt in terms of neighborhood in an anonymous dispatch from Jerusalem, published in *The Constitutional Whig*. Turner "had acquired a great influence over his neighbourhood acquaintance," Gray wrote. More specifically, "in his immediate neighbourhood, he had acquired the character of a prophet." Gray mentioned one informant who clued him in to Turner's reputation as a prophet in the neighborhood, a woman who turned over evidence of his visions, "some papers given up by his wife, under the lash—they are filled with hiero-glyphical characters." It was slaves like Turner's wife who had introduced the language of neighborhood to Gray's thinking about the revolt long before he met Turner. *The Confessions* is rife with talk of neighborhood because Turner and other slaves had talked about the revolt as a story of neighborhoods all along. To understand Nat Turner's rebellion, we need to remap it along neighborhood lines, as Turner himself did.[8]

If the conceit of all prophets is that they are born, the truth, of course, is that they are made, and it was Nat Turner's neighborhood that made him a prophet. This mantle was not his inspira-tion, and he assumed it slowly and reluctantly. He was prepared to accept the reputation of a gifted child arising from his precocious ability to spell, but his neighbors' faith in him surpassed his own, for they also believed his good sense "was perfected by Divine inspiration." Yet Turner, demanding further signs, held himself aloof from his neighbors and "wrapped myself in mys-tery." In the meantime he fasted and prayed and reflected on the scriptures. A verse from the Sermon on the Mount struck Turner most powerfully. He prayed upon it daily, even at the plow, and there "[t]he Spirit that spoke to the prophets in former days" appeared to Turner and spoke the words himself: "Seek ye the kingdom of Heaven and all things shall be added unto you." Only after two more years of prayer did the Spirit reveal himself a second time, and only then was Turner at long last convinced of what his neighbors had known all along: His "wisdom came from God." But now his faith surpassed theirs, for he also believed God had chosen him for "some great purpose." And Turner "now began to prepare them for my purpose."[9]

Of all the people in Turner's neighborhood, why did he become the object of his neighbors' spiritual ambitions? One reason they may have expected great things of him was that Turner's neighborhood was bigger than theirs. The boundaries of neighborhood were clear, but they varied. Neighborhoods in the Natchez District were adjoining plantations. Neighborhoods in Turner's region may well have been larger, if only because slavery was extensive there a half-century earlier. Yet in every neighborhood, there were people who worked over a larger terrain and whose neighborhood grew in proportion. Most of these slaves had occupations that demanded mobility: preachers, midwives, body servants, artisans, carriage drivers, team-sters, and the like. Historians long believed Turner was one of these mobile slaves, an artisan, but he was a plow hand, in fact. He came to have an extended neighborhood not by trade but through an unusual geography of ownership. Turner was sold four times and changed his place of residence three times. Yet all his owners and residences covered a vicinity of just a few miles square. So Turner was a rare man with unusually strong ties to a great many people in several neighborhoods. His neighborhood, in effect, encompassed several neighborhoods. Perhaps his reputation as a prophet acquired a ring of truth to his neighbors because he knew more people than they did, because he knew the local terrain better than they did, because his horizons seemed broader than theirs, and because his knowledge of strange people and strange places sometimes seemed uncanny.[10]

Turner's reputation as a prophet may also have gained credence from white people who had long thought he was gifted too. Slaveholders were part of slave neighborhoods, as far as slaves were concerned, and by Turner's account, owners had a hand in fashioning his stature as a prophet. Turner counted his owner "and other religious persons who visited the house" among those who had first taught him his prayers as a child. They agreed with his grandmother that he possessed powers of understanding beyond a slave's. As Turner mulled over his visions of the Spirit, he recalled these people's remarks from time to time and took strength from them.[11]

Yet church was no place for a man of Turner's spiritual gifts. As Randolph Scully points out, Turner steered well clear of churches, and not because he rejected their standards of evangelical authority. On the contrary, Turner's account of his rise as a prophet depicted milestones widely recognized by evangelical churches as signs of authentic conversion. From his resolution not to steal as a child to his periods of solitude and fasting, he displayed a self-control worthy of evangelical manhood. Communications with the Spirit were Turner's own direct experience of grace. The sanctified common ground Turner shared with the churches suggests he was striving not for autonomy but recognition. Scully's account of the travails of slave preachers suggests Turner was wise to avoid entangling himself in the churches. If their white overseers would have readily recognized the forms of Turner's claim to evangelical authority, they could hardly have put their imprimatur on its content. His visions were about to take a dark, sanguinary turn that church patriarchs would not have appreciated as acts of grace. Slave preachers like Tom and York, forbidden to preach by South Quay Baptist Church in the 1810s and 1820s, offered an object lesson, if Turner needed one, that recognition by the disciplinary apparatus of the churches was impossible for the likes of him. Given this spiritual terrain, Turner understandably cast his lot with the neighborhoods, although this arena had its own constraints.

Turner's neighborhood, like all slave neighborhoods, was complex. Slaves did not consider their neighborhoods entirely their own, for owners were inextricable figures here, but these were places of profound solidarities nonetheless. In Turner's case, they wrought the man into a prophet. For most of Turner's days, his spiritual powers were his neighborhood's idea, not his. Yet tensions ran deep in neighborhoods too. His neighbors' faith was never enough for Turner. When he finally came around to their way of thinking, he went them one better: Not only was he touched by God, but He also had some purpose to achieve through Turner. What the neighborhood gave Turner in stature, it soon took away.

Turner was sidetracked from his "great purpose" for some six years because the neighborhood that first exalted him then brought him low. Around 1822, just as he began to confide intimations "something was about to happen," he absconded to the woods for thirty days. Fellow slaves assumed he had followed in the footsteps of his father, who had run away years before never to return. Another group of slaves whom Turner did not mention in *The Confessions* had their own stake in his attempt to remain at liberty. After all, he could hardly find food or safe haven for weeks at a time without the aid of other slaves in the neighborhood. So bondpeople who knew Turner, whether they had harbored him or assumed he was safely on free soil, had cause for disappointment when he reappeared, quoting the Spirit: "For he who knoweth his Master's will, and doeth it not, shall be beaten with many stripes, and thus have I chastened you." Fellow slaves understandably rebuked him, "murmurred against" him, as Turner put it. With that phrase, he cast himself as Moses, his neighbors as the ungrateful Israelites, who "murmured" against Moses for lack of food and water after he parted the Red Sea. Of course, the Spirit's words were open to interpretation. So it may have disappointed Turner, for his part, that fellow slaves assumed slaveholders were the only master he had in mind.[12]

Turner thus conceived his plot in earnest now, at the moment he was scorned by his neighborhood. After this reproach, perhaps in response to it, he had his most vivid revelation: a battle between white spirits and black spirits that eclipsed the sun; blood and thunder streamed across the sky. When he saw drops of blood fall like dew upon a corn field, he revealed the vision to "many, both white and black, in the neighborhood," but it did little to uplift his fallen standing. Only a reprobate white man was suitably impressed by these visions, and Turner took him down into a creek, where the Spirit baptized them, and onlookers "re-viled us." In May 1828 the Spirit told Turner, when he saw another sign in the sky, to begin "the great work" and commence the "fight against the Serpent." Upon a solar eclipse on February 12, 1831, he confided his purpose to four slaves. He identified them with the neighborhood only obliquely, counting them among those from whom he had kept aloof "years before," but all four were from there. Hark Travis lived on the same farm as Turner, while Sam Francis, Henry Porter, and Nelson Edwards belonged to owners nearby. These men, all from his neighborhood, were the people "in whom I had the greatest confidence."[13]

Neither the political character of neighborhoods nor *The Confessions* preclude the possibility, as Peter H. Wood and Scot French have suggested, that Turner's rebellion was part of a wider conspiracy. Beck, a young house servant on a plantation straddling the county line between Southampton and Sussex, offered the most concrete evidence of such a plot in her trial testimony about conversations on her owner's place. A week before the revolt, Beck testified, she overheard two defendants say they would join rebels who came to their vicinity. Another man ventured that his master had "crossed him and he would be crossed" before the year was out. According to the trial record, Beck said she had heard three other men say much the same "some time previously in the neighborhood." The defendants, Beck noted, lived about a mile from her owner's plantation—north of Turner's neighborhood, that is.[14]

Beck's testimony is, as Scully suggests, inconclusive evidence of a conspiracy in her neighborhood. To be sure, she persuaded the court in Southampton to convict all three defendants and another in Sussex to find seven others guilty. In 1835, however, eighteen citizens of Sussex questioned her credibility and petitioned the governor to commute the death sentence of a defendant convicted on her testimony who had not yet been executed. Turner, asked directly by Gray whether he knew of "any extensive or concerted plan," replied with a rhetorical question of his own: "can you not think the same ideas, and strange appearances about this time in the heaven's might prompt others, as well as myself, to this undertaking." Turner knew of no plans in other neighborhoods, but he could not rule out the possibility. The boundaries of neighborhood did not necessarily prevent the plot from extending into another neighborhood. But they underscored the difficulties of melding rebels from different neighborhoods into a cohesive force.[15]

Nat Turner's rebellion, by his account, took root in neighborhood soil. That was the field where he first gained recognition for his uncommon abilities, steeled himself for battle against slavery, and finally cultivated his authority as a prophet, such as it was. It did not bode well for his revolt that he could never quite align his neighbors' faith in him with his own faith in himself. When theirs approached its apogee, he awaited further signs. When his faith was strong enough to confide intimations of his plans, theirs tumbled. Rebuked by his neighborhood for returning to it, he looked to the sky. Yet when the time came to find comrades-in-arms, he looked to his neighborhood, and there he found them. In the event, the progress of his rebellion turned sharply on neighborhood lines too.

On Sunday afternoon, August 21, Turner joined his four confederates around 3 o'clock for a dinner at Cabin Pond, less than a mile north of his owner's house. Turner found two other slaves from the neighborhood there as well: Jack Reese, the brother of Hark Travis's wife, and Sam Francis's fellow slave Will. Turner dismissed Reese as Travis's "tool." Will proved his mettle in the revolt, but Reese deserted early (at Whitehead's farm) and alerted his owner. It did not take long for the assembly to settle on a time and place to begin the rebellion: that very night at the home of Turner's owner. They then fortified themselves with brandy and roast pig past midnight before proceeding south to the Travis house. Turner entered first, silently to avoid provoking "alarm in the neighborhood."[16]

One of the most curious features of the rebellion was Turner's own reluctance to kill. Of the sixty people slain by the rebels, only one died by Turner's hand, and his hesitation was, perhaps in part, a neighborhood hesitation. His rage against slaveholders was second to none, but killing them was no simple matter. They were the serpent, the Spirit told him, but they were fixtures in Turner's neighborhood too. By Turner's account, some even had a hand in fashioning his stature as a prophet, and they, too, earned his "greatest confidence." His hesitation was evidently palpable to his comrades, for they insisted he kill the first victim. Inside the Travis house, after they collected firearms downstairs, "It was then observed that I must spill the first blood." Upstairs in his owners' bedroom, Turner struck his owner but only landed a glancing blow. It was Will Francis—"Will the executioner," Turner later called him—who "laid [Joseph Travis] dead, with a blow of his axe."[17]

As the rebels made their way across their neighborhood, the revolt moved swiftly, gained recruits and momentum. After Turner had his men perform a few military drills, they proceeded to another farm, belonging to his owner's kin, just 600 yards distant. They struck next at the nearest farm of any account, Piety Reese's place two miles away, and then another mile to that of Turner's former owner, Elizabeth Turner, by around sunrise Monday morning. (The Turner place appears on the map on p. 720 as "Samuel Turner.") There Turner divided his forces, which now numbered fifteen, and they quickly attacked two adjoining farms before reconnoitering at Whitehead's, where Turner killed his one and only victim, a daughter in the Whitehead family, with the blow of a fence rail. By then, fifteen corpses marked their path through the neighborhood.[18]

As the rebels pressed on outside their neighborhood, the revolt began to unravel. At the Whitehead place, they divided into two forces again. One headed due north to Nathaniel Francis's farm, the second traveled over a mile northwest to Howell Harris's. Somewhere between the Francis and Harris farms, the second detachment crossed into another neighborhood. When Turner went after them, he told the first detachment en route to the Francis place that he would rejoin them "in *that* neighborhood." The first detachment veered northeast from Francis's and overran three farms before Turner caught up with what was by then a forty-man force at Newit Harris's. They cheered Turner as he rode up, but news of the revolt was traveling fast in the daylight, among owners as well as slaves.[19]

The rebels had ventured a good way off from Turner's neighborhood by now, and he modified their tactics to navigate the new terrain. Instead of a stealthy, silent advance and attack by surprise, he concentrated his forces and ordered them to charge at full gallop and in full cry to exaggerate the size of their ranks and paralyze the enemy in fear, to "carry terror and devastation wherever we went." For a time, the stratagem seemed to work, drawing ten to twenty more slaves into the uprising.[20]

But as the ranks grew, they combined several neighborhoods and pulled the rebellion in different directions. Traveling east, Turner wanted to march on to Jerusalem, where he mistakenly believed a large store of arms could be had. Other rebels, newcomers perhaps, wanted to stop three miles outside of town at the Parker farm, where they had "relations." Turner and a half dozen men stayed behind at Parker's gate while others went recruiting in the slave quarters. It is unclear whether the rebels bent on recruiting there lived in that neighborhood, in Turner's, or in a third. The boundaries of neighborhoods, after all, were permeable and overlapping. In any case, there was no point to Turner joining them to recruit. They were in someone else's neighborhood now, and he was a stranger to slaves here. Meanwhile slaveholders from across Southampton County marshaled to attack and caught up with Turner's men at Parker's gate, where the rebels had their first skirmish with local militia.[21]

When Turner tried to reconsolidate his forces, he decided to withdraw to familiar neighborhood grounds. Having escaped from Parker's farm with about twenty men, he headed toward a bridge three miles south of Jerusalem. Realizing the rest of his men had scattered, he was sure "they would make back to their old neighborhood," and he fixed upon rejoining them there to enlist new recruits and march on Jerusalem again. Along the path of his retreat, however, Turner began to pick up new recruits. Passing through several farms, his force of twenty had increased to "about forty strong" by the time they rested in a wood at the edge of the Ridley farm that night. But the new followers did not stick around for long. Turner awoke to an attack on his men, many of whom fled, and his forty men were back down to twenty. Turner thought he could pick up more recruits back on the several farms he had passed through and decided "to rally in the neighborhood, I had left," but to no avail. Gunfire met them at the first plantation, Blunt's. By the time Turner reached the next estate, his company had dwindled to two.[22]

Turner returned to his neighborhood as soon as he could. At nightfall on Tuesday, August 23, he sent his two remaining men to find the four neighbors in whom he had first confided his plan, with instructions to convene as many men as possible back at Cabin Pond. Turner arrived at the pond alone that night and waited until the following evening, when he dug a cave under a pile of fence rails, but no one came. Hark Travis had been shot and captured back on the Blunt plantation. Turner's three other neighbors, on the run from militia rampaging over Southampton, were in no position to join him, and they all were taken up during that first panicked week after the insurrection. The militia killed Henry Porter and Nelson Edwards, who was beheaded, his skull claimed by a unit from Norfolk as a macabre icon of the rebels' defeat. Sam Francis was jailed on August 30, held for trial and represented by the ubiquitous Thomas Gray. Francis and Travis were tried the same day, both convicted, and sentenced to hang on September 9.[23]

During the ten weeks between the rebellion and Turner's capture on October 30, rumor had him far afield of Southampton, but he was in his neighborhood all along. A month after the rebellion a newspaper from Richmond received a report from a correspondent in Botetort County, 180 miles west of Southampton, that Turner had been spotted near a crossroads tavern heading west toward Ohio. Others speculated, more plausibly, that Turner was hiding to the east in the Great Dismal Swamp where boggy terrain with dense stands of reeds, shrubs, and woods could offer an opportune, if unlovely, hiding ground. As late as October though, Turner hid himself on the Francis place, less than two miles from Travis's, where the revolt began.[24]

Turner knew the solidarities of neighborhood could not help him now. Even as he hid out there, he did all he could to keep out of sight. By his account, he ventured out only for water and, after six weeks, to "eaves drop the houses in the neighborhood." Turner insisted no one had yet laid eyes on him when the meat in his cave was sniffed out by "a dog in the neighborhood." We need not take at face value Turner's account of his perfect solitude while he was at large to recognize the inherent limits of neighborhood solidarities under the circumstances. If Turner received any help from slaves in the neighborhood, and it seems improbable he did not, during those ten long weeks, keeping the secret returned the favor. By the same token, given the conflicts that prevailed in neighborhoods during the best of times, it is not surprising some neighbors recoiled from him during this moment of crisis. The dog returned a couple of nights later, accompanied by two people whom Turner identifies only as "negroes." But as the dog was from the neighborhood, presumably they were too. Turner begged them not to give him away, but "they fled from me." Certain they would reveal his sanctuary, he left the cave and was caught in another hovel. In the end, Turner felt abandoned by his neighborhood, even if he did not put too fine a point on it in The Confessions.[25]

Neighborhoods, in all their complexity, clarify much that is puzzling about Turner's revolt—why he hid out so close to where it started, why his forces stopped before they reached his objective, why he changed tactics in midstream, how he selected his initial comrades, and, most important, why his ranks grew along the way, albeit modestly. The boundaries of neighborhoods were hard to fix as were the loyalties within them. Divisions were evident from the outset. In Turner's younger days, his neighbors had more faith in him than he had in himself, and they broke faith with him when he returned home a seemingly repentant runaway. Yet he also turned to his neighborhood when he resolved to find collaborators for his great work and convened them at Cabin Pond. Turner pointed to the boundaries of neighborhood in his extemporaneous instructions to the detachment headed toward the Harris farm. And the boundaries of neighborhood kept him out of the Parker quarters, waiting at the gates.

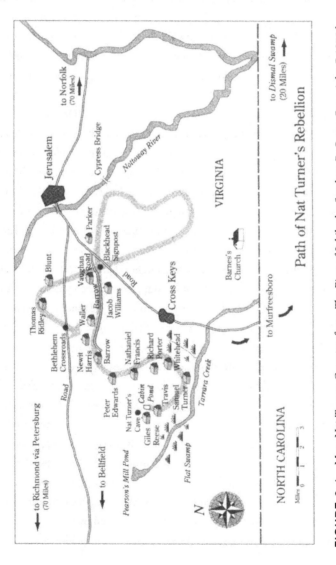

FIGURE 6-1 Map: Nat Turner Country from *The Fires of Jubilee* by Stephen B. Oates Copyright C 1975 by Stephen B. Oates. Reprinted by permission of HarperCollins Publishers

He changed tactics after he left his neighborhood, but no shift in tactics could close the breach between neighborhoods on the path to Jerusalem. When he sought fresh troops, he retreated to his neighborhood because that was the only place where he could raise them. Yet he hid from his neighbors, even as he hid amongst them. Turner's rebellion arose from the solidarity of neighborhoods, and it broke apart on the shoals between them.

NOTES

Anthony E. Kaye is assistant professor of American history at the Pennsylvania state University, University Park. He would like to thank the Institute for the Arts and Humanities for a grant in fall 2004, when this article was written; members of the panel and audience at SHEAR and an anonymous reviewer for the *JER* for helpful comments.

1. *The Confessions of Nat Turner* is collected most conveniently in Kenneth S. Greenberg, ed., *The Confessions of Nat Turner and Related Documents* (Boston, MA, 1996), 37–58. For the quotation above, see ibid., 45. The most extensive collection of primary sources remains Henry Irving Tragle, comp., *The Southampton Slave Revolt of 1831: A Compilation of Source Material* (Amherst, MA, 1971). In the notes below, citations to *The Confessions of Nat Turner* and other documents available in both volumes will refer to Greenberg; documents cited to Tragle are not available in Greenberg.

2. These issues are explored in Anthony E. Kaye, "Neighbourhoods and Solidarity in the Natchez District of Mississippi: Rethinking the Antebellum Slave Community," *Slavery & Abolition* 23 (Apr. 2002), 1–24; Kaye, *Joining Places: Slave Neighborhoods in the Old South* (Chapel Hill, NC, 2007). For discussions of slave neighborhoods in various regions of the South, see ch. 1; Frederick Douglass, *My Bondage and My Freedom*, ed. William L. Andrews (Urbana, IL, 1987), 27–28; Israel Campbell, *An Autobiography Bond and Free: Or, Yearnings for Freedom, from My Green Brier House* (Philadelphia, PA, 1861), 76–94, 105–9; John W. Blassingame, ed., *Slave Testimony: Two Centuries of Letters, Speeches, Interviews, and Autobiographies* (Baton Rouge, LA, 1977), 128–41, 151–64, 213–16.

3. *The Richmond Enquirer*, Aug. 26, 1831; Diary of Governor John Floyd, Aug. 26, 29, 1831, in *Southampton Slave Revolt*, comp. Tragle, 46, 252, 254.

4. *Richmond* (VA) *Compiler*, Aug. 24, 1831; Norfolk (VA) *American Beacon*, Aug. 26, 1831; *Richmond* (VA) *Enquirer*, Aug. 30, 1831, in *Southampton Slave Revolt*, comp. Tragle, 36–38, 40–42, 43. For discussions of the extent of the rebellion in terms of "neighborhood," see *The Petersburg* (VA) *Intelligencer*, Aug. 26, 1831; *The Lynchburg Virginian*, Sep. 8, 1831, in *Southampton Slave Revolt*, comp. Tragle, 38, 73. On attempts to craft an official narrative assuaging fears of a widespread rebellion, including the role of John Hampden Pleasants and Thomas R. Gray, see Scot French, *The Rebellious Slave: Nat Turner in American Memory* (Boston, MA, 2004), ch. 2.

5. Richmond (VA) *Constitutional Whig*, Aug. 29, 1831, Sep. 3, 1831; *Richmond Enquirer*, Aug. 30, 1831, Sept. 27, 1831, Nov. 15, 1831, in *Southampton Slave Revolt*, comp. Tragle, 51, 54–55, 70, 99–100, 139.

6. Richmond *Constitutional Whig*, Sep. 26, 1831, and "To the Public," both in *The Confessions of Nat Turner*, ed. Greenberg, 81, 40, 42; Thomas C. Parra-more, *Southampton County, Virginia* (Charlottesville, VA, 1978), 105–7; David F. Allmendinger, Jr., "The Construction of *The Confessions of Nat Turner* in *Nat Turner: A Slave Rebellion in History and Memory*, ed. Kenneth S. Greenberg (New York, 2003), 24, 26–27. The court sentenced all five slaves represented by Gray to execution but recommended that the governor commute the sentence of three of the men—Jack, Nathan, and Moses—to transportation out of state. "Summation of Trials," in *Southampton Slave Revolt*, comp. Tragle, 230–31, 233–34, 243.

7. Greenberg, ed., *The Confessions of Nat Turner*, 40, 44, 46, 47, 48, 51, 52, 53; Allmendinger, "Construction of *The Confessions*," 32.

8. Richmond *Constitutional Whig*, Sep. 26, 1831 in *The Confessions of Nat Turner*, ed. Greenberg, 81. Allmendinger persuasively attributes this dispatch to Gray in "Construction of *The Confessions*," 31–34. See also, *Richmond Enquirer*, Sep. 2, 1831, in *Southampton Slave Revolt*, comp. Tragle, 58. Greenberg suggests Turner maneuvered the revolt to avoid the farm where his wife lived. See "Introduction: Text and Context," in *The Confessions of Nat Turner*, ed. Greenberg, 11–12.

9. Greenberg, ed., *Confessions of Nat Turner*, 45–46. For a nuanced account of the travails of Turner's relationship to the slave community, see Patrick H. Breen, "A Prophet in His Own Land: Support for Nat Turner and His Rebellion within Southampton's Black Community," in *Nat Turner: A Slave Rebellion*, ed. Greenberg, 103–18.

10. Allan Kulikoff, *Tobacco and Slaves: The Development of Southern Cultures in the Chesapeake, 1680–1800* (Chapel Hill, NC, 1986), 92–96, 141–48, maps 2, 8; Parramore, *Southampton County*, 76–77.

11. Greenberg, ed., *The Confessions of Nat Turner*, 44–46. Turner also implied white people had wondered at his precocious ability to spell, noting it "was a source of wonder to all in the neighborhood, particularly the blacks," 45.

12. Greenberg, ed., *The Confessions of Nat Turner*, 46; Breen, "Prophet in His Own Land," 109–10; Allmendinger, "Construction of *The Confessions*," 39. Turner was quoting scripture in regard to those who "murmurred"; paraphrasing it when quoting the Spirit. See Exodus 15:24, 16:2, 17:3; Luke 12:47.

13. Greenberg, ed., *The Confessions of Nat Turner*, 47–48; Breen, "Prophet in His Own Land," 111–13; Parramore, *Southampton County*, 78–79, 85, 247n42; Parramore, "Covenant in Jerusalem," in *Nat Turner*, ed. Greenberg, 63.

14. Greenberg, ed., *The Confessions of Nat Turner*, 100; Wood, "Nat Turner: The Unknown Slave as Visionary Leader," in *Black Leaders of the Nineteenth Century*, ed. Leon Litwack and August Meier (Urbana, IL, 1988), 34–36; French, *Rebellious Slave*, ch. 2, esp. 37–41.

15. Greenberg, ed., *The Confessions of Nat Turner*, 54, 100–101; French, *Rebellious Slave*, 41, 60–64.

16. Greenberg, ed., *The Confessions of Nat Turner*, 48–49; Allmendinger, "Construction of *The Confessions*," 28; Parramore, *Southampton County*, 79, 85. Reese was then employed by Jordan Barnes, to whom Reese had been hired out by his owner, Joseph W. Reese. Ibid, 85.

17. Greenberg, ed., *The Confessions of Nat Turner*, 44–45, 46, 49.

18. Parramore, *Southampton County*, 83; Parramore, "Covenant in Jerusalem," 60.

19. Greenberg, ed., *The Confessions of Nat Turner*, 50, emphasis added.

20. Ibid., 50–51; Parramore, "Covenant in Jerusalem," 63.

21. Breen, "Prophet in His Own Land," 118; Greenberg, *The Confessions of Nat Turner*, 51–52. The forces that attacked the rebels at Parker's gate may have included citizens as well as local militia. They are variously identified in primary and secondary sources as a "white patrol" and "local militia, or citizens of the county," initially under the command of Captain Arthur Middleton of the county militia, later in the day under Alexander P. Peete, whom Gray refers to, parenthetically, as "Captain Alexander P. Peete," 51; Parramore, "Covenant in Jerusalem," 27; *Richmond Enquirer*, Sep. 27, 1831, in *Southampton Slave Revolt*, comp. Tragle, 100; Stephen B. Oates, *The Fires of Jubilee: Nat Turner's Fierce Rebellion* (New York, 1975), 85.

22. Greenberg, ed., *The Confessions of Nat Turner*, 52–53.

23. Ibid; Richmond *Constitutional Whig*, Sep. 3, 1831, in ibid., 73. *The American Beacon*, Aug. 29, 1831; *The Richmond Enquirer*, Sep. 2, 1831; Trial Record, Sep. 3, 1831, in *Southampton Slave Revolt*, comp. Tragle, 49–50, 58–59, 191–93.

24. *The Richmond Enquirer*, Oct. 4, 1831, Nov. 15, 1831; Samuel Warner, *Authentic and Impartial Scene of the Tragical Scene Which Was Wintesses in Southamton County*, both in *Southampton Slave Revolt*, comp. Tragle, 116–18, 139–40, 296–98.

25. Greenberg, ed., *The Confessions of Nat Turner*, 53.

7

Libby Prison Break

By Virgil Carrington Jones

A noise in the night around Libby Prison at Richmond, Virginia, was never, as a rule, something for the Confederate guards on duty to get excited about. This resulted from the fact that rare was the hour a moan or pitiful cry did not come out of the walls of the old building from some inmate stirred in sleep by sickness, inertia, or worry over loved ones at home. These wails were part of the natural atmosphere, a blending of the babble by day that at bedtime quieted to a restless protest of murmuring voices. By understanding, it was each sentry's responsibility to sift the echoes seeping from the darkness and to recognize those with a warning of danger or trouble. This they had to do by instinct rather than military handbook, and it was well done, as part of a conscientious and thorough job. No matter how much corruption and intrigue were spawned by the war, there was never a taint upon these men who paced away tortuous hours on the outside of the old ship chandler's warehouse. Praise was earned by them from friend and foe alike.[1] And their efficiency, saluted by official record, would have accounted for the promptness with which a guard, one night in early February, 1864, jerked his gun to firing position and blurted:

"Hush! What's that noise?"

A second sentinel, just beginning another lap of his post, stopped, swung about, and stared at the speaker in the faint glow from a gas light at the street comer.

"What noise?"

"Didn't ya hear it—a strange noise? Seemed to come out of the ground oyer there. Kind of like a faint rumbling."

The other guard stood in silence and listened. Above him towered the prison, a giant four-story, brick building, each floor divided into three huge warehouse rooms. Its front was on Cary Street and its rear a story lower on Canal. A few feet back flowed the muddy James River, turbulent stream at times, and between them lay the Kanawha Canal, a narrow band of water so still the moon seemed carved into the smooth opaqueness of its mirrory surface.

"I don't hear nothin'," the second guard said. "Must be rats. Got millions of 'em along this wharf."

The suggestion settled well with the alarmed sentinel. Slowly he turned and resumed his monotonous pacing, his form changing gradually into a silhouette as he moved out of the pale of the street lamp.

But the second guard was mistaken about the rats. No rodent was involved in the strange disturbance that had come to the alert ears outside of Libby. This noise was man-made, and it was not intended to have happened. Stealth was the keynote of what was going on under ground, for there, only a few feet beneath the paths of the sentries, Union prisoners were digging to freedom. The sound they had unintentionally created was evidence of their inability to direct a tunnel with accuracy. Almost tragically demonstrated was the tendency of the human mole to turn upward. That was what had happened—too soon.

It was like the birth of an uprising, this effort to break away from the clutches of the Rebels. It began with one man, and he, a volunteer from the coal mining area of Pennsylvania, kept the plot to himself until convinced in his own mind it would succeed. After that he slowly bared his plans, cautiously hand-picking those to whom he talked. Secrecy and stealth, patience and steel nerves, ability to endure hard labor and discomfort—these were the qualities he looked for in the small circle of prisoners he took into his confidence.

The Pennsylvanian was Colonel Thomas Ellwood Rose, thirty-three years old. He had started out a private in the Twelfth Pennsylvania Infantry, and soon was promoted to a captaincy in the Seventy-seventh Pennsylvania Volunteer Infantry.[2] With the latter regiment he stormed through Georgia and Tennessee, making some mistakes for which he was catechised in official reports, but amassing over-all a record for bravery that jumped him two ranks to brigade command, by special commission from the governor of his home state. Then had come Chicamauga, where something went wrong, innocently or otherwise, and before he knew it he and most of his men were surrounded so completely by the enemy that nothing but surrender was left to them. And now he was in his fifth month at Libby, sleeping on the floor, subsisting on meager rations, longing to get back to the field of action.

One of the first men he told of his plan of escape was Major Archibald G. Hamilton of the Twelfth Kentucky Cavalry. This officer had the qualities Rose sought. The two stretched on a blanket one day while the Pennsylvanian whispered what he had in mind, and from then on they were together often.

Silently and secretively they plotted and schemed. In carrying out this risky business their first goal was to acquaint themselves thoroughly with the layout and routine of the prison. Every comer of the drafty old building to which they could gain access was carefully examined. The two top floors were used as quarters for the inmates. On the next, flush with the ground level of Cary Street, the west room was used as an office by the Libby superintendent, the center as a kitchen where the inmates could cook their meals if they desired, and that on the east as hospital quarters. The cellar below also was divided into three chambers and was reserved largely for storage purposes.

Obviously, to tunnel out of the prison, they would have to find some means of reaching the basement. This must be done in so secret a manner the guards and the other prisoners would not be aware of what they were about. To find an answer, they carefully studied the movements of the inmates, and determined that the kitchen was the least frequented of all the rooms, especially at night But how to get from there to the cellar? This problem they studied for hours, and it was Hamilton who finally came up with the solution. He led Rose to one of two huge fireplaces in the chamber and, squatting, explained: take the bricks loose at the back and make an opening through the chimney, extending it downward into the basement. Make it just large enough to admit the body of a man. Twelve bricks in the back wall would do it, he estimated. Such an aperture would permit them to crawl down into the east room of the cellar, where they could do their work at night, and, upon returning, replace the outer bricks in the fireplace to cover the trail during the daytime. Guards were on duty only on the outside of the building during the period while the inmates were sleeping, and they should have no reason to suspect what was going on inside.

The next problem was where to conceal the dirt if they succeeded in getting through to dig a tunnel. That answer was more readily found. The east room was known as Rat Hell because its floor was covered with about two feet of packing straw, some cast aside from the beds of the hospital room above, a major portion taken from the huge boxes in which the Union government had sent mercy shipments of food and clothing. Under this straw the dirt could be hidden as excavated. Guards rarely entered Rat Hell, so there would be little likelihood the plot would be discovered.

With these details worked out, Rose organized his crew. Thirteen other men were carefully picked.[3] Individually they were given instructions. They would work in shifts of five men, one to dig while the others disposed of the dirt and fanned air into the tunnel as it lengthened.

Christmas cheers of 1863, dispirited and marked by cups nowhere near running over, had barely faded from the streets of Richmond when the project got under way. It had an optimistic start. The scheme for reaching the cellar worked well. A rubber blanket was obtained, and into it was swept the soot from the fireplace, after which the bricks were dislodged by aid of a chisel and two kitchen knives. Two nights of careful labor were required to chop out an opening large enough to serve their purpose. At the basement end of this aperture was suspended a ladder made of rope shrewdly confiscated from some of the bales of clothing shipped from the North.

Once the way was cleared to the basement, the nightly stint became routine. From 10:00 p.m. until 4:00 a.m. they worked, shift succeeding shift.[4] Through the east wall of the prison eight feet below the street level they cut a hole scarcely more than two feet in diameter. As the brick and dirt were loosened in crumbs and hunks, they were scattered over the floor beneath the straw in the huge cellar room.

After the digging progressed beyond the cellar wall, some sort of carrier to convey the dirt from the man pecking away in the cramped quarters of the tunnel to the men waiting at its mouth had to be devised. This problem brought into use an old wooden spittoon from the prison quarters. By means of pieces of clothesline attached to opposite sides, it was drawn back and forth as needed, a silent but useful partner in a desperate scheme.

As originally planned, the tunnel would turn southward after it cleared the prison wall and proceed in the direction of a large street sewer paralleling the canal. The prisoners had seen city workmen descend into this conduit back of the Libby, and it was recognized as a possible subterranean channel by which escapees might flee to another section of Richmond before coming above ground.

Night after night the work progressed. Back into the tunnel, wedging himself along by pushing and pulling with hands, feet, and elbows, moved the man whose turn it was to do the digging. Always with him he carried a short piece of candle, the spittoon, and the tools, which now consisted of a broken shovel in addition to the chisel and knives. As he advanced, he kept the shovel in position to fend off any of the huge wharf rats which might be lurking in his path. Fights with these pests were numerous, and sometimes spirited. Always there was danger. One bite, they knew, could mean a fatal infection.

Reaching the end of the shaft, the digger lay on his belly and chipped away at the earth, cupping it up in his hands or scooping it with the shovel to transfer it to the cuspidor. When this was full, he gave a tug on the clothesline to signal for the container to be drawn out into the cellar and emptied. Carefully it was spread under the straw, after which another tug was given in the opposite direction to start it back for refilling. Over and over this went on throughout the dead of night while prisoners slept and guards walked their posts overhead, all in complete ignorance of what was going on down below. Final chores as the hour of 4:00 a.m. approached consisted of covering the tunnel opening with straw, drawing the rope ladder up into the chimney, replacing the bricks in the back of the fireplace, and dusting them over with the soot gathered in the blanket. There was little fear that this break in the fireplace would be discovered The prison was kept indifferently clean by a detail of Negroes who swept the floors every morning and sloshed them with James River water twice a week. Never beyond this routine were their endeavors extended. And in their lack of work initiative they set no precedent. It was jokingly related that a part of the soot captured in the blanket had been left by the first fire ever ordered built by Libby & Son, ship chandlers and grocers who had erected the building.

The man who went most often into the tunnel was Rose. Again and again he crawled down into the shaft to see how it was proceeding. He was there when it got below the level of the canal and water began to seep in—and he was there chipping away when a deluge suddenly broke through the wall and almost drowned him.

This unexpected development called for a serious pooling of ideas. The fifteen men gathered in the darkness of the rat-infested cellar to talk over the matter, and decided to turn the tunnel in the direction of a small sewer extending from the southeast comer of the prison toward the larger sewer. By such means they hoped to avoid the water danger.

But again they were foiled. First they encountered wooden piling fully a foot in diameter, a barrier that caused a delay of several nights while an opening was pecked through with the tools at hand. But water continued to seep into the tunnel, and with it came a stench so sickening one man fainted while digging and was drawn out with great difficulty. After that the plan was abandoned.

Another conference was held. This time it was decided to dig directly eastward, below the street, in the hope of coming up beneath an old floorless carriage shed used for storing the boxes in which mercy shipments from the North had arrived. It stood on a vacant lot surrounded by a high board fence.

Work was resumed. For days it went on without mishap, and the tunnel became so long it was increasingly difficult to fan air back to the man on duty as digger. Every few minutes he would have to wriggle out into the cellar, feet first, to catch his breath. In addition, the dirt beneath the straw became deeper, and more care had to be taken to see that it was properly covered.

Rat Hell thus was converted into a hell of painstaking labor. Sore muscles, aching shoulders, bruised elbows, skinned knees became a badge of merit. Hour after hour men sweated in the tunnel, talking little, and that in whispers. It was serious business. One slip and their efforts would be wasted, their chances of escape thwarted, and they would be placed in solitary confinement. Greater care was maintained as the work progressed. Toward the last, for instance, those who were not on duty took turns upstairs at watching from the windows on the east side for indications that the guards had become suspicious.

As weeks went by and the tunnel lengthened, members of the fifteen-man party found it a growing strain to control their impatience. During the daytime, looking down from the windows on the east, they could see the guard pacing directly above the earth where they had lain, cramped and uncomfortable, the night before. But the view across the street gave them courage. There they could see the empty lot into which they hoped to escape, and beyond that lay dingy buildings and more empty lots, all part of a landscape marked by a confusion of roofs and chimneys. Perhaps some night soon they would be scampering across those lots, hidden by those roofs and chimneys and dingy houses, on their way to freedom. They would choose a route, once clear of the tunnel and the shed, away from the assembly of guard tents at the intersection of Twentieth and Cary. As they stared from the windows they could see in the distance rolling hills, far down along the banks of the river, and, closer at hand, spanning the stream between Richmond on the north side and Manchester on the south, long white bridges, the nearest partially hidden by green trees on a little island midway of the James.

All of this they drank in, and then turned smugly to look with pity at the hundreds of their fellow inmates who had no knowledge of what was going on down in the earth yards below, of the toil and suffering a handful of stalwarts were enduring to accomplish a goal that on the surface might seem impossible. One look about the prison was enough to spur the hapless fifteen to greater impatience, to make them long for the hour when they once more could squeeze through the fireplace opening and drop down the rope ladder into Rat Hell. Everywhere there was evidence of boredom, and nothing marked it more clearly than the haggard expressions on the faces of once active officers now confined in close quarters against their will. Some were emaciated, some dirty, and nearly all unkempt. There was little incentive to waste time on personal toilets when one day was like another. The rooms in which they waited for death or freedom were forty feet wide and one hundred feet long. Walls were of bare brick, floors of rough plank, and windows narrow, dingy, and left with only an occasional pane. At one end of each was a row of tin wash basins and a wooden trough that served as a bathtub. The only furniture consisted of stools and hard-bottom chairs.[5]

Monotony was a prisoner's greatest foe. It seemed to tear into his soul, to take away his hope and determination, converting him into the sort of individual he most likely despised in normal life. And it made heroes of those who could supply any form of diversion, including the patient individual who trained captive mice in a treadmill fashioned of tin cans.

These sights above, where twelve hundred men were crowded into quarters intended for scarcely one-third that number, made the fifteen work harder when they slithered back into the tunnel at night. It was possible every unfortunate devil in the place might get away if they ever extended the shaft as far as the shed in the vacant lot.

Renewed vigor went into the digging as February appeared on calendars, and at last came the day when there was talk of turning upward. But Rose wanted to be certain; it was his argument they had worked too long and hard and had too much at stake to risk it by a foolish miscue. How to make sure? They debated the question over and over, and in the end the plan accepted came from Captain John Gallagher, jolly Irishman of the Second Ohio Regiment. His jovial nature had put him on good terms with the guards, and he was positive he could get them to let him go across to the shed, using the pretense of looking for a box sent from the North. It was a gamble, but it seemed a safe one.

So Gallagher was detailed to make the attempt, and his presumption was correct. A guard marched along behind while he ostensibly went across in search of the box. When he returned—from a fruitless trip, so far as the Confederate who accompanied him knew—he had acquired a measurement. His steps, as best he could calculate, placed the distance to the shed at about fifty feet.

That night when the conspirators crawled down into Rat Hell, their first act was to measure the length of the tunnel. According to their method of figuring, they were directly beneath the shed. It had to be that way. So they turned upward. And that was the occasion when the guard walking post heard the strange noise.

Rose had taken upon himself the responsibility of this test, and he it was who burrowed toward the surface until a part of the street fell in, bringing about the narrowest escape of the entire undertaking. Through the hole, in the faint light from the gas lamp, he could see the two guards as they stood listening for a repetition of the noise. He held his breath in hopeful suspense, praying no more dirt would collapse. When the sentinels turned away from each other, mentally cursing wharf rats, the colonel immediately backed out of the tunnel and made plans to shore up the hole.

One benefit had resulted from this experience in digging upward: it was clear now that the shaft would have to be extended about fifteen feet before it would reach the shed.[6]

The following morning prisoners in Libby heard firing in the direction of Bottom's Bridge, a short distance to the east of the city. They listened, and cheers came involuntarily from their throats, for they recognized battle action and realized that at least some of the shots were coming from friendly guns. This was the first shooting they had heard in weeks, since severe winter weather had enveloped the area. The two armies grappling with each other in Virginia had not come together in a death struggle since Gettysburg, the preceding summer. Throughout the fall and winter they had toyed with each other in the northern part of the state, waiting, rebuilding, getting ready for a new offensive when the roads opened. And now that time might have come!

The gunfire from Bottom's Bridge—caused by an abortive effort of Union General Benjamin F. Butler to send troops storming into Richmond—was on the minds of the prisoners as they went down into the tunnel to dig that night. Things were beginning to happen again on the outside, out there where their old units were facing Southerners across the mud which came with winter—and this knowledge gave them renewed incentive to burrow to freedom. Back and forth moved the wooden spittoon, at shorter intervals. Also with greater persistence pecked the chisel and the knives and the broken shovel. And more often the different diggers backed out in the candle's light to draw fresh air into their lungs.

This night the dirt seemed to come away more easily, now that they knew where they were and how much farther they had to dig. A few more feet and freedom! No more lying on their backs, their sides, their bellies, to hack away at the earth barrier between them and the life they craved. No more straining of eyes in the faint reflection from the brave little pieces of candle. No more sore elbows, tired muscles, aching backs.

As the night advanced, Rose crawled into the tunnel at frequent intervals to measure. He was jubilant but calm, a man of achievement, his hour at hand. Long years afterward the soldiers around him would talk of the cool-headed persistence, the dogged determination of this officer who singlehandedly spearheaded one of the greatest prison deliveries of the war. It was a second effort at escape for him. Shortly after Chickamauga he had fled his captors at Weldon, North Carolina, only to be retaken the next day. A few days later he was transferred to Libby, and now he would try again.

Some time after midnight Rose crawled in and took over the digging. He had decided to burrow upward again. Busily he went about it, and at one-thirty o'clock in the morning, sweaty, mud-caked, breathing hard, he was able to pull head and shoulders above ground in the shed where the boxes were stored.[7]

There he rested and breathed deeply of the fresh air, aware of a temptation to free the remainder of his body and flee. At last he was on the outside looking in, a prisoner no longer. His final barrier to liberty, the guards pacing along the streets, had been passed. All he would have to do would be to melt into that confusion of rooftops and chimneys he had stared at many times from the upper floor of Libby, and the goal he had been working toward through-out those long, terrible nights down in Rat Hell would be his.

But Thomas E. Rose was an honorable man, and in this moment of temptation his thoughts turned to the other men who had made his dream possible, who, each night, had slaved and suffered and sacrificed along with him. After listening for a time to the pace of the sentry on the other side of the board fence, he pulled his head and shoulders back into the hole, squirmed down onto the floor of the tunnel, jerked the cord that would signal for the spittoon to be withdrawn, and followed along, dragging the tools behind him.

Now to work out the final details of escape. A whispered council in Rat Hell, hurried and excited, brought this decision: they would lie in prison until darkness settled again before attempting escape, thus gaming advantage of a full night in which to make good their flight. Meanwhile, each man would have the privilege of telling one friend of the existence of the tunnel.[8] Those who made up the second party thus formed were to wait one full hour before starting on the trail of the others.

The daylight period of February 9, 1864, seemed the longest of any of their prison experi-ence to the men involved in the plot. It was made worse by their inaction. Before dawn their plans had been perfected, and then there was nothing to do but wait. Precious belongings were in bundles. Bits of food were scraped together. And the entire group—at least those who could—dressed in clothing that would be inconspicuous. They were facing the moment they had dreamed of as they sweated in the stinking, damp, close tunnel, the goal they had longed for and thought of, and which had kept them diligently at work despite almost insurmount-able obstacles.

Darkness approached. As Richmond slowly disappeared into the blackness of night, Rose checked to make sure of every detail. The fifteen friends had been selected and taken into confidence. Standing by as their leader, to make sure they waited an hour before following was Colonel Harrison C. Hobart of the Twenty-first Wisconsin.[9]

At seven o'clock, shortly before nightfall had completely blacked out the view from the windows, the original fifteen gathered in the kitchen. When they were all accounted for, Rose got down on hands and knees and backed into the fireplace. One by one the others followed, feet first, through the narrow opening until they got a foothold on the rope ladder. There was desperation in their movements, the tragic air of men about to go into battle, as they quietly came together again down in the basement. Still ahead of them was the worst part—the squeeze through the tunnel. There they would have to take off their heavier garments and push them along in bundles before them.

As they milled about the mouth of the tunnel, they could hear rising noises on the floor above. These, it was realized, were made by the second party of fifteen, up there trying to divert attention while the escape was in progress. A banjo player had been enlisted, and around him there was music and dancing, whooping and hollering, an all-male hoedown with a purpose. He who called the figures had a stentorian voice that carried well into the surrounding streets and lots, and forth it came with all its volume.

"It was a living drama," wrote an eyewitness. "Dancing in one part of the room, dark shadows disappearing through the chimney in another part, and the same shadows reappearing upon the opposite walk."[10]

But this drama could be only momentarily concealed. The excitement of the fifteen left behind soon spread as word got around that an escape was in progress. The leak had been stimulated by some of the dancers themselves. It was beyond their power to suppress cheers when they observed from the upstairs windows, with the aid of the street lights, that members of the first group to go through the fireplace were walking away into the darkness beyond the carriage shed on the vacant lot.

In the room directly above the kitchen Captain John W. Lewis of the Fourth Kentucky Cavalry, a prisoner from Chickamauga, was preparing to lie down for the night when his blanket mate, Captain Rogers, another Kentuckian, whispered: "Lewis, the boys have a tunnel open and are getting out; shall we go?"

John lay stunned, unable to believe what he heard. He turned and studied his friend. "Yes," he said at last, his voice barely audible. "Let's make the trial."

They gathered up their most precious things, what little food they could lay their hands on, and went down toward the fireplace at the back of the kitchen.

"It was very dark," Lewis recorded, "and there seemed to be great confusion, and all at once a stampede occurred and almost everyone started on the run for the stairs at the other end of the room. Much to my surprise, no alarm of the guard ensued and I could presently hear our people coming back and evidently going through with the programme, whatever that might be. I placed myself among a little squad of four men just then crawling by me, and, squeezing in behind No. 2 of the party, I inserted my legs into the back of the fireplace and my foot finding a hole on a rope ladder, I soon reached the floor of the cellar. As I crossed the floor in search of the tunnel, I could see the legs of the sentry on Cary Street, who walked his beat in blissful unconsciousness of what the 'Yankees' were doing almost under his feet."[11]

Midway of the tunnel, as Lewis crawled through, he had to lie flat and squeeze under what he assumed was a water main. It seemed to him the point of no return, but he wriggled past and kept crawling.

Emerging in the carriage shed, Lewis found a bright moon shining. This, coupled with the light from the gas lamps at the street corners, cast a baleful glow along the ground over which he must pass. But with four others he went Indian file across the lot, passed under an arched gateway and emerged into Canal Street scarcely a hundred feet from a sentry. If the guard saw them he gave no alarm, apparently taking them to be hungry Rebel soldiers who had gone into the carriage shed in search of some overlooked item of food in the boxes.

One hundred and nine men wriggled free of the tunnel and melted into the darkness—on their way to freedom, of short or long duration. Most of them made their way eastward, toward the coast, hoping to reach General Butler's lines at Fortress Monroe. Soon Union cavalry was scouring the Virginia peninsula as far up as the Chickahominy, striving to rescue as many of them as possible, and a gunboat was sent up the James River for the same purpose.

But the complete success of this prison break extended no farther than the carriage shed. The trek beyond was too full of difficulties. Forty-eight of the escapees were recaptured, some within a matter of hours, and two were drowned. Among those retaken was Colonel Rose, a man fate had decided would not flee his captors, though he had worked hard to provide himself with a second chance. Fifty-nine of those who fled into the night made their way across the Potomac to their homes in the North. And some of them stopped in Washington to pour into the ears of Abraham Lincoln the plight of the fellow officers they had left behind.

NOTES

1. Capt. John W. Lewis of Co. I, 4th Ky. Cavalry, in "Libby," E. R. Hutchins, comp., *The War of the Sixties* (New York: Neale Publishing Co., 1912), p. 377, said: "The regular guard around Libby was one of the best organizations of the kind I ever knew of; they performed their duties right up to the handle, in a soldierly manner, and they were entirely incorruptible."

2. After the war, Rose became a captain in the 16th U.S. Infantry and survived for many years. See Frank E. Moran, "Colonel Rose's Tunnel at Libby Prison," in *Famous Adventures and Prison Escapes of the Civil War* (New York: The Century Co., 1911), p. 242.

3. *Ibid.*, 210, lists them as Capt. Terrance Clark, 79th Ill.; Maj. George H. Fitzsimmons, 30th Ind.; Capt. John F. Gallagher and Capt. W. S. B. Randall, 2nd Ohio; Capt. John Lucas, 5th Ky.; Capt. I. N. Johnson, 6th Ky.; Maj. B. B. McDonald, 101st Ohio; Lt. M. S. McKean, 21st Ill.; Lt. David Garbett, 77th Pa.; Lt. J. C. Fislar, 7th Ind. Artillery; Lt. John D. Simpson, 10th Ind.; Lt. John Mitchell, 79th Ill.; and Lt. Eli Foster, 30th Ind.

4. *Brave Deeds of Union Soldiers* (Philadelphia: George W. Jacobs Co., 1915), p. 29.

5. Nelson Monroe, *The Grand Army Button* (Boston: Rockwell and Churchill Press, 1893), p. 64.

6. The actual length of the tunnel was estimated at sixty to seventy feet.

7. Reports on the length of time required to dig the tunnel vary. A majority of those participating, however, place the period at forty-two nights.

8. Moran, *op. cit.*, p. 242, reports that in 1893 eleven of the men who dug the tunnel were still alive. They were: Randall, Clark, Foster, McKean, Fislar, Lucas, Simpson, Mitchell, Hamilton, Johnson, and Rose. Mitchell, then living in Pomeroy, Wash., wrote in 1909, in *The Confederate Veteran*, XVII, 114, that he was the last survivor.

9. Hobart, who later was brevetted brigadier general, had been among those captured with Rose at Chickamauga. His experiences in the escape were related in a paper read before the Commandery of the State of Wisconsin, Military Order of the Loyal Legion, and later compiled with others in book form under the title *War Papers* (Milwaukee: Burdick, Armitage and Allen, 1891). See also Gen. Luther S. Trowbridge, *The Operations of the Cavalry in the Gettysburg Campaign* (Detroit: Ostler Printing Co., 1888), p. 22.

10. Hobart, *op. cit.*

11. Capt John W. Lewis, *op. cit.*, p. 378.

8

John Schofield as Military Director of Reconstruction in Virginia

By James L. McDonough

I n 1895 when a bill was before Congress to revive the grade of Lieutenant General for the benefit of John M. Schofield, then commanding general of the United States Army, a former Confederate general, Senator Eppa Hunton from Virginia, supported Schofield unreservedly. Hunton stated on the Senate floor that as virtual governor of Virginia during Reconstruction Schofield had "left behind him none but friends."[1] That this northern general who commanded in the Cavalier State during the "Dark and Bloody" days of Reconstruction received such praise from a former rebel officer is indeed interesting and prompts this examination of Schofields service.[2]

As Commander of the XXIII Army Corps, Schofield had been with Sherman when the latter received Joe Johnston's surrender in North Carolina. Schofield was then left in command of the Department of North Carolina and confronted with the problem of restoring civil government. The thirty-three-year-old general soon demonstrated a moderate attitude toward the South. His military campaigns had afforded him an opportunity to observe the southern people, Negroes and whites, and he had become convinced that moderation was the only sane policy.

James L. McDonough, "John Schofield as Military Director of Reconstruction in Virginia," *Civil War History, vol. 15, no. 3*, pp. 237-256. Copyright © 1969 by Kent State University Press. Reprinted with permission.

His views are set forth in a letter to General Grant on May 10, 1865. He would place the southern states under military government and declare existing state laws in force, excepting those which conflicted with Federal laws and the Constitution. Persons who took an amnesty oath would be permitted to elect members to a convention which should repudiate the doctrine of secession, abolish slavery, and restore the state to constitutional relations with the Federal government. He then would allow the people to approve or disapprove the action of the convention and at the same time elect state officers. If the required actions of the convention were approved the state would be readmitted. He would leave the conditions of suffrage up to the state, as guaranteed in the Constitution. He doubted both the wisdom and legality of attempting to force the South to accept Negro suffrage. The Negroes were not prepared for suffrage. They could neither read nor write, had no knowledge of law and government, and needed education before being granted such a responsibility. To "raise the Negro," he concluded, "in his present ignorant and degraded condition," to political equality with the whites would be to enslave the latter and would tend to incite them to rebellion.[3]

Schofield was relieved of Reconstruction responsibilities in North Carolina, however, and after a mission in Europe he was assigned, in August, 1866, to command the Department of the Potomac, which included the state of Virginia. He soon showed that he intended to be reasonable and impartial in his dealings with both races. Eleven days after assuming command he reported that there was a well-founded feeling of insecurity among the whites caused by their being destitute of arms while a considerable portion of the Negro population possessed weapons, many of them of a military nature. Since Negroes were guaranteed the constitutional right to bear arms, the insecurity of the whites could be corrected, Schofield believed, only by organizing volunteer militia companies throughout the state under authority of Governor Francis H. Peirpoint. Membership in these companies should be limited to men who were loyal and well-disposed toward the freedmen. And the Army should supply the arms and ammunition for these companies.[4]

Neither did Schofield intend to favor whites at the expense of Negroes. His impartiality was evident in December, 1866, in the case of a killing of a freedman by Dr. James L. Watson, of Rockbridge County. The Negro had run into Watson's vehicle, whereupon the doctor shot him. The Rockbridge court acquitted Watson of the charge of murder,[5] but Schofield apparently believed that the evidence did not justify the decision. He had Watson arrested and ordered him to be tried by a military commission.[6]

Schofield may have had a dual purpose in doing this: redressing a miscarriage of justice and testing the legality of the new Freedmen's Bureau Act.[7] On April 2, 1866, President Johnson had proclaimed that the insurrection was over and that "standing armies, military occupation, martial law, military tribunals, and the suspension of the privilege of the writ of *habeas corpus*" were ended.[8] This proclamation was supplemented by an executive order which forbade trial of citizens by military tribunals where civil courts were in existence. This order was in harmony with the Supreme Court decision of April 3, 1866, in the case of *ex parte Milligan*. But the Freedmen's Bureau Act gave the Bureau "military jurisdiction over all cases and questions" concerning the right of freedmen "to have full and equal benefit of all laws and proceedings, concerning personal liberty, [and] personal security."[9] It was under the provision of this Act that Schofield proposed to try Dr. Watson before a military commission. Thus the case would test the constitutionality of the freedmen's bureau bill in light of the presidential order and the Supreme Court decision in *ex parte Milligan.*

When the military commission assembled it was served with a writ of *habeas corpus* from the circuit court of Richmond. Schofield refused to comply with the writ. Then President Johnson, upon the advice of Attorney General Henry Stanberry, concluded the case by dissolving the commission and discharging Watson from custody.[10] Schofield's efforts to bring the murderer to justice thus came to naught.

When the state legislature convened on December 2, 1866, Schofield's interest, like that of most Virginians, turned to its proceedings. The most important question up for consideration was the ratification of the Fourteenth Amendment. Schofield believed the Amendment was unjust and unwise. He prepared a written argument on the subject which shows that he was especially opposed to section three. This section, he said, disqualified from office nearly everyone "whose social position, intellectual attainments and known moral character entitle him to the confidence of the people." He argued that it was

> folly to attempt to bring back a revolted people by disfranchising all leaders in whom they trust and confide. These leaders if they will act in good faith [and Schofield believed a sufficient number would] can bring their people back to their allegiance. Without them it can not be done during the existing generation.[11]

Schofield also objected to the national government prescribing qualifications for state offices or for voting in state elections. Section three was also unfair to Negroes, he said, since its effect would be to allow more of the "poor whites" to hold local office, thus putting the Negroes in the hands of their only real enemies in the South. Any thought of universal suffrage, without regard to intelligence or other qualifications, was absurd. Northern politicians might "theorize as much as [they] pleased about the criminality of the late rebellion," but, Schofield contended, it was "folly to suppose that the present generation of Southerners can be made to acknowledge or believe that it was anything more than a legitimate war for the settlement of a great political question left unsettled by the framers of the constitution ... " Therefore, looking at the matter in "a practical common sense light," the Federal government should not demand "repentance in sack cloth and ashes" when any show of such repentance would be "the purest hypocrisy."[12]

In spite of these objections, Schofield strongly urged that Virginia ratify the Amendment. He believed that it offered the best terms on which the state could be restored. He warned that failure to ratify probably would cause Congress to impose harsher conditions. In addition, he claimed that Congress could hardly refuse to recognize the existing state government if the Amendment were ratified. In fact, Schofield visited Washington and received assurances to that effect from leading Republicans in Congress.[13] His advice was not heeded. The state senate voted unanimously against the Fourteenth Amendment and the margin in the House of Delegates was 74 to 1.[14]

When the Virginia legislature began its extra session on March 4, 1867, the accuracy of Schofield's prediction had become apparent. Two days earlier the United States Congress had passed over Johnson's veto the first of a series of measures prescribing the mode of action which southern states must follow to be readmitted to the Union. The Reconstruction Act of March 2, 1867, declared that except for Tennessee no legal governments existed in the former Confederate states. These states were to be apportioned into military districts until good order and "loyal and republican" governments could be established in them. The Act established five military districts, each under a general officer of the army who was to be the supreme authority in each state under his command in accordance with the laws of the United States. Each state was to hold a constitutional convention, with delegates to be elected by all male citizens of the state of voting age, regardless of color, except those disfranchised for participation in the rebellion. This convention should frame and the voters should ratify a constitution extending the franchise to those persons entitled to vote for delegates to the convention. The state legislature elected under the new constitution then should ratify the Fourteenth Amendment. The state might be readmitted to the Union after the Fourteenth Amendment had become law, and after Congress had approved these actions and had declared the state entitled to representation in Congress.[15]

On March 23, 1867, Congress passed a supplementary Reconstruction Act ordering the district commander to direct the entire process of state action in carrying out the provisions of the first Act. He was to establish voting districts, supervise registration of voters, conduct an election on the question of calling a constitutional convention and choosing delegates to it, and submit the proposed constitution to the voters for ratification or rejection.[16]

President Johnson vetoed both bills, attacking the infringement upon state powers and the establishment of military government as unconstitutional and dangerous. He denied the right of Congress to grant Negro suffrage in the South and claimed that the nature of the acts indicated that such was their true intent and purpose. He also denied the constitutionality of imposing military government on the southern states in time of peace and warned that the relatively unlimited authority entrusted to the military commanders would be a real danger to the people of these states. Johnson asserted that this authority made the military commander "an absolute monarch."[17] Congress passed both bills over the President's veto.

As Johnson indicated, the far-reaching authority entrusted to military commanders meant that mildness or harshness, justice or injustice, would largely depend on the character of the commander. Virginia was fortunate to have Schofield as her commander. He regarded the Reconstruction Acts as a terrible oppression which was not "appreciated by even the most enlightened and conservative people of the North," and could only be realized by "those who actually suffered the baneful effects of the unrestrained working of those laws."[18] Schofield's moderate attitude and just treatment of the citizens had already made a favorable impression on Virginians who only a few months before had complained bitterly about the actions of his predecessor, General Alfred H. Terry. In fact, the Virginia state legislature petitioned the President to appoint Schofield as district commander because of the "great impartiality" with which he had "discharged his duties ... toward all classes."[19]

Schofield officially assumed command of the First Military District on March 13, 1867.[20] His first general order did much to gain the respect and confidence of the people. Officers of the existing provisional government were to continue performing their duties, unless otherwise directed in individual cases, until their successors were duly elected and qualified under the Reconstruction Act of March 2, 1867. The order further stated:

> It is desirable that the military power conferred by the before mentioned act [of March 2, 1867], be exercised only so far as may be necessary to accomplish the objects for which that power was conferred, and the undersigned appeals to the people of Virginia, and especially to Magistrates and other civil officers, to render the necessity for the exercise of this power as slight as possible, by strict obedience to the laws, and by impartial administration of justice to all classes.[21]

"In common with the public journals in every portion of the State," responded the Lexington *Gazette*, "we express our decided gratification, that if we are to be subjected to military rule, we are at least to have the consolation of being governed by a gentleman. ..."[22] Similar statements were expressed by the Lynchburg *Virginian*, the Norfolk *Journal*, the Richmond *Whig*, and the Abingdon *Virginian*. Available evidence seems to indicate that these sentiments were shared by most conservatives in the state.[23]

But the satisfaction over Schofield's appointment did not remove the outraged feelings of most white Virginians over the Reconstruction Acts. The Lynchburg *Virginian* declared that it preferred a military dictator over the entire country rather than rule "by that mob at Washington." The Staunton *Spectator* considered Congress' action with respect to Virginia parallel to rape, and it advocated that Virginia should resist the outrage and retain her honor, rather than submit and become party to the act. And the Charlottesville *Chronicle* said that the South, now that the war was over, was asked "to love, to kiss the hand that wielded the lash," and the penalty for not doing so was "to be ruled by the blacks."[24] Many newspapers advised conforming to the Reconstruction Acts, however, as there seemed no reasonable alternative. Negro suffrage was an outrageous measure for many to accept and conservative whites feared that the freedmen's vote would be controlled by radicals and adventurers. But suffrage for the former slaves was regarded as a fixed fact.[25]

Several times Schofield invoked his authority as commanding general to preserve the peace or to insure against violations of the Reconstruction Acts. When Negro votes were rejected at a city election in Alexandria on March 5, he issued orders prohibiting any further elections under the provisional government until registration was completed.[26]

Schofield also sought to prevent inciting disorder through speeches or newspaper editorials. Schofield warned the Richmond Times that he would not tolerate any more of its articles which fostered enmity, created disorder and led to violence. He sustained the action of General O. B. Wilcox, sub-district commander at Lynchburg, who forbade a public lecture by H. Rives Pollard, a man who had openly declared his hostility to the national government. But he also told Wilcox that he would prefer not to interfere with freedom of speech or the press. He desired rather to wait until an offense was committed and then to punish the offender.[27]

A riot occurred in Richmond in May which was quelled only by intervention of the military. When the Richmond *Dispatch* reported that a Massachusetts man named Jedekish K. Hayward had delivered incendiary speeches tending to incite the Negroes to riot, Schofield summoned the reporter, ascertained the truth of the report, arrested and turned Hayward over to Mayor Mayo for trial and punishment. As an additional preventive measure he ordered the Negro "Lincoln Mounted Guard" to cease parading or drilling under arms. A detachment of Federal cavalry was assigned to patrol the city night and day.[28]

Meanwhile, Schofield was busy preparing for the approaching registration and election. Existing state office holders continued to exercise the duties of those offices unless removed for disloyalty, misdemeanor or by death. When vacancies did occur Schofield appointed someone to temporarily fill the position. He left control of civil affairs to the people, if at all possible, by selecting replacements on the concurrent recommendations of county courts or city councils and the president of the board of registration for the county or city. These appointees had to swear that they had not been disfranchised for participating in the war and would not be denied the right to hold office by the proposed Fourteenth Amendment.[29] Such appointees were to be replaced, as soon as new office holders were elected under the provisions of the Reconstruction Acts.

On April 2, 1867, Schofield began the process of appointing three- man boards of registration for Virginia's counties and cities. He designated a five-man panel of army officers to select and recommend persons for appointment to the boards. An officer of the army or bureau was to be selected as a member of each board, wherever possible, and the remaining two members were to be selected in order of preference from the following groups: honorably discharged United States Army officers, loyal citizens of the county or city for which they were selected, or other loyal citizens having the proper qualifications. Schofield insisted that the men appointed must be of unwavering loyalty to the Union, of high character, impartial judgment, and possess the confidence of the people.[30] This order is important because it gave preference for appointment first to officers, past and present, of the Union Army, second to the native loyal whites, and last of all to those who might be "carpetbaggers." All but twenty-seven who were appointed presidents of the boards of registration in the ninety-nine counties, and the cities of Richmond, Petersburg, and Norfolk, were army officers. And three of the non-army appointees were civilian agents or former agents of the Freedmen's Bureau.[31] The presidents, aided by their two subordinates, directed the registration at the county seat and exercised supervisory jurisdiction over subordinate boards of registration in each magisterial district.

Registration began in late June, 1867. In an effort to insure a fair and just registration Schofield provided that three white and three Negro voters in each election district might serve as challengers for the purpose of detecting any person who fraudulently attempted to register. The names of voters, white and Negro, were entered on separate lists, as were the names of persons registered after challenge and persons denied the right to register. In the latter two cases Schofield required that the cause of challenge and the grounds for refusal of registration should also be entered on the lists.[32]

In compliance with the Reconstruction Act of March 23, 1867, Schofield declared that all male citizens of the United States twenty-one years of age or older, who were residents of the state for at least one year, were entitled to vote unless they were disfranchised for felony or for participation in the rebellion. All persons were disfranchised who at any time had served as members of Congress, as civil or military' officers of the United States, or in any official capacity which had required taking an oath to support the Constitution of the United States, as legislative, executive or judicial officers of a state, and afterwards had participated in the rebellion. Schofield drew up a specific list of executive and judicial officers who would be disfranchised by the law.[33]

Great political excitement was expected as Negroes and whites, radicals and conservatives, campaigned and voted on the heated issues. Schofield therefore took measures to preserve peace and maintain order if the necessity arose. He issued an order designed to protect the personal and property rights of all persons "in cases where the civil authorities may fail, from whatever cause, to give such protection, and to insure the prompt suppression of insurrection, disorder and violence." The order provided for the appointment of army officers and Freed-men's Bureau officials as military commissioners in the state's seven sub-districts. To ensure that the commissioner's orders would be complied with, police officers, sheriffs, constables, and other law enforcement officials were required to obey their orders. The commissioners were also given judicial powers in the counties and cities. Civil trials were preferred, but if the commissioner believed such would result in a miscarriage of justice, he was empowered, subject to Schofield's approval, to call upon a military commission. Civil officers were ordered to continue to discharge the functions of their offices and were assured that they would not be superseded except in cases of necessity.[34] Thus, when Schofield began the registration process, he possessed almost absolute control over the state of Virginia.

For purposes of Army administration and command, Schofield divided the state into seven sub-districts, each of which had seven or eight military commissioners, with each commissioner responsible for one or more counties.[35] Through the military commissioners and bureau agents he exercised supreme judicial power, while his right to remove from office any state officers and replace them with men of his choice gave him complete executive power. He also exercised supreme legislative power through his right to suspend any law and issue any new regulations which he considered necessary for the accomplishment of his work.

Schofield exercised his power as little as possible and in the best interests of the state. He permitted the civil authorities to continue to function with little hindrance, appointed men to office who, in most cases, were recommended by state officials and could, at the same time, take the iron-clad oath.[36] And he reported that "No case arose in Virginia in which it was found necessary, in my opinion, to supersede the civil authorities in the administration of justice. Not a single citizen of that state was tried by military commission."[37]

The registration seems to have been conducted in an impartial and orderly manner. Relatively few complaints of injustices to either whites or Negroes were received by the registration boards.[38] The official returns listed 227,376 voters in the state, 121,271 of whom were whites and 106,105 Negroes.[39] Comparing these figures with the tax list for 1867 Schofield reported that 17,649 more Negroes had registered than were contained on the tax list. This fact prompted him to order a census conducted by a board of army officers in a Richmond ward where the disparity was greatest. The registration was found to be "very nearly correct" while the tax list was "quite erroneous."[40] Schofield was convinced that nearly all the people who were entitled to register had done so.

Attention was soon focused on election day (designated by Schofield for October 22) when the voters would decide for or against holding a constitutional convention, and elect delegates to the convention if it was approved. Voting was to be by ballot and conducted at the same places and by the same army officers, bureau agents and civilians who had conducted the registration.[41] Separate ballot boxes were to be maintained for whites and Negroes. All sales of liquor were to be suspended on election day, and civil police officers were required to maintain good order. Any person who attempted to prevent any qualified voter from casting his ballot, whether by fraud, force, or intimidation, was to be tried for the offence by a military commissioner, and registering officers were authorized to exercise all the powers of a military commissioner during the time of election and counting of ballots. Registering officers and their assistants were to count the returns, certify the results of the election, and turn over all books, papers, and ballots to the president of the board of registration for the county or city. Having tallied the reports, the latter would deposit the ballots in a safe place, and forward his tally, along with all rejected ballots, to the commanding general. Schofield warned that if ballot boxes or poll books should be lost or destroyed a new election would be held in the district or ward affected, but he expressed the hope that there would be "full and free exercise of the elective franchise."[42]

Schofield provided that 105 delegates should be elected to the constitutional convention, or one for every 2,061 electors. His apportionment gave forty-seven delegates to election districts with white majorities and fifty-eight to districts having Negro majorities. Since there was a white majority in the state, this action led to charges that he had gerrymandered the state in favor of the radicals. But his explanation for this apportionment disproves such an assertion. There were fifty-two counties and cities with white majorities, Schofield said, and fifty with Negro majorities. In the former there were only 90,555 voters, both white and colored, while in the latter there were 125,895. On that basis, since the number of electors entitled to elect one delegate was 2,061, the white counties would have elected forty-four delegates and the Negro counties would have elected sixty-one.[43] Apportionment by the congressional districts of 1860 would have resulted in thirty-four delegates from white counties and seventy-one from Negro counties. By congressional districts of the provisional government the numbers would have been thirty-two and seventy-three respectively. By following the state senatorial districts as a basis of apportionment, the number of delegates from Negro and white districts would have been the same as by Schofield's apportionment, but many large fractions would have been unrepresented and many districts would have had greater representation than they wrere strictly entitled to. Therefore, Schofield apportioned delegates on a county or city basis, and when necessary, combined several counties and cities into election districts when each, individually, was entitled to fractional representation, but lacked a large enough fraction to justify its having another delegate.[44] Schofield's plan of apportionment seems to have been as fair as any that could have been worked out, and was at least as favorable to the whites as any existing method of apportionment—obviously more favorable than some.

On October 22, the radicals registered a decisive victory, approving the holding of the convention by a vote of 107,342 to 61,887, and electing seventy-three delegates to the conservatives' thirty-two.[45] Whites could hardly blame the result upon Schofield's reapportionment. Of 121,271 registered white voters, more than one-third, or 44,017, failed to vote, while only 12,687 of 106,105 registered Negroes neglected to vote. And only 638 freedmen in the entire state voted against the convention.[46]

Charming the Negroes with glowing promises of social equality, con-fiscation and free land, the extreme radicals had forged a tightly knit, compact party of Negroes, carpetbaggers, and radical white Virginians. The extent and thoroughness of the organization was not realized by most conservatives, and they had no single political leader or any fixed political policy—except opposition to radicalism. The conservatives were divided over whether to vote for the convention, whether to ally with political parties of the North, and whether to oppose or submit to the congressional plan of Reconstruction.[47] That the radicals won is hardly surprising.

Feelings ran high in Richmond where Schofield allowed the polls in certain wards to reopen an extra day in order to poll a complete vote.[48] He was accused of doing so in order to insure a radical victory. The Richmond *Southern Opinion*, perhaps the most "unreconstructed" paper in Virginia, denounced him for this "marvellous, stupendous and utterly unparalleled atrocity," and thanked him for "yet another lesson in that intricate infinite maze of confounded villainy with stealth—the Yankee character."[49] The defeated conservative candidates also protested against keeping the polls open, and charged voting frauds.

Schofield defended himself well, saying that the purpose of keeping the polls open was to record the fullest possible vote. His critics' position, he continued, seemed to be token on the erroneous premise that the "party is entitled to the victory which can poll the greatest number of votes in a given number of hours." He also denied that any voting frauds had taken place.[50] It is highly unlikely that Schofield's action was motivated by a desire to secure a radical victory. The men elected in Richmond were extreme radicals while Schofield's views were moderate. The Richmond *Whig* stated that Schofield "personally strongly desired the defeat of the Hunnicutt [extreme radical] ticket."[51] And Schofield also kept the polls open an extra day in Norfolk, which gave the whites an additional opportunity to poll their votes.[52]

The Negroes and radical leaders were jubilant over the victory. They had defeated several moderate Republicans as well as conservative whites. Their triumph seemed to be a heady wine, as some of the radical leaders were soon delivering incendiary speeches. James W. Hunnicutt was arrested on a warrant of the Charles City county court for inciting Negroes to insurrection against whites and charged with having advised Negroes to bum the homes of their enemies.[53] Also arrested for incendiary language was Lewis Lindsay, Negro delegate to the convention from Richmond. He proclaimed that the streets of Richmond would "run knee-deep in blood" before any of his children would suffer for food. He also thanked the Almighty "that the Negroes had learned to use guns, pistols and ram rods."[54] Negro military organizations again were formed, in violation of Schofield's orders, and he used troops to disarm them.[55]

Moderate Republicans were unhappy over the radical victory and conservative whites were appalled as they thought about the constitution which this convention might adopt. Now aroused from relative apathy, they issued a call for a convention of conservative white men from throughout Virginia, to be held on December 11, 1867.[56] This convention would attempt to unite all whites before the expected radical constitution would be submitted to the electorate for ratification. Hopefully, it might then be defeated.

The constitutional convention assembled in Richmond on December 3, 1867. In order to be as fully informed as possible about what to expect from it Schofield investigated the political background of its members. His description of them is interesting and enlightening. He characterized Charles H. Porter and John Hawxhurst as political adventurers. David S. White was a Methodist minister and political adventurer who associated "entirely with Negroes." James H. Platt was a speculator and former Union army officer. The outstanding Republican leader was Judge Edward Snead, a native of Virginia and a consistent Unionist. The leading convervatives were James C. Southall, editor of the Charlottesville *Chronicle*; Jacob W. Liggett, member of the recent House of Delegates, and James M. French, former colonel in the Confederate army.

The outstanding "unreconstructed" delegates (Schofield used the term "unreconstructed" to refer to those unalterably opposed to the Reconstruction Acts and determined to retain political power exclusively in the hands of whites) were John L. Marye, Jr., of Fredericksburg; Norval Wilson, a Methodist minister and former abolitionist who became a violent secessionist during the course of the war; J. C. Gibson, who had killed a man in a street fight; and Eustace Gibson, a former Confederate army officer. The most influential Negro delegates were "Dr." Thomas Bayne of Norfolk, who was illiterate; William A. Hodges of Princess Anne County, who irritated radicals by denying that Negroes were indebted to the North for their freedom; and Lewis Lindsay, previously mentioned, who had thanked God that Negroes had learned how to use firearms.

Other important delegates were William James, a radical from England who had been dismissed from his post as collector of internal revenue in Richmond for alleged malpractices; James C. Toy, recently acquitted on a charge of stealing hogs (Schofield thought he was guilty); Edgar Allan, a radical who later joined the moderate Republican ranks; Edward W. Massey, a former Confederate, but now a bitter radical; Daniel M. Norton, a self-styled Negro physician whom Schofield described as a "sharp trickster and schemer"; Sanford M. Dodge, adventurer from the North who was employed in a distillery; John Robinson, Negro and former slave-trader; and C. L. Thompson, illiterate tobacconist from Albermarle County who received only three white votes in his native town but still won the election as a delegate to the convention. Altogether there were, he wrote, fifty-one radicals, twenty-two Republicans, thirteen conservatives, and nineteen unreconstructed.[57]

The convention lasted until April 7, 1868, with the exception of a Christmas recess, and the resulting constitution, as had been expected, was highly objectionable to most whites. All persons were disfranchised who had ever held any state or Federal office, had taken an oath of such office, and afterward had participated in the rebellion.[58] No person could hold office unless he first took the iron-clad oath. Sections concerning ownership of church property, provisions for local government and homestead exemptions, also created considerable dissatisfaction.[59] The constitution provided, significantly, for a state-wide system of free public schools—the first such provision in Virginia's history—for equal and uniform taxation on property, and for a tax on incomes exceeding $600 per year.[60]

The commendable provisions of the constitution do not negate the fact that it represented an attempt to establish Negro and radical supremacy in the state. Its office-holding and disfranchisement provisions would make it very difficult in many places to carry on the government efficiently. Negro enfranchisement, coupled with disfranchisement of many whites and restriction of office holding to persons who could take the iron-clad oath, would mean that many state offices would be filled by carpetbaggers, unqualified Negroes, and scalawags. Well aware of the difficulties which the new constitution could create Schofield addressed the convention and warned the delegates that if the proscriptive measures were carried out, many counties would be without a sufficient number of men eligible for and capable of filling the offices. They would probably result in the defeat of the constitution when submitted for ratification.[61] Schofield's words were in vain. In a letter to Grant he reported that his speech

> seemed not to have the slightest influence. ... The same baneful influence that secured the election of a majority of ignorant blacks and equally ignorant or unprincipled whites to the convention, has proved sufficient to hold them firmly to their original purpose. They could only hope to obtain office by disqualifying everybody in the state who is capable of discharging official duties, and all else ... was of comparatively slight importance.[62]

Thus, "villifying General Schofield for giving them good advice and driving them from the treasury which they wished to empty," said the Richmond *Enquirer*, "the Negroes and carpet-baggers ... adjourned."[63]

Schofield's efforts in the latter case probably saved the state a large sum of money. The constitutional convention soon used up the $100,000 which had been appropriated for its expenses by the state legislature in March, 1867. It then passed an ordinance to levy a tax on the people for another $100,000. Since the Reconstruction Act of March 23, 1867, placed no limit on the amount to be collected in taxes levied by the convention, Schofield feared an endless taxation process for as long as the convention stayed in session. Determined to prevent such a drain on the state treasury, he told General Grant: "The sum already expended ought to have been ample—more than was necessary—to defray all their expenses. ... They ought in my opinion to be debarred from the exercise of the authority given them by Congress to levy and collect a special tax."[64] With Grant's approval, Schofield negotiated a loan to pay convention expenses up to April 6, 1868. It seems likely that Schofield's actions helped bring the convention to a conclusion sooner than would have been the case otherwise.

Besides the proscriptive measures of the constitution, Schofield also objected to the county organization section which provided for the election of city, town, and county officers. In more than half of these places Negroes were in the majority. In view of "their present temper," he said, they could be expected to elect "persons of their race who can neither read nor write to fill the majority of those offices."[65]

If Schofield could not persuade the convention to modify the constitution perhaps he could prevent it from going into effect. The wisest course, he believed, was not to submit it to the people for ratification at all, thus letting "the thing fall and die where it is." Then, he wrote Grant, he could go on putting Union men in office and reorganize the provisional government upon a loyal basis, "until the friends of reconstruction get control of the state." Then a convention could be called which would frame a constitution fit to be ratified by the people, and approved by Congress and the country at large. The Republican party, he continued, could only be damaged by endorsing such a constitution as that framed by the recent convention. It would be necessary, however, for Congress to modify the iron-clad oath and provide greater latitude for the selection of officers before another constitution could be framed.[66]

Since neither Congress nor the constitutional convention had appropriated money to pay the expenses of an election on the proposed constitution Schofield told Grant that he intended to postpone the election until Congress made an appropriation. As Congress knew the contents of the constitution, Schofield said he would regard congressional action in appropriating money, or failure to act, as indicating his duty in the matter.[67] Apparently Grant and the Republican leaders approved his plan to circumvent the constitution. At any rate, on April 24, 1868, Schofield issued an order suspending the election until further notice.[68]

A number of newspaper editors believed that the constitution would have been defeated if submitted to a vote, while Schofield feared it would have been adopted. However, his motives were misinterpreted. The editors charged that he had acted so that separate votes could be taken on the objectionable provisions and the constitution would thus be approved.[69] He did later recommend that the constitution be submitted to the electorate with provision for a separate vote on the section requiring office holders to take the iron-clad oath. But his correspondence indicates that this action was primarily designed to defeat the iron-clad oath and save the state from the results of adopting the unexpurgated constitution, rather than to insure that the constitution would be adopted. He himself said that he would have preferred drawing up a new constitution. He recommended a separate vote on the test oath provision because it was the maximum concession which friends of the constitution would accept, while further concessions would "produce discord among the friends of reconstruction."[70]

It should be remembered that Schofield's primary responsibility as district commander was to enforce the Congressional Reconstruction Acts. These directed that "loyal and republican" state governments must be established and Congress was to decide when such governments existed. Schofield realized that to an overwhelmingly Republican Congress Republicanism was as much a criteria for readmission as loyalty to the Union. Therefore if he were going to secure Virginia's readmission to the Union he would have to sacrifice his own wishes in order to secure the greatest possible support from the friends of Reconstruction. He personally disliked the Reconstruction Acts and would have liked to expurgate other provisions of the constitution, but this was not within his power.

Meanwhile he was facing another difficult problem—what to do about elections for state, city, and municipal offices. On April 2, 1867, he had issued an order suspending all elections for these offices until the registration had been completed.[71] These offices were greatly desired by the radicals and now pressure was being exerted to get Schofield to remove the incumbents and replace them with "loyal" men. But Schofield was convinced that most of these offices could not be filled by competent persons. The men who were most zealous for Negro suffrage and most clamorous for offices, he wrote to Grant, were in many cases "entirely unfit for the offices they aspire to." Schofield decided to appoint Republicans to the vacant offices in "all cases where respectable and competent persons of that party could be found." "If by this course I incidentally give strength and influence to the respectable Republicans as against the lower class of men who have acquired control over the mass of colored voters," he continued, "I am sure I shall thereby render the country an important service and not be justly subject to the charge of partisanship."[72]

He then asked Grant's opinion on whether he should remove from office the disfranchised persons whose terms had not expired. Grant approved Schofield's plans and suggested that no removals be made "except for cause" until the vacant offices had been filled. It would then be possible to better judge the wisdom of further removals and appointments, "and also as to whether they are required to a proper administration of the reconstruction acts."[73]

On the basis of this ruling, Schofield, on April 4,1868, made what was probably his most important appointment to office. He declared the office of governor vacant by reason of the expiration of Francis Peirpoint's term of office, and appointed Henry H. Wells, a native of New York, former member of the Michigan legislature, and recent general in the Union

Army, as governor of Virginia.[74] Schofield had been considering removing Peirpoint for several months. He advised Grant that by his official conduct and influence, Peirpoint had done more "to prevent the proper execution of the acts of Congress than all the disfranchised office-holders in Virginia combined."[75] Recently the governor had made extensive use of his pardoning powers in freeing Negroes who had been convicted by state courts—and this while Schofield's military commissioners were supervising the actions of the civil courts.

Peirpoint's term of office had expired on January 1, 1868, and under the state constitution he was ineligible to succeed himself. Schofield had recommended that Grant issue an order appointing Schofield to discharge the duties of governor. This would relieve the state of the burden of the governor's salary, and relieve Schofield of the necessity of making an appointment to the office of governor that likely would not "be acceptable to any considerable proportion of any party."[76] Scho-field's recommendation was not followed and Peirpoint continued to hold office after the expiration of his term. By April, 1868, Schofield was convinced that Peirpoint was using his official position "for no other apparent purpose than to secure his renomination and election" to the office of governor in spite of the constitutional prohibition against successive terms. Therefore, Schofield wrote Grant that he believed it was his duty "to appoint a successor who is eligible under the laws of the state ... , who will be more acceptable to the people and who can and will aid us instead of being a dead weight or worse in the work of reconstruction."[77]

The appointment was first offered to Judge Alexander Rives, a native Virginian and prominent Republican who, Schofield said, "would have been invaluable to the Union cause." But Rives preferred to retain his judgeship.[78] Therefore, after consulting with leading Republicans, Schofield proposed to Grant that Wells be appointed.[79] Grant approved and Wells became governor.

Peirpoint did not give up without a struggle, however. Charging that Schofield's action was made "in the interest of the rebels" to defeat the adoption of the constitution, the ex-governor tried to get Grant to countermand Schofield's order.[80] Grant refused, but Peirpoint continued his efforts to reclaim the office. He accused Schofield of subverting the Reconstruction laws to give state offices to Confederates and outsiders. This was especially true, claimed Peirpoint, in Schofield's appointment of tobacco inspectors. There were to be two inspectors at each warehouse and these could nominate deputy inspectors. Inspectors were required to take the test oath and therefore Schofield had appointed only one inspector at each warehouse, allowing this inspector to appoint deputies who would do the work of the second inspector, but would not be required, as subordinate officers, to take the test oath.[81]

Schofield did make appointments just as Peirpoint stated,[82] but it hardly seems likely that he was acting to aid the "rebels." It seems much more reasonable to conclude that he did so in the interest of good government and to keep such offices from falling into the hands of extreme radicals. Besides, Grant ordered an investigation made of accusations that Schofield was selling out to conservatives, and Schofield was exonerated.[83]

Peirpoint also charged that Schofield, with his conservative friends, was discriminating against Virginia Unionists and placing "strangers [carpetbaggers] in all the important offices, State and Federal."[84] These charges were repeated by extreme radicals who, though pleased by Peirpoint's removal, were displeased that a man of their own persuasion was not appointed in his place.

Peirpoint's charge that Schofield's action was a deliberate attempt to favor carpetbaggers over Virginia Republicans has persisted in several accounts of the Reconstruction period in Virginia.[85] But such a conclusion is not adequately supported by the facts. While it is true that Governor Wells was not a Virginian, and that many of Schofield's appointments did go to so-called "carpetbaggers," it is equally true that Schofield's correspondence with Grant about appointments to office, particularly Wells' appointment, makes it clear that the basic consideration was "respectable" or moderate Republicanism plus the ability to take the test oath and perform the duties of office. The fact that the governor's office was first offered to Judge Rives—who was preferred by Schofield—and that it was only after Rives refused the position that it was awarded to Wells, seems to disprove the charge that Wells' appointment was part of Schofield's "carpetbagging" plans. And, of course, the fact that Wells later came to uphold the extreme radical position does not negate the fact that at the time of his appointment he was widely recognized as a moderate Republican.[86]

The appointment of Wells was the first of a long list of military appointments to replace incumbent state officials. By May 15, 1868, Schofield reported that he had already appointed nearly five hundred officers and would have appointed more if qualified persons could have been found. But now the Fourteenth Amendment was about to become law. All office holders disqualified under its provisions were to be removed immediately from office and all men appointed to fill the vacated offices would have to take the iron-clad oath. Schofield wrote Grant that he already had appointed nearly all available men who were competent to fill these offices, and the Fourteenth Amendment would create several thousand more vacancies. It appeared to Schofield that these offices would have to remain vacant unless Congress made some special provision to avert the situation.[87]

But Schofield was spared solving this problem when he was confirmed as the new Secretary of War following the failure of the impeachment proceedings against President Johnson. On June 1, 1868, he was relieved as Commander of the First Military District and assumed the office of Secretary. He had demonstrated an outstanding administrative ability as district commander, creating a systematic and well developed administrative plan. The hallmark of his success was his realistic good sense, together with attention to avoiding mistakes, and an ability to remain above personal prejudices.

He was motivated by an understanding and sympathy for the defeated southern people. He desired to prepare Virginia for readmission to the Union as soon as possible, on the best terms possible, and with a minimum of hardship. There is no evidence that he was vindictive. He believed that many former Confederate civil and military officials would faithfully serve the Union (and if some of them did not, the United States Army would be present to deal with them). Without the services of such men many offices would inevitably be filled by the untrained, incapable, or self-seeking.

While it is true that Schofield opposed universal male Negro suffrage, there is no evidence that would warrant the conclusion that he was a racist. His opposition was partially on Constitutional grounds. And he was convinced that most Negroes, being illiterate, were not prepared to accept the suffrage responsibility. He believed that granting immediate, unqualified Negro suffrage could only be detrimental. In his opinion, the Negroes were incapable of exercising the new privilege wisely, and the disfranchised whites, observing their failures, would develop a bitterness which, in the long run, would create a more difficult situation in race relations.

Though convinced that the civil authorities in Washington were pursuing an unfortunate course in these matters, Schofield also believed that the military should be subordinate to civil authority. He would use such influence as he possessed to change what he considered an unwise policy, or soften its blow, but as a soldier it was his duty to carry out the national policy defined by the civilian heads of government.

As military commander of the First District, Schofield was industrious, reasonable and properly motivated. In a difficult situation, he performed admirably.

NOTES

1. *Congressional Record*, 53 Cong., 3 sess., p. 1898.
2. The author wishes to acknowledge a special debt of gratitude to Dr. William T. Alderson, Executive Director of the American Association for State and Local History, whose suggestions and doctoral dissertation were particularly helpful in the preparation of this article. The author, of course, is responsible for all statements of fact or opinion.
3. John M. Schofield, *Forty Six Years in the Army* (New York, 1897), pp. 373–376.
4. Schofield to Maj. George K. Leet, Aug. 27, 1866, Dept, of the Potomac, Office of the Adjutant General or the Army. mss. National Archives, Washington, D. C. The records of the Department of the Potomac, the Adjutant General's Office and the First Military District, will hereafter be abbreviated respectively as: Dept. Potomac, A.G.O., 1st Mil. Dist.
5. Alrutheus A. Taylor, *The Negro in the Reconstruction of Virginia* (Washington, 1926), p. 26.
6. Spec. Ord. 186, Dec. 14, 1966, Schofield mss, Library of Congress. All the Schofield mss hereafter cited are in the Library of Congress.
7. Oliver O. Howard to Schofield, Dec. 10, 1866, Schofield mss.
8. James D. Richardson (comp.), *A Compilation of the Messages and Papers of the Presidents, 1789–1902* (New York, 1903), VI, 429–32.
9. Gen. Ord. 61, Aug. 9, 1866, A.G.O.
10. Hamilton J. Eckenrode, *The Political History of Virginia During the Reconstruction* (Baltimore, 1904), pp. 50–51.

11. Schofield, "Reconstruction," Schofield mss. William M. Wherry, aide-de-camp to Schofield, in an attached statement, says the essay was written in the winter of 1866–67.

12. *Ibid.*

13. Schofield, *Forty Six Years*, pp. 394–395.

14. William T. Alderson, "The Influence of Military Rule and the Freedman's Bureau on Reconstruction in Virginia, 1865–1870," (Ph.D dissertation, Vanderbilt University, 1952), pp. 133–134.

15. *The Statutes at Large of the United States 1789–1873* (Boston, 1846–73), XIV, 428–429. Act of Mar. 2, 1867. Hereafter cited as *U.S. Statutes at Large.*

16. *Ibid.*, XV, 2–5. Act of Mar. 23, 1867.

17. Richardson, *Messages and Papers*, VI, 498–511, 531–535.

18. Schofield, *Forty Six Years*, pp. 395–396.

19. Francis Peirpoint to Andrew Johnson, forwarding a petition of the Virginia General Assembly, Mar. 8, 1867, Johnson mss, Library or Congress.

20. Gen. Ord. 10, Mar. 11, 1867, A.G.O.; Gen. Ord. 1, Mar. 13, 1867, 1st Mil. Dist.

21. Gen. Ord. 1, Mar. 13, 1867, 1st Mil. Dist.

22. Quoted in Alderson, "Military Rule in Virginia," p. 151.

23. *Ibid.*, pp. 150–151.

24. *Ibid.*, p. 152.

25. *Ibid.*, p. 153.

26. Schofield to John C. Underwood, Mar. 16, 1867, 1st. Mil. Dist. Eckenrode, *Virginia During Reconstruction*, pp. 65–66.

27. Alderson, "Military Rule in Virginia," p. 154.

28. *Ibid.*, p. 155.

29. Gen. Order 9, Apr. 5, 1867, 1st Mil. Dist.; Gen. Ord. 16, Apr. 20, 1867, 1st Mil. Dist.

30. Spec. Ord. 16, Apr. 2, 1867, 1st Mil. Dist.

31. Gen. Ord. 15, Apr. 20, 1867, 1st Mil. Dist.

32. Gen. Ord. 28, Mar. [May] 13, 1867, 1st Mil. Dist.

33. *U.S. Statutes at Large*, XV, 14–16. Act of July 19, 1867. Gen. Order 47, July 26, 1867, 1st Mil. Dist.

34. Gen. Ord. 31, May 28, 1867, 1st Mil. Dist.

35. Gen. Ord. 33, June 3, 1867, 1st Mil. Dist.

36. Gen. Ord. 9, Apr. 5, 1867, 1st Mil. Dist.; Gen. Ord. 48, July 26, 1867, 1st Mil. Dist.

37. Schofield, *Forty Six Years*, p. 399.

38. Alderson, "Military Rule in Virginia," p. 168.

39. Memorandum, May 10, 1869, 1st Mil. Dist.

40. Schofield to Adj. Gen. of the Army, Dec. 13, 1867, 1st Mil. Dist.

41. Gen. Ord. 65, Sept. 12, 1867, 1st Mil. Dist.

42. Gen. Order 68, Oct. 4, 1867, 1st Mil. Dist.

43. This was due to the fact that the western counties had large white majorities while the more heavily populated eastern counties had very small Negro majorities.

44. Alderson, "Military Rule in Virginia," p. 183.

45. *Ibid.*, p. 184.

46. Schofield, "Personnel of the Virginia Convention," Schofield mss.

47. Alderson, "Military Rule in Virginia," pp. 169–180.

48. Gen. Ord. 65, Sept. 12, 1867, 1st Mil. Dist.; Spec. Ord. 154, Oct. 23, 1867, 1st Mil. Dist.; Richmond *Whig*, Oct. 25, 1867.

49. Richmond *Southern Opinion*, Oct. 26, Nov. 2, 1867, quoted in Alderson, "Military Rule in Virginia," pp. 184–185.

50. Schofield to Thomas J. Evans and others, Now. 7, 1867, 1st Mil. Dist.

51. Richmond *Whig*, Nov. 1, 1867, quoted in Alderson, "Military Rule in Virginia," p. 185.

52. Alderson, "Military Rule in Virginia," p. 186.

53. Richmond *Enquirer*, Dec. 3, 1867, quoted in Alderson, "Military Rule in Virginia," p. 191.

54. Richmond *Whig*, Nov. 15, 1867; Richmond *Enquirer*, Nov. 15, 1807; quoted in Alderson, "Military Rule in Virginia," p. 191.

55. Schofield to George Stoneman, Dec. 16, 1867, 1st Mil. Dist.

56. Richmond *Whig*, Nov. 11, 1867; Alderson, "Military Rule in Virginia," p. 112.

57. Schofield, "Personnel of the Virginia Convention," Schofield mss.

58. The list of such officers included all those disfranchised by the Reconstruction Act of July 19, 1867, with the addition of members of the city council.

59. The section on church property stated that title to such property was not affected by the late war, by an antecedent or subsequent event, or by any legislative enactment, but was to be vested in the parties originally holding the title, or their assignees. The title of northern church organizations to much property that had been taken by southern churches was thus confirmed.

60. Sen. Exec. Doc., 40 Cong., 2 sess., No. 54 (Serial 1317), 1–26.

61. Richmond *whig,* Apr. 21, 1868, quoted in Alderson, "Military Rule in Virginia," P. 204.

62. Schofield to Grant, Apr. 18, 1868, Schofield mss.

63. Richmond *Enquirer*, Apr. 23, 1868, quoted in Alderson, "Military Rule in Virginia," p. 204.

64. Schofield to Grant, Mar. 21, 1868, 1st Mil. Dist.

65. Schofield to Grant, Apr. 19, 1868, Schofield mss.

66. Schofield to Grant, Apr. 18, 1868, *ibid*.

67. *Ibid.*

68. Schofield to the People of Virginia, Apr. 24, 1868, 1st Mil. Dist.

69. Richmond Enquirer, Apr. 30, 1868, Harrisonburg *Rockingham Register*, Apr. 30, 1868; Charlottesville *Chronicle,* May 2, 1868; Lexington *Gazette,* May 6, 1868; Harrisonburg *Old Commonwealth,* Apr. 29, May 6, 1868; Richmond *Whig*, Apr. 28, 1868; Norfolk *Journal*, Apr. 27, 1868; cited in Alderson, "Military Rule in Virginia," p. 211.

70. Schofield to Grant, May 6, 1868, Schofield mss.

71. Gen. Ord. 33, Mar. 30, 1868, 1st Mil. Dist.

72. Schofield to Grant, Apr. 2, 1868, Schofield mss.

73. Grant to Schofield, Apr. 3, 1868, *ibid.*

74. *Ibid.*; Gen. Ord. 36, Apr. 4, 1868, 1st Mil. Dist.

75. Schofield to Grant, Apr. 2, 1868, Schofield mss.

76. Schofield to Grant, Dec., 1868, *ibid.*

77. Schofield to Grant, Apr. 2, 1868, *ibid.*

78. Schofield to Grant, Apr. 24, 1868, *ibid.*

79. Schofield to Grant, Apr. 2, 1868, *ibid.*

80. Grant to Schofield, Apr. 6, 1868, *ibid.*

81. Francis Peirpont to Grant, Apr. 23, 1868, *ibid.*

82. Gen. Ord. 15, Feb. 14, 1868, 1st Mil. Dist.

83. Alderson, "Military Rule in Virginia," p. 220.

84. Francis Peiipont to Grant, Apr. 23, 1868, Schofield mss.

85. Eckenrode, *Virginia During Reconstruction*, p. 105; W. Asbury Christian, *Richmond Her Past and Present* (L. H. Jenkins, 1912), p. 300; Nelson M. Blake, *William Mahone of Virginia, Soldier and Political Insurgent* (Richmond, 1935), p. 99.

86. Alderson, "Military Rule in Virginia," p. 222.

87. Schofield to Grant, May 15, 1868, 1st Mil. Dist.

9

Baseball, The Lost Cause, And The New South In Richmond, Virginia, 1883–1890

By Robert H. Gudmestad

O n 4 September 1883, Charles F. Johnston took down the Confederate battle flag that hung in the window of his store on Main Street. Johnston, a veteran of the Army of Northern Virginia, sold newspapers, musical instruments, "Fancy Articles," stereoscopic views, and season tickets for Richmond's professional baseball team. He needed to use the flag, because he and fellow members of the R. E. Lee Camp No. 1, a local veterans' organization open to all men who had fought for the South, were marching to the fairgrounds.[1]

That afternoon, almost 3,000 spectators watched Johnston and his wartime comrades file past in old Confederate uniforms that were too tight. Later, they saw "knights" on horseback use lances to capture rings balanced on the top of poles, cheered at horse races, and watched veterans shoot pigeons and glass balls. The daylong celebration closed with a grand ball in the evening. Such commemorations recalled memories of earlier days and invited the citizens of Richmond to honor publicly the memory of the men who had fought for the Confederacy.[2]

This celebration, however, incorporated an element foreign to antebellum southern society and the Confederate war effort—baseball. Union veterans of the Phil Kearny

FIGURE 9-1 In the former capital of the Confederacy, baseball and the evolution of the Lost Cause seemed intricately intertwined. At least six officers and directors of the Virginia Base-Ball Association were Confederate veterans enrolled in the R. E. Lee Camp No. 1. This veterans' organization, founded in April 1883, was a prominent fixture in Richmond life until 1941, when the soldiers' home maintained by the camp closed its doors.

Post, a chapter of the Grand Army of the Republic, which hallowed the sacrifices of northern soldiers, played a baseball game with the Lee Camp veterans. In sweet revenge for the war's outcome, the southerners won, 6–4. In a later contest that same day, members of the Richmond Virginias, the team for which Johnston sold tickets and was the official scorer, tangled with a club from nearby Manchester.[3]

In many ways, the Richmond Virginias baseball team became representative of the city during the first half of the 1880s. Because many of the men who formed the Virginia Base-Ball Association had fought in the Civil War, the club served as a tangible link to the conflict, not yet two decades distant. Baseball in the former capital of the Confederacy fit neatly with romantic conceptions of war that began to emerge with the mythology of the Lost Cause.[4] Those who directed the club used the game to promote the veneration of the Confederacy, while the team itself became a visible reminder of the recent struggle. At the same time, however, the club's owners embodied many values of the New South and of the nation's growing middle class. They represented thriving professional ranks that stressed uniformity, standardized business practices, and the need for experts to make difficult decisions in a competitive business. In a state that had recently rebelled against national authority, management tried to integrate the team into a national system.[5]

The members of the Virginia Base-Ball Association also recognized and capitalized on the demands of the working class for entertainment. The increasingly repetitive and boring tasks in Richmond factories made urban laborers desire more stimulating forms of amusement to distract them from the cares of everyday life. This growing population of city dwellers who craved excitement was a natural audience for the team's games. Baseball in Richmond thus became one way to defuse class tensions.[6]

As it did in most of the South, the appearance of baseball in Virginia's capital coincided with the Civil War. Henry Chadwick, an Englishman who did much to promote the game during its infancy, had tried to introduce team sports to Richmond in the 1850s. He failed, but after the war he noticed that the people of Richmond were excited about baseball. The Civil War had provided opportunities for southerners to learn the game, either when confined in prison camps or while guarding northern prisoners of war, and they continued to play after they returned home. Within a year of Appomattox, Alexander G. Babcock established a team. He probably had become familiar with the game during his service in the Confederate artillery. The sport quickly grew in popularity and became the favorite recreation of young men. By the 1880s, there were more than a dozen clubs in the city. Teams were organized along neighborhood, ethnic, and occupational lines.[7]

One of Richmond's young enthusiasts was Henry C. Boschen, a shoe manufacturer. Local legend has it that Boschen, advised by his doctor to get some exercise, secured a bat and a ball and went to a vacant lot. He hit the ball, retrieved it. and hit it again. Soon growing weaiy of his solitary exertions, Boschen organized the Pacific Baseball Club in 1875 and served as its first president. He then recruited a team from the workers in his factoiy. Whenever he spotted a promising young player, Boschen offered the man a job and a chance to play ball.[8] In this fashion, he identified four players who eventually had solid careers in the major leagues. The best, pitcher Charley Ferguson, played on Boschen's team until the Philadelphia Athletics of the National League purchased his services. His promising career lasted only five years before he died of typhoid fever at the age of twenty-five.[9] Originally a shortstop, Billy Nash switched to third base after the first baseman complained that the velocity of the youngster's throws left his hands sore. Nash played eleven years with the National League's Boston Beaneaters, where he became captain and helped his team win the pennant three times. Outfielder Eddie Glenn went on to play for three years in the major leagues before dying from an injury sustained during a collision on the basepaths. Edward Christopher "Pop" Tate, a Richmond native like Nash and Glenn, was the team's catcher. He later joined Nash in Boston.[10]

By 1881, Boschen and his team, known as the Virginians, were competing against strong amateur teams and major league clubs. The game they played differed from modern baseball, although the basic rules were the same. Pitchers delivered the ball on the run from the pitcher's box, a six-foot-long rectangle. They could not throw overhand, so pitches above the shoulders were balks and automatically walked the batter. Hitters called for either a high or low strike, and seven pitches outside the proper zone led to a walk. Catchers stood from six to fifty feet behind home plate and caught the ball after it bounced if there were no men on base. They were the only players to wear gloves, which were made of stiff leather with the fingers cut off at the joints. As a result, fielders commonly suffered from split fingers or broken hands.

FIGURE 9-2 After the Civil War, young southerners, including these unidentified Virginia amateurs, embraced baseball as their favorite recreation. Another contemporary enthusiast. Henry C. Boschen, became the father of organized baseball in Richmond. He is sometimes credited with inventing the spitball and the bunt.

Substitutions were rare, though, so an injured player stayed in the game even if, as happened to one hometown player, "the blood was continually dropping from his hand." A coin toss determined which team batted first, while a bell summoned the other squad to the field.[11]

Boschen's semiprofessionals played at the Richmond Base-Ball Park, located at the corner of Clay and Lombardy streets, opposite the Richmond, Fredericksburg, and Potomac Railroad yards. The facility eventually had a "beautiful grand stand with two private boxes on each end ... expressly for the ladies." Although Boschen charged admission to his team's games, apparently much of the money for the club's operations came out of his own pocket.[12]

Boschen directed the Virginians until June 1883, when several gentlemen organized a joint stock company called the Virginia Base-Ball Association. All ten of Boschen's players deserted him and signed contracts with the new association. Apparently the wholesale exodus caught the shoe manufacturer by surprise. He published a statement in the local papers angrily complaining how "the nine" were "suddenly taken from me." Boschen indicated his desire to build another team and respectfully asked citizens to continue to patronize his games, even though the quality of play would not be as high.[13]

WM. C. SEDDON.   C. M. BRUCE.

SEDDON & BRUCE,

Nos. 102, 104, 106 VIRGINIA ST.,   RICHMOND, . . . VIRGINIA,

Offer to the TRADE a Large and Fine Assortment of

GROCERIES,

TOBACCO, SOAPS,

Canned Goods, Wines, Liquors, Etc.

Possessing extensive facilities for BUYING and SELLING GOODS, we respectfully solicit the continued favors of our friends, feeling confident of giving satisfaction in the future as we have endeavored to do in the past, by attending to your orders promptly, and guaranteeing everything to be as represented.

Especial attention paid to the Consignment of

GRAIN AND TOBACCO.

Virginia Historical Society

FIGURE 9-3   William C. Seddon, the first president of the Virginia Base-Ball Association, linked the Confederate legacy to the New South. The son of a Confederate secretary of war, Seddon operated a wholesale grocery, which he advertised in *Richmond, Va., as a Manufacturing and Trading Centre* (1880). Thomas L. Alfriend, Seddon's successor as president, publicized his fire, marine, and life insurance agency in the same directory.

The men who organized the Virginia Base-Ball Association were mainly wealthy professionals. William C. Seddon, the association's president, operated a wholesale grocery and expanded his business in 1881 to include speculation as a stockbroker. Most Richmond residents knew Seddon as the son of James A. Seddon, former Confederate secretary of war. Because the father used his influence to help his son's fledgling business after the war, James and William were closely identified. Known as a man of "sterling integrity and rare ability," the younger Seddon was also wealthy. His personal income totaled $2,400, while his company was worth $5,000. He grew up at Sabot Hill, a manor twenty miles outside Richmond on the James River, and the family owned a sugar plantation in Louisiana as well.[14]

The association's other officers and board members did not come from backgrounds as privileged as Seddon's, but most were affluent, socially prominent businessmen. They were, most agreed, the "best people of all classes." Frank D Steger and Thomas L. Alfriend, the secretary and treasurer, respectively, sold insurance. A pork packer, a railroad and machinist supplier, a judge on the 7th circuit court, three merchants, and a stockbroker also sat on the board. Only Charles H. Epps, the captain of the police force and a former janitor at City Hall, was not securely ensconced in the professional class.[15]

These respected civic leaders who founded the Virginia Base-Ball Association also were closely connected to the memory of the Confederacy. Seddon, although he had been too young to enlist, was linked to the war effort through his father's officeholding. Eight of the eighteen men who served as directors of the association had worn a Confederate uniform, as had the team's official scorer. Charles Epps, for instance, enlisted within a week of the firing on Fort Sumter, served as color bearer for the Richmond Light Infantry Blues, and was left for dead on the field of Hatcher's Run in 1865. George A. Smith, a second lieutenant in the president's guards, accompanied Jefferson Davis in the closing days pf the Confederacy.[16]

Not only did these men fight in the war, but they also kept its memory alive by joining veterans' organizations. At least six officers or directors of the Virginia Base-Ball Association enrolled in the Lee Camp, organized only two months before the formation of the association Charles R. Skinker, who helped quell John Brown's insurrection at Harpers Ferry and joined Confederate service soon after the outbreak of hostilities, was frequently elected president of the F Company Association of the First Virginia Volunteers. Peyton Wise, known as "general" because of his postbellum commission in the Virginia State Line, went on to chair arrangements for the United Confederate Veterans' reunion in 1896 and was one of the organizers of the Jefferson Davis Monument Association. Such men were typical of the veterans of their day. During the 1880s and 1890s, large numbers of Civil War veterans, South and North, joined organizations such as the Association of the Army of Northern Virginia and the Grand Army of the Republic. Such societies led the efforts to erect monuments on battlefields and town squares and planned reunions that commemorated both armies.[17]

In stark contrast to the management of the team under Boschen, the former Confederates used the Virginias to promote the memory of those southerners who fought in the war. Besides the game during the celebration at the fairgrounds in September 1883, the Virginias played a benefit contest with a local amateur team to raise money for the Lee Camp soldiers' home. Beverley Randolph Wellford, Jr., who sat on the board of directors of both the home and the Virginias, helped make the arrangements.[18] Like the home it was building, the Lee Camp provided a place of refuge from the bitter effects of the war.

Furthermore, just as the soldiers' home paid homage to the sacrifices of those who had fought for the Confederacy, the bodies of the veterans themselves made anyone who saw them remember the war. Skinker lost the lower portion of his left leg at Hatcher's Run, while Smith had his left arm blown off at Fredericksburg. When these men attended the games and sat together, the absence of their limbs was a poignant and constant reminder of the suffering of the Confederate soldier.[19]

Wise's appearances as an official spokesman for the team reaffirmed the visibility and authority of Confederate leadership in the city. No doubt he wore his uniform for occasions such as the presentation of a gold watch and chain to Eddie Glenn in recognition of the speedy left fielder's outstanding play. After the club joined the American Association in 1884, Wise headed up the solicitation committee in charge of encouraging more people to buy stock. His chairmanship echoed the practice common throughout the South of using a Confederate general's blessing to raise subscriptions. Spectators at the games were reminded of the service of veterans in another way when the Stonewall Brigade Band from Staunton played before some of the contests. The twenty-member band entered the northeast corner of the stadium and marched to the grandstand. Such a ceremony had several meanings. It was a tangible link to the men who fought in the war, it honored the Confederate dead, and it brought more people to the ballpark to see the popular musicians. It was difficult not to remember the Confederacy when attending a Virginias' game.[20]

It was, in part, the team's identification with the Confederacy that made the Virginias so widely accepted in the city. Baseball became popular throughout the country after the Civil War partly because it validated the experience of that conflict. The game allowed veterans to affirm their wartime actions while encouraging younger fans to praise their accomplishments. Like the military, players wore uniforms, engaged in physical training, and developed a sense of cohesiveness as a unit. The game, like war, demanded precision, organization, and teamwork to defeat the enemy. It also promoted such values essential to traditional notions of masculinity as courage, initiative, self-control, and competitive drive.[21]

All of the rituals employed by the Virginia Base-Ball Association strengthened the feelings of social solidarity, deference to leadership, and homage to the common soldier. Confederate veterans controlled the team and used it as a vehicle to promote the memoiy of the war and the celebration of veterans' sacrifices. Part of that effort embraced sectional reconciliation, rather than confrontation. Members of the Lee Camp promised "not to prolong the animosities engendered by the war." The celebration at the fairgrounds in September 1883 included a ballgame with Federal veterans, in contrast to the attitudes of a Richmond team in 1866. The earlier club refused to play the city's Union team, composed of businessmen and Federal officials. Furthermore, instead of seeking membership in a league composed of southern

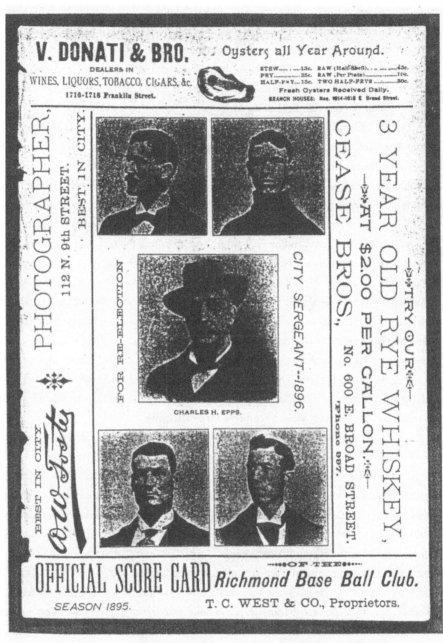

FIGURE 9-4 Richmond's captain of police from 1865 to 1869 and again from 1870 to 1890 was Charles H. Epps (1840–1897). He became city sergeant in 1890, and when he came up for reelection in 1896, he made sure he promoted his candidacy on the Richmond Base Ball Club's scorecard.

teams, the Virginias allied with leagues dominated by northern squads. Even before it played clubs from around the United States, the team hired "foreign players" from everywhere but the South. By the beginning of the 1885 season, only three players were born or had grown up south of the Mason-Dixon Line, a stark contrast from just two seasons earlier, when the entire team was from the Richmond area. Ironically, the father of one of the new players had died in Andersonville.[22]

Even as much of the leadership of the Virginias was closely tied to the Confederacy, they were also keen businessmen, judging from the reports of R. G. Dun & Co. Seddon was "a young man of excellent character] & business] habits," who, according to Dun's Richmond correspondent, ran a "First class house." The informant universally praised the business acumen of the officers and board members. For instance, he described Thomas L. Alfriend, who later became president of the association, as an honorable man of "integrity & character" and John L. Schoolcraft as a "man of fair business] qualifications, good character], steady habits, and deemed honest." The general assessment was that the board members were reliable businessmen who enjoyed the respect and trust of the community.[23] They were "some of the best men—that is if the best men are those who have comfortable bank accounts." Even *Sporting Life*, a weekly paper with a national circulation, noted that the Virginia club was "supposed to be well heeled financially." These astute businessmen believed in the possibilities of baseball and considered it a sound investment.[24]

Once the association acquired the team, it immediately set out to improve the quality of the club. One of management's first actions was construction of the Virginia Base-Ball Park. In good bureaucratic fashion, the stockholders appointed a three-man committee to "secure suitable grounds" for the team's new playing field. Within two weeks, the association purchased a lot and put up a fence. Construction of the grandstands soon followed. Located just outside the city limits and across the street from Richmond College, the former pasture

PEYTON WISE

Virginia Historical Society

FIGURE 9-5 Baseball and veterans' activities were only two of the postwar interests of Peyton Wise (1838–1897). The Accomack County native operated a tobacco firm, became an inspector for Richmond's tobacco exchange, and from 1870 served as ranking major general of the state militia.

was stony, rough, and uneven.[25] It was prone to dust storms that choked the players, drove dirt into spectators' faces, and occasionally delayed games. Low spots in the infield caused the ball to bounce erratically, a condition worsened by the fact that the fielders played their positions barehanded. The park was so large—485 feet on a side—that wealthy fans parked their carriages along the outfield fence. This arrangement forced players to thread their way through horses and buggies in order to track down a well-hit ball. Because it was nearly impossible to knock the ball over the fence, outfielders ran long distances "hunting the sphere in all directions." On one occasion, a visiting player was credited with a home run after the Virginias' outfielders lost the ball in high grass.[26]

Although Richmond's diamond was primitive by modern standards, residents eagerly paid a quarter to see games in this beautiful park that had "first-class, comfortable seats for ladies as well as gentlemen." In order to get to the grounds, most spectators took a streetcar to the end of Broad Street, where they boarded a horse-drawn omnibus that whisked them to the gate. An awning that shielded spectators in the grandstand from the unrelenting summer sun made this section worth the extra fifteen-cent admission price. Ladies and their escorts sat in a reserved portion of the western end of the grandstand, presumably to protect them from those in the general admission section who engaged in such vulgar habits as spitting, drinking, and cursing. Although ladies received a cooler of ice water on hot days, the men went beneath the grandstand to buy beer and whiskey. Truly devoted patrons bought scorecards for the games, and those who preferred comfort rented seat cushions. Spectators who could not afford to pay the extra price to sit in the grandstand were relegated to the general admission sections along the first and third baselines. Attendance at the park, including African Americans, who had their own area, swelled to 3,000 on holidays or when a well-known opponent came to town.[27]

In order to help attract fans to the new ballpark, the association used creative methods to promote the club and raise money for operations. A horse-drawn bandwagon rolled through Richmond on game days to remind people of the event. The team also played benefit contests with local amateur clubs. During an Independence Day moonlight excursion on a steamer, patrons could enjoy music, dancing, and refreshments while getting to meet the players. Before some games, the Virginias competed in throwing matches and running contests.[28] Such promotions sponsored by the association helped to finance the club, because the sales of stock only covered the initial expenses of the team. The twenty-five-cent admission boosted attendance but limited revenue; even top-notch competition brought in gate receipts of only $500. Guarantees for visiting teams, league dues, equipment, and traveling expenses all cut into the profit margin. By far the biggest expenditure was player salaries, which, on a national basis, doubled during the decade. At a time when an average laborer took home less than $40 a month, several members of the 1885 Virginias team made up to four times that amount.[29]

An even better way to ensure high attendance was competition with worthy adversaries. As a temporary measure for the remainder of the 1883 season, the association notified fans that it was making arrangements to "play match games with professional clubs from the North and West" in an effort to bring in teams of higher caliber. Seddon scouted out opponents during his trips to sign players and then used the telegraph to arrange games. It was a haphazard system and one that sometimes hindered the club's ability to draw large numbers of fans because of the unknown quality of the visitors. The Philadelphia Southwarks, for example, agreed to play three games with the Virginias in August. When the visitors arrived in town, it became apparent the team was full of "scrub-players," so management called off the games. Likewise, when Our Boys of Baltimore proved to be inferior, Seddon told the fans "that if they did not wish to witness the game under such circumstances, their money would be refunded," and he promptly canceled the next day's scheduled meeting.[30]

A better solution to the problem of finding quality opponents was joining a league, in which a screening process took place. Seddon traveled to Philadelphia in September 1883 and met with delegates and proxies from eleven other cities across the country. Eight of these clubs ultimately gained entry into the Union Association, one of three major leagues that operated the next year. Richmond joined with seven other teams, including some from the erstwhile Inter-State Association, to form the Eastern League of Professional Base-Ball Clubs. In it, the Virginias played teams from Baltimore, Harrisburg, Reading, Allentown, Wilmington, Trenton, and Brooklyn.[31]

Joining a league was a big step toward ensuring the quality and uniformity of baseball in Richmond. Annual dues were $100, enough to discourage all but serious competitors. League members adopted the reserve rule, a clause that bound players to one team until that management gave the player his release, either outright or through a trade. Players, therefore, could not jump from club to club in an effort to increase their salaries. The rule created continuity within a team by keeping players attached to it but also reduced the players to an untenable bargaining position when it came time to renegotiate salaries. League play also brought a semblance of order to a haphazard scheduling system. As a member of a league, each team had a schedule two months before the first pitch was thrown. Fans knew exactly when the games would be played and could plan accordingly. Joining a league was the club owners' attempt to bring order and predictability to the chaotic world of baseball.[32]

Later, in 1884, the club jumped to the American Association, and Richmond became the first city in the former Confederacy to have a major league baseball franchise.[33] Associating with a major league brought prestige to the city, because the club could measure itself against the best teams in the country. Even before the Virginias entered a league, the *Whig* proudly informed fans that the Baltimore papers "speak of the Richmond Base-Ball Club as being the strongest in America outside of the [National] League and American Associations." Success on the diamond gave the city bragging rights. The *Dispatch* reprinted the backhanded compliment of a Toledo paper that noted the team did not "present an especially fine appearance upon the field, but if they do not look like hay-makers, their play is such as to put them in the first rank of base-ballists. Everybody was agreeably surprised."[34]

Competition with teams from the North and Midwest helped the city shed some of its insularity. Just as the club eventually traveled to nine other states, players from across the country took the field in Richmond. The team exemplified the New South creed of progress

FIGURE 9-6 *Left*: A Charlottesville native, Charley Ferguson (1863–1888) began playing for Henry Boschen's club in 1882. He later signed with the Philadelphia Athletics and remained with them until 1888, when he died of typhoid fever. Experts maintain that if Ferguson had continued his level of performance for another ten years, he would have been one of the top twenty pitchers of all times. *Right*: Richard F. Johnston (1863–1934) joined the Virginias in 1884 but was dealt to Boston the next year. After seven years in the major leagues, he was forced to retire because of a "drinking problem. He returned to his hometown of Kingston, New Jersey, to coach.

coming from a small group of merchants, industrialists, and planters who were not hesitant to seek ties with the North.[35]

Management proved adept at running the business aspects of the club but recognized the need for a baseball expert to assemble and direct the team, To that end, the members of the Virginia association sought an experienced baseball man who could make decisions in matters they knew nothing about. In October 1883, Theodore P. "Ted" Sullivan, who had guided the St. Louis Browns of the American Association to a second-place finish that year, agreed to manage the team for the 1884 season. About a month before the season started, however, Sullivan reneged on his contract. The St. Louis Maroons of the Union Association had offered him $1,000 more than he could earn with the Virginias and also gave him the opportunity to manage a team that would compete against his former boss, a man Sullivan loathed. He refused to report to Richmond. Forgetting how the Richmond players had abandoned Boschen, the *Dispatch* complained that "Ted is like all the rest. It is not so much his word as somebody else's money that controls him!" When Sullivan decided to stay in St. Louis, the team brought in Myron S. Allen, who had managed the Kingston Leaders of the Eastern League. He lasted less than a month. Failure to find an adequate manager bedeviled

FIGURE 9-7 *Left*: William M. Nash (1865–1929), a Richmond native, began his baseball career as a teenager on Henry Boschen's team. Considered one of the best third basemen of the nineteenth century, Nash played for Boston, 1885–95. After three years in Philadelphia, he became a National League umpire. *Right*: Another native of Richmond, E. C. "Pop" Tate (1860–1932) played for Henry Boschen before joining the Richmond Virginias in 1885. The left-handed catcher wore a Boston Beaneaters' uniform from 1885 to 1888.

the team throughout 1884. The absence of a professional left ultimate direction to Seddon and Felix I. Moses, the association's secretary, who became the team's manager by default.[36]

Seddon conducted a frantic search for new talent and signed several men from northern cities. Moses did not settle on a consistent lineup and frequently used players who lasted only for a few weeks. Twenty-one new players joined the team, and twenty-eight different men wore a Virginias' uniform for the 1884 exhibition, Eastern League, and American Association seasons, a total of 130 games. This high turnover brought instability to the team and weakened its performance.[37]

Seddon was even willing to sign Edward J. and William H. Dugan, two brothers who had earned notoriety in Richmond-when their team played the Virginias the year before. They drew much criticism in the local press for protesting the umpire's calls. The most egregious mistake, however, was signing Frank S. "Terry" Larkin, an infielder with a questionable past. He had played for at least six other clubs before joining the Virginias. One day in 1883 Larkin first tried to kill his wife, then a policeman, and finally himself. He earned six months in the penitentiary, but this lesson did not cure his alcoholism. Once Larkin joined the Virginias, he performed adequately at second base but for ten days in August went unaccounted for. Such was the quality of players brought in by a wholesale grocer and a fertilizer salesman.[38]

Virginia Historical Society

FIGURE 9-8 On 13 June 1885, Richmonders celebrated the Virginias' record of 24–5 with a series of comic sketches on the front page of the *Dispatch*.

The difficulty in securing talented players meant that the decision to join the American Association was a disastrous one. Richmond stumbled to a tenth-place finish in the thirteen-team league. Observers in other cities commented on the poor play of the Virginias. One paper noted that "there is some good material in the Virginians, but it needs bringing out badly."[39] Although a contemporary publication maintained that "the new comers made a very good record," the numbers told otherwise. The Virginias' 12–30 finish translated into a pitiful 286 winning percentage, at a time when talent in the league was down because too many teams competed in too many leagues. The Virginias batted poorly and fielded worse. The best that can be said for the team is that it performed better than Washington, the squad it replaced. Not surprisingly, the American Association dropped Richmond from the league during the winter meeting. Not only was the club an embarrassment on the field, but having to take the train to New York, Columbus, Louisville, St. Louis, Cincinnati, Baltimore, Philadelphia, Toledo, Brooklyn, Pittsburgh, and Indianapolis also drained the Virginia association's treasury.[40]

Management, however, did not dwell on its errors but took steps to fix the team's problems. Seddon resigned as president, probably with the mutual consent of the board. Most likely, the directors wanted Seddon out because of his questionable decisions, but he had also married the daughter of a leading New Orleans merchant and moved to Louisiana. Richmond joined Norfolk, Washington, Baltimore, Lancaster, Trenton, Newark, and Jersey City in the new Eastern League. After the disastrous 1884 season, the club hoped to cut down on travel expenses by playing teams closer to home. The most important change came even before the team stowed its gear for the winter, when it began looking for "a first class manager," which was, according to *Sporting Life*, "something that it has been in need of the past season." Management learned from its mistakes and knew that it had to import an expert to oversee the team or it would repeat the ruinous performance in 1884.[41]

Joseph Simmons agreed to guide the Virginias, and the board of directors gave him full control of the team. Simmons, who had managed the Wilmington Quicksteps to the pennant in the 1884 Eastern League, immediately cleaned house. He retained only four players from among those who had finished the regular season. In marked contrast to the previous year, the Virginias did not make a roster change until after the eighty-third game.[42]

A surprisingly good addition was George W. Latham, nicknamed "Jumbo" because he packed 250 pounds onto his five-foot, eight-inch frame and "Juice" because of his "extensive and inelegant vocabulary" that infuriated opponents. Although opposition players and fans taunted Latham as being washed up, he proved to be a good player who was a superb coach on the field.[43] Simmons also signed Samuel J. Kimber, who lacked control of both his temper and his pitches. While playing for the National League's Brooklyn Dodgers, Kimber pitched ten no-hit innings, but in a Virginias' uniform he hit two batters in the head in a single game, causing one to quit the contest and leaving the other unconscious for fifteen minutes. The patience of Simmons paid off, as the erratic Kimber posted an earned run average of 1.52 for the year, sixth best in the league.[44]

The team opened the 1885 exhibition season by taking two of three games from the Providence Grays, champions of the National League in 1884 and winners of the first fully sanctioned World Series. The Virginias started quickly and amassed a 23–5 record by 12 June. When the club returned to Richmond that day, a crowd of 500 and George Voelker's brass band greeted them at the train station. Team members climbed into two wagons, built by Lange Brothers, a grain and feed distributor, especially for "base-ball transportation purposes." The vehicles were adorned for the occasion with banners that read, "We Have Met the Enemy and They Are Ours" and "A Clean Sweep from Jersey City to Home-Plate." Twelve brooms, one for each player and the manager, jutted from the wagons, while evergreens, flags, and streamers fluttered in the breeze. The crowd trailed the team as it rode across town to William J. Manning's saloon. In the short ceremony that preceded lunch, each player received a bouquet. The next day, six humorous sketches depicting the fine art of baseball graced the front page of the *Dispatch*.[45]

Simmons's ability to assemble a quality team is apparent upon examination of the club's record in the Eastern League. Richmond consistently won games and finished the year with sixty-five victories and twenty-six losses, a .691 winning percentage. It was an impressive improvement over its performances in the 1884 Eastern League and American Association.[46]

Even as the Virginias competed on the diamond, they played an important role in introducing Richmond to the practices of the emerging middle class and the values of the New South. Baseball acquainted fans with the growing emphasis on standardized business practices. Regular procedures, such as the official rain-out policy, became widely known. Although indignant fans may have wanted their money back when a game was canceled, the posting of placards at the park effectively insulated the association from having to give refunds. In a similar fashion, spring practice introduced the idea that teamwork, self-sacrifice, discipline, and the development of corporate values did not just happen but had to be cultivated. Before the 1884 season, curious spectators attended practices, and the consensus was that the training put the Virginias "in excellent trim."[47]

People also came to recognize the importance of rules within an organization. When the manager disciplined players for violating a team rule, such as the time Simmons suspended Charlie Householder for staying out too late and fined Bill Greenwood for heavy drinking, fans learned the necessity of adhering to standard policies. Richmonders absorbed the lessons of management so well that when the Newark team forfeited its game with the Virginias because the manager could not locate all of his players, one paper commented that the incident "goes for nothing, merely showing bad management." Such negligence on the part of the Virginias had become unthinkable.[48]

Fans of the national game understood and accepted the way baseball incorporated rationality and accentuated cooperation within groups to attain competitive ends. Individual players were accountable for their own actions while trying to succeed in a group setting. People eagerly followed the results of the team but also wanted specific information on the performance of each of the players. As the game increased in popularity, both of the city's

FIGURE 9-9 Henry Boschen's semiprofessional squad posed with the National League's Detroit team during the celebration of the Yorktown centennial in 1881. The Virginians' mismatched uniforms contrast with the regularity of those of their opponents. Seated in the front row are Knight (Detroit), Henry C. Boschen (Richmond), Sam Trott (Detroit), and Eddie Glenn (Richmond). In the middle row are Dinks Napier (Richmond), Barker (Richmond), an unidentified Detroit player, Jim Powell (Richmond), Sadie Hauck (Detroit), an unidentified Detroit player, and Manny Ralston (Richmond). Standing in the rear are Herbert Hankins (Richmond), Wesley Blogg (Richmond), an unidentified Detroit player, Powell (Detroit), Charlie Bennett (Detroit), Edward Hanlon (Detroit), and Billy Nash (Richmond).

major dailies gave a detailed and complex rendering of the previous day's games, complete with notations for bases-on balls, first base-on errors, strikeouts, doubles, triples, home runs, and earned runs. Fans loved the order and efficiency of the game, so statistics became the standard measure of performance. They expected such statistics to be precise. On one occasion, when the *Dispatch*'s correspondent questioned the accuracy of the "so-called 'official' scorer" of the Virginias, Charles Johnston "positively refused" to release the record. Baseball, especially when played by professionals, reproduced many of the characteristics required by industrial capitalism.[49]

Uniformity was another value that came to be championed. A photograph of Boschen's semiprofessional club taken in 1881 for the Yorktown centennial celebration shows a motley collection of players. Some of them have no discernible uniforms, while others have the letter "R" crudely drawn or sewn onto their shirts. Their caps do not match, either. The club's appearance contrasts sharply with the matching caps, shirts, and sweaters worn by the Detroit players. By 1883, however, uniforms became emblematic of being a good team. The *Dispatch* criticized the image projected by one "so called" professional squad from Washington that had lost two games to the Virginias by the combined score of 49–8. "The appearance of the visitors plainly indicated that instead of being a professional nine (as was claimed for them) ... they were the most indiffrent kind of amateurs," the paper asserted. "Their uniforms, in which there was an entire lack of *uniformity* (some being white, others gray, and others still different shades—representing, in fact, all the recognized colors), told as much." The clear lesson was that a team that did not pride itself on its public image was likely to play poorly. One of the first actions of the Virginia Base-Ball Association was purchasing fancy, uniforms that made its squad look like the National League teams it played in exhibition games. All agreed that the Virginias presented a "'splendid appearance on the field." Uniformity, symbolized by the presence of uniforms, became a value to be esteemed and pursued.[50]

Just as baseball introduced many of the values of the New South to Richmond's citizens, it also enabled industrial laborers to adapt to the new urban milieu. The game was a soothing way of recalling traditional patterns of life that smoothed out some of the differences in society. The movement toward industrial capitalism and bureaucratic methods altered America drastically in the late nineteenth century. Such marked changes led many individuals to perceive disorder in society. Baseball was one method of coping with these changes. It blended many rural elements—open space, warm weather, and a grass field—with the urban setting. Fans in Richmond used baseball as a means of identification with one another, a way to establish rituals of mutual dependence in an increasingly fragmented community. Just as identification with Confederate veterans' organizations provided a shelter from the growing confusion of industrial society, so, too, did identification with the Virginias. True fans shared a vocabulary of such terms as "flys, fouls, base-hits, put-outs, spheres, sent-to-earth, [and] daisy grass-cutters." Instead of celebrating the Fourth of July with pageants and military parades as in antebellum days, people in the New South came together through "base-ball and private pic-nics." Baseball, a local paper concluded, was the "common plane upon which this democracy could meet, shake hands, and readjust the business difficulties of the city." The sport became a common denominator through which fans from all stations in life could share a mutual interest.[51]

Richmond residents identified so much with baseball that passion for the game w;as raised to a "fever-heat." One publication found it "[s]trange how a furore will take hold of an entire city," while another marveled at how the town "has gone wild, and nothing can be heard but base ball." People flocked to see the Virginias. Although few attendance figures are available, the team averaged more fans under the association's leadership than under Boschen's. Attendance of 1,000 at one of Boschen's games had been considered outstanding. By contrast, the Virginias averaged just over 1,000 spectators a game at the Virginia Base-Ball Park throughout the 1883, 1884, and 1885 seasons and drew 2,000 fans or more on thirteen occasions.[52]

When the team took to the road, large crowds assembled at various sites around the city to learn the scores of the games as they came over the telegraph wires. The Richmond Theatre exploited the excitement by creating a minstrel show about "the cunning base stealers, artistic muffers, impartial umpires, [and] chronic kickers." Residents of the capital were so smitten with baseball that even some of the city's ministers attended the games, despite general misgivings among clergy about the corrupting effects of organized sport. They probably objected to the gambling that took place on the games. On one occasion, a public outcry followed an allegation that more than $3,000 changed hands when the Virginias lost to the Ross Club of Pennsylvania.[53]

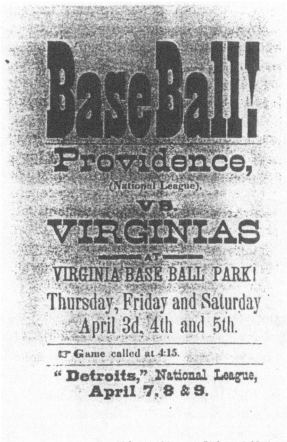

Valentine Museum, Richmond, Virginia

FIGURE 9-10 Local print shops capitalized on fan enthusiasm by issuing broadsides and scorecards. The Virginias lost all three of these advertised games to the Providence Grays in 1884. Providence went on to capture the National League pennant that season and won the first fully sanctioned World Series.

Excitement for the team translated into greater profits for local merchants. Newspapers benefited from increased advertising revenue, local print shops kept busy issuing posters and scorecards, and cigar dealers sold more of their products on game days. It was obvious to the *Daily Dispatch* that a "good game of ball attracts not only our own citizens, but outsiders as well." County merchants arranged to stay an extra day in the city in order to watch a game.[54]

Andrew Krouse and William J. Manning capitalized on the team's success as well. In an early version of a sports bar, Manning posted inning-by-inning reports of away games on a blackboard in his billiard hall. The hundreds of enthusiasts "anxiously awaiting" the scores blocked Broad Street when they could not cram into the building. Fans became so intent on getting up-to-the-minute reports that some accused Manning of withholding information so that he could bet on the results of the games. Krouse posted the "correct score, by innings—with 'struck outs,' base hits, and errors" on a bulletin board outside his saloon.[55]

Audiences at the Virginias' games were primarily from the working class, mainly because the ballpark was one attraction that laborers could afford. The twenty-five-cent admission compared favorably with other amusements. Games with better opponents, though, brought "ladies, professional] men, merchants, mechanics, and others" to the ballpark.[56] Richmond crowds were an unruly bunch. The Wilmington *Sunday Critic* described them as "beyond description for rowdyism." It noted that visiting teams had to endure "the vilest abuse from all classes." At a time when cheering, booing, and whistling were being relegated to saloons, burlesque, and sporting events, the behavior of the fans is not surprising. The baseball park was one of the few remaining places where they could freely express themselves.[57]

Although Richmond crowds sometimes cheered the good plays of visiting clubs, they gained a reputation for being obnoxious. Not only did the crowds bait opponents, but on occasion they taunted the Virginias as well. They laughed at Jim Powell, a Richmond native and the team's captain, when he struck out. The ridicule was so intense that when Powell came to bat a second time and hit the ball to the fence, he retaliated by allowing himself to be tagged out as he strolled to second base. Richmond crowds once jeered Kimber so badly the manager sent police into the stands to restore order.[58]

Fans were offensive when cheering players, as well. A favorite means of expression was tossing rented seat cushions in the air, a practice so common that the papers feared for the safety of ladies at the games and called for authorities to stop the culprits. The fans were venting frustration with the increased tedium of urban life and the doldrums of daily toil. They took advantage of the sense of increased anonymity at the park to let off steam.[59]

Richmond fans' greatest outbursts of hooliganism, however, were reserved for the umpires. In this they were not alone, as game officials became "a convenient target" for the irritation and frustrations of working-class crowds. Because only one umpire worked the game, he frequently had poor views of close plays and as a result made many questionable calls. The crowds at the Virginia Base-Ball Park responded with "howls, hoots, and hisses." When a ball struck an umpire and injured him, the spectators "instead of sympathizing with him, laughed at his mishaps." Once the game continued, the attempts of an officer of the Virginia Base-Ball Association to quiet the fans only made them rowdier.[60] Another time, Richmonders berated an American Association umpire so mercilessly that he "very foolishly faced the whole crowd" and tried to single out the worst of the hecklers. His actions exacerbated the situation, and had "it not been for the prompt exercise of the police authority in silencing the crowd it is hard to say what might have ensued." The crowds were so bad that the team's manager wrote a letter to the editor asking patrons to stop "hooting and hissing" the decisions of the umpire.[61]

Such incidents occurred only after the team went professional and entered a league. This development suggests that fans took the game more seriously once the Virginias signaled their intentions to play a better brand of ball. As the game passed from an a'mateur amusement to a professional business, the spectators took the liberty to engage in behavior that stretched the bounds of decency.

African Americans were part of these clamorous crowds. During the 1880s, segregation was the rule in the city, although such arrangements had not yet been codified. African Americans who attended games probably did not sit in the grandstand but stood alongside the fence instead. These spectators made their presence known at the games by "always hurrah[ing] for the visiting club. They yell with delight when the home club gets a setback." Such behavior, the *Dispatch* complained, was not "in good spirit." A tantalizing clue to the actions of African Americans is found in a description of a game at Boschen's park,

National Baseball Hall of Fame Library, Cooperstown, N.Y.

FIGURE 9-11   In 1884 Moses Fleetwood Walker (1857–1924) became the first African American to play in the majors when the Toledo Blue Stockings joined the American Association. When the Blue Stockings scheduled an appearance in Richmond, a letter to the Toledo manager threatened bloodshed if the black catcher suited up. Confrontation was avoided only because Walker, a frequent target of deliberately mispitched balls and unduly vicious spiked slides, had received broken ribs and had been released from the team when the Blue Stockings arrived in town.

where "the colored part of the crowd yesterday cheered the home-boys on every good play." This response was "quite different" from that at games at the Virginia Base-Ball Park. It is quite possible that blacks were answering the tangible and visible links of the Virginias to the Confederacy. Forms of covert resistance, such as refusal to yield to whites on the sidewalk or cheering for the opposing team, were ways in which African Americans asserted their claims to equal civil and political rights. It was one means of declaring their humanity while registering their disagreement with those groups they opposed.[62]

Although African Americans might be able to watch games in the Virginia Base-Ball Park, they certainly could not play there. In Richmond there were at least two baseball teams composed entirely of blacks, one of which played "colored" teams from other cities, and the city council authorized the purchase of bats and balls for the "colored poor-house." A game between one of these clubs and the Virginias, or any other white team, was unthinkable.[63] As Richmond swiftly moved toward a more segregated society, African Americans were not welcomed as participants in the all-white domain of the baseball diamond, something made perfectly clear in October 1884.

The Toledo club of the American Association was set to close out its season in Richmond with a three-game series against the Virginias. One of the better players on the visiting team was catcher Moses Fleetwood Walker, the first African American to play in the major leagues. About a week before the series, Charlie Morton, Toledo's manager, received a letter, signed by four people, that warned him not to allow Walker to take the field. According to the letter, seventy-five "determined men" had sworn to "mob Walker if he comes on the ground in a [baseball] suit." Although the letter hoped there would be no trouble, it promised "much bloodshed" if the manager did not pay heed. In fact, the signatories' resolution was not tested. Walker did not play in Richmond because a rib injury sustained in July led to his release. Enthusiasm for baseball was not allowed to cross the color line in later years, either. In 1889 city leaders asked the Detroit Club of the National League to cancel its games with the Cuban Giants, an African-American team. The locals did not want "colored and white clubs to play there [in Richmond] against each other."[64]

Even though the ballpark provided a refuge for fans and the Virginias had a first-rate club in 1885, the association ran into financial difficulties in July of that year. The team became a victim of its own success. Victory on the field led to a noticeable drop in attendance. One resident noted that the club was "vastly too strong for the other clubs" in the Eastern League, so fans stayed home because they "take it for granted that the club will win easily and there is no use in going out" to the games.[65]

If the combination of low revenue and high player salaries was not enough to bring the team to financial ruin, the actions of Thomas Carpenter were. Carpenter, the club's secretary-treasurer, cleaned out the safe and fled to Canada. He took what little cash the club had, and his theft exposed the critical state of the Virginias' finances. The crisis forced the association to sell the team's best players, Nash and Richard F. Johnston, to the Boston Beaneaters of the National League just as the club left for its final road trip of the year. The two had been the main offensive weapons of the Virginias, and their transfer had immediate effect. In Richmond's first game after the transaction, Washington allowed no hits and then went on to sweep the three-game series. Eight games ahead of Washington when the pair were shipped off, the Virginias suddenly looked vulnerable. A local resident reflected popular sentiment when he confided to a friend that he was "beginning to fear that after all the Virginias will loose the penant."[66] His apprehensions were realized. The squad saw its lead over Washington evaporate, and the Nationals ultimately captured the Eastern League pennant.[67]

When a committee of the players went to Alfriend's house demanding payment of the team's salaries from the previous month, he maintained the association did not have the

FIGURE 9-12 In May 1890 citizens prepared for the unveiling of Marius-Jean-Antonin Mercié's statue of R. E. Lee. The imposing bronze was erected on the site of the central gate of the Virginia Base-Ball Park.

money. Alfriend surrendered the treasuiy, and each player received $7.50. The team withdrew from management's control in order to finish the season on its own. A "right much demoralized" club played one more game, in which it lost to Bridgeport, before disbanding on 19 September 1885.[68]

Baseball clubs folded with regularity in the 1880s, and so it is not . surprising that the Virginias did not last. The team, after all, was invited to join the American Association only because the Washington Nationals failed. Clubs from Jersey City, Atlantic City, Lancaster, and Norfolk bowed out of the 1885 Eastern League because of financial difficulties. In the case of the Virginias, the club's president bitterly pointed out that "the public had themselves to blame" for the team's demise. People, he maintained, asked themselves, "[W]ho wants to see a one-sided game? We know who will win without going to the grounds." The game had lost its appeal in Richmond because it ceased to be exciting and unpredictable. Watching the Virginias play was no longer entertaining for the working class because they assumed the outcome was a foregone conclusion. Attending a baseball game had become a monotonous event, too much like the tedious work the spectators wanted to leave behind.[69]

Although fans stopped coming to the park, they closely scrutinized the treatment the players had received. Most of the team members did not have enough money to pay their hotel bills or buy train tickets but eventually managed to drift to other cities and play for other ball clubs. As Simmons tried to leave town, he was arrested for an unpaid debt of $48 for the printing of scorecards. The hardheaded business decision of the association to withhold player salaries did not sit well with Richmond citizens. One resident felt the club should have paid the players "instead of throwing them out in the cold at this stage of the season." It was an anticlimactic end to a promising year.[70]

Less than five years after the Virginias folded, Marius-Jean-Antonin Mercie's statue of Robert E. Lee was erected at the edge of Richmond's city limits. The Lee Camp took the lead in arranging the dedication ceremonies and asked citizens to drag the monumental bronze from the railroad depot to its pedestal. This ritual deliberately mimicked the method used to move Thomas Crawford's equestrian statue of George Washington from the waterfront to its site next to the state capitol in 1857. Nearly 9,000 people took a turn at the ropes that pulled Lee's statue. Marshals who led the citizens in their efforts included Smith and Epps, both of whom squeezed into their Confederate uniforms once again and both of whom had served on the board of directors for the Virginias.[71]

Once the statue was in place, 100,000 spectators witnessed the four- mile-long parade that preceded the dramatic unveiling. Marching in the procession were Smith, Epps, Alfriend, and Wise. Skinker drew special notice for being able to keep up with his old unit despite using crutches. All of these men had been closely affiliated with the Virginias and doubtless realized that the new statue had been erected on the site of the central gate of the Virginia Base-Ball Park. It is somehow fitting that the ultimate monument to the Lost Cause stands on the former ballpark, because the Richmond Virginias helped to promote simultaneously the New South and the veneration of the Confederacy.[72]

NOTES

1. For Johnston's background, see Richmond *Daily Dispatch*, 14 Sept. 1883; *Richmond Daily Whig*, 18 Oct. 1883; J. H. Chataigne. comp., *Chataigne's Directory of Richmond, Va., ... 1882–3* (Richmond, 1882), p. 228 (quotation); and Jane B. Hewett, ed., *The Roster of Confederate Soldiers, 1861–1865* (16 vols.; Wilmington, N.C., 1995–96), 8:504. On the R. E. Lee Camp No. 1, see R. B. Rosenburg, *Living Monuments: Confederate Soldiers' Homes in the New South* (Chapel Hill and London, 1993).

2. Richmond *Daily Dispatch*, 5 Sept. 1883; *Richmond Daily Whig*, 5 Sept. 1883. On veterans' celebrations, see Gaines M. Foster, *Ghosts of the Confederacy: Defeat, the Lost Cause, and the Emergence of the New South, 1865 to 1913* (New York and Oxford, 1987), pp. 93–95, 100–101,107–8, 112, 137–40.

3. Richmond *Daily Dispatch*, 5 Sept. 1883; *Richmond Daily Whig*, 5 Sept. 1883. The standard work on the GAR is Stuart McConnell, *Glorious Contentment: The Grand Army of the Republic, 1865–1900* (Chapel Hill and London, 1992).

4. Foster, *Ghosts of the Confederacy; Charles Reagan Wilson, Baptized in Blood: The Religion of the Lost Cause, 1865–1920* (Athens, Ga., 1980); William B. Hesseltine, *Confederate Leaders in the New South* (Baton Rouge, 1950).

5. Richmond *Daily Dispatch*, 2 Aug. 1883; C. Vann Woodward, *Origins of the New South, 1877–1913*, in Wendell Holmes Stephenson and E. Merton Coulter, eds., *A History of the South*, 9 (Baton Rouge, 1951); Edward L. Ayers, *The Promise of the New South: Life after Reconstruction* (New York and Oxford, 1992); Paul M. Gaston, *The New South Creed: A Study in Southern Myth-Making* (New York, 1970); Don H. Doyle, *New Men, New Cities, New South: Atlanta, Nashville, Charleston, Mobile, 1860–1910* (Chapel Hill and London, 1990); James Tice Moore, "Redeemers Reconsidered: Change and Continuity in the Democratic South," *Journal of Southern History* (hereafter cited as JSH) 44 (1978): 357–78.

6. Robert Wiebe, *The Search for Order, 1877–1920* (New York, 1967), esp. pp. 111–63; John F. Kasson, *Amusing the Million: Coney Island at the Turn of the Century* (New York, 1978); Gunther Barth, *City People: The Rise of Modem City Culture in Nineteenth-Century America* (New York, 1980), pp. 148–91. Robert F. Burk and John Rickards Betts discuss the interaction of baseball and industrialism, but not in the South (Robert F. Burk, *Never Just a Game: Players, Owners, and American Baseball to 1920* [Chapel Hill, 1994]; John Rickards Betts, "The Technological Revolution and the Rise of Sports, 1850–1900," *Mississippi Valley Historical Review* 40 [1953–54]: 231–56).

7. Ayers. *Promise of the New South*, pp. 310–11; Henry Chadwick, "Baseball in the South," in George B. Kirsch, ed., *Sports in North America: A Documentary History*, vol. 5: *Sports Organized, 1880–1900*, ed. Gerald R. Gems (Breeze, Fla., 1996), p. 114; George B. Kirsch. "Bats, Balls, and Bullets: Baseball and the Civil War," *Civil War Times Illustrated* 37 (May 1998): 30–37; Louis A. Brown, *The Salisbury-Prison: A Case Study of Confederate Military Prisons, 1861–1865*

(Wendell, N. C., 1980), pp. 136–37. On Chadwick, see Charles C. Alexander, *Our Game: An American Baseball History* (New York, 1991), pp. 10–13; Bernard J. Henley, "The Early Years of Baseball in Richmond," *Richmond Quarterly* 1 (Winter 1978): 48; Richmond *Daily Dispatch*, 19 July 1867, 1 May 1875; Michael B. Chesson, *Richmond after the War, 1865–1890* (Richmond, 1981), p. 82; and Walter S. Griggs, Jr., "From the Lads of Sheep Hill to the Braves of the Diamond: The Story of Professional Baseball in Richmond," n.d., pp. 1–21 (typescript), National Baseball Hall of Fame, Cooperstown, N.Y. (hereafter cited as NCooNa). On Babcock, see Hewett, ed., *Roster of Confederate Soldiers*. 1:280. One explanation of why baseball was not popular in the South before 1861 is that it did not fit into the southern code of honor. See Kenneth S. Greenberg. *Honor & Slavery: Lies, Duels, Noses, Masks, Dressing as a Woman, Gifts, Strangers, Humanitarianism, Death, Slave Rebellions, the Proslavery Argument, Baseball, Hunting, and Gambling in the Old South* (Princeton, 1996), pp. 115–25.

8. Chataigne, comp., *Richmond Directory, 1882–83*, p. 121; *Richmond Dispatch*, 22 Oct. 1898; *Richmond Times*, 22 Oct. 1898; G. Watson James, "It's 'Batter Up!' Time on the City's Sandlots," *Richmond Times-Dispatch*, 31 Mar. 1935, magazine section, pp. 5–6; A Woolner Calisch, "The Birth of Baseball in Richmond: Game's History in Early Days Is Recalled," *Richmond Times-Dispatch*, 10 Sept. 1935, magazine section, pp. 2–3. Businesses in the nineteenth century commonly sponsored baseball teams. Examples are found in Steven M. Gelber, "'Their Hands are all out Playing': Business and Amateur Baseball, 1845–1917," *Journal of Sport History* 11 (1984): 22–25; Jacquelyn Dowd Hall, James Leludis, Robert Korstad, LuAnn Jones, and Christopher B. Daly, *Like a Family: The Making of a Southern Cotton Mill World* (New York, 1987), pp. 135–36; and Thomas K. Perry, *Textile League Baseball: South Carolina's Mill Teams, 1880–1955* (Jefferson, N.C., 1993).

9. Information on Ferguson and the other players mentioned in this study is found in the Lee Allen Notebooks and Vertical Files, NCooNa; index cards, Swales Baseball Collection, New York Public Library, New York, N.Y. (hereafter cited as NN); Jeanine Bucek et al., eds., *Baseball Encyclopedia* (10th rev. ed.; New York, 1996); and Marshall D. Wright, *Nineteenth Century Baseball: Year-by-Year Statistics of Major League Teams, 1871–1900* (Jefferson, N.C., 1996). For additional information on Ferguson, see Harry Clay Palmer, J. A. Fynes, Frank Richter, and W. I. Harris, *Athletic Sports in America, England and Australia* ... (Philadelphia, 1889), p. 115; Hiram T. Askew, "Charley Ferguson: A Baseball Star to Remember," *Richmond Quarterly* 5 (Spring 1983): 50–51; Allison Danzig and Joe Reichler, *The History of Baseball: Its Great Players, Teams and Managers* (Englewood Cliffs, N.J., 1959), p. 178; and Robert L. Tiemann and Mark Rucker, eds., *Nineteenth Century Stars* (n.p., 1989), p. 42. While with Philadelphia, Ferguson pitched complete game shutouts on successive days, the first a three-hitter and then a no-hitter. The next year he pitched both games of a doubleheader and gave up only one run in each.

10. On Nash, see Hiram T. Askew, "Billy Nash: First Richmond Baseball Great," *Richmond Quarterly* 3 (Spring 1981): 34–36; Dan Abramson, "When Richmond Was in the Major Leagues." *Richmond Surroundings* 15 (Sept.–Oct. 1992): 48; George V. Tuohey, *A History of the Boston Baseball Club* (Boston, 1897), pp. 222–23; David Nemec, *The Beer and Whiskey*

League: The Illustrated History of the American Association—Baseball's Renegade Major League (New York, 1994), p. 61; David Uuentin Voigt, *American Baseball*, vol. 1: *From Gentleman's Sport to the Commissioner System* (Norman, Okla., 1966), pp. 243, 262, 276; Harold Seymour, *Baseball*, vol. 1: *The Early Years* (New York, 1960), pp. 280, 297; and *St. Louis Post-Dispatch*. 19 Sept. 1884. Glenn died in Richmond in 1892 at the age of thirty-one (*Richmond Dispatch*, 11 Feb. 1892; Richmond Times, 11 Feb. 1892; Richmond *State*, 10 Feb. 1892). Tate was a rarity, a left-handed catcher. Evidence of his prowess may be found in *Richmond Dispatch*, 13 June 1885.

11. *Richmond Daily Whig*, 19 June 1884 (quotation); *Richmond Daily Dispatch*, 4 May, 4 June, 6 July 1880,22 July, 12 Aug., 19 Oct. 1881, 5 July 1885; Nemec, *Beer and Whiskey League*, pp. 28–29; Voigt, *American Baseball*, 1:205–9; Seymour, *Baseball*, 1:176–81; Joseph Durso, *Baseball and the American Dream* (St. Louis, 1986), p. 32; Alexander, *Our Game*, pp. 45–46.

12. Richmond *Daily Dispatch*, 22 May 1881, 7, 22, 27 (quotation) Apr. 1883; Michael Benson, *Ballparks of North America: A Comprehensive Historical Reference to Baseball Grounds, Yards and Stadiums, 1845 to Present* (Jefferson, N.C., 1989), p. 330.

13. Richmond *Daily Dispatch*, 21 (quotation), 22 June 1883; *Richmond Daily Whig*, 21, 25 June 1883; Robert L. Scribner, "Two Out, and——? The Richmond 'Virginians' Need Not Feel Unfamiliar in the International League. They Have Been There Twice Before," *Virginia Cavalcade* 3 (Spring 1954): 18–22. Boschen did scrape together a new team and continued to play through 1885. He even adopted some of the Virginias' attractions: new uniforms, an expanded ballpark, membership in the Union League as an alliance club, and players from other cities (Richmond *Daily Dispatch*, 27 June 1883, 27 Mar., 30 Apr. 1884; *Sporting Life*, 19 Mar. 1884, p. 3; ibid., 26 Mar. 1884, p.3). After 1885, Boschen does not appear in any more accounts of baseball in Richmond, although he lived until 1898.

14. A. J. Reach, ed., *Reach's Official American Association Base Ball Guide for 1884* (Philadelphia, 1884), p. 23 (quotation); Richmond, Personal Property Tax Book, 1883, Library of Virginia, Richmond (hereafter cited as Vi).

15. Richmond *Daily Dispatch*, 21 June, 24 Aug. (quotation) 1883. The information on occupations is derived from various city directories of the period.

16. The list of officers and members of the board of directors who served in the Confederate military includes Thomas L. Alfriend (treasurer 1883–84, president 1885), W. Miles Cary (director), Charles H. Epps (vice-president), S. A. Ellison (director), Charles F. Johnston (scorer), Charles R. Skinker (director), George A. Smith (director), Beverley Randolph Wellford, Jr. (director), and Peyton Wise (director). Their records of service are in Hewett, ed., *Roster of Confederate Soldiers*, 1:100. 3:279, 5:320, 345, 8:504, 14:162. 218. 16:106. 430; and Clement A. Evans, ed., *Confederate Military History Extended Edition* (hereafter cited as *CMHEE*) (17 vols., 1899; Wilmington, N.C.. 1987), 4:859–60, 1171–72.

17. Foster, *Ghosts of the Confederacy*, pp. 104–12; Ayers, *Promise of the New South*, pp. 333–34. Skinker's exploits are found in *Southern Historical Society Papers* (hereafter cited as *SHSP*) 2 (1875): 317; ibid. 22 (1894): 285; *CMHEE*, 4:1170–71; Chataigne, comp., *Richmond Directory, 1882–83*. p. 30; and J. H. Chataigne, comp., *Chataigne's Directory of Richmond, Va., ... 1885*

(Richmond, 1885), p. 81. Wise is noted in *SHSP* 25 (1897): 14; *CMHEE*, 4:1280–81; and *Confederate Veteran* 5 (May 1897): 206. Alfriend, W. Miles Cary, Epps, and Smith were the other members of the Lee Camp (*Charter, By-Laws, Rules of Order and List of Officers and Members of R. E. Lee Camp. No. 1, Confederate Veterans* ... [Richmond. 1884], pp. 29. 31, 33–34, 37–38). Johnston, the scorer, was also a member. For more evidence of the emphasis on sectional reconciliation among Civil War veterans, see Foster, *Ghosts of the Confederacy*, pp. 67–70, 112–14; Wilson, *Baptized in Blood*, pp. 28–32; McConnell, *Glorious Contentment*, pp. 185–93; and Nina Silber, *The Romance of Reunion: Northerners and the South, 1865–1900*, Civil War America (Chapel Hill and London, 1993).

18. *SHSP* 20 (1892): 323. The veterans' home is described in Foster, *Ghosts of the Confederacy*, p. 93; Archer Anderson, *Address on the Opening of the Lee Camp Soldiers' Home, May 20th, 1885* (Richmond, 1885); Richmond *Daily Dispatch*, 26, 27 Apr. 1884; and Rosenburg, *Living Monuments*, pp. 26–28, 93, 96, 99, 112. 114, 127, 142–43, 147–49. Wellford, a judge on the 7th judicial circuit embracing Richmond and Henrico County, was married to a niece of James Seddon and served for many years as the recording secretary of the Virginia Historical Society.

19. *CMHEE*, 4:1170, 1172.

20. Gaston, *New South Creed*, p. 184; *Richmond Dispatch*, 3 Aug. 1884, 11 Aug. 1885; *Richmond Daily Whig*, 20 Sept. 1884.

21. David Lamoreaux, "Baseball in the Late Nineteenth Century: The Source of Its Appeal," *Journal of Popular Culture* 11 (1977): 597–613; Michael S. Kimmel, "Baseball and the Reconstitution of American Masculinity," in Alvin L. Hall, ed., *Cooperstown Symposium on Baseball and American Culture* (Oneonta, N.Y., 1989), p. 292.

22. *Charter, By-Laws, Rules of Order and List of Officers and Members of Lee Camp*, p. 3 (first quotation); Wilson, *Baptized in Blood*, pp. 37–38; Foster, *Ghosts of the Confederacy*, pp. 79–103, 137–43; Gaston, *New South Creed*, pp. 167–77; Hesseltine, *Confederate Leaders*, pp. 93–147; Richmond *Daily Dispatch*, 7 Apr. (second quotation), 5 Sept. 1883, 8 Mar. 1885; George B. Kirsch, *The Creation of American Team Sports: Baseball and Cricket, 1838–1872* (Urbana and Chicago, 1989), p. 209. All three southern players on the 1885 squad—Glenn, Tate, and Nash—were Richmond natives. The player whose father died at Andersonville was Dick Johnston, who joined the team in 1884 (Lee Allen Notebooks and Vertical Files, NCooNa). Richmond contemplated joining the Southern League for the 1886 season but folded before that time (*Richmond Dispatch*, 18 Aug. 1885; Bill O'Neal, *The Southern League: Baseball in Dixie, 1885–1994* [Austin, Tex., 1994]).

23. E. R. Chesterman, "Ball in Other Days: History of the National Game as Played Here in Richmond ... ," *Richmond Dispatch*, 16 Sept. 1894, p. 1: Virginia. Vol. 43, p. 503 (first and second quotations), Vol. 44. p. 212 (third quotation), Vol. 45, p. 277 (fourth quotation), Vol. 43. p. 23, R. G. Dun & Co. Collection. Baker Library, Harvard University Graduate School of Business Administration, Boston, Mass. The members of the board were Valentine H. Hechler, Jr., Felix I. Moses, Otho O. Owens, John L. Schoolcraft, Charles K. Skinker, George A. Smith, Charles E. Straus, Simon Sycle, and Beverley Randolph Wellford, Jr.

24. Richmond *Daily Dispatch*, 2 Aug. 1883 (first quotation); *Sporting Life*. 13 Aug. 1884, p. 6 (second quotation).

25. Richmond *Daily Dispatch*, 21, 24, 27 June 1883; *Richmond Daily Whig*, 21 June 1883; J- Thompson Brown & Co., "Cities of Richmond and Manchester, Va.," 1886 (manuscript map), Vi; Benson, *Ballparks of North America*, pp. 330–31; Chataiene. comp., *Richmond Directory*, 1885, p. 420; James, " 'Batter Up!' Time," p. 6.

26. Richmond *Daily Dispatch,* 25 July 1883, 25 Mar. (quotation), 25 Apr., 15, 24 May, 30 June, 5 July, 3, 31 Aug. 1884, 15 May, 16 June 1885.

27. James, "'Batter Up!' Time," p. 6; *Richmond Daily Whig*, 11 July 1883 (quotation), 21 June, 7 July, 26 Sept. 1884; Richmond *Daily Dispatch*, 20 Apr., 2, 5 July, 25 Sept. 1884, 7 Apr. 1885. The park was typical of its day. See Alexander, *Our Game*, pp. 46–49; Seymour, *Baseball*, 1:193–206; Nemec, *Beer and Whiskey League*, pp. 25–28; and Philip J. Lowry, *Green Cathedrals: The Ultimate Celebration of AU 273 Major League and Negro League Ballparks Past and Present* (Reading, Mass., 1992).

28. *Richmond Daily Whig*, 21 July, 18 Sept. 1883; Richmond *Daily Dispatch*, 9 Sept. 1883, 27 June 1884, 1 Aug. 1885.

29. *Richmond Dispatch*, 18 Sept. 1885; Chesterman, "Ball in Other Days." p. 1; J. Scott Gross, "Wilmington Quicksteps—Glory to Oblivion," *Baseball Research Journal* 15 (1986): 50; Alexander, *Our Game*, p. 45; United States Bureau of the Census, *Historical Statistics of the United States: Colonial Times to 1970*, Bicentennial Edition (2 vols.; Washington, D.C., 1975), 1:168.

30. Richmond *Daily Dispatch*, 21 June (first quotation), 9 Oct. 1883, 18 Mar. 1884; *Richmond Daily Whig*, 7 (second quotation). 11 (third quotation) Aug., 10 Oct. 1883.

31. Richmond *Daily Dispatch*, 14 Sept., 21 Oct. 1883, 6 Jan., 18 Apr. 1884; *Sporting Life*, 7 Sept. 1883, p. 2; ibid., 9 Jan. 1884, p. 2; Albert G. *Spalding*, ed., *Spalding's Official Base Ball Guide and Official League Book for 1884* (Chicago, 1884), pp. 68–69; Reach, ed., *Base Ball Guide for 1884*, pp. 22–23; Joshua B. Orenstein, "The Union Association of 1884: A Glorious Failure," *Baseball Research Journal* 19 (1990): 3–5; Alexander, *Our Game*, p. 38; Seymour, *Baseball*, 1:148–51; Voigt, *American Baseball*, 1:130–36. Chicago, Philadelphia, Baltimore, Washington, St. Louis, New York, Brooklyn, Pittsburgh, Hartford, Milwaukee, and Indianapolis formed the Union League. The other two major leagues were the American Association and the National League. The Eastern League is the ancestor of the International League, current home of the Richmond Braves and the oldest active minor league (*International League of Professional Baseball Clubs, 1983 Record Book* [47th rev. ed.; n.p., 1983], p. 1; Neil J. Sullivan, *The Minors: The Struggle and the Triumph of Baseball's Poor Relation from 1876 to the Present* [New York, 1990], p. 20).

32. Richmond *Daily Dispatch*, 6 Jan., 18 Mar. 1884; Reach, ed., *Base Ball Guide for 1884*, p. 23; Seymour, *Baseball*, 1:151. Robert F. Burk characterizes the formation of leagues and the reserve rule as a "search for order," borrowing Wiebe's famous phrase (Burk, *Never Just a Game*, pp. 82–85 [quotation on p. 82]). The reserve rule lasted until 1975, when a labor arbitration panel struck it down. Its demise led to free agency and higher player salaries (David Quentin Voigt,

American Baseball, vol. 3: *From Postwar Expansion to the Electronic Age* [University Park, Pa., and London, 1983], pp. 161, 211–14).

33. On the American Association, see *Richmond Dispatch*, 5 Aug. 1884; Nemec, *Beer and Whiskey League*; Alexander, *Our Game*, pp. 35–40; Burk, *Never Just a Game*, pp. 69–74; Seymour, *Baseball*, 1:137–47; Voigt, *American Baseball*, 1:122–28; and David Pietrusza, *Major Leagues: The Formation, Sometimes Absorption and Mostly Inevitable Demise of 18 Professional Baseball Organizations, 1871 to Present* (Jefferson, N.C., 1991), pp. 61–79.

34. *Richmond Daily Whig*, 30 Apr. 1883 (first quotation); *Richmond Dispatch*, 30 Sept. 1884 (second quotation). The papers printed only positive assessments of the squad, rather than relaying negative descriptions. For accounts that criticize the Virginias and were not reprinted, see *New York Times*, Sept. 1884; Louisville *Courier-Journal*, 13 Sept., 11 Oct. 1884; and *Washington Post*, 25 Aug. 1885.

35. Gaston. *New South Creed*, p. 219.

36. Richmond *Daily Dispatch*, 2 (quotation). 13 Apr. 1884; *Richmond Daily Whig*. 1, 4, 7, 18 July 1884; Tiemann and Rucker, eds.. *Nineteenth Centiuy Stars*, p. 120; Theodore P. Sullivan file. Lee Allen Notebooks and Vertical Files. NCooNa; Bucek et al., eds.. *Baseball Encyclopedia*, pp. 178, 184, 710, 730, 1645. Sullivan played three games for the Virginias, as shortstop and pitcher. The *Whig* petulantly noted that "neither in the field nor at the bat did he display any particular ability" (*Richmond Daily Whig*, 4 July 1884). Sullivan is said to have coined the word "fan," short for fanatic. He was replaced as manager in St. Louis by Charlie Comiskey. Moses is named as manager in all the official records and accompanied Seddon to Eastern League functions. See Bucek et al., eds., *Baseball Encyclopedia*, pp. 183, 704; Reach, ed., *Base Ball Guide for 1884*, pp. 23, 111; *Richmond Dispatch*, 18 July 1884; Chataigne. comp., *Richmond Directory*, 1882–83, p. 269; and *International League Record Book*, p. 7.

37. Those players added to the team during the 1884 Eastern League season were Myron S. Allen (who played two games as player-manager), John A. Doyle. Edward J. Dugan, William H. Dugan, Richard F. Johnston, Frank S. '"Teriy" Larkin, Marshall J. Quinton, William G. Schenk, W. E. Stratton, Theodore P. Sullivan (who played three games as player-manager), Washington J. Williams, and men named Devine, Hardie, Hetcher, and Shay. Those who joined the club during the stint in the American Association were Wesley Curry, Walter H. Goldsby, John Hanna, Michael R. Mansell, Peter J. Meegan, and Andy Swan. They joined Edward L. Ford, Edward C. Glenn, Paul Latouche, Henry W. Morgan, William M. Nash, James E. Powell, and William B. Smiley, who were holdovers ffom 1883. Those players not from Richmond boarded at the St. James Hotel on 12th Street.

38. Richmond *Daily Dispatch*, 16 Sept. 1883. The Dugans were the first brother pitcher-catcher combination in major league history. After the Washington Nationals released Larkin, he came home drunk and shot his wife in the mouth. Mistakenly thinking he had killed the woman, Larkin cut his throat with a razor. When a policeman arrived on the scene. Larkin fired two shots at the officer and wounded him. While in the hospital recovering from his self-inflicted injury, Larkin thought his wife would die, so he again tried to kill himself by jumping off his bed

and bashing his head against a steam register. Police had to restrain him while doctors strapped him into his hospital bed to prevent other outbursts. "For God's sake," Larkin begged, "hit me in the head and put an end to my suffering." After his release by the Virginias, Larkin was arrested for drunkenness in Brooklyn and eventually killed himself in 1894 (index cards, Swales Baseball Collection, NN; Lee Allen Notebooks and Vertical Files, NCooNa; Wright, *Nineteenth Century Baseball*, pp. 43, 47–48, 53, 58, 64, 119; Bucek et al., eds., *Baseball Encyclopedia*, p. 1253; Bill James, *The Bill James Historical Baseball Abstract* [New York, 1986], p. 37; Nemec, *Beer and Whiskey League*, pp. 47, 52; *Washington Post*, 29 Apr. 1883; *Sporting Life*, 6 Aug. 1883, p. 3; ibid., 22 Oct. 1884, p. 5; Richmond *Daily Dispatch*, 3 June 1884). For a Richmond fan's allegations concerning Larkin's problems with "muddy" water and the player's response, see *Sporting Life*, 11 Feb. 1885, p. 4; and ibid., 18 Feb. 1885, p. 3.

39. Louisville *Courier-Journal*, 13 Sept. (quotation), 11 Oct. 1884; *New York Times*, 9 Aug. 1884; New York *Tribune*, 13 Sept. 1884.

40. *Richmond Daily Whig*, 11 Aug. 1884; *Richmond Dispatch*. 5. 9 Aug., 21 Oct. 1884; *Sporting Life*. 13 Aug. 1884, p. 5; ibid., 20 Aug. 1884, p. 6; Bucek et al., eds., *Baseball Encyclopedia*, pp. 183–84: Albert G. Spalding, ed., *Spalding's Official Base Ball Guide for 1885* (Chicago, 1885), pp. 31. 36–54 (quotation on p. 36). For the record, the Virginias surrendered seven runs per game, committed 6.7 errors per game, and batted 220 as a team. Their hurlers allowed more runs per contest than any other staff. In Seddon's and Moses's defense, Richmond had less capital stock with which to work than did the other teams in the American Association (Nemec, *Beer and Whiskey League*, pp. 5, 72: A. J. Reach, ed., *Reach's Official American Base Ball Guide for 1885* [Philadelphia, 1885], pp. 11. 73–74).

41. "Genealogy: The Bruce Family," *Virginia Magazine of History and Biography* 11 (1903–4): 443; *Richmond Dispatch*, 8 Mar. 1885; *Sporting Life*. 22 Oct. 1884, p. 5 (quotations). The old Eastern League became the New York State League (*International League Record Book*, p. 1).

42. *Sporting Life*, 31 Dec. 1884, p. 4; ibid., 14 Jan. 1885, p. 4; Gross, "Wilmington Quicksteps," pp. 49–51. After clinching the Eastern League crown, the Quicksteps jumped to the Union Association and posted a 2–16 record under Simmons's guidance. The 111 percentage was the worst ever in major league baseball (Bucek et al., eds., *Baseball Encyclopedia*, p. 186). Simmons kept Nash, Glenn, Johnston, and "Steady" Pete Meegan, but the last refused to sign with the team for $1,000 (*Sporting Life*, 20 May 1885, p. 6). The team comprised Nash, Tate, George W. Latham, Samuel J. Kimber, John Corcoran, William Greenwood, William Higgins, Charles Householder, Richard F. Johnston, and Harry "Shadow" Pyle.

43. *Sporting Life*, 24 June 1885, p. 5; ibid., 22 July 1885, p. 6 (quotation); ibid., 8 Sept. 1885, p. 6; *Richmond Dispatch*, 24 Mar., 6 Apr., 21 July 1885; *Richmond Daily Whig*, 10 Apr. 1885; Nemec, *Beer and Whiskey League*, pp. 31–32. 40–41, 50.

44. Lee Allen Notebooks and Vertical Files, NCooNa; Swales Baseball Collection, NN; *Richmond Daily Whig*, 17 June 1885; *Richmond Dispatch*, 19 Sept. 1885; *Sporting Life*, 19 Aug. 1885, p. 2.

45. *Richmond Dispatch*, 4–8 Apr., 12,13 (quotations) June 1885; *Richmond Daily Whig*, 12, 13 June 1885; Seymour, *Baseball*, 1:185–86; Voigt, *American Baseball*, 1:109. Players of the opposing

team commonly rode from their hotel to the ballpark in wagons, as there were no dressing facilities for visiting clubs at the park. During such trips, fans of the home team often hurled taunts or even objects such as rotten vegetables at the visitors (Alexander, *Our Game*, p. 46; Seymour, *Baseball*, 1:204–6).

46. *Richmond Dispatch*, 16 Sept. 1885; *Sporting Life*, 4 Nov. 1885, p. 4. The Virginias' 909 fielding average and .353 batting average placed them second in the league. Richmond could make a claim to being the best fielding team, because the first-place club played only eighteen games in the league.

47. *Richmond Dispatch*, 2 July, 23, 27 Mar. 1884, 24, 27 Mar. 1885; *Richmond Daily Whig*, 5 Apr. 1884 (quotation); Barth, *City People*, pp. 148–91; Lamoreaux, "Baseball in the Late Nineteenth Century," pp. 597–602; S. W. Pope, *Patriotic Games: Sporting Traditions in the American Imagination, 1876–1926* (New York, 1997); Allen Guttman, *From Ritual to Record: The Nature of Modern Sports* (New York, 1980).

48. *Sporting Life*, 29 July 1885, p. 2; *Richmond Dispatch*, 31 May, 1, 5, 22 July 1885; *Richmond Daily Whig*, 1 July 1885 (quotation); Gaston, *New South Creed*, pp. 167–77. On the ways the middle class was able to inculcate its values, see Olivier Zunz, *Making America Corporate, 1870–1920* (Chicago and London, 1990).

49. Richmond *Daily Dispatch*, 21 May 1884 (quotations); Steven M. Gelber, "Working at Playing: The Culture of the Workplace and the Rise of Baseball," *Journal of Social History* 16 (1983): 3–20; Gelber, "Business and Amateur Baseball," pp. 5–27; Kimmel, "Baseball and the Reconstitution of American Masculinity," pp. 281–97. The *Dispatch* increased its coverage of baseball in part because of a letter to the editor (Richmond *Daily Dispatch*, 26 May 1883). For a progression of the coverage of the games, see *Richmond Daily Wiig*, 4, 23 May, 24 July 1883. For another incident of the scorer being sensitive to criticism, see ibid., 3 July 1885.

50. Richmond *Daily Dispatch*, 5 (first, second, and third quotations; emphasis in the original), 6, 24 (fourth quotation) June 1883. The team picture is located in the Photograph Collection, NCooNa. and is incorrectly dated 1883.

51. Guttman, *From Ritual to Record*; Foster, *Ghosts of the Confederacy*, pp. 79–80; Richmond *Daily Dispatch*, 2 Aug. 1883 (first and third quotations); *Richmond Daily Whig*, 7 July 1885 (second quotation). Michael S. Kimmel argues that baseball supporters asserted the game was democratic when it really was not (Kimmel, "Baseball and the Reconstitution of American Masculinity," p. 293). For an explanation of the appeal of rural recreation and one that could help explain baseball's allure, see Ted Ownby, *Subduing Satan: Religion, Recreation, and Manhood in the Rural South, 1865–1920* (Chapel Hill, 1990).

52. Richmond *Daily Dispatch*, 10 July 1883 (first quotation); *Richmond Daily Whig*, 2 Apr. 1884 (second quotation); *Sporting Life*, 17 Sept. 1884, p. 5 (third quotation). Few of Boschen's games had attendance figures (see, for example, Richmond *Daily Dispatch*, 14, 15 Apr. 1883). Ninety-four of the Virginias' 161 home games had attendance figures; a total of 95,600 spectators witnessed those contests.

53. *Richmond Daily Whig,* 3 Apr. 1884 (quotation); Richmond *Daily Dispatch,* 2, 24 Aug. 1883. The term "muffers" refers to players who made fielding errors, while "kickers" denotes players who argued with the umpire's decisions. Incidents of gambling can be found in Richmond *Daily Dispatch,* 2 Aug. 1883, 18 June 1885; and *Richmond Daily Whig,* 2 June, 2 Aug. 1883, 3 Apr., 26 May, 16 June 1884. The entire Virginias team signed an affidavit that the players did not throw the game. For more on the intersection of morality and sport, see William J. Baker, "Disputed Diamonds: YMCA Debate over Baseball," *Journal of Sport History* 19 (1992): 257–62.

54. "BaseBall!" broadside, Apr. [1884], Valentine Museum, Richmond, Va., reproduced in Ben W. Blake, "Uncovering a Diamond: A Major League Club on Park Avenue," *Richmond Times-Dispatch,* 9 Aug. 1981, p. B-2; *Richmond Daily Dispatch,* 25 July 1883 (quotation), 25 Sept. 1884.

55. *Sporting Life,* 20 Aug. 1884, p. 3 (first quotation); Richmond *Daily Dispatch,* 30 May 1884 (second quotation), 1 May 1885; *Richmond Daily Whig,* 25 June 1885.

56. Patricia C. Click, *The Spirit of the Times: Amusements in Nineteenth-Century Baltimore, Norfolk, and Richmond* (Charlottesville, 1989), pp. 95–96; Seymour, *Baseball,* 1:76; Richmond *Daily Dispatch,* May 1884 (quotation).

57. Wilmington, Del., *Sunday Critic,* n.d., quoted in Richmond *Daily Dispatch,* 30 May 1884. John Kasson describes the changing codes of conduct (John Kasson, *Rudeness & Civility: Manners in Nineteenth Century Urban America* [New York, 1990], pp. 239–51).

58. *Richmond Dispatch,* 9 Oct. 1884, 7 Apr. 1885: *Richmond Daily Whig,* 7 July, 18 Sep. 1885. For examples of Richmond crowds cheering the good play of the other team see Richmond *Daily Dispatch,* 25 May, 17 June 1884.

59. *Richmond Dispatch,* 5 July 1885; Kasson, *Amusing the Million.*

60. Barth, City People, p. 173 (first wuotation); Alexander, *Our Game.* p. 47; Richmond *Daily Dispatch,* 20 Apr. 1884 (second and third quotation).

61. Richmond *Daily Dispatch,* 17 Apr., 9, 10 July, 31 Aug., 10, 14 (first and second quotations) Oct. 1884, 9 July, 13 Aug. 1885 (third quotation); *Richmond Daily Whig,* 9 July 1884. Richmond fans were not alone in their rowdy behavior. During a game with the Nationals in Washington, a spectator assaulted the umpire. The Virginias "went to the rescue of the umpire and released him from his assailant" (*Washington Post,* 10 May 1885).

62. Richmond *Daily Dispatch,* 20 Apr. (first and second quotations), 1 May 1884 (third and fourth quotations); Jane Dailey, "Deference and Violence in the Postbellum Urban South: Manners and Massacres in Danville, Virginia," *JSH* 53 (1997): 555–57; Chesson, *Richmond after the War,* pp. 101–2, 160–61, 191–96; C. Vann Woodward, *The Strange Career of Jim Crow* (3d rev. ed.; New York, 1974), pp. 31–65; Howard N. Rabinowitz, *Race Relations in the Urban South, 1865–1890* (New York, 1978), p. 189; Charles E. Wynes, *Race Relations in Virginia, 1870–1902* (Charlottesville, 1961), pp. 79–88.

63. Richmond *Daily Dispatch,* 15 July 1880, 22 May 1881; *Sporting Life,* 24 Sept. 1884, p. 3 (quotations).

64. *Richmond Dispatch*, 2 Sept. 1884; David W. Zang, *Fleet Walker's Divided Heart: The Life of Baseball's First Black Major Leaguer* (Lincoln, Nebr., and London, 1995), p. 42; Robert Peterson. *Only the Ball Was White: A History of Legendary Black Players and All-Black Professional Teams* (New York, 1970), pp. 23–24 (first, second, and third quotations); Seymour, *Baseball*, 1:334; Jerry Malloy, comp., *Sol White's History of Colored Baseball, with Other Documents on the Early Black Game, 1886–1936* (Lincoln, Nebr., and London, 1995), p. 136 (fourth quotation). The local papers made no mention of the Walker incident. The Richmond correspondent of *Sporting Life* recognized none of the four names signed to the letter.

65. *Sporting Life*, 3 June 1885, p. 3 (quotations). Before 24 July, the team averaged 1,345 spectators at home games. After that date, it averaged 670. Total attendance for the year was more than 49,000.

66. *Sporting Life*, 12 Aug. 1885, p. 1; *Richmond Dispatch*, 22 Aug. 1885; David K. Walthall to Guy Reeves London, 24 Aug. 1885 (quotation), London Family Papers, 1864–94, Virginia Historical Society, Richmond.

67. *Richmond Dispatch*, 1 Sept. 1885.

68. Ibid., 18, 19, 20 (quotation) Sept. 1885; *Richmond Daily Whig*, 18 Sept. 1885; *Sporting Life*, 23 Sept. 1885, p. 1.

69. Nemec, *Beer and Whiskey League*, p. 5; Albert G. Spalding, ed., *Spalding's Official Base-Ball Guide and Official League Book for 1886* (Chicago, 1886), p. 67; *Richmond Dispatch*, 22 Aug. 1885 (quotations).

70. *Richmond Dispatch*, 24, 25 Sept. 1885; *Sporting Life*, 30 Sept. 1885, p. 1 (quotation). Simmons denied the charge and pledged to fight it in court, but the case's final disposition is unknown. He stayed in baseball. In 1891 he managed the Syracuse Stars, a team whose catcher was Moses Fleetwood Walker (Zang, *Fleet Walker's Divided Heart*, p. 76). Richmond fielded several amateur teams in the late nineteenth century before a professional team joined the Virginia State League in 1894 (Calisch, "Birth of Baseball," pp. 2–3).

71. *SHSP* 17 (1889): 187–335; Foster, *Ghosts of the Confederacy*, pp. 100–103; Chesson, *Richmond after the War*, pp. 205–6.

72. *SHSP* 17 (1889): 275–78, 285; Watson, "'Batter Up!' Time," p. 6; J. Thompson Brown & Co., "Cities of Richmond and Manchester, Va." 1886 (manuscript map), Vi.

10

Woman Suffrage in Virginia

THE EQUAL SUFFRAGE LEAGUE AND PRESSURE-GROUP POLITICS, 1909–1920

By Sara Hunter Graham

I n 1920 Tennessee became the thirty-sixth state to ratify the Nineteenth Amendment, and woman suffrage became the law of the land. Conspicuously absent from the list of the thirty-six ratifiers were nine southern states that refused to grant the vote to women. Virginia was one of the nine. Because the Equal Suffrage League of Virginia (ESL) was one of the most vital suffrage organizations to emerge in the South, a study of its failure to win the vote for women in the Old Dominion offers insights into several important questions. What was the relationship between national reform movements and regional political dynamics? Was the strategy formulated by the national suffrage association and adopted by the ESL suffragists appropriate for the South's one-party political system? How did the Virginia suffragists fare when they attempted to follow this strategy? Most important, why did pressure politics, pioneered by the National American Woman Suffrage Association (NAWSA) and highly successful in many states, result in frustration and defeat in Virginia and much of the South? Using the Equal Suffrage League of Virginia as a test case, this essay will examine the strengths and weaknesses of pressure-group tactics and chart the course of a democratic movement in a region dominated by antidemocratic sentiments. Although the experience of the Virginia suffragists was in

Sara Hunter Graham, "Woman Suffrage in Virginia: The Equal Suffrage League and Pressure-Group Politics, 1909-1920," *The Virginia Magazine of History and Biography, vol. 101, no. 2*, pp. 227-250. Copyright © 1993 by Virginia Historical Society. Reprinted with permission. Provided by ProQuest LLC. All rights reserved.

many ways unique, their eleven-year crusade and subsequent defeat may suggest common problems shared by women throughout the South in their battle for the vote.

To understand the difficult path that the Virginia suffrage movement traveled, a brief overview of the national votes-for-women campaign is necessary. During the years 1896–1910, no state legislature passed suffrage resolutions, a circumstance that led historians to label that period "the doldrums."[1] In fact, nothing could be further from the truth. Beginning in the mid-1890s, the National American Woman Suffrage Association worked tirelessly to achieve a respectable public image through a variety of methods. Parlor meetings brought to the cause society women, a constituency that would lend legitimacy and finance the burgeoning movement. College women were recruited by the College Equal Suffrage League, a NAWSA affiliate. These young activists helped to conduct the mass enrollment drives that boosted NAWSA's membership totals over the one hundred thousand mark by 1912. Progressivism also played an important role in the emergence of what might be called "the new suffragism" of the twentieth century. Suffragists began to play down their radical past by gradually eliminating all references to such controversial issues as divorce reform and racial equality. They also endorsed a number of progressive causes such as the abolition of child labor, pure food and drug legislation, and other municipal housekeeping reforms.

Respectability produced results. By 1916, NAWSA commanded a professional congressional lobby, a publicity bureau the equal of those serving the national political parties, and a million-dollar campaign fund with which to press their case in Congress. The movement was also a force to be reckoned with in many states and localities, where suffragists had spent a decade or more educating the public and enrolling support for their cause. By the second decade of the twentieth century, NAWSA was widely recognized as one of the most powerful single-issue pressure groups of the time. But even at the peak of their power, suffrage leaders such as NAWSA President Carrie Chapman Catt were well aware of a critical weakness within the movement. This weakness was the South.[2] During the first years of the new century, a time when many state suffrage societies began the crucial tasks of building constituencies and publicizing their cause, the majority of southern states had weak or nonexistent suffrage organizations. Not until the second decade of the twentieth century did stable suffrage societies appear in the South, fully ten years after such associations emerged elsewhere.[3]

Virginia is a case in point. The woman suffrage movement came to the commonwealth when a small group of Richmond activists met in 1909 to found the Equal Suffrage League of Virginia.[4] Their first meeting took place in a rented parlor; in the twilight, some twenty women discussed the cause before a flickering fire, a scene that one member later described as "a lovingly touched and shaded picture of the beginnings of things."[5] Respectability was the league's unstated byword, underscored by the group's choice of president. Lila Meade Valentine was one of the Virginia elite both by birth and by marriage. Described by her husband as "a flower gently moving in the wind" and as a "piece of Dresden China," she embodied the attributes of the southern lady.[6] Beneath her genteel exterior, however, Valentine possessed a natural flair for organization and a quiet strength of purpose that won her a loyal following.

Valentine was not the only Virginia suffragist with impeccable social credentials. Among the many women who joined the ESL were writers Ellen Glasgow and Mary Johnston, artists Adèle Clark and Nora Houston, and Dr. Kate Waller Barrett, one of Virginia's first woman physicians and president of the National Florence Crittenton Mission, as well as a number of teachers, club women, journalists, and businesswomen. The league also counted as members the great-great-granddaughters of Thomas Jefferson and George Mason.[7] Thanks in part to the social prominence of these early Virginia suffragists, the ESL enrolled almost 120 members in the first year of its existence. Of that number, however, the vast majority lived in Richmond, leaving most of the state without suffrage societies.[8] Therefore, recruitment and organizing became the primary focus of the ESL in its early years.

Recruitment of new members proved to be one of the most difficult tasks that the Virginia activists faced. In 1910, when ESL Secretary Alice Tyler wrote to prominent women across the state to ascertain suffrage sentiment, the replies she elicited were often discouraging. Some responded that their efforts to recruit for suffrage had aroused no interest. Others met with parental opposition; one activist recruited several young women, only to find that their fathers refused to permit them to attend a single suffrage meeting. Even Tyler's effort to

Virginia Historical Society

FIGURE 10-1   As late as 1911, Mary Johnston worried that "the League *as a body* is pretty well confined to four walls." By 1915, the year this picture was taken on Capitol Square in Richmond, however, ESL members had taken their message to schools, fairs, union meetings, and city streets.

enlist the prosufifrage principal of Stuart Hall, a girl's school in Staunton, resulted in a bleak response. "We women of Virginia are so absolutely ignorant of the question, and I should say indifferent," wrote Maria Pendleton Duval, "that I believe we would not meet with success until they are enlightened." Moreover, Duval proved to be unable to suggest a single person in her area who might initiate a suffrage club, because she had "never heard any one express an opinion on the subject."[9]

The task of awakening suffrage spirit was therefore a daunting one. Outside the South, the national organization had worked with renewed vigor for more than a decade to enlist members, acquire adequate financial backing, and build a network of local and state societies to lobby for the vote. By 1910, as these components fell into place, NAWSA moved into the realm of "practical politics"—exerting pressure on politicians, organizing by electoral district, and staging massive publicity campaigns. In Virginia, however, Valentine and her aides faced a wall of public apathy and possessed none of the financial or organizational tools with which to bring it down. Only through persuasion and publicity—what suffragists called "education"— would suffrage become a viable political issue, but both took years to accomplish. In a sense, Old Dominion suffragists faced a twofold challenge: they had to initiate an education campaign to enlighten the public, while simultaneously belonging to a national organization that was completing the education stage and moving on to pressure-group politics.[10] From its very origins, then, the ESL was out of step with the mainstream of the suffrage movement and as a result could count on little help from its parent organization.

Undaunted, Virginia suffragists began their campaign to arouse public interest in their cause. The Richmond league served as the heart of the state movement for the first two years of the ESL's existence, and the group's Thursday afternoon meetings were well attended. But as one Richmond member reported in 1911, "the League *as a body* is pretty well confined to four walls."[11] Before the year's end, however, activists had established a state headquarters and had stepped up their efforts to spread the suffrage gospel throughout the commonwealth. Suffragist Mary Johnston visited women's colleges, speaking to faculty and students on the virtues of woman suffrage and enrolling converts to the cause. League President Lila Meade Valentine met with a group of prominent Richmond businessmen and persuaded them to found the Men's Equal Suffrage League of Virginia.[12] Suffragists also took their message to schools, fairs, union meetings, and city streets by distributing literature and taking turns at impromptu speech making. Soon the Richmond league membership had climbed to 290, and four newly established branches boasted more than a hundred recruits.[13]

Public apathy, however, was quickly replaced by a far more troublesome demon: active opposition. By 1912, the Virginia Association Opposed to Woman Suffrage (VAOWS) had formed to "rouse the people of Virginia … to keep the burden of government from being forced on an unwilling majority."[14] In a series of pamphlets and leaflets, VAOWS attacked the votes-for-women campaign with a variety of arguments. Some VAOWS propaganda came from antisufifrage organizations as far away as New York and expressed themes used by antisuffrage groups nationwide. More common, however, were pamphlets drafted by the Virginia antis with arguments tailored for southern audiences.

One such pamphlet, entitled "Why Women Should Oppose Equal Suffrage," maintained that biological and functional differences between the sexes prevented women from engaging in "political strife with calm minds."[15] In another, women were held to be easily excitable and impractical, not "disposed to bother their heads with the actual facts of politics," and thus unsuited for the franchise. The author asserted that the women engaged in the suffrage movement "are prepared to fall back on the conclusive feminine argument 'because'! No other argument, however profound, is quite so convincing or fascinating as that word 'because', accompanied by some pouting or alluring scarlet lips—especially if there be dimples by way of re-enforcement."[16] By evoking the stereotype of the southern belle, a willful, illogical creature bent on getting her own way with a flutter of eyelashes and a rustle of crinolines, the VAOWS pamphleteers skillfully called forth an image of womanhood that was uniquely apolitical—and distinctly southern.

Antisuffrage propaganda contained more than misogynist appeals. VAOWS also used a combination of political and racist arguments to discredit the suffrage campaign. One of the antis' most effective tactics concerned the threat of federal interference in state franchise restrictions. The majority of Virginia's blacks, poor whites, and Republicans had been disfranchised in 1902, when a state convention had imposed residency, literacy, and poll tax requirements on would-be voters.[17] Democratic leaders, however, continued to fear federal scrutiny, which in turn might lead to judicial review of Virginia's restrictions on the franchise. To play upon white fears of black political domination should these voting requirements be removed, the antisuffragists repeatedly incorporated states' rights rhetoric into their literature. One pamphlet distributed widely in Virginia warned that the passage of the federal woman suffrage amendment would "trample and destroy the soul and purpose of State rights."[18] Pressing home the danger of federal intervention, antis labeled the suffrage amendment a "force bill" and drew parallels between it and the Fifteenth Amendment.[19]

Another political argument used by Virginia antisuffragists centered on the fate of the Democratic party in the South and in the nation. After asserting that the suffrage amendment "invites revival of the fifteenth amendment," the author of one pamphlet suggested a consequence equally unsettling to Virginia Democrats. If woman suffrage were to be enacted by constitutional amendment, the pamphleteer warned, Republicans could demand that the southern states offer full suffrage to blacks of both sexes or face a reduction in congressional representation as mandated by the Fourteenth Amendment. According to the pamphleteer's calculations, the latter option would cost the state six out of ten of its representatives and reduce Virginia's vote in the electoral college by half.[20]

On the other hand, enfranchising both male and female blacks seemed to be an even worse option for most white Virginians. One of VAOWS's most effective pieces of propaganda specifically addressed the question of how woman suffrage would affect black voting and white supremacy at the county level. A flier entitled "Virginia Warns Her People Against

Votes for Women a Success

The Map·Proves It

Alaska 1913

WHITE STATES: Full Suffrage   SHADED STATES: Taxation, Bond or School Suffrage
DOTTED STATE: Presidential, Partial County and State, Municipal Suffrage   BLACK STATES: No Suffrage

Suffrage Granted

1869—WYOMING

1893—COLORADO
    Bounds Wyoming on South

1896—UTAH
    Bounds Wyoming and Colorado

1896—IDAHO
    Bounds Wyoming and Utah

1910—WASHINGTON
    Bounds Idaho on West

1911—CALIFORNIA

1912—OREGON
    Bounds California on North

1912—ARIZONA
    Bounds California on East

1912—KANSAS
    Bounds Colorado on East

1913—ILLINOIS
    Starts a New Cycle

1913—ALASKA

Would any of these States have adopted EQUAL SUFFRAGE if it had been a failure just across the Border?

NATIONAL WOMAN SUFFRAGE PUBLISHING COMPANY, INC.
PUBLISHERS FOR THE
NATIONAL AMERICAN WOMAN SUFFRAGE ASSOCIATION
505 Fifth Avenue   PUBLISHED FEBRUARY, 1914   New York City

Broadside Collection, Virginia Historical Society

FIGURE 10-2 This broadside, printed in New York by the National American Woman Suffrage Association, circulated in Virginia in 1914.

Woman Suffrage" charged that if black women were added to the number of black male voters, "Twenty-nine Counties Would Go Under Negro Rule."[21] Antisuflfrage propagandists dwelled on this "negro rule" theory and called up a variety of statistics to demonstrate the fragility of white supremacy in Virginia and other southern states. If black women became voters, one antisuffragist fretted, "it would be ten times as difficult to deal with colored women and keep them from the polls as it ever was with colored men. The woman of the African race has her share of pertinacity too and would be exempt from fear of physical consequences."[22] If woman suffrage came to Virginia by federal amendment, VAOWS activists asserted, the work of the 1901-2 disfranchising convention would be undone, the door opened to federal intervention, and white supremacy placed in jeopardy. And if threats of racial disharmony and federal action were not enough to frighten Virginians, VAOWS pamphleteers also linked class conflict to woman suffrage. One VAOWS flier urged citizens of the commonwealth to "work with all your might against Socialism's vanguard, woman suffrage."[23]

Class, racial, and sexual stereotypes intertwined to form Virginia antisuffragism. These fears reflected sentiments shared by many southerners and, more damaging to the suffragists, institutionalized in the Virginia political settlement of 1902. Leaders of VAOWS therefore remained wedded to these arguments throughout the entire suffrage campaign, their propaganda deviating only in degree of virulence as the years passed. On the other hand, Virginia suffragists based their claim for the vote on a series of changing, and occasionally contradictory, themes. In the first years of its existence, the ESL often used conservative appeals based on woman's traditional role as wife and mother. "The child is the heart of the equal suffrage movement," began one of Lila Meade Valentine's most successful recruitment speeches, which ended with a plea for the vote for the sake of home and family.[24] Sometimes ESL propaganda was difficult to distinguish at first glance from antisuffrage material. One prosuflfrage flier baldly stated that "the place of the woman is in the HOME," before going on to argue that the vote was necessary because many family responsibilities lay outside the home. "Women are, by nature and training, housekeepers," the flier continued. "Let them have a hand in the city's housekeeping, even if they introduce an occasional house-cleaning."[25]

By using the "municipal housekeeping" argument, Virginia suffragists chose to uphold conventional gender stereotypes rather than to ground their reform on the basis of sexual equality. In part, Valentine and her lieutenants doubtless chose this strategy to avoid challenging the status quo and provoking more opposition. A second motive for the group's initial conservatism, however, is less obvious but no less important. As a fledgling movement, the ESL had to educate not only the people of Virginia but its own members as well. As feminists learned in the 1960s, self-education is a necessary first step to the formation of a movement psychology. During the early years of their campaign, Old Dominion suffragists underwent a gradual shift from acceptance of traditional gender definitions toward a growing perception of the need for female equality.[26] Moreover, as the group's awareness of women's legal, economic, and social disabilities grew, the scope of its activities and interests widened to include a truly progressive agenda with strong feminist components.

One source of enlightenment for many suffragists was the weekly ESL meetings that featured speakers on such diverse topics as labor conditions for women and children, public health, and city planning, as well as woman suffrage.[27] By 1913, the league's horizons had expanded far beyond the woman's sphere of old. At their state convention that year, suffragists passed a slate of feminist resolutions that endorsed equal pay for equal work, a single moral standard, university education for the state's women, and equal guardianship of children. Progressive reforms such as the eight-hour day, abolition of child labor, public health funding, prohibition, and compulsory education were listed along with the feminist resolutions in the group's platform.[28] The ESL did not, however, entirely abandon its conservative appeal based on traditional female roles: as late as 1917, for example, Virginia suffragists met to hear a speaker address the topic, "How to Overcome Catering Difficulties at the Breakfast Table."[29] For the most part, however, the ESL increasingly supported a serious reform agenda to promote both women's status in particular and the public welfare in general.

As for antisuffrage "negro rule" and states' rights propaganda, Virginia suffragists at first elected to ignore their opponents' arguments. "If it wasn't the negro woman (Poor soul!) it would be something else," Mary Johnston noted to Lila Meade Valentine in 1913. Johnston speculated that voting restrictions would doubtless be imposed on black women if the federal woman suffrage amendment was ratified, but she urged that the ESL continue to demand universal female suffrage. "I think that as women we should be most prayerfully carefull," she wrote, "lest, in the future, women—whether coloured women or white women who are merely poor—should be able to say that we had betrayed their interests and excluded them from freedom."[30] Although Valentine and the other ESL suffragists may or may not have agreed with her, they knew full well that endorsing universal suffrage would not be easy. Even winning suffrage might be accompanied by the extension of traditional electoral restrictions. Warning the group that victory depended on overcoming "the difficulty of the negro question," one well-wisher speculated that "people are going to hang on to old ways of thinking and feeling longer in that subject than most others."[31]

The "old ways of thinking" would indeed be a stubborn foe, especially in state political circles. Despite steady gains in membership and increased efforts at public awareness, the ESL had little effect on Virginia politicians as the years passed.[32] In both 1914 and 1916, ESL activists watched state woman suffrage resolutions go down in resounding defeat.[33] One of the many causes of the twin losses was a matter of timing. All reform movements, whether social or political, have their own unique stages of development. As has been seen, the Virginia suffragists lagged far behind the national movement from the very beginning of their campaign. In terms of practical politics, this backwardness had serious consequences.

In 1910 Carrie Chapman Catt had created an innovative plan for political organization at the state, county, and city levels based loosely on the structure of New York's infamous political machine, Tammany Hall. NAWSA urged its affiliates to adopt the scheme, and by 1916, the year in which the ESL leadership began to consider such tactics, virtually all suffrage associations outside the South as well as a few within the region had adopted the

FIGURE 10-2   Carrie Chapman Catt, president of the National American Woman Suffrage Association, sat for this portrait by Mary Foote in 1927, after the successful conclusion of the national votes-for-women campaign.

new organizational plan. Catt recognized that merely lobbying politicians for the vote was ineffective without what she called "home pressure"—pressure supplied by constituents in politicians' home districts. When implemented, Catt's plan paid high dividends. With house-to-house enrollment drives, petition and letter-writing campaigns, and personal delegations from their home districts to provide tangible evidence of suffrage support, lobbyists steadily converted congressmen and state legislators to the cause in the second decade of the century.[34]

After the defeat of woman suffrage at the hands of the Virginia legislature in 1916, Lila Meade Valentine at last called for a full-scale remodeling of the Equal Suffrage League based on NAWSA guidelines. "The simple fact is that we have got to begin at the very beginning," Valentine admitted in a letter to Catt, because "nine out of ten audiences in Virginia have to be converted to woman suffrage itself, and would positively refuse a federal amendment."[35] As a first step, ESL members voted to drop their campaign for a state amendment in favor of the federal suffrage amendment because the process to amend the Virginia constitution was an extremely difficult one. A proposed state amendment had to be approved by two consecutive legislatures and a public referendum before becoming law. This requirement meant that in order to win the vote by state amendment, suffragists not only had to obtain both public and legislative approval, but also had to sustain that support over a period of years. In practical terms, such a process made it virtually impossible to pass a state suffrage amendment, regardless of what the ESL did or did not do. Consequently, after 1916 Virginia suffragists worked for the passage of the federal woman suffrage amendment, a move that placed them in compliance with NAWSA strategy but at odds with the states' rights advocates who formed the backbone of the state Democratic party.

Valentine and the ESL activists also adopted Catt's organizational plan, which divided the state into congressional, county, and city districts, with chairmen to steer the campaign at each level.[36] Even though this innovation at last placed the ESL in step with NAWSA policy, the Virginia suffragists still faced serious obstacles in their attempts to implement the plan. A precondition of Catt's political organization was a core of constituents, educated to the virtues of the issue and eager to support it. Because the ESL had only embarked on the educational stage about the time that the majority of suffrage societies had begun to move into the

Foster Studio Collection, Virginia Historical Society

FIGURE 10-3   In 1916 Lila Meade Valetine, shown here with her husband, Benjamin Batchelder Valentine, called for a full-scale remodeling of the Equal Suffrage League based on NAWSA guidelines. "The simple fact is that we have got to begin at the very beginning," she told Carrie Chapman Catt.

second or more political stage of the movement, the group's education program was far from complete in the Old Dominion. All too often Virginia suffragists found little understanding and less support for their cause at the county and local levels. "Women must be organized into an effective unit, eager for the franchise, before legislation can be seriously attempted," one prosuffrage editor cautioned a prominent suffragist. His assessment of the state of the Old Dominion's suffrage crusade in 1916 was pessimistic: "Virginia women in the mass not only are not anxious for the vote, but they have very little conception of the whole movement."[37] Without proper education and publicity campaigns and a nucleus of support at the local, county, and district levels, the implementation of Catt's plan of political organization was practically impossible.

Consequently, the ESL attempted to follow NAWSA's guidelines regarding political organization while simultaneously continuing their program of suffrage education.[38] As a result of intensive effort, membership totals increased from 9,662 in 1916 to almost 16,000 by the next year.[39] Other signs were not so optimistic. Although the league continued to send more than six thousand press releases per year to state newspapers, the effect, as one discouraged suffragist put it, was "very like shooting an arrow in the air, it falls to earth we know not where."[40] Without doubt, some of the prosuffrage news items made their way into print, but many of the state's most prestigious papers, including the *Richmond Times-Dispatch,* remained obstinately opposed to woman suffrage. Politicians as well were often impervious to suffrage activities. When ESL Congressional Committee Chairman Elizabeth Lewis mailed suffrage questionnaires to all Democratic candidates in 1916, only two bothered to respond. In part, the politicians' apathy stemmed from the failure of the ESL to convert the public and to generate home pressure. Lewis succeeded in appointing chairmen for nine of the state's ten congressional districts, but she found few volunteers at the county or local levels willing to assume positions of authority. Consequently, some counties remained unorganized, and others had only a handful of individuals who would work for woman suffrage.[41]

Even if the problems of education and organization had disappeared, however, institutional and political obstacles remained to block the suffragists' path to victory. The very nature of Virginia politics conspired against the suffragists. NAWSA strategy was based on the premise of pressure-group politics, a political art form that the national suffrage association had helped to pioneer. According to NAWSA's plan, growing numbers of recruits generated by Catt's reorganization would bring political pressure to bear on legislators and congressmen. By creating a bandwagon effect, suffragists at state and local levels would promote the image (if not the reality) of mass support for prosuffrage candidates. Pressure politics, however, cannot work where reformers find neither allies of conviction nor of convenience within the established political system. Such was the case in Virginia.

In the Old Dominion, the political settlement enacted by the 1901–2 constitutional convention nearly eliminated a viable two-party system. With the majority of blacks, poor whites, and Republicans robbed of the franchise, and with only about 30 percent of the adult male population registered to vote, the Democratic machine maintained an iron grip on Virginia politics from statehouse to courthouse. Moreover, as historian Raymond H. Pulley has noted, "the restrictions imposed upon Virginia politics during the first years of the twentieth century made insurgency or political nonconformity virtually impossible."[42] Neither could the ESL expect to exploit factional divisions within the Democratic party itself. In some one-party states, suffragists were able to ally themselves with progressive factions within the Democratic party to the benefit of their cause.[43] Virginia Democrats, however, had almost eliminated factional strife by adopting a policy of flexible response to issues that attracted widespread public support.[44] Potentially divisive issues such as prohibition, corporate regulation, and child labor had been endorsed by the Democracy during the years 1902–9, leaving no vital progressive faction within the legislature with which the suffragists could associate themselves. Without either an opposition party or a powerful party faction to support their cause, and faced with a public mandate for suffrage restriction on the basis of class, race, and gender, the ESL could find no political division to exploit with pressure politics.

Thus, when the federal suffrage amendment passed the United States Senate in June 1919, Virginia suffragists faced the prospect of waging a ratification campaign without public approval or political support in the state legislature. Lila Meade Valentine had no false hopes. Despite the dismal prospects for success, she insisted in a letter to Carrie Chapman Catt that the ESL would continue to canvass house by house and to work for victory: "We are proceeding on the assumption that in the suffrage movement even the improbable can be attained."[45] But could the improbable in fact become reality? With the ratification campaign, the national suffrage movement entered a third and final stage, built on decades of education, organization, and publicity. In order to assure ratification of the federal amendment, state suffrage leagues needed an educated public ready to supply home pressure, monetary reserves to finance the campaign, the support of leading newspapers, an experienced and influential lobby to pressure legislators, and powerful prosuffrage politicians to lead the fight in both houses of the legislature. The Equal Suffrage League of Virginia had none of these forces at its command.

After ten years of recruiting, ESL membership stood at roughly thirty thousand. Of that number, according to one authority, the percentage who were enfranchised men and who thus could actually vote for suffrage remained very small.[46] Thus, home pressure was virtually impossible to bring to bear on the General Assembly. Money with which to finance the Virginia ratification effort was also in short supply. The NAWSA executive council estimated that ratification campaigns waged in certain difficult states, including nearly all of the South, would require a minimum of forty thousand dollars per state. Although there are no existing records of a separate ESL ratification campaign fund, the organization's operating budget during the period 1916–19 hovered between one and two thousand dollars per annum, a figure far below the amount suggested by NAWSA for ratification expenses.[47] Prosuffrage publicity, too, was sparse. Suffragists could count on only a few newspapers to support their cause, while the list of influential antisuffrage periodicals was a long one.[48] As for the suffrage lobby, it was composed of sincere but for the most part inexperienced women who had little clout

(Extracts from the Messenger)

THE NEGRO

AND THE

NEW SOCIAL ORDER

*A Reconstruction Program, Prepared by Chandler Owen
and A. Philip Randolph (negroes),
Editors of the Messenger
March 10th, 1919*

THE MESSENGER PUBLISHING CO.
2305 SEVENTH AVENUE   NEW YORK CITY

POLITICAL PROGRAM

Page 6—Political action must go hand in hand with industrial action. A class of people without the vote or the privilege of determining the kind of government under which they live, has neither security of life nor property from which liberty proceeds.

In view of the foregoing WE DEMAND the rigid enforcement of the 13th, 14th and 15th amendments to the Constitution which were primarily framed to give protection to Negroes.

WE DEMAND the reduction of representation in the South upon the basis of actual voting population. The Negro is not allowed to vote, which is in criminal violation of the federal constitution.

We condemn all property and educational tests for suffrage.

WE DEMAND *universal suffrage without regard to race, color, sex, creed or nationality.*

WOMAN SUFFRAGE

We favor the adoption of the Susan B. Anthony amendment to the Constitution, granting suffrage to women—both white and colored.

("Suffrage democracy knows no bias of race, color, creed or sex."—*Mrs. Carrie Chapman Catt*.)

SOCIAL EQUALITY

Page 9—*We favor "Social equality" in every sense of the phrase.* WE DEMAND a new order based upon a society of equals. Evasions, pretexts and excuses cannot explain away the fact that no genuine brotherhood can exist so long as the issue of social equality is not squarely met.

SOCIAL EQUALITY has grown out of the two cardinal and corollary principles of *identity of treatment* and *free interchangeability.*

INTERMARRIAGE

We now approach the American bugaboo—the question upon which Negroes and whites alike set up false theories in flagrant violation of the most fundamental principles of social evolution. *We refer to intermarriage between the whites and Negroes.* WE FAVOR THE INTERMARRIAGE between any sane, grown persons who desire to marry—whatever their race or color. WE FAVOR THE INTERMARRIAGE OF WHITE MEN WITH COLORED WOMEN AS WELL AS COLORED MEN WITH WHITE WOMEN, because there is no natural or instinctive aversion.

Race purity is both a myth and without any value.

WE THEREFORE DEMAND THE REPEAL OF ALL LAWS AGAINST INTERMARRIAGE AS BEING INIMICAL TO THE INTERESTS OF BOTH RACES. We further call attention to the fact that there is no desire to check the association of white men with colored women, colored women with white men, nor to serve any interests of Negro men. And inasmuch as no law requires any woman under any circumstances to marry a man whom she does not will or want to marry, these laws narrow themselves down to the *prevention of WHITE WOMEN MARRYING COLORED MEN whom they desire to marry.*

WE DEMAND as much intercourse—economic, political, and social as is possible between the races

Issued by
THE MEN'S ANTI-RATIFICATION LEAGUE OF
MONTGOMERY, ALA.

Reject the Anthony Amendment. Do not Give Congress Control of Your State Suffrage

Broadside Collection, Virginia Historical Society

FIGURE 10-4 One of the most potent weapons in the arsenal of the antisuffragists was the threat of "negro rule" if a federal amendment granted women the vote. This broadside, which on first glance advocates woman suffrage, black social equality, intermarriage, and racial amalgamation, was in fact issued by the Men's Anti-Ratification League of Montgomery, Alabama, to frighten readers into "rejecting] the Anthony Amendment." The flier circulated in Virginia.

within the legislature.[49] Finally, there were no prominent Democrats in the General Assembly willing to speak in behalf of suffrage or to lead the fight; only a handful of legislators could be counted on to vote for the reform at all.[50]

Although the fate of the suffrage amendment in Virginia was virtually decided before the ratification proceedings began, both sides campaigned aggressively. The antisuffragists redoubled their efforts to discredit their adversaries by flooding the state with fliers that linked the federal amendment with "negro rule" and an end to white supremacy. Nor did the ESL's strategy of ignoring the race issue quell VAOWS's vituperative propaganda. One pamphlet summed up white southerners' objections to woman suffrage in a single sentence: "Every argument for sexual equality in politics is, and must be, an argument also for racial equality."[51] Given the simple truth of this statement, its implications for the woman suffrage campaign were bound to be devastating in a state devoted to institutionalized inequality based on race, class, and gender.

Since the early days of the suffrage campaign, Virginia suffragists had refrained from responding to antisuflfrage racial propaganda. With the vote on ratification of the Nineteenth Amendment scheduled for the regular legislative session in January 1920, however, the ESL adopted a new tactic that had first been articulated in 1917 in an address to league members by President Lila Meade Valentine. In her speech, Valentine rejected the "negro rule" theory as a legitimate objection to woman suffrage, because the federal amendment "leaves absolutely intact all the other qualifications which the State Constitution provides for a voter." All restrictions such as literacy requirements and poll taxes could be applied to women just as to men, she continued. She called "farcical [the] assumption of the antis that, if women were given the ballot, the negro women would learn to read and write over night [and] 'would go hungry to pay their poll tax of $1.50'" and concluded "it is quite obvious, therefore, that white men and women together" would continue to control the state.[52]

Not until 1919, however, was this argument publicly endorsed by the ESL. With the onset of the ratification campaign, the Old Dominion's suffragists began with increasing frequency to maintain that woman suffrage could be modified to exclude black women as easily as male suffrage had been manipulated to disfranchise black men. Writing in October 1919, ESL Secretary Ida M. Thompson instructed organizer Mary Elizabeth Pidgeon on the proper response to antisuffragists' charges that the amendment would inaugurate "negro rule":

> The negro woman is no more of a menace than the negro man. White supremacy is maintained in both cases by the restrictions imposed by each State Constitution. It goes without saying that each State Legislature will take all necessary steps to make these restrictions apply to the woman voter when the federal amendment is ratified. That is all we need to say.[53]

Throughout the remaining months of 1919, Lila Meade Valentine personally wrote to various suffragists and influential politicians explaining the new ESL position.[54] Moreover, the ESL prepared a "Brief for the Federal Suffrage Amendment," a packet that included a variety of arguments, statistics, and instructions for use by those working for ratification. Among the pages of the brief was one labeled "SITUATION WITH REGARD TO THE NEGRO" and

FIGURE 10-5 Many of the ESL leaders continued their political activism by organizing and taking office in the state's League of Women Voters. The delegation from the league that visited Virginia senators Claude Swanson and Carter Glass in Washington in November 1923 included former suffragists Adèle Clark, Mary Elizabeth Pidgeon, Roberta Wellford, and Nora Houston (second, third, fourth, and seventh from the left).

subtitled "SUFFRAGE WILL HELP MAINTAIN WHITE SUPREMACY." According to this document, white supremacy would be preserved by the fact that Virginia's white women outnumbered the total black population, as well as by such devices as the poll tax and other voting restrictions. Ratification lobbyists could also turn to a list of canned responses to challenges to the federal amendment raised by states' rights advocates.[55] In the last months of the ratification campaign, then, the Virginia suffragists sought to undermine the opposition by offering a way simultaneously to enfranchise some and disfranchise other women in the name of expediency.

Despite the Equal Suffrage League's new argument for the vote, the federal woman suffrage amendment failed in Virginia by large majorities in both houses.[56] With the blessing of the ESL, a "Machinery Bill" was passed later in the year that extended existing male voting restrictions to women, with the stipulation that the act would go into effect only if the Nineteenth Amendment was ratified by the requisite thirty-six states.[57]

Thus, when the amendment finally became law in August 1920, a list of voter qualifications placed the Virginia ballot box out of the reach of many black women. Nevertheless, during the September registration drive, the *Richmond Times-Dispatch* reported that long lines of both white and black women formed in city hall to pay their poll taxes and to register to vote. Although the number of white women registering surpassed that of blacks, the newspaper described throngs of black women who "evinced great earnestness and eagerness to get their names on the polling books." Ironically, another group of women who added their names to the registration rolls was the Virginia Association Opposed to Woman Suffrage. VAOWS officials grumbled that the vote had been forced on them but urged their coworkers to do their duty, register, and vote.[58]

The Equal Suffrage League's failure to win the vote for Virginia women may be blamed in part on NAWSA's strategy of pressure-group politics, a strategy that disregarded regional political dynamics in favor of a monolithic vision of national reform. Faithful to its parent organization, the ESL followed guidelines designed for two-party states, with disastrous results. The drawbacks of inappropriate tactics were compounded by delayed implementation. In Virginia, the first decade of the twentieth century could indeed be labeled "the doldrums"; national suffrage momentum had already swept the movement far beyond the first timid steps at education and organization that were only begun in the Old Dominion in 1909.

But the primary cause of the Virginia activists' difficulties was internal. The convention of 1901–2 had perpetuated an oligarchic system that permitted the adoption of progressive reforms, so long as those reforms did not challenge the political status quo. Certain reforms were enacted in order to dissipate political insurgency, but the system as a whole remained impervious to democratic change. In the absence of an opposition party or significant factional division within the Democracy, suffrage pressure tactics, even if implemented fully, were doomed. The race issue was determinant, and from the point of view of white supremacist politicians, woman suffrage offered them no benefits and grave problems. Virginia's political system withstood a federal amendment designed to enfranchise all women, regardless of race. In this sense, the 1902 "race solution" was also a gender solution.

Within a few weeks of the national victory, the Equal Suffrage League disbanded. Although many ESL leaders—including Adèle Clark, Mary Elizabeth Pidgeon, Lila Meade Valentine, and Roberta Wellford—continued their political activity by organizing and taking office in the state's League of Women Voters, in time the great woman suffrage crusade vanished from all but the memories of a dedicated few. Today, some might ask why the Virginia suffragists waged a campaign that seemed doomed to failure. Others might point to the ESL's support of the Machinery Bill as a loss of faith in the full meaning of the Nineteenth Amendment. Without doubt, the Old Dominion's suffragists harbored some if not all of the racist sentiment of their times, and although their ranks held women like Mary Johnston, others supported the racial and class restrictions implemented in 1902. If the woman suffrage movement offered a new vision of democracy for all women regardless of race and class, the majority of ESL activists remained blinded to this promise by the constraints of time and place.

The salient point here, however, is not to hold the Virginia suffragists to some modern yardstick of conviction, but rather to observe the change over time brought about by their involvement in a national democratic reform movement. Founded in 1909 by a handful of women meeting in a rented room, the Virginia suffrage headquarters by 1920 had become the center of a vital reform organization boasting more than thirty thousand recruits. For some ESL members, the suffrage crusade was complementary to other progressive reforms.

With the vote, women could easily enact child labor legislation, pure food and drug laws, and other social justice measures. For other ESL activists, however, suffrage work initiated a transformation in sentiment and understanding that would sustain them as suffragists and as women. Through meetings, speakers, canvassing, and exposure to the world outside the home, they learned of societal ills and endorsed a progressive agenda far in advance of public opinion. This transformation also included a deepening awareness of the concerns of women, reflected in a feminist agenda that surpassed mere suffrage. The Virginia campaign for the vote failed, but the suffrage movement did not. Woman suffrage invited the women of Virginia to extend the boundaries of women's sphere to encompass the world of politics, progressive reform, and feminism. Their acceptance of this invitation opened a new chapter in the history of Virginia women.

NOTES

1. The "doldrums thesis" may be found in Eleanor Flexner, *Century of Struggle: The Woman's Rights Movement in the United States* (Cambridge, Mass., 1959), p. 256.

2. The southern suffrage crusade has received little attention in recent years. For book-length studies of the movement in the South, see Paul E. Fuller, *Laura Clay and the Woman's Rights Movement* (Lexington, Ky., 1975); and A. Elizabeth Taylor, *The Woman Suffrage Movement in Tennessee* (New York, 1957). Maijorie Spruill Wheeler's *New Women of the New South: The Leaders of the Woman Suffrage Movement in the South* (New York and Oxford, forthcoming) should rectify this recent neglect. A useful discussion of ideological issues that characterized the southern movement may be found in Aileen S. Kraditor, *The Ideas of the Woman Suffrage Movement, 1890–1920* (1965; New York, 1981), chap. 7.

3. Efforts to organize suffrage clubs in the South were made in the late nineteenth century, but most of these organizations had either ceased to exist or were small and unstable by the turn of the century. Despite some progress by the second decade of the twentieth century, a *Woman's Journal* survey conducted in 1912 showed the relative weakness of southern suffrage organization compared to most states outside the region. Of the six southern states that responded to the survey, only Virginia and Kentucky listed memberships of more than one thousand; only Virginia had established a state headquarters. Five southern states failed to respond to the survey at all, indicating at the very least disorganization within those states' suffrage societies. The survey may be found in the proceedings of the 44th annual NAWSA convention, 21–26 Nov. 1912, Breckinridge Family Papers, Box 701, Library of Congress, Washington, D.C. (hereafter cited as DLC). For more on the nineteenth-century movement in the South, see A. Elizabeth Taylor's many articles, including "The Woman Suffrage Movement in North Carolina," *North Carolina Historical Review* 38 (1961): 45–62, 173–89; "The Origin of the Woman Suffrage Movement in Georgia," *Georgia Historical Quarterly* 28 (1944): 63–80; and "The Woman Suffrage Movement in Texas," *Journal of Southern History* 17 (1951): 194–215.

4. There were two active suffrage associations in Virginia by the second decade of the twentieth century: the Equal Suffrage League of Virginia, a NAWSA affiliate and the larger of the two groups, and the National Woman's Party (NWP), with a small active membership in Norfolk and perhaps elsewhere in the state. The NWP is not included in this essay for two reasons. First, there are only scattered references—mainly in the ESL records—to NWP activity in Virginia, and because the two groups had little affection for each other, these references present a one-sided picture. Second, the NWP was primarily a militant pressure group based in Washington, D.C., with negligible influence at the state level until the ratification campaign of 1919–20. Its part in the Virginia ratification lobbying resulted in confusion, crossed signals, and hard feelings between ESL and NWP activists but had no discernible bearing on the Virginia legislature or on the failure of woman suffrage in Virginia. For more on the NWP, see Sally Hunter Graham, "Woodrow Wilson, Alice Paul and the Woman Suffrage Movement," *Political Science Quarterly* 98 (1983–84): 665–79; and Christine A. Lunardini, *From Equal Suffrage to Equal Rights: Alice Paul and the National Woman's Party, 1910–1928* (New York, 1986).

5. Nora Houston, "History of the Equal Suffrage League of Virginia," 2 May 1914 (clipping), in Ida M. Thompson Papers (also called the Suffrage Collection), Box 4, Virginia State Library and Archives, Richmond.

6. Benjamin B. Valentine, undated fragment, and "The organization of the Men's Equal Suffrage League of Virginia," n.d., Lila Meade Valentine Papers, Sec. 2, Virginia Historical Society, Richmond (hereafter cited as ViHi). On Valentine's qualities as a leader, see Ellen Glasgow to Lila Meade Valentine, 17 Sept. 1920, ibid., Sec. 3. The best overview of Valentine's career is Lloyd C. Taylor, Jr., "Lila Meade Valentine: The FFV as Reformer," *Virginia Magazine of History and Biography* (hereafter cited as *VMHB*) 70 (1962): 471–87. For Valentine's work in woman suffrage, see Elizabeth Dabney Coleman, "Genteel Crusader," *Virginia Cavalcade* 4 (Autumn 1954): 29–32.

7. Brief biographies of prominent suffragists may be found in the Thompson Papers, Box 3. Dorothy M. Scura provides a perceptive account of Ellen Glasgow's part in the suffrage movement in "Ellen Glasgow and women's suffrage," *Research In Action* 6 (Spring 1982): 12–15. For more on Mary Johnston, see Elizabeth Dabney Coleman, "Penwoman of Virginia's Feminists," *Virginia Cavalcade* 6 (Winter 1956): 8–11; John R. Roberson, ed., "Two Virginia Novelists on Woman's Suffrage: An Exchange of Letters between Mary Johnston and Thomas Nelson Page," *VMHB* 64 (1956): 286–90; and Marjorie Spruill Wheeler, "Mary Johnston, Suffragist," *VMHB* 100 (1992): 99–118. On Lucy Randolph Mason, see Jolin A. Salmond, *Miss Lucy of the CIO: The Life and Times of Lucy Randolph Mason, 1882–1959* (Athens, Ga., and London, 1988).

8. Alice Tyler to Frances Squire Potter, 19 Mar. 1910, Adèle Clark Papers, unmarked box, "Equal Suffrage League of Virginia—Correspondence 1910" folder, Virginia Commonwealth University, Richmond. One of the richest sources for the Virginia suffrage movement (as well as the national suffrage crusade and the League of Women Voters), the Adèle Clark Papers are unfortunately uncataloged at the present time, and there are no plans to rectify this situation. Because several unmarked boxes in this collection contain valuable insights into the Virginia campaign, some material cited in this essay can be identified only by folder rather than the usual box number.

9. For a sample of the responses to Tyler's recruitment initiative, see Louise Cadot to Alice Tyler, 11 Dec. 1910, and Maria Pendleton Duval to Alice Tyler, 31 Aug. 1910, both in Clark Papers, unmarked box, "Woman's Equal Suffrage League of Virginia—Correspondence 1910" folder.

10. This is not to say that NAWSA had entirely abandoned suffrage education; the organization provided literature and other educational matter to suffrage societies throughout the votes-for-women campaign. NAWSA leaders believed that suffrage education was the crucial precondition to pressure-group politics. Once a sizable constituency had been developed through suffrage education, pressure could then and only then be exerted on politicians. Although suffrage education continued throughout the entire campaign, especially in the South, many suffragists outside the region began to turn their attention away from education and toward direct political action as a result of the successful educational efforts conducted in the 1900–1910 period.

11. Mary Johnston to Lila Meade Valentine, 23 Apr. 1911, Valentine Papers, Sec. 3.

12. Valentine, "The organization of the Men's Equal Suffrage League of Virginia."

13. Although a common strategy in other regions, recruitment of trade union members was unusual for southern suffragists. The ESL's efforts gained the endorsement of at least one union, but Valentine and her staff left no indication of public response to the recruitment attempts. For more on the suffragists' recruitment activities, see Lila Meade Valentine, annual presidential address to the Equal Suffrage League of Virginia, 1911, and Alice Tyler, report of the corresponding secretary, 1911, both in Clark Papers, Box 53-A.

14. Jane M. Rutherford, president of the Virginia Association Opposed to Woman Suffrage, form letter, 1912, Thompson Papers, Box 4.

15. "Why Women Should Oppose Equal Suffrage," n.d., pamphlet issued by the Virginia Association Opposed to Woman Suffrage, Thompson Papers, Box 4.

16. "Virginia Warns Her People Against Woman Suffrage" (pamphlet), n.d., Clark Papers, Box 130.

17. For accounts of the 1901–2 convention, see Andrew Buni, *The Negro in Virginia Politics, 1902–1965* (Charlottesville, 1967), chap. 2; J. Morgan Kousser, *The Shaping of Southern Politics: Suffrage Restrictions and the Establishment of the One-Party South, 1880–1910* (New Haven, 1974), pp. 171–81; Allen W. Moger, *Virginia: Bourbonism to Byrd, 1870–1925* (Charlottesville, 1968), chap. 9; and Raymond H. Pulley, *Old Virginia Restored: An Interpretation of the Progressive Impulse, 1870–1930* (Charlottesville, 1968), chap. 4.

18. "The Virginia Assembly and Woman Suffrage," n.d., pamphlet issued by the Advisory Committee Opposed to Woman Suffrage, Clark Papers, Box 130.

19. "That Deadly Parallel," n.d. (flier), and J. S. Eichelberger to unidentified addressee, 21 Mar. 1918, both in Clark Papers, Box 130. In all probability, the states' rights posture of the antis was one of expediency, not of principle. When all but one of Virginia's congressional delegation voted in favor of the Eighteenth Amendment (Prohibition), no protest was mounted against the amendment on the grounds of federal interference with state prerogatives. Apparently, states' rights was an argument used predominantly when race was the issue.

20. "The Virginia Assembly and Woman Suffrage" (pamphlet).

21. "Virginia Warns Her People Against Woman Suffrage" (pamphlet). "Negro rule" was a common theme in antisuffrage propaganda. See, for example, "The Virginia Assembly and Woman Suffrage" (pamphlet); and American Constitutional League Field Secretary J. S. Eichelberger's fact sheet and form letter, 21 Mar. 1918, both in Clark Papers, Box 130.

22. "The Virginia Assembly and Woman Suffrage" (pamphlet).

23. "Woman's Suffrage The Vanguard of Socialism," n.d. (flier); see also "The Red Behind the Yellow: Socialists Working for Suffrage," 1915, flier issued by the New York State Association Opposed to Woman Suffrage, both in Clark Papers, Box 130.

24. Speech typescript and *The Charlotte News*, 2 Nov. 1913 (clipping), both in Thompson Papers, Box 3. Virginia suffragists were not alone in using this type of argument; see Kraditor, *Ideas of the Woman Suffrage Movement*, chap. 5.

25. "Women in the Home," n.d., flier originally issued by NAWSA and reprinted by the Equal Suffrage League of Virginia, copies in both the Broadside Collection, ViHi, and Thompson Papers, Box 4.

26. Without doubt, some if not a majority of the ESL members used the term "female equality" to mean equality for whites only. Mary Johnston was one of the few Virginia suffragists to state in writing her belief in suffrage for both black and white women. Although she may have had some support for her views, it is likely that the majority of her suffrage colleagues hoped for some type of electoral restrictions that would limit the number of black female voters.

27. A list of topics presented to ESL members on a weekly basis during the years 1913–18 may be found in the ledger book of the ESL corresponding secretary, Clark Papers, Box 51.

28. "Resolutions Adopted by the ESL at the Third Annual Convention," Oct. 1913 (pamphlet), Thompson Papers, Box 4.

29. Ledger book of the ESL corresponding secretary, Clark Papers, Box 51.

30. Mary Johnston to Lila Meade Valentine, 5 Jan. 1913, Valentine Papers, Sec. 3.

31. Lewis Parke Chamberlayne to Lila Meade Valentine, 23 Feb. 1912, ibid., Sec. 3.

32. For membership figures, see Charlotte Jean Shelton, "Woman Suffrage and Virginia Politics, 1909–1920" (M.A. thesis, University of Virginia, 1969), pp. 27–29. According to Shelton, by 1915, the league counted seven thousand members; four years later, this figure had risen to thirty thousand. For lists of street meetings and other publicity stunts, see ledger book of the ESL corresponding secretary, Clark Papers, Box 51.

33. A joint resolution was defeated in 1914 by a vote of 74 to 13. In 1916 another resolution was voted down 52 to 40. A good description of both contests may be found in Shelton, "Woman Suffrage and Virginia Politics," pp. 36–43. Shelton accounts for the seeming increased support for the suffrage resolution in 1916 by the fact that the resolution simply referred the issue to the voters and thus was supported by many legislators who did not favor suffrage per se.

34. The best description of Catt's plan, called "the Woman Suffrage Party," is Mary Gray Peck, *The Rise of the Woman Suffrage Party*, Series V-H, Woman and Government Series, ed. Myra Hartshorn (Chicago, 1911), in the National American Woman Suffrage Association Papers, DLC (microfilm ed.), reel 49. See also Sally Hunter Graham, "Woman Suffrage and the New Democracy" (Ph.D. diss., University of Texas, 1988), chap. 4, for a description of the plan's implementation.

35. Lila Meade Valentine to Carrie Chapman Catt, 14 Nov. 1916, Clark Papers, Box 3.

36. A congressional committee, made up of the congressional district chairmen, was charged with interviewing all incumbents and congressional candidates regarding their stand on woman suffrage (Equal Suffrage League of Virginia, *Yearbook, 1916* [Richmond, 1916], pp. 10–15).

37. Richard Hawn to Mary Day Winn, 9 Mar. 1916, Clark Papers, unmarked box, "Press Bureau— ESL" folder. Hawn was the editor of the Pulaski *Southwest Times*.

38. To inject a quick dose of suffrage propaganda, some organizers turned to street meetings in town squares, while others held impromptu rallies at county fairs. The state ESL headquarters acted as the league's official publicity and propaganda bureau, distributing more than two hundred thousand pieces of prosuffrage literature in 1916 alone. For a complete description of ESL activities in 1916, see Equal Suffrage League of Virginia, *Yearbook, 1916*, pp. 12–15.

39. ESL annual report, 1917, Thompson Papers, Box A.

40. Edith Clark Cowles, report of the executive and press secretary, ESL annual report, 1917–19, ibid., Box 1.

41. Elizabeth Lewis, report of the chairman of the state congressional committee, 1916, ibid., Box A.

42. Pulley, *Old Virginia Restored,* p. 111.

43. In Texas, for example, suffragists had formed an alliance with other progressives who hoped to impeach the corrupt governor, Jim "Pa" Ferguson. After the impeachment had been accomplished, grateful progressive legislators ratified the Nineteenth Amendment, in part because they recognized that many women voters would continue to support their agenda and their bids for re-election.

44. Prohibition is a case in point. When the Democratic party observed that support for prohibition was growing throughout the state in 1908, party chieftains endorsed a "dry" candidate for governor and carried the election—with the help of large blocks of "wet" votes in the cities. Cooperation for the sake of electoral supremacy and party unity meant that prohibition came to Virginia without the party strife that characterized similar crusades elsewhere. See Pulley, *Old Virginia Restored,* pp. 156–62 and chap. 8.

45. Lila Meade Valentine to Carrie Chapman Catt, 28 May 1919, Clark Papers, unmarked box, "Lila Meade Valentine clippings, National Suffrage Association" folder.

46. Shelton, "Woman Suffrage and Virginia Politics," p. 28. Shelton also speculates that suffrage sentiment in Virginia "remained virtually unknown to both suffragists themselves and their opponents."

47. NAWSA ratification guidelines are detailed in NAWSA Bulletin 15, 3 June 1919, Breckinridge Family Papers, Box 703. For ESL finances, see Equal Suffrage League of Virginia, *Yearbook, 1916;* ESL annual report, 1917, Thompson Papers, Box A; and E. G. Kidd, treasurer's report, 7 Nov. 1917–7 Mar. 1919, Thompson Papers, Box 4. The league's headquarters showed a balance of $259 on 1 January 1920, a sum that had declined by some fifty dollars by mid-February of that year. Whether this sum was the treasury balance for the entire organization or for the Richmond headquarters alone, the paucity of the amount indicates a severe financial shortage

for a state organization engaged in a ratification campaign. See Ida M. Thompson, ESL head-quarters report, 11 Jan-10 Feb. 1920, ibid., Box 1.

48. Ida M. Thompson to Mrs. C. E. Townsend, 5 May 1919, ibid., Box A.

49. Adèle Clark was the ratification committee chairman and head of the ESL lobby. Although she had served as an ESL lobbyist for several years, her expertise remained questionable. One of many scattered references that indicate her lack of effectiveness may be found in Adèle Clark to Lila Meade Valentine, 1 July 1919, ibid., Box 1. In this letter, Clark related how a prosuffrage state senator who had agreed to head the ratification fight in the Senate provided her with the names and addresses of prominent women in his district and instructed her to organize a campaign there so he "would have some ground to stand on." In most states, this step had been accomplished by suffragists long before the ratification stage and without the prodding of politicians. Clark also seemed perplexed about what Senate faction her champion belonged to, thus revealing a rather dim understanding of legislative dynamics.

50. As late as February 1919, Lila Meade Valentine confessed to Carrie Chapman Catt that "unhap-pily we have no Democrats of prominence in the State who could be induced to speak in behalf of the Federal Amendment" (Lila Meade Valentine to Carrie Chapman Catt, 3 Feb. 1919, Clark Papers, unmarked box, "Lila Meade Valentine clippings, National Suffrage Association" folder).

51. "The Virginia Assembly and Woman Suffrage" (pamphlet).

52. Lila Meade Valentine, presidential address to the 7th annual ESL convention, 12–14 Nov. 1917, Valentine Papers, Sec. 5. In an *Answer to Anti-Suffragists*, printed at about the same time, Valentine elaborated: "But, cry the Antis in a still further effort at camouflage, the South is in danger of negro domination if women be given the vote. A bogey—a mere bogey, this. There is no such danger. The state constitutions provide amply for restricting the shiftless, illiterate vote. To assume that only the women of the negro race would be sufficiently interested in citizenship to register and vote is to gratuitously insult the white women of the South. To assume that white women would be less interested than white men in maintaining white supremacy is equally wide of the mark" (Lila Meade Valentine, *Answer to Anti-Suffragists* [n.p., c. 1917], p. 2).

53. Ida M. Thompson to Mary Elizabeth Pidgeon, 11 Oct. 1919, Thompson Papers, Box 4.

54. See, for example, Lila Meade Valentine to Gertrude Brown, 27 Nov. 1919, ibid., Box 4.

55. "Brief for the Federal Suffrage Amendment" (probably Jan. 1920), Clark Papers, Box 150.

56. On 7 February 1920, after more than twelve hours of debate, the Virginia Senate voted to reject the Nineteenth Amendment, 24 to 16. Five days later, the House voted 62 to 22 against ratifica-tion. For a complete account of the legislative debates and votes, see Shelton, "Woman Suffrage and Virginia Politics," pp. 61–64. See also *Richmond Times-Dispatch*, 7–13 Feb. 1920.

57. A copy of the Machinery Bill may be found in Thompson Papers, Box 4. Unlike the ill-fated federal amendment that had few supporters in the legislature, this bill boasted twenty-five patrons in the Senate and twenty-six in the House (ESL Headquarters Bulletin 6,27 Feb. 1920, ibid., Box A).

58. *Richmond Times-Dispatch*, 29 Sept. 1920; see also 28, 30 Sept. 1920, and "To the Woman Citizen," n.d., flier issued by the League of Women Voters, ViHi.

11

V for Virginia

THE COMMONWEALTH GOES TO WAR

By Charles W. Johnson

Men do not control modern war; it controls them. … It has become so all-encompassing and demanding that the mere act of fighting it changes the conditions under which men live. Of all the incalculables which men introduce into their history modem warfare is the greatest. If it says nothing else it says this, to all men involved in it, at the moment of its beginning: Nothing is ever going to be the same again.

Bruce Catton, *America Goes to War* (1958)

B ruce Catton was writing some thirty years ago about a war that had occurred almost a century earlier, but his words could easily apply to World War II. Before it was over, fifty million people had died, and the world was changed forever. For the American people, too, the war altered everything. For Virginians, the changes were profound, pervasive, and long lasting.

In the 1930s three countries—Japan, Italy, and Germany—viewed themselves as "have-not" nations and were willing to use force or the threat of it to gain what they felt was their rightful place in the sun. After years of mounting tension, World

FIGURE 11-1   At the onset of World War II, bucolic scenes such as this mountain farm and A. H. Gray's service station in Upper Zion in Caroline County were commonplace throughout Virginia. As more and more Virginians entered the war, either in branches of the military or as civilians doing their part for the war effort, these places often languished, depending on the crops or services produced. Some farms were razed to make room for fast-rising military bases.

FIGURE 11-2 To bring the scattered 24,000 people working for the War Department together, Col. Leslie R. Groves of the Corps of Engineers built the Pentagon, then the biggest office building in the world. Arlington County swampland and Hell's Bottom slum gave up their existence for the four-million-square-foot concrete structure. The area of Northern Virginia surrounding the Pentagon changed dramatically during the war, as housing for military personnel became critical. Fairlington, a 3,439-unit housing tract carved out of Fairfax and Arlington counties, was built by the Defense Homes Corporation.

War II formally began in Europe when Adolf Hitler's Germany invaded Poland in September 1939. Britain and France honored their treaty obligations and declared war on Germany, only to see the Poles quickly defeated by the Nazi *Blitzkrieg* ("lightning war"). Norway, Belgium, Holland, and France fell in spring 1940. Forced off the Continent at Dunkirk, the British stood alone, though under the new and more determined leadership of Winston Churchill.

Failing to defeat the Royal Air Force—a necessary condition for the invasion of England—Hitler focused his air assault on the terror bombing of British cities. He also turned his attention eastward, where his real interest lay, and in June 1941 launched his forces in an enormous invasion of the Soviet Union. By December the Germans had besieged Leningrad and were within sight of the spires of the Moscow Kremlin before being halted by a combination of distance, attrition, resistance, and the Russian winter. By then all the major nations of the world except the United States were at war.

Library of Congress

FIGURE 11-3

In the twenty-seven months between the assault on Poland and the bombing of Pearl Harbor, the United States edged closer to conflict. Convinced that a German victory in Europe would threaten national security, President Franklin D. Roosevelt found ways to help the British. The United States slowly became the Arsenal of Democracy. At first America sold the British weapons and other necessities of war. In the year following Dunkirk, the British bought 600,000 rifles, 80,000 machine guns, 900 field guns, and hundreds of merchant ships. It was not nearly enough, however, and the British were running out of money. Appealing to Congress to find a way to send ships, planes, tanks, and guns, FDR introduced the Lend-Lease bill. It passed Congress in March 1941 by a vote of 60 to 31 in the Senate and 317 to 71 in the House. Virginia's delegation—reflecting party loyalty to their recently reelected Democratic president and a genuine outpouring of goodwill toward Britain— voted for the bill. This action was followed two weeks later by an initial appropriation of $7 billion, a down payment on more than $50 billion in aid given during the war to America's allies. Churchill called the program "the most unsordid act in history" and "an inspiring act of faith." No one could be sure, however, that either the British or the Russians would hold out.

Aid to Britain was opposed by those who believed the United States had made a mistake in 1917 by entering the Great War. They did not want to pull English and French chestnuts out of the fire again. That cynical attitude did not find much support in Virginia. The English

FIGURE 11-4 In the early 1940s, as existing Virginia military installations expanded and new ones were built, more and more farmers were asked to leave their homesteads. Caroline County families such as the one pictured on the opposite page moved their belongings to make room for Camp A. P. Hill. Makeshift communities sprang up almost overnight to accommodate the displaced families and the incoming defense workers. The single-family prefabricated housing offered few amenities but did boast small yards. Often workers had to settle into trailer camps, similar to the one for employees of the torpedo factory in Alexandria.

roots of families tracing their ancestry back to colonial times ran deep, and many members of the Episcopal, Methodist, and other churches had vital emotional and institutional ties to England. Most Virginians looked at the German advances as unprovoked aggression and were horrified by attacks on civilians from the air. (This latter sensitivity did not survive the war.)

FIGURE 11-5 Because of the housing shortage, many owners of multiroom homes were asked to rent out surplus rooms. This husband and wife moved to Newport News from South Carolina for employment at the shipyard. They rented a one-bedroom apartment for $8.00 a month.

As the nightly German bombing of England worsened, Virginians in Richmond and Lynchburg and Bristol sat around their radios and listened through the crackle of transatlantic static as Edward R. Murrow began each of his broadcasts in his resonant voice with the words, "This ... is London." He told them of the bombers and the antiaircraft fire, the slow arc of the tracer bullets, the labors of firemen and volunteers digging the living and the dead out of the rubble. Listeners heard the crump of bombs and the shrill of sirens. They learned of thousands of British children evacuated from London and other cities to the relative safety of the countryside. Red Cross chapters throughout the state began a campaign to place some of these young evacuees in Virginia homes for the duration. The people of Petersburg, for example, made arrangements to take in twenty children. Bundles for Britain and other clothing drives found willing hands to help.

During 1940 America also began to build up its own military and industrial strength. Defense budgets rose, production plans increased, and military and naval forces expanded. Virginians all over the state, but especially in the east, only needed to look around to see evidence of the frantic enlargement of old military and naval facilities or the creation of new ones. Fort Monroe saw most of its prewar cadre shipped off to Puerto Rico after the Nazi

FIGURE 11-6 Splashing through the mud and rough terrain at Fort Myer in Arlington County, the U.S. Army Command Reconnaissance General Purpose truck was given a successful test drive in 1941. During the war, more than 600,000 of these quarter-ton GP trucks were produced. Engineers predicted the versatile vehicle would replace the motorcycle and sidecar. Although the public relations designation was "blitzbuggy," the truck became familiarly known as the jeep. Whether the moniker derived from the blurring of the initials GP or from a character in the Popeye cartoon who could "go anywhere and do anything" is not known.

invasion of Poland. Additional units were raised to replace them as training staff, including some of the 246th Coastal Artillery, a Virginia National Guard unit from the Shenandoah Valley. Fort Eustis, a creation of the Great War, was reopened in 1941 as part of the Coastal Artillery School.

The most famous resident of Fort Myer, just southwest of Washington, D.C., was the vehicle that was officially called the "U.S. Army truck, 1/4-ton, 4 × 4, Command Reconnaissance (General Purpose)." The army's public relations designation—"blitzbuggy"—thankfully never caught on, and throughout the war the GP was, for everyone, the "jeep." Tested extensively at Fort Myer in 1941, it saw service in every theater of the war.

Langley Field, created near Hampton during the First World War and used as a blimp base since then, became home to the 25th Anti-Submarine Warfare Wing and squadrons of B-17 bombers. To Langley fell the responsibility of guarding six hundred miles of coast. When Camp A. P. Hill was carved out of quiet agricultural land in Caroline County, the displaced farmers, many of them African-Americans, were assisted in their relocation by members of the Civilian Conservation Corps. Camp Lee, another World War I site, returned to duty in 1940 as a medical facility and as the new home for the Quartermaster Corps School.

In early 1941 a marine parachute battalion was established at Quantico. These "paramarines" left Virginia before Pearl Harbor, but the facility housed thousands of other marines during the war, including the First Battalion of the newly formed Marine Raiders. On the streets of Norfolk and Newport News sailors' uniforms were already a familiar sight, but as 1940 turned into 1941 their number mushroomed, as did that of shipyard workers.

Even before Pearl Harbor, 24,000 people worked for the War Department in buildings scattered around the Washington metropolitan area. The vast expansion of the armed forces increased the need for administration to be centralized. Beginning in September 1941 Colonel Leslie R. Groves of the Corps of Engineers undertook one of his two famous wartime projects (the other one being in Alamogordo, New Mexico). As a conservation measure, the Pentagon was constructed with reinforced concrete, which saved 43,000 tons of steel, enough to build a battleship. Much of the land was drained and filled swampland; part came from the destruction of Hell's Bottom, an Arlington slum. The four-million-square-foot structure was the largest office complex in the world, with twice as much space as the Empire State Building. Designed so that no two offices would be more than half a mile apart, the building was originally restricted in height to three stories to avoid interfering with the new Washington National Airport. The Pentagon became an instant symbol of the massive American war effort and, after the war, of the military-industrial complex that affected all states but especially Virginia.

As Germany advanced in Europe, its Oriental ally continued expanding in Asia. In the face of growing American economic and diplomatic pressure opposed to this expansion, Japanese naval strategists began to consider how best to neutralize American power in the Pacific. Failing a diplomatic resolution, they decided to destroy the American fleet with a surprise blow delivered by aircraft launched from carriers. For Americans, whether they realized it or not, the world was fast becoming a more dangerous place.

Defending the country, even if America managed to stay out of the war, required a larger army and navy. When General George C. Marshall took over as acting chief of staff in summer 1939, the army contained 174,000 enlisted men. With the outbreak of war in Europe, Roosevelt authorized expansion of the army to 227,000 men and the National Guard to 235,000. In September 1940—given impetus by the fall of France and the German threat to invade Britain—a bipartisan coalition in Congress passed the Selective Compulsory Military Training and Service Act providing for America's first peacetime draft. Virginia's congressional delegation unanimously supported the measure. On the more controversial extension resolution passed the following August by a vote of 203 to 202 in the House, Virginia's representatives remained solid.

FIGURE 11-7 The defense buildup of the early 1940s increased shipbuilding at Hampton Roads ports. Newport News Shipbuilding and Dry Dock Company went from a work force of 13,000 in 1939 to 70,000 by 1943. Workers leaving the shipyard gates at the end of the day to board the Washington Avenue streetcars were a familiar sight.

FIGURE 11-8 Newport News saw the launching of many famous warships. The USS *Ticonderoga* was sent on her way by workers knocking free the undertimbers in February 1944.

To supplement the original draft act, a joint resolution of Congress in August 1940 authorized the call-up of the National Guard. Among the men inducted that first year were nearly all of the Virginia Guard, called up between September 1940 and February 1941. Most began their training at Fort Meade, Maryland, and many of them were part of the 116th Regiment, 29th Infantry Division.

Just before FDR ordered the Virginia National Guard to undergo a year's training, Governor James H. Price oversaw the organization of the Virginia Protective Force late in 1940. Under the command of Brigadier General Edward E. Goodwyn, the VPF was designed to assume the guard's role in an emergency. If necessary, the governor could have drafted men to fill the VPF's ranks, but there were more than enough volunteers. The original complement of 200 officers and 3,100 men stayed fairly constant during the war in spite of losses of men who were drafted or who volunteered for active duty. Officers received training at the Virginia Military Institute and Virginia Polytechnic Institute, and there were training classes at the weekly drills for enlisted men.

The VPF was organized into twelve battalions made up of companies formed by cities, towns, and counties from all around the state. They were armed with a variety of weapons from shotguns and submachine guns to World War I-vintage rifles, and their uniforms were made by inmates of the state penitentiary system. The Virginia Flying Corps, consisting of pilots flying their own planes, was added to the VPF in late 1941. These volunteers were particularly effective in supplementing the Civil Air Patrol's coastal patrolling activities.

Even with the rapidly enlarging military force in 1941, it had been possible to keep hoping that the United States would not be dragged into war. When the Japanese attacked Pearl Harbor on Sunday morning, the seventh of December 1941, and the news came flashing back to the United States, that hope was smashed. Those who heard the news would always remember where they were when they learned it.

Caught up in the war at last, the people of the United States experienced profound changes in their personal lives and sensed that their nation was being altered as well. Some things would stay more or less the same, of course, but sixteen million American men and women put on their country's uniform, and millions more took new jobs in war industries and in the massive governmental machinery required to organize the war effort. New factories or retooled older ones provided work for many who had never been "on the line" before. There were opportunities for women as well as men, African-Americans as well as whites, although publicity implying equal opportunity and good pay for all often was at odds with reality.

Virginians shared the common wartime experiences of Americans all over the nation. Parents in Iowa and New Mexico said good-bye to their sons and daughters at train and bus stations just as they did in Richmond and Roanoke. Women in Seattle and San Diego took new jobs or expanded responsibilities in the same way women did in Norfolk and Radford. Men, women, and children from every part of the Old Dominion volunteered for the myriad civilian tasks that had to be done in the same way that civilians from Alabama and Idaho did.

In the military, draftees and volunteers from Abingdon and Arlington shivered in the same kinds of lines waiting for physical examinations as did their peers from Portland, Maine, and Ironwood, Michigan. They trained and marched, studied and dozed, fought and died or survived with the husbands and fathers and sons of every color and ethnic background from every state. In these ways World War II provided an integrating experience in the life and memory of the nation.

In other ways, however, Virginia's experience was different from that of other states. The location of the nation's capital put the state near the center of Allied planning for the war that spread all over the world. The large number of bases meant that soldiers, sailors, marines, and airmen from across the nation trained in and passed through the commonwealth. The seacoast put Virginia in the forefront of naval construction, of the battle for the Atlantic, and of preparations for the invasions of North Africa and occupied Europe.

In the course of the war, 300,000 Virginians served in the military. Some never left the Zone of the Interior, as military planners called the continental United States, and significant numbers stayed close to home in the Pentagon and elsewhere in Washington to plan, coordinate, and administer the massive increase in America's martial power. Others shared burdens overseas. Virginians probably watched the 116th Infantry more closely than any other single unit because it embraced so many of their National Guard, but men and women from the state were in every service and in every theater of the war.

Virginians served in every rank from the highest to the lowest. Admiral John Lesslie Hall of Williamsburg commanded the USS *Arkansas*, the oldest battleship in the fleet, in June 1940 but was promoted to chief of staff for the battleship division of the Atlantic fleet. In the first American amphibious operation of the war, he oversaw the landing of marines in Iceland to relieve British forces. Promoted to rear admiral, he trained General George S. Patton's 35,000 men for the invasion of North Africa in November 1942. Hall and his people learned from the inevitable mistakes of war and used training camps in North Africa to prepare troops for the invasions of Sicily and Italy. The 11th Amphibious Force that came ashore in Normandy on D-Day was under Hall's command. Later he shifted oceans and commanded the landing force at Okinawa. Appropriately, the first American troops to come ashore in Japan as part of the army of occupation were Hall's Tokyo Bay Force.

Ralph Lee Edwards, a farm boy in Stafford County, had a draft exemption as "an essential farmer" and worked hard to keep his family fed. Because Edwards took odd jobs on the side, a neighbor reported him to the local draft board, which decided to change his status. He received the standard form induction letter that began with the words, "The President of the United States to Ralph Lee Edwards, Greeting." Edwards reported to Parris Island for training in June 1944 and by Thanksgiving was in Hawaii with the 4th Marine Division as part of a draft designed to replace marines killed or wounded. Assigned to the 24th Marine Infantry Regiment as an ammunition carrier in February 1945, he and the other members of I Company fought their way through the black sands of Iwo Jima to clear the caves of Japanese soldiers. When the company left the island in March, 81 percent of its 278 men had become

FIGURE 11-9   Navy Construction Battalions (Seabees) were ail-volunteer forces of highly trained men from civilian life. During the war years, nearly a quarter of a million men were organized by the navy into 338 battalions. These Seabees from the Norfolk Naval Base created a road through the sand dunes by putting down twenty-foot wire mesh sections that were then welded together.

casualties. Edwards survived this, his only action of the war, but Iwo Jima cost the marines 6,000 dead and the Japanese more than 22,000.

Virginians in the navy served in the air, on shore, on board ships, and under the sea. The so-called "Lee Volunteers" joined the navy in a recruiting drive in August and September 1942. More than a thousand strong, they received their basic indoctrination at the Norfolk Training Center before being sent off to a variety of schools to learn specialty skills.

"Seabees" was the nickname given to the Navy Construction Battalions (CBs). By the end of the war, this all-volunteer force numbered nearly a quarter of a million men organized into 338 battalions. These volunteers were usually older than the average sailor or marine they worked with. "Don't let them shoot a Seabee—he might be your uncle" was a popular watchword. Admiral William Frederick Halsey listed the bulldozer after the submarine, radar, and the airplane as one of the four decisive weapons in the Pacific war. At Virginia's Naval Construction Training Station Peary, Seabees received three weeks of basic and five of specialized training in all aspects of construction. Two other camps, Allen and

FIGURE 11-10 Lt. Harold McKnight Leazer (fifth uniformed figure from the left) from Remington, Virginia, commanded the 454th Bomb Group of the 736th Squadron. In June 1944 his family received the news that his B-24 had been shot down over St. Polten, Austria. Leazer, at first listed as missing in action, did not survive the crash and was posthumously awarded the Air Medal. His tailgunner, Jennings H. Titus of Petersburg (squatting on the right), survived and spent the rest of the war as a prisoner. Before going overseas, the squadron posed at Sloppy Joe's Bar in Havana, Cuba.

Bradford, were set up as temporary facilities before Peary was ready, but increasing demand kept these camps open as well.

It was truly a world war. Virginians sweltered in the heat of Port Moresby and elsewhere on the coast of New Guinea and the other Pacific islands unloading supplies for General Douglas MacArthur's drive north. They also endured fog and cold in the Aleutian Islands. Halfway around the world, after an evening at the theater in bombed-out London, Virginians with the 8th Air Force could, the next day, be looking down on central Germany from their B-17s and B-24s. From 25,000 feet they could see the smoke and watch the bombs explode and look straight ahead and see the ugly puffs of flak reaching up for them. Under the sea they sweated out the depth-charge attacks from enemy destroyers and felt the same fear as soldiers who looked out across the snow-covered fields and fir forests around Bastogne.

Sacrifices in war are always made unevenly. Some families sent their sons and daughters, husbands and fathers, off to war and after years of worry saw them return safe and whole. Others knew the pain of deep, unrelieved loss when the dreaded telegram came that began, "The Secretary of War regrets to inform you that your son. ..."

Virginia State Library and Archives

National Archives

FIGURE 11-11 *Above*: When German submarines mined the entrance to the Chesapeake Bay in early 1942, the war at sea was brought close to the Virginia shoreline. The American tanker *Tiger* sank off Virginia Beach in April 1942 after being struck by a German torpedo. Eight ships were sunk off the Virginia-North Carolina coast in January 1942; that number rose to nearly one a day in March. *Below*: Also in April, the German submarine U-85 sank in the bay. Military prisoners from Fort Monroe dug graves in the Hampton National Cemetery for the twenty-nine recovered bodies. The German sailors were the first foreign enemy soldiers interred in American soil since the War of 1812.

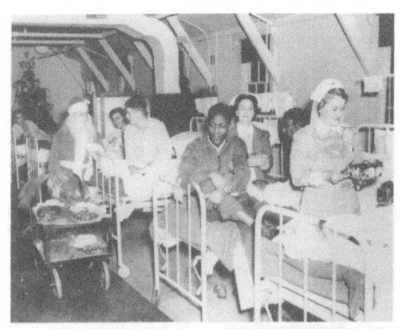

Virginia State Library and Archives

Virginia Historical Society

FIGURE 11-12 Although many Virginia women joined the war effort in the traditional role of nursing, such as these Gray Ladies giving out Christmas treats to the wounded at Camp Patrick Henry Hospital (above), others actively served in the military. They volunteered for the WACs, WAFs, and WASPs and performed shore duty in administrative positions in the Women Reserves. Margaret Curry of Richmond joined the WAVES in March 1943. After attending boot camp at Hunter College in The Bronx, Curry went on to navy training school at Iowa State Teachers' College in Cedar Rapids. She became a yeoman second class and was stationed in the detail office of the Receiving Station, NOB/ Norfolk, where Chief Yeoman Sidney Cohen oversaw her work (below).

The Virginians of Company A, 116th Regiment, 29th Infantry Division, who went ashore on Omaha Beach early on D-Day, 6 June 1944, were especially ill-starred. Their six landing craft came under accurate fire while still far offshore. One craft simply disappeared. Another foundered. The men on the other four heard machine gun bullets ricochet off the front ramps before they were lowered. The craft were still several hundred yards from the seawall when the ramps fell and the men began to die. Flogged by fire from German rifles, machine guns, artillery, and mortars, they absorbed punishing casualties. Within ten minutes, every officer and NCO was dead or wounded. Within ten more, the company virtually ceased to exist. Ninety-six percent of the 197 men in the company were casualties. Forty-six of them came from Bedford (population 3,800). Twenty-three died. With replacements, the company went on to fight its way across France and into Germany, but for the soldiers nothing would ever be the same again.

Virginia provided extensive training for military personnel, especially those on the way to the Mediterranean or the European Theater of Operations. Hampton Roads Port of Embarkation in Warwick County saw many come and go. Camp Patrick Henry, close by, was a major staging area for HRPE. Capable of housing 35,000 men, the camp and its operations benefited from the extensive labor of German and Italian prisoners of war, who did much of the laundry and the KP. Among the notable groups to pass through were Nisei units, composed of Americans of Japanese ancestry, and the 92d "Buffalo" Division, made up of black troops.

Women in uniform served in every branch. The Women's Army Auxiliary Corps (WAAC), which became the WACs when it was made an integral part of the army, was established in May 1942. Serving in almost all military jobs except combat, WACs were present in every theater of war. Top WAC strength was 99,000 in April 1945. The WAVES (Women Accepted for Volunteer Emergency Service) provided comparable services for the navy by performing shore duty primarily in administrative positions. The peak number of Women Reserves, as they were called after 1944, was 90,000 in July 1945. Two groups of women worked in or with the air force, the Women's Airforce Service Pilots (WASP) and the Women's Auxiliary Ferrying Squadron (WAFS). Mainly employed to ferry planes from plants to airbases, these women pilots also towed targets for gunnery practice, made weather flights, and carried out a variety of other noncombat but frequently dangerous duties. When the WASPs were deactivated in December 1944, 916 women were on duty. Although the Marine Corps had enlisted women in World War I, it was the last service to admit women during World War II. The Women's Reserve of the United States Marine Corps was established in February 1943. By the end of the next year there were more than 1,000 women at Quantico. The highest strength of these women marines was more than 18,000 in the summer of 1945.

As in past conflicts, women performed in more traditional roles as nurses. In hospitals such as those at Fort Eustis and Camp Pickett, on hospital ships, in forward aid stations and rehabilitation centers all around the world, women worked to repair the physical and emotional wreckage caused by combat, stress, and accident.

For those who remained at home as civilians, the war in Virginia was as close as the coast. German submarines ravaging American and Allied shipping were literally right offshore and in early 1942 even mined the entrance to the Chesapeake Bay. Debris from ships sunk within sight of the beaches floated ashore on the incoming tide. Eight ships were sunk off the Virginia-North Carolina coast in January 1942, and the number rose to nearly one a day in March.

After the shock of Pearl Harbor, Americans all over the nation responded to appeals for blackouts against air raids and caution against saboteurs. People on both coasts answered the call with special urgency. Virginians had reason to be particularly wary. The nation's capital was in their backyard, and vulnerable shipyards and port facilities dotted the coast.

Faced with these uncertainties, in May 1942 the governor created yet another paramilitary force called the Virginia Reserve Militia (VRM). Known as the Minute Men, they were an auxiliary of the VPF and were intended to delay an enemy attacking force until better-equipped troops arrived. Averaging in age between forty-five and fifty, they furnished their own uniforms, weapons, and ammunition. The state supplied only the idea and the insignia. Unlike the VPF, they were not required to serve outside their communities. Every county was supposed to have at least one company and every city a company for each 30,000 people. Eventually the VRM comprised 117 companies and three troops of cavalry numbering more than 8,000 officers and men. Though not disbanded until the end of the war, these units, armed with shotguns and target rifles, were thankfully never called on to face Axis paratroopers.

Others wore different uniforms and insignia. The Red Cross, the USO, air raid wardens, and plane spotters all participated in the war effort. Across the commonwealth Red Cross volunteers rolled bandages, collected blood, and conducted first aid courses. Working with the International Red Cross, they made it possible for prisoners of war and their families to communicate and for families to send badly needed food parcels to American captives of Germany and Japan. Red Cross workers formed support groups for relatives of POWs and shared information through newsletters. With the wartime shortage of doctors, volunteers worked in military hospitals visiting wounded GIs and helping with rehabilitation programs. Red Cross volunteers also staffed canteens and participated in war bond drives.

The United Service Organizations (USO) was made up of six national welfare associations: the YMCA, the YWCA, the Jewish Welfare Board, the Salvation Army, the National Travelers Aid Association, and the National Catholic Community Service. These groups united to provide recreation and various comforts to servicemen and women as well as war workers. Beyond such well-known efforts as dances and entertainments, the USO developed hobby projects, fishing trips, talent shows, visits to historical sites, and even taffy pulls. Mobile units went to more distant outposts with movies, cigarettes, games, puzzles, and books. At Union Station in Washington, D.C., what had been the president's reception room was turned over to the USO to be used as a servicemen's lounge. The Norfolk "Y" set up cots for servicemen, and the USO also provided dance lessons, camera clubs, and community sings at twenty centers. Richmond's Jewish Community Council sponsored Saturday night dances

FIGURE 11-13 After the attack on Pearl Harbor, Virginia joined the rest of the country in dividing itself into air raid warning centers. These centers were further subdivided into zones, precincts, and sectors, all staffed by volunteers. The commonwealth had twenty-six centers, each equipped with air raid shelters, trucks, and observation posts, similar to the one seen in Emporia on Tillar Street.

FIGURE 11-14 Air raid wardens were supplied with sirens and flashlights and sported armbands with the Civil Defense insignia. This employee of the Newport News Shipbuilding and Dry Dock Company volunteered in May 1942 to help sound the alarm if enemy planes were sighted.

and Sunday afternoon buffets and issued a general invitation to "servicemen and women of all faiths" to visit "the oldest servicemen's center of this war in the U.S."—"The Center of Southern Hospitality." The Richmond USO provided female escorts for servicemen who wanted to attend area churches.

The fear of direct attack from German or Japanese bombers was a real one all over the nation in 1941–42, especially on the coasts.

Plane-spotting stations staffed by volunteers were set up to warn of impending attack. Virginia's plane spotters were drilled by pilots from nearby airfields who simulated enemy raids. In areas believed to be particularly vulnerable, the British system of air raid wardens

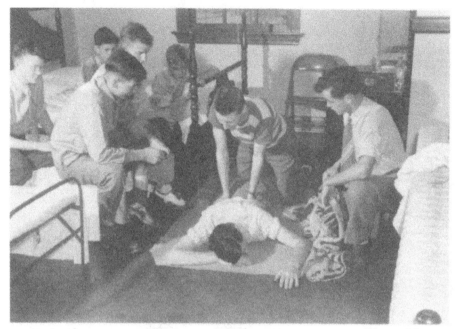

WAR STAMPS
FOR
VICTORY

Compliments of
THALHIMERS
RICHMOND, VIRGINIA

FIGURE 11-15 The young people of Virginia also became actively involved in the war effort. A first aid demonstration was given at Randolph Henry High School dispensary in Keysville in June 1940. Youngsters were encouraged to buy war stamps—green stamps were priced at 25 cents, red at 10 cents—that would eventually add up in value to a war bond.

was adopted. These volunteers worked with Civil Defense authorities to ensure the safety of American civilians by enforcing blackouts and providing information on air raid shelters. The Virginia Defense Council published recommendations for organizing the state's air raid warning system just three days after Pearl Harbor. Twenty-six air raid warning centers were set up in the commonwealth, each subdivided into zones, precincts, and sectors. Volunteers were investigated by the military to make sure that they were not enemy agents.

The dangers to civilians in modern war were brought home in countless ways, from air raid drills, blackouts, testing of sirens, and headlight covers for automobiles to gas masks for noncombatants and plane spotter cards in bubble gum packages. Miller and Rhoads employees in fireproof suits were trained to put out incendiary bombs if any fell on the roof of the department store in Richmond.

The dollar cost of the war was enormous. The national budget for 1941–42 appropriated $14.6 billion for the army alone. Income and other taxes could not cover it all, even though World War II saw the beginning of payroll deductions to prepay the annual income tax a paycheck at a time. The government also sold bonds to individuals. Bond sales brought the war home to everyone, soaked up excess wages, dampened inflation, and raised revenue. A national advertising campaign urged Americans to put 10 percent of their income into war bonds. A billboard exhorting tourists to buy bonds appeared on Natural Bridge in Rockbridge County. Celebrities on national tours made appeals. Children could help by purchasing green (25 cents) or red (10 cents) war stamps to put into books that, when filled, would buy a $25 or $50 war bond.

Much of that money went for the multitude of matériel that the military needed to carry on the war. Because of the comparatively limited industrial capacity of the southern states in the 1940s, the majority of the total of $300 billion in war contracts went to other parts of the nation. By early 1943, however, Virginia firms held nearly $2 billion in contracts, second only to Texas among southern states. Virginia's economy boomed. The military posts and bases needed thousands of civilian workers. Governmental administrative activity spilled out over Northern Virginia. The state produced immense quantities of the munitions and ships vital for success in the war. Newport News Shipbuilding and Dry Dock Company expanded from 13,000 workers in 1939 to 70,000 in 1943. Factories of all sizes produced everything from parachutes, tents, plastic hoses for bombers, uniforms, paper, ice, and shoes for the navy to tire fabric, cargo covers, and lawn chairs for military clubs.

The Radford Arsenal was one of many examples of the wartime industrial expansion in Virginia. Because American production of explosives was so limited when war began in Europe, Congress authorized a massive enlargement of munitions facilities. Construction began at Radford Ordnance Works in September 1940, and the arsenal was producing smokeless powder within seven months. Radford ultimately employed more than 22,000 workers.

Because war production made labor an increasingly valuable commodity, salaries rose as employers bid for workers' services. Why work for the prevailing wage of 35 cents an hour at Colonial Williamsburg or the College of William and Mary when nearby Yorktown

FIGURE 11-16 Boy Scouts from Gloucester helped to conduct a scrap metal drive. The metal was sold to a scrap dealer, who turned it over to appropriate parts-making companies.

Naval Weapons Station paid 58 cents an hour? Rising wages combined with frequently noisy, unsafe, and repetitive working conditions meant that there was a great deal of jumping from job to job. During one three- month period Newport News Shipbuilding hired 8,400 new workers, but 8,300 others quit.

The expansion of facilities and shortages of male employees created new opportunities for women, although they were most likely to find work at plants that had traditionally hired women. Some factories, such as DuPont's Spruance Rayon Plant, employed women in many new jobs, however. An individual example was Thelma Stern, employed at the Norfolk Navy Yard in Portsmouth as ship's draftsman. She became the first woman allowed to go aboard ships to collect data on the weight and location of items being added to or removed from the vessel. Up to this time, work rules, male prerogatives, and superstition kept women on land. Opportunities for promotion for women were limited, however. Few became supervisors except in industries employing large numbers of women. Although women were frequently paid less than men, at federal installations equal pay for equal work was the rule.

For Virginia's farmers, World War II brought both good times and troubles. Lend-Lease and military consumption drove farm prices up. The demand for cigarettes caused tobacco to be declared an essential crop, and its growers and harvesters were given liberal exemptions from military service. Though farm workers' wages rose to four times prewar levels,

FIGURE 11-17   In preparation for an exam at the Virginia Mechanics' Institute, these members of the Motor Corps of the Volunteer Service Bureau of the Richmond Community Council studied the undercarriage of a truck with the guidance of state trooper John Clinely.

farmers lost laborers to the draft and defense jobs in the cities. As in much of the rest of the nation, Virginia farmers employed high school students and prisoners of war for harvesting.

Probably most important in the long run, the increased demand and labor shortage spurred mechanization of agriculture. Because fewer laborers were needed, the depopulation of rural Virginia accelerated and was never reversed. In the 1950 census for the first time urban dwellers outnumbered rural Virginians. By fostering a mechanical revolution on farms, World War II freed labor for a retail and service economy and proved to be a catalyst for far-reaching changes that continued for the next half century.

The federal government tried to provide adequate supplies for the armed forces and American allies, to assure fair distribution of scarce items, and to control inflation. It gradually introduced price controls and rationing measures supervised by the Office of Price Administration. Among the many items that were placed on the ration list were shoes, leather, sugar, rubber, gasoline, some meats, nylon items, some canned goods, liquor, and coffee. Men's suits no longer came with vests or two pairs of pants.

Local boards issued ration books with coupons to residents. Drivers were allocated A, B, or X stickers—depending on their occupations— that determined the amount of gasoline that they could purchase each week. Rationed items had to be paid for with both money and ration coupons. The OPA set ceiling prices to keep profiteering to a minimum, but the black market and forged coupons could not be completely eliminated. The shift in production by many prewar distillers to ethyl alcohol was especially painful to some and led to a resurgence of moonshining and bootlegging. Rationing meant that the war was present for everyone, every day.

FIGURE 11-18   In 1940 the War Department desperately needed new powder production plants for ammunition. To avoid costly delay and red tape, the army contracted with the Hercules Powder Company in Radford and built onto the existing plant to form the Radford Ordnance Works. The site was chosen because the plant was protected from attack by the nearby mountains. Even so, security inspections of all the workers were standard procedure.

The news media naturally covered the war in great detail. In both their stories and their advertising, news magazines focused primarily on the conflict. Newspapers expanded their coverage of local men and women in the service and traced the course of the war on every front. The war's domination of the front pages led one nine-year-old in 1944 to ask, "Mom, are there going to be headlines after the war is over?" By mid-1942 it was almost impossible to turn a page in *Life* magazine without finding the war. Advertisers in print and on the radio asked for the indulgence of their customers because so many products were limited or unavailable for the duration. The Ford Motor Company jingle sung on the radio was typical: "There's a Ford in your future,/ But the Ford in your past/ Is the one you have now,/ So you better make it last."

Appeals to everyone to conserve, recycle, share rides, "use it up, wear it out, make it do, or do without" brought the population into the effort in a way that was unique in American history. Virginians were challenged, for example, by the information that the people of Nebraska had collected 136 million pounds of scrap (103 pounds per person) and told that they should be able to do better. Boy Scouts pulled wagons full of newspapers on paper drives.

FIGURE 11-19   Part of the work done at the Norfolk Naval Air Station involved the repair of damaged planes. Workers were reminded by signs on the planes to treat them with tender loving care, because many people depended on the workers' expertise in restoring the aircraft to fighting shape.

The Richmond Pigeon Fanciers Concourse Association gave the government two hundred birds for breeding. Victory gardens increased food supplies nationwide more than anyone in government had anticipated. In August 1943 Inez Goddin Freeman of Richmond, the wife of historian Douglas Southall Freeman, won a prize of one hundred pounds of fertilizer for having the largest victory garden in an exhibition. Residents of towns and cities across Virginia worked side by side in community victory gardens. That sense of community and shared effort remain for many the primary memory of what Studs Terkel called "the good war."

World War II, however, did not end or even suspend the tensions between labor and capital, between the races, and between political parties. The tensions were often submerged but surfaced, for example, when John L. Lewis took his United Mine Workers out on strike in 1943. He won a small raise for the coal miners and the unremitting hostility of most Americans. Both labor and management demonstrated a willingness to use the pressures of war to advance their causes.

Competition between blacks and whites for housing, recreation facilities, and jobs led to tensions in Washington, D.C., and other cities crowded with newcomers. Jim Crow on military bases and a segregated military establishment led blacks to promote a Double V

U.S. Army Quartermaster Museum, Fort Lee

Courtesy of Vivian Morris

FIGURE 11-20 Virginia housed German POWs during the war in camps throughout the state. At Bellwood (above), a 3,000-man camp in Chesterfield County, a German prisoner gave the Nazi salute to Maj. Gen. Philip Hayes, who was there to inspect the installation. Because of the acute labor shortage, prisoners of war from Camp Pickett (below) helped load hay into a baler.

FIGURE 11-21 To encourage local food production, Mervin A. McKenney (rear center standing in front of the window) founded a community cannery at Mathews High School. Canning was conducted on segregated shifts. Although publicity for jobs in new factories boasted equal opportunity and good pay for all, the reality was often much different.

FIGURE 11-22 By 1942, food rationing was in force. Families grew their own food supplies in victory gardens similar to the one tended by this trailer park resident in Arlington. Communities often had contests for the best home-grown produce.

FIGURE 11-23 This group of fifth graders at a Roanoke elementary school was shown the importance of recycling old rubber tires. Rubber was used in the making of gas masks, and one tire would supply enough material for twelve masks.

campaign to defeat fascism abroad and racism at home. Through the expanded opportunities and broadening experiences that World War II provided them, black Americans began the first stirrings of the civil rights movement that transformed Virginia and the rest of the South in the following decades.

Politicians, not surprisingly, were unable completely to disregard the possibility of gaining political advantage from the war. Despite all the griping and fear and upheaval for Virginians and for Americans generally, the period from Pearl Harbor to V-J Day marked a special time. They looked back on it as one when the nation was more united than at any other time that they remembered.

And then it was over. The fighting in Europe ended in May 1945. Some units remained as part of an occupying force, while others were in the process of transshipment to the Pacific for the expected invasion of Japan. Suddenly that conflict was over too. The atomic bombs dropped on Hiroshima and Nagasaki ended the four-year effort by millions of men and women in the services, and millions more at home, to destroy the will and capacity of Japan to make war.

During those years, the nation and the Old Dominion had changed. The state's population had grown dramatically, especially in Northern Virginia, where the nerve center of the war effort continued to be the center of the nation's response to the Cold War. The great increase in industrial production and jobs in Virginia was another legacy of the conflict.

The war on the home front was more than statistical increases, however. Americans had changed in ways that prove harder to measure. They fought and prevailed as part of the greatest

Kirn Memorial Library, Norfolk

Courtesy of Laura Dervishian; Courtesy of Richard M. Hamrick, Jr. (inset)

FIGURE 11-24 The end of the war in both Europe and Japan brought celebrations in Virginia. Sailors snake-danced down Granby Street in Norfolk, and a woman in Staunton expressed her pleasure at the banner headlines. Richmond's own Lt. Ernest Dervishian, a Medal of Honor recipient, was welcomed back with a homecoming parade in 1945.

FIGURE 11-25 A wartime wedding between Mabel Elizabeth Barlow and Leon Jenkins was performed at Richmond's Tabernacle Baptist Church in June 1944. Both served in the military— Jenkins as an aviation machinist for the USNR in Norfolk and Barlow as a yeoman second class in the WAVES—although the bride was married in a traditional white dress and not her uniform.

FIGURE 11-26 By the war's end, rural Virginia suffered depopulation. The 1950 census showed, for the first time, that urban dwellers outnumbered those who lived on farms. Early temporary housing set up for defense workers grew into communities of suburban homes with wooded properties.

FIGURE 11-27   On 8 March 1946 Winston Churchill stepped off the train in Williamsburg to tour the historic capital. Army chief of staff Dwight D. Eisenhower accompanied him. Earlier that day, Churchill had addressed the Virginia General Assembly; he praised Eisenhower and said that Great Britain and the United States should "forge a new union of hearts based upon conviction and common ideals."

coalition in the world's history, provided weapons and supplies for themselves and their allies, overcame the last vestiges of the Great Depression, and defeated powerful enemies. Both civilians and those in uniform contributed to the victory and could share a justifiable pride. What Americans had seen in the opening of Buchenwald and Auschwitz, however, told also of the depravity to which human beings could descend and tempered any excessive optimism. The bombings of Tokyo and Dresden and Hiroshima led, for the thoughtful at least, to a more somber assessment of the victory. The war cost all participants dearly.

Of the Virginians who went off to war, more than seven thousand never came home. Many of those who survived came back to parades and the welcome of a grateful nation. Others returned quietly to a country that was rapidly moving on to peacetime pursuits and expected veterans to get on with making a life in civilian society. The GI Bill gave many of them an opportunity that would have been unavailable otherwise to attend college and build a better future for themselves and for the nation. They flooded the campuses from the largest universities to the smallest schools. Whether they stayed at home during the war or went to the ends of the earth, they saw with new eyes a future and a state that had been profoundly changed.

12

Civil Rights and Memory: 1948–1970

By Matthew Mace Barbee

I n 1948, white dominance of electoral politics was briefly interrupted by the election of lawyer Oliver Hill to the Richmond City Council. Hill would lose reelection in 1950, but his brief success was the first step in the slow dismantling of disenfranchisement. In the ensuing years of active work for full civil rights, African American political action groups and civic associations worked tirelessly to expand voter registration. As schools were desegregated and as suburbanization altered the demographics of Richmond's electorate, these political changes looked to become more permanent and the patient efforts of the early-century middle class would pay off. However, fear of the loss of political control spurred Richmond's traditional white elite to action. Through a combination of legal and illegal anti-integration efforts, the white elite worked to perpetuate their control. Their fears were manifest in the resurgence of Confederate heritage and a new-found competition with Northern Virginia and Norfolk for dominance within the state. And, just as the anti-integration movement worked to slow the tide of political change, throughout the 1950s and '60s Richmond's civil rights movement used a range of tactics to counter these legal and illegal actions and take advantage of demographic change and the larger national tide of political change. In the 1970s, largely through the efforts of a working-class African American man, Curtis Holt, the illegal actions of the anti-integration movement were brought before the U.S. Supreme Court and Richmond was prevented from holding municipal elections for seven years. This moratorium on local elections ended, and, at last, Richmond's African American community gained a majority on the City Council in 1978. The 1980s saw the continued influence of this community, culminating in the election of African American Richmonder L. Douglas Wilder as state governor in 1989. By this time, the energies that had been dedicated to shifting Richmond's political culture were invested in revising the memorial landscapes of Richmond and Monument Avenue. While the resurgence of Confederate heritage had been a key cultural symbol for the anti-integration movements, the reimagination of Richmond's and Virginia's historical identity became a crucial site of negotiation as the echoes of the civil rights movement continued and the region took note of the waves of globalization that were eroding the surface of traditional Southern identity.

MEMORY AND ELECTORAL POLITICS IN THE CIVIL RIGHTS AND ANTI-INTEGRATION MOVEMENTS

This period, 1948–1970, was marked by expanded political franchise and social citizenship that followed the paths opened by the social, cultural, and economic upheaval of World War II. As political historian Alexander Keysar argues in his important political history of the franchise, *The Right to Vote: The Contested History of Democracy in the United States*, "nearly all the major expansions of the franchise that have occurred in American history took place during or in the wake of wars."[1] It is nearly impossible to recruit and motivate legions of soldiers, many of whom come from disenfranchised, subaltern groups, if those same groups are denied full citizenship. World War II, like the Civil War before it, was a key event in the social and political histories leading up to African American franchise. In Virginia, African Americans had been almost uniformly disenfranchised under Jim Crow. In 1940, of 364,224 African American Virginians over the age of twenty-one, only 30,967 were registered to vote.[2] This small fraction, a mere eleven percent, had begun the historic shift from the Republican coalition to the Democratic coalition. According to historian Andrew Buni, African American Virginians' distrust of the Byrd machine did not prevent their overwhelming support for Roosevelt.

This shift had a larger resonance in the imagination of the white elite than it did at the polls. Even if all 30,967 registered African American Virginians voted for FDR, they formed only a small portion of his resounding victory over Wilkie in Virginia in the 1940 election, 235,961 to 109,363.[3] However, as World War II progressed, African American civic associations worked to register voters. From 1941 to 1944 the number of African American Virginians who were registered to vote grew from 30,748 to 32,889. And, as the war ended, and servicemen returned home, those figures grew to 38,020.[4] The enrollment of African American voters would continue after the war as civic associations mobilized community support. Between 1945 and 1948 African American Richmonders had more than doubled their presence in the electorate, with the number of registered voters expanding from 6,374 to 11,127.[5]

As described by Randolph and Tate and sociologists John V. Moeser and Routledge M. Dennis, the late 1940s was an era in which African American Richmonders made political strides through community mobilization and advancing a moderate agenda supported by the dominant white elite. Importantly, increased African American political mobilization was also born out of the stifling climate of Jim Crow segregation. In terms of leadership, many African American legal and political leaders had been trained in historically black colleges and universities, settings in which they were taught to be committed to African American rights. For example, both Thurgood Marshall and Oliver Hill went to Howard University's law school and were there influenced to take on civil rights activism.[6] In more general terms, the closely knit communities of African American Richmond had developed close social ties and civic associations that were crucial for the motivation and organization of a large- scale social movement. For many young people who went on to play a significant role in the movement in Richmond, this community was central to the formation of a generation committed to African American rights. As Jean Ellis Harris recalled,

> All of the individuals with whom I came in contact during my early and forma-
> tive years whether they were my mother's friends, relatives, teachers, principal,
> members of my church—everyone took an interest in exhorting all of us as
> young people to excellence, and instilling in us a sense of responsibility for the
> well being of future generations of black people.[7]

This generation built upon and drew from the same community institutions that defined their childhoods. In 1946, the Richmond Civic Council (RCC), an association of over eighty church, civic, fraternal, labor, business, and educational groups, started a massive voter registration drive. The RCC also supported efforts in 1947 for city charter reform spearheaded by the Richmond Citizens Association (RCA), the political body of the local white elite. The RCC reasoned that if they supported the RCA's charter reform they would ensure both the possible support of the white elite and would be able to encourage measures within the new charter that would allow for African American representation.

This was a crucial moment for African Americans in Richmond and it was seized by the man who would, for the better part of the twentieth century, prove to be the major thinker and leader of that movement. Oliver Hill graduated from Howard University Law School, where he was second in the class of 1933 behind Thurgood Marshall. Hill practiced law in Richmond before serving in World War II. After the war, he began in earnest his activism for African American civil rights and in 1947 ran for City Council. He lost, but his showing and the passage of the new city charter were encouraging for the RCC, who foresaw great potential for collaboration with the RCA. In 1948 Hill was elected, primarily due to the success of voter registration drives.

These voter registration drives involved more than simply having men and women sign up. While the RCC and other affiliate groups faced great opposition in the form of disenfranchisement practices, they made use of African American media and social networks to both enable and encourage voter registration. Virginia did not hinder registration in ways common across the South—by having registration offices that were off- limits to African Americans or with limited hours, for example—and the main barriers were a poll tax and a form with twelve questions that tested the respondent's "understanding" of the law. Because the poll tax was high, community organizers such as Dr. W. Ferguson Reid began by encouraging those people who could afford the tax. And, Reid explains, since

> the poll tax list was public knowledge, and they had people listed by blacks and whites, so it made it easier for us to identify the blacks who had paid the poll tax. So we had that reproduced and we put it in all the barbershops and beauty shops. We had signs made don't talk politics in here if you don't vote. And under that we had the poll tax list so that the barbers would be encouraged to vote and register themselves so that when anybody got in a political discussion the first thing they would do is go to the book to see whether you are qualified to make a statement or not. Also, we got the Afro [the *Richmond Afro-American* newspaper] to publish the list of people that had paid the poll tax. [8]

The publication of the poll tax list in barbershops and beauty parlors had the desired effect. Because barbershops were an important site in voter registration drives and a central space for dialogue among African American men, the posting of the poll tax list created a sense of purpose and motivation for men to register to vote. In an interview with the Church Hill Oral History Project through Virginia Commonwealth University's Virginia Black History Archives, Douglas Wilder recalled spending time in the barbershop next to his childhood home. He remarked that the barbers

> used to say when someone opened his mouth, "Douglas, look in the book and see if you see his name." And if his name wasn't in the book we wouldn't let him talk so he couldn't talk because he was not a registered voter and we didn't allow it and so he just couldn't do it, and that little gimmick was so embarrassing to so many people that they would immediately go and register to vote and then come back and if their name wasn't in the book they would pull out their card and slip and say I can do it because I can vote. [9]

Of course, these voter registration drives did face other challenges, including the bureaucratic barriers put into place to limit the African American franchise. In the same interview, Reid remarked that

> On the blank paper registration you also had to have it notarized, so there were not many black notaries at that time, so we encouraged blacks to become notaries so with the understanding they would notarize the papers without charging the blacks, so we flooded the—city hall with people applying for notaries. When they found out we were becoming notarized, and there were not that many white notaries they did away with that.[10]

Despite the challenges the RCC and later groups faced in their efforts to register African American voters, through creative problem-solving which involved tapping into the strong communal ties of African American Richmond, they were able to greatly increase the size of the African American electorate.

Throughout this era, the Byrd machine continued its domination of Virginia and Richmond politics. While committed to segregation, Byrd was opposed to overt displays of violence and opposed voter intimidation and other tactics that, historically and in other parts of the South, were used to discourage African American voters.[11] While they faced procedural challenges, Hill and the RCC were not threatened with the large-scale violence brought upon activists in other areas of the South. The RCC harnessed this limited participation, endorsing no other candidates in the at-large city elections. By putting their entire electoral strength behind a single candidate, rather than a full slate, the RCC hoped to ensure Hill's endorsement by the RCA.[12] They hoped that this tactic, combined with Hill's moderate political stances and his support by some whites, would win the RCA's endorsement. However, the RCA failed to include Hill on their slate of candidates, a move which angered the leadership of the RCC and made clear the complexities of developing biracial political coalitions. While the RCA did include Hill on their 1950 slate, he failed to win reelection.[13] These failures made clear that while RCA may have been invested in allowing moderate, conservative African Americans to form a minority within the city government, they did so on their own terms. Moreover, Hill's failure to win reelection pointed to internal fractures within the RCC that would eventually lead to its premature demise, enabling the rise of the more aggressive Richmond Crusade for Voters (RCV), a political action group with closer ties to the burgeoning civil rights movement.[14] In the past African Americans had lacked the foothold to mount political campaigns that were openly opposed to the local elite. However, the voter campaign drives of the 1940s and '50s had established a large enough electorate and provided the motivation necessary for the germination and perpetuation of the African American political action groups that did not answer to the interests of white elites.

Through the 1950s, no other African American gained political office in Richmond. However, the political mobilization of voters and communities combined with Richmond's shifting demographics, urban development, and economic prospects to keep the possibility of African American political involvement and control at the center of political and cultural conflict. As was common across the nation, postwar Richmond experienced widespread sub-urbanization that was facilitated by federal economic, housing, and transportation policies and the mobilization of our national "possessive investment in whiteness."[15] Suburbanization drew white voters out of the city and into surrounding Henrico and Chesterfield counties. Faced with a declining population, Richmond's elites attempted to revivify the city through urban renewal plans; repeatedly, Norfolk was held up as a model of those plans, in part because of its relative rise within the state. Urban development and transportation projects led to decline of Jackson Ward, the historic center of Richmond's African American community.[16]

In the 1950s, Hill worked closely with the NAACP and Thurgood Marshall and legally challenged those social structures and institutions that exacerbated the political disenfran-chisement of African Americans. As the NAACP lawyer for Virginia, Hill and his staff filed more civil rights suits for equal education than were filed in any other Southern state in this period.[17] In one of these cases, *Davis v. County School Board of Prince Edward County*, Hill represented a well-organized group of Moton High School students who had walked out of the tar-paper shack that served as their school. That case wound its way through the courts and became one of the five cases that Marshall and the NAACP Legal Defense Fund team brought before the U.S. Supreme Court and which would, in time, be known as *Brown v. Board of Education*. Hill's role in this landmark case is indicative of his life's work, challenging racism through the courts, and although his time in the City Council was very short-lived, he remained committed to augmenting legal action with political and social action. It was in this era that he recruited a young Howard Law graduate, Henry Marsh, into his firm. Marsh would go on to further the goals of the movement in a long career in the City Council and state General Assembly that has lasted from 1978 until the present day. Hill's commitment to political and social change was also evident in a speech he gave to the very people he had represented in *Davis v. County School Board of Prince Edward County*. Hill called for his listeners to lessen their dependence on legal decisions and to augment those gains by voting. More important, Hill urged his audience to get over old patterns and habits of social behavior that enabled racism. He criticized the old habit of "playing dumb," which Hill described as "a hangover from the slavery days when you could always fool a white man by playing dumb ... now you must show that you want to be a first-class citizen."[18] While Hill placed his legal expertise in the service of the NAACP and the greater cause of civil rights, he urged the greater community to take personal action through voting and changing patterns of behavior. Civil rights would only come through personal responsibility and respectability.

As these demographic shifts occurred, *Brown vs. Board of Education* exacerbated the growing spatial segregation of the city by encouraging suburbanization and engendering racial fear. Harry Byrd, through his influence as a long-tenured senator, issued calls for Southern governments to use policy, legal, and constitutional measures to fight the forced segregation of schools. As a leader of massive resistance, Byrd worked with George Wallace,

Strom Thurmond, and other segregationist politicians. While he continued to embrace more benign practices than his colleagues, his steadfastness and his efforts to use legal measures resonated deeply across Richmond's civil rights movement. As the fight against segregation became more heated, it transformed into a dual-front struggle that was fought through the courts and legislative bodies and in street protests. The RCC, while somewhat successful in making slow gains in the 1940s, was unable to carry on this campaign and was replaced by the RCV, which, through ties to the NAACP, was able to wage court battles and successful protests, boycotts, and strikes. The RCV used a structure similar to that of a political machine; thorough top-down organization kept all the members on message and coordinated toward the same goals. This strategy proved effective and the massive resistance campaign lost its traction in Richmond during the 1960s.[19]

The rise of the RCV in place of the RCC and the NAACP is also evidence of the ways civil rights activists responded to the politically entrenched segregationist activists who enjoyed broad legal and judicial powers because of their positions in state and local government. After the *Brown* decision, the state government organized a series of General Assembly committees that were tasked with designing a response to school integration. Some of these committees, such as the Gray Commission, used their powers to hinder the work of the NAACP and other organizations. According to Ferguson Reid, NAACP organizers in Virginia

> couldn't operate because the NAACP was also under attack by the Virginia General Assembly. They were trying to get the membership list of the NAACP because they knew most of the members were rural people who depended on a livelihood of whites, if they could get the membership list they could put pressure on the members not to participate, threaten to fire them and so forth.[20]

Since it was near impossible for the NAACP to operate in Virginia, Reid and other Richmond organizers decided that for their work to be "the most effective we should separate from the NAACP and operate under a different name, and it came about that we were named the Crusade for Voters, and the main effort would be to register voters and educate them on politics."[21]

Throughout the 1960s, Richmond's white elite clung to power but remained well aware that their grasp was loosening, in large part because of the efforts by the RCV and continued white-flight suburbanization. By 1960, Richmond's African American population accounted for 42 percent of the population; the number of African American voters had risen from 12,486 in 1957 to 16,396 in 1961.[22] Census data indicated that by 1968 Richmond's population would have a majority African American population. Suburbanization also led to an imbalance of city and suburban services and infrastructures without suburban tax outlays. Richmond needed a larger tax base and land for development if it was going to expand and continue the services its metropolitan region needed.[23] In order to secure a larger tax base and prevent the dominance of local government by African Americans, Richmond's political leadership began proceedings to merge with Henrico County; when these attempts failed in 1965, Richmond's elite turned to Chesterfield County and, through closed door proceedings, were able to secure a portion of that county's land and population in 1970. The area of land annexed was almost wholly white and dramatically shifted the population of Richmond from the feared African American majority back to a white majority.[24] The subtext of racial segregation resonated in the 1968 election of two conservative African American candidates, B. A. Cephas and Winifred Mundle, to City Council. Both Cephas and Mundle were supported both by the RCV and a new group, Richmond Forward (RF) which had replaced the RCC.

RF was formed in 1963 by a group of business and community leaders.[25] Initially chaired by the aptly named, retired General Edwin Conquest, RF began as a social network of like-minded white men who worked together to develop a sustainable political network and organization. RF began through a series of casual meetings among concerned and like-minded Richmonders. Many of these founding members were local business leaders such as Samuel Bemiss, Harry Schwarzschild, and William Thalhimer and future Virginia Senator Willis Robertson.[26] Clandestinely calling themselves "The Group," in August 1963 they established a statement of purpose. Noting that while Richmond had grown over its 200-year history, it has always moved forward in services such as "protection from lawlessness and calamity, of public improvements and facilities, and of education and welfare. This forward movement was possible only because there were always leaders willing to give more of themselves for the cause of good government than they expected of others."[27] Adopting the name Richmond Forward, The Group agreed to pledge their "time, talent and resources" to encourage the most capable men and women to run for office, support those candidates, and to advise them on matters and help the City Council "discharge its duties in an efficient businesslike manner."[28] That fall RF began recruiting members. General Conquest asked members to search out prospective members among "individuals in second and third echelon positions in your own and other organizations" since, he felt, RF would already have identified and recruited company presidents.[29]

In November of that year RF held a dinner meeting followed by a recruitment presentation. The dinner was a success, and RF was able to recruit enough members and donors to launch an aggressive political movement in 1964. RF's initial strengths lay in Richmond's West End. The West End was a predominantly white, affluent area of families that had moved out of the central city toward the suburbs. This area of Richmond abuts Henrico County, which, at the time, was in negotiations for a merger with the city of Richmond. Had the merger gone through, Richmond's West End would have been linked with suburban areas with which it was demographically and economically similar; the West End would have become the new center of political power. RF reached out to that potential power center and recruited members among residents of the greater Richmond area, including Henrico and Chesterfield counties. In a newsletter sent out in 1964, the RF leadership stated that while RF did not anticipate merger or annexation with Chesterfield and Henrico counties, those counties and their residents "have an obvious stake in Richmond's progress. Many hold jobs in

Richmond, shop in the downtown area, use library facilities and entertainment facilities, and receive city services. ... A progressive, well-run Richmond is as important to these people as it is to Richmond citizens."[30]

While RF claimed that they did not anticipate merger or annexation, they did everything within their power to make it so. While David Mays and others worked behind closed doors to negotiate the merger, the platform RF developed in 1964 was heavily pro-merger. On April 7,1964, the RF finalized a platform which included a plank calling for the expansion of city boundaries. On the grounds that community interests transcended the city's legal boundaries, RF called for the expansion of boundaries "in order to incorporate those areas which should be a part of the City for the future betterment of a greater Richmond." Pledging themselves to giving "true representation" to those residents of areas that would be incorporated, RF argued strongly for local control of the greater Richmond area.[31]

RF's platform also included planks calling for the betterment of schools and the development of stronger technical training and improved housing and industrial development through the development of a more business-friendly city government. While the RF platform made no claims regarding race, a close analysis of it and other internal documents from 1964 points to the social and political values that were deeply embedded and depend upon ideals of paternalistic white privilege.

In January 1964, RF prepared a document to help its City Council candidates prepare for public debates. A series of expected questions are followed with suggested answers. While the answers are evidence of the image RF wanted to present to the electorate, the questions can help us gauge the challenges RF felt it faced in developing a politically viable image. In this document, RF attempted to prepare its candidates for hard questions regarding their political and personal feelings on African American civil rights. For example, RF prepared its candidates to deal with questions that asked how they felt "about better jobs in the city government for Negroes?" The recommended response to that question diverts attention away from the subject of race and emphasizes an ideal of a colorblind, merit-based polity: "I feel now and have always felt that every citizen should have an equal opportunity for employment and that jobs should be awarded on the basis of qualifications and not race, creed or color."[32] RF also prepared its candidates to deal with questions as to whether or not they employ African Americans in their businesses. The suggested responses do not include any in the affirmative; rather, candidates were given the option of simply stating "At the present time my company does not employ any Negro personnel" or amending that statement by adding that "my company has no policy restricting the employment of Negroes. When job vacancies occur within our organization, those jobs are filled on the basis of qualification and merit, and not because of a man's religion or his race."[33]

It is important to remember that in much of the South in 1964 segregation was still a violently enforced social order based upon myths of color. However, working to maintain a centuries-old hold on local government, Richmond's predominantly white business elite carefully avoided the stark racial hierarchies espoused by political leaders in other Southern states and deployed a rhetoric that displaced race as a salient term in the debate and instead employed merit and qualification as the basis for full citizenship and entry into business and polity.

This rhetoric drew from the centuries-old practice of maintaining white privilege by investing political power within state and local governments. For example, while the anti-integration movement had worked tirelessly to preserve racial segregation and white privilege, it had done so through claims to a conservative interpretation of federalism. By claiming states' rights, anti-integrationists could resist federally enforced integration without vocally espousing segregation. This strategy was evident in RF's campaign documents. In April, in an internal memo circulated among members, RF's leadership argued strongly against federal urban renewal plans. These plans and the federal Civil Rights Act were attacked not for their content but because they were attempts to undermine local control and centralize power in Washington, DC. These rhetorics were manifest in the previously discussed notes on approaching debates. RF indicated that a likely question would ask how candidates felt "about the recent [City Council] proposal on Urban Redevelopment and Renewal?" RF candidates were encouraged to respond that while they had not yet studied the proposal in great detail, they could say that

> I favor a vigorous attack on our slum problem in Richmond. Almost every municipality has to look to their state and Federal government for help in these projects. However, I believe that we may be able to interest local private capital in underwriting some slum clearance projects once they have confidence in our dty council. The present city council certainly doesn't inspire much confidence in anyone.[34]

When asked to speak about current plans for urban development, RF encouraged its candidates to take the opportunity to attack the credibility of the current council and the role of the state and federal government in local growth. The speaker positions himself as concerned with a "slum" problem, thereby distancing himself from and evoking images of decay and violence associated with poor, African American neighborhoods. He uses this position to indicate that he, and other RF candidates, will be able to foster the confident environment in which local, private capital can be used for local development. Nowhere is race mentioned; rather, the images implicit in the word "slum" remind potential listeners of the fears associated with blackness. Moreover, by dismissing the current City Council and its assumed embrace of federal oversight, the RF candidate paints his opposition as ineptly enabling those fears. Thus, without mentioning race, the RF candidate positions himself as the confident, inspiring protector of Richmond from the encroachment of those fears embodied in African Americans.

In positioning themselves against the RCV, RF necessarily created an image of the RCV and its policies. The RCV's take on similar issues can be garnered from responses to a questionnaire the League of Women Voters distributed to 1964 council candidates.[35] Howard Carwile, a major political activist associated with RCV in the 1960s, gave strongly worded answers that are remarkable not only for their insight into the ramifications of urban renewal programs but also for the degree to which they stand apart from the policies endorsed by other candidates. Joining Carwile on the ballot was Ronald Charity,[36] who was endorsed by Voters' Voice, an organization of middle-class and professional African American activists led by future governor L. Douglas Wilder. Charity's positions were similar to, if less forcefully presented than, Carwile's. In most questions regarding the development or expansion of city services and amenities—for example, an expanded civic center and the creation of more public pools—RF candidates argued that better services would attract more business for the city. In response to questions regarding urban renewal, those candidates argued, as above, for increased private investment. Charity and Carwile, however, stated that while attractive, increased services would undermine funding for schools and educational programs. In fact, both embraced policies diverting city moneys to education and the development of the Richmond Professional Institute.[37]

More important, Carwile and Charity campaigned against all urban renewal programs. When asked about urban renewal projects, RF candidates stated that the city should strictly enforce housing codes and, when codes were violated, allow private enterprise to take over. Carwile and Charity, recognizing that such policies would make home ownership impossible for African Americans, argued that the city should encourage the development and improvement of private homes by owners. Carwile was direct in this, stating that the city need "absolutely not resort to any aspect or facet of cooperation with such groups, but encouragement for neighborhood improvement groups and cooperation with such groups in securing liberal credit for home and business repair."[38] Later in the same questionnaire, candidates were asked to comment on the major issue facing Richmond in 1964. RF candidates invariably said that the city needed to annex parts of Henrico or Chesterfield counties. Carwile and Charity, however, argued that the city needed better vocational training schools and needed to redirect its urban renewal policies. Carwile strongly stated that

> Richmond should abandon every phase of urban renewal. Urban renewal is the key issue in this campaign. It is not a slum-clearance program. It is a slum-producing program. It is not progressive, but shockingly retrogressive. It relegates every democratic and humanitarian concept to a status of blight and decay in order to make way for the god of mammon.[39]

Carwile and Charity clearly understand that the loss of Richmond's home-owning, African American middle class and the loss of a strong, African American working class with marketable skills would drastically undermine the future of Richmond's historically cohesive African American community. The fiscally conservative policies they called for would have helped perpetuate the tradition of African American enterprise that had long existed in the city and would have stemmed the tide of the dilution of African American franchise posed by the destruction of African American neighborhoods and the annexation of white suburbs. The threat, for Carwile and RF, is posed by the business elite against the city's poor and African American communities.

Though both RF and the RCV were, essentially, fiscally conservative groups—nobody was proposing anything approaching socialization of housing or jobs—both groups put forward policies that would have lasting impacts on Richmond's electorate. RF's policies would perpetuate a business-friendly environment in which white voters would hold a majority. The RCV would have expanded the city's African American electorate while reestablishing the threatened stability of that electorate's community and its organizations. Moreover, both groups expressed their policies in language that avoided direct mention of race while defining their opponents as a threat to the city. Recall that RF presented themselves as protecting the city from poverty and slums while the RCV employed militaristic language in discussing present urban renewal plans.

RF's position on the threat posed by the RCV was not simply a campaign tactic; it seems, from internal documents, to have been a belief RF held of African American political leaders that was well calculated for use in campaigns. After a 1964 meeting with the leadership of the RCV, the RF leadership noted that their African American candidate, B. A. Cephas, had proven popular among the RCV and that Henry Marsh was a figure who deserved respect. Overall, though, the memo paints a grim picture, indicating that "the opposition is against everything" and would impede any growth within the city. This practice of using fear and spreading rumors of negativity has proven an effective campaign tool and cultural logic in the advancement of privatization. While its slippery nature obscures the reentrenchment of racial difference, the metaphoric separation based upon associations with race was clearly becoming manifest in Richmond. A key site of this transformation was in the resurgence and reinvigoration of modes of historic remembrance.

RACE, ECONOMICS, AND THE CIVIL WAR CENTENNIAL

The marriage of urban policy with claims of progress and metaphorical reminders of racial hierarchy was well underway in Richmond politics in the 1960s. And, as was increasingly common across the South, this marriage was facilitated and expressed through the resurgent presence of Confederate emblems, such as the Confederate flag, which became popular symbols of anti-integration movements. These emblems often gained greater visibility through the nationally organized celebrations of the Civil War centennial from 1961 through 1965.[40]

The Civil War centennial was a nationally organized program that sought to remind all Americans of the national sacrifices and strife that lay 100 years in the past. According to the *Civil War Centennial Handbook*, a guide written by William Price and published by the national Civil War Centennial Committee, state centennial programs were encouraged to work together to create events and programs that would emphasize both the strife of the war and the long intranational cold war that followed.[41] That national committee worked to coordinate programs among the various state and local chapters and keep those programs within a narrative of American national exceptionalism in which two distinct parts were torn apart and, after 100 years, brought back together.

As Jon Wiener has noted, this narrative of national reunion takes on special significance when placed within the historical contexts of the height of the Cold War and against the backdrop of civil rights struggles.[42] This narrative of reunion was a crucial public spectacle that was designed to remind all Americans of their place within a nation that was, now, at odds against a dangerous foe. And, while the national committee did stress the massive losses incurred by the Confederate states during the war, it sought to downplay any lasting regional loyalties and sectional identities in its celebrations.

This project was most successful within Virginia, in large part because the state had seen deeply concentrated military action during the war and was littered with the spaces associated with its memory. The Virginia Civil War Centennial Commission was led by an executive committee of members of the Virginia General Assembly and Virginia historians. Its executive director, James J. Geary, had served for some time as the Associated Press correspondent in Richmond and was familiar with the inner workings of Virginia's governmental and business institutions. In a July 2001 article for *Virginia Cavalcade*, Geary reflected on the opening of the centennial in April 1961:

> it felt like a dream. Here was Virginia, the defeated standard-bearer of the Confederacy, beginning an observance already planned to be long and inclusive. And the agency I headed had done the planning. It would turn out to be far and away the largest and most elaborate Civil War centennial observance of any state, North or South. Our commission studiously would avoid and discourage any refighting of that fateful conflict.[43]

Geary's commission achieved the elaborate centennial by undertaking a "grassroots program" that was designed for a broad audience, not simply Civil War buffs. By fostering the work of local chapters and encouraging statewide participation in the centennial, the state commission worked to build a broad base for the centennial. In the same article, Geary notes that the state faced a number of challenges in awakening interest in the Civil War. Chief among these was a deep ambivalence and "opposition engendered by the strong feelings about civil rights and the public's submersion in the battles over school desegregation. Richmond was a hotbed of these sentiments. ... The strong currents gave many people pause about having a centennial. ... They expressed fears of further divisiveness, of the rise of hate groups, of waving the bloody flag."[44]

This ambivalence colluded with a general waning of local interest in the Civil War. As Geary notes, interest in the Civil War had been generationally defined. Veterans of the conflict and their children had placed the war and the Lost Cause firmly in the center of Richmond's and Virginia's public memory. But, as those populations passed on and as other moments gained greater currency with historical identities, the Civil War had drifted and been pushed to the background. Geary notes that "people got tired of hearing the old veterans talk end-lessly about the war. … They don't want to hear any more about it." But, "now the old veterans were gone; their voices had been stilled; the reunions were no more. The old soldiers, tugging on sleeves to get attention, were not even a memory for most people."[45] The centennial, then, had to reawaken local investment in the Civil War and acknowledge deep ambivalences awoken by the climate of the 1950s and 1960s. To do so, Geary and the Virginia commission worked closely within the nationalist structures set forth by the U.S. commission to bring the public back to the Civil War. The result was the "big, public oriented, but tasteful Virginia centennial program."[46]

Virginia's program stands out as the largest and most successful of the state programs. Size and success, however, are not the only facets that separated Virginia from other Southern states. When discussing the Civil War centennial in Virginia (or for that matter, Virginia in general), South Carolina is a useful counterpoint. While both states claimed, rightfully perhaps, a position of primacy within the former Confederacy, South Carolina remained and remains much more committed to a politics of states' rights and anti-integration. As Prince points out, South Carolina politicians used the centennial to rally support for the contin-ued segregation of public schools. And, just as Virginia would distance itself from the deep South, South Carolinians would point to Virginia as a failed Southern state. For example, when Virginia first integrated some public schools in 1959, South Carolina state Senator John Long commented from the senate floor that "Virginia needed another Stonewall. … South Carolina has segregation in the public schools and South Carolina intends to keep it."[47]

The South Carolina commission, as Prince points out, was willing to admit that the war was a civil war and not, as regional parlance had it, a war of rebellion or secession; however, South Carolina's Centennial Commission included in its official publications reminders that, for that state, the war was one of states' rights and came out of the failures of the U.S. Constitution."[48] Prince deftly traces the ways that the Civil War centennial became a major period of resurgence for Confederate emblems—it was in this period that the Confederate battle flag returned to the State House, a place it would occupy into the twenty-first cen-tury—and those emblems were taken up by modern states rights' and anti-integration politicians, such as Strom Thurmond in his 1948 presidential campaign with the States' Rights Democratic Party or Dixiecrats.

While South Carolina's centennial commission belligerently resisted the approach embraced by the national commission, Virginia welcomingly embraced it. While South Carolina placed multiple Confederate flags throughout the statehouse, and kept them there, Virginia's General Assembly allowed the battle flag to be flown over the statehouse, but only during the years of the centennial and only when the assembly was not in session. Virginia embraced the symbolic power of Confederate emblems, but was careful to keep those emblems located within nationally acceptable frames. While the centennial and the emblems associated with it did resonate with Virginia's and Richmond's racial politics, the connections, though oftentimes personal, were rather obtuse and shrouded through the careful footwork of creating a nationally marketable image.

Market value would be the crucial and central concern that runs throughout the records of the Virginia and Richmond centennial commissions. While the programs would resurrect a stagnant moment in local historical identity and public memory, their ultimate value was increased tourist revenue that would come through the careful marketing and branding of Virginia with national identities and memories of the Civil War. The state commission orchestrated grassroots efforts and local celebrations through a number of pamphlets and booklets that encouraged and gave guidelines for the creation of county, city, and town centennial programs. The most comprehensive of these, *The Civil War Centennial: An Opportunity for All Virginians*, bore a frontispiece that called the centennial an opportunity "TO HONOR OUR HEROES/TO PROMOTE/Virginia as the place to come to during the Civil War Centennial/TO TELL/the true story of Virginia's People—Peacemakers, Warriors, Restorers and rebuilders/TO DRAMATIZE/The great ideas that are the basis of our freedom and tradition—individual responsibility, faith in God and service to country."[49] Throughout these materials, folded into evocative phrases describing a memory of the Civil War as a time of great heroes during which Virginians took the national lead, is a primary call for increased tourism.

Within Virginia, this marketable image would largely be coordinated by local chapters and facilitated by the state commission. Virginia hosted a few major events over the course of the centennial, including reenactments of the Battle of First Manassas/First Bull Run, Jefferson Davis' inauguration as president of the Confederate government, and Lee's surrender at Appomattox, as well as the publication of a number of scholarly books. Much of this work was done along with the national commission. The only major disagreement the Virginia commission had with the national program was in scheduling the opening of the centennial. While the national committee wanted centennial programs to start in April 1961 with recreations of the attack on Fort Sumter and other pivotal events, the Virginia commission pushed hard to have the official opening be a national day of prayer on the 100th anniversary of the ill-fated Peace Convention. In February 1861, a contingent of Virginia politicians led by former president John Tyler, organized a meeting to discuss ways to prevent secession and regional hostility at the Willard Hotel in Washington, DC. The national committee did agree to call for a national day of prayer on February 5, 1961, to co-host services at Washington National Cathedral, and to place a plaque at the Willard Hotel. However, it did not agree to open the centennial on that date, which would have further positioned Virginia as the true preserver of the Union that was, unfortunately, stuck between an aggressive North and the reactionary Deep South.[50]

The Virginia commission used these projects as the center points of a range of programs that were undertaken by local commissions which were encouraged to establish wide-reaching public relations and educational campaigns. Suggested programs included developing outreach in schools, the creation of discussion and reading groups, and facilitation of reenactment of local battles. The highlight of local programs, however, was to be the rededication of any local Confederate memorials in a tasteful ceremony that promoted national unity. State guidelines suggested that these ceremonies include the playing of both "The Star Spangled Banner" and "Dixie" and that all members of the community be invited "as the observance is intended to bring all the people together" to "encourage a greater appreciation of courage and a firmer dedication to high ideals, to remind ourselves of the mutual sacrifices made all over the nation and to bring a deeper understanding of the causes of division and war."[51]

Alongside coordination and facilitation of local events, the state commission's primary project was the construction of the Virginia Civil War Centennial Center. Opened in October 1961, the center was a domed hall with two stories that served as both museum and tourist center. Tourists would enter the hall and be able to sit through a series of orienting films highlighting Virginia's role during the Civil War. Afterward, they would be directed to rotating museum exhibits as well as information booths where they could gather maps with suggested tours of the state and informational pamphlets. Located in the heart of downtown Richmond, the center was adjacent to the Richmond-Petersburg Turnpike, a roadway that became Interstate 95. Because traffic moving along the East Coast had to take the turnpike when crossing Virginia, the center was ideally situated to draw in a wide swath of potential tourists who might be resistant to traveling deep into Richmond. This location proved hospitable and, by all accounts, the Centennial Center drew in huge numbers of visitors who, oftentimes, went on to visit other centennial sites and programs across Richmond and Virginia. Moreover, the center was not an unwieldy financial undertaking for the state because after the centennial ownership of the site would transfer to the Medical College of Virginia, which would use the building for its purposes.

Many areas of Virginia benefited from the centennial. The Shenandoah Valley saw a huge upswing in its tourist revenues and the creation of permanent museums. Alexandria was able to complete important preservation and museum-building projects that increased its overall tourist development. But, of all the local chapters, Richmond gained the most from the centennial. The Centennial Center built off of Richmond's central location as a regional crossroads and drew visitors into the city. The Richmond Centennial Commission began their work well aware of this central location and the lucrative tourist dollars that could well come into Richmond via the centennial. Their work also resonated with the political activities that were arising contemporaneously in response to Richmond's burgeoning African American electorate and would continue on after the centennial concluded in a number of symbolically potent acts of public memory.

Including Robert Throckmorton, a Richmond banker, and India Thomas, a national leader of the UDC, the Richmond centennial committee also had representation from historians James J. Geary, J. Ambler Johnston, and Hobson Goddin.[52] While the majority of the committee was invested in traditional political structures of elite white rule through paternalism and a Lost Cause-dominated historical identity, the secretary of the committee, Robert Waitt, came from outside elite social circles.[53] The grandson of Union officers and Union sympathizers, Waitt was a major figure in Virginia's Republican Party at a time when the Democratic Party was still very dominant. A former head of the Virginia Young Republicans and Virginia secretary for Richard Nixon's 1960 presidential campaign, Waitt had entered politics in 1952 when he ran for lieutenant governor. Although he lost that election, the number of votes he received, 75,000, was a rather startling result in deeply Democratic Virginia. The success of his campaign came, in part, from the fact that he campaigned on issues that spoke directly to the growing African American electorate. His platform was defined by calls for the repeal of the poll tax, the standardization of voting registration and voting machines across the state, and the repeal of all Jim Crow laws.[54] As secretary of the committee, Waitt was responsible the day-to-day operations and the programs that Richmond produced during the centennial. The committee published over twenty pamphlets and books that highlighted Richmond's history during the Civil War. Many of these were written by Goddin, Johnston, and Geary and stressed the national importance of Richmond before, during, and after the war. In addition, Richmond hosted a number of commemorative events, placed plaques and markers around the city, and hosted re-enactments, many in conjunction with the UDC. While Waitt's politics were not congruent with those of the majority of the body, he was generally praised for his work and received praise from within Richmond and from the national centennial commission, which gave him three awards for his work. The only contingent that openly resisted his leadership was the UDC, "who urged him to resign and denounced him, his grandfathers, and Union sympathizers in general."[55] The UDC's calls went unheeded as Richmond's political parties found common cause in commemorating the Civil War and developing the local tourism industry. [56]

This common cause extended past the 1965 closing of the centennial. Business and political leaders recognized that the centennial had both branded Richmond as a tourist destination and provided the impetus for building projects and institutional changes that would enable the reinvig-oration of Richmond's tourist industry. Business and political leaders both sought to continue some of the more effective marketing schemes and tourist attractions that originated during the centennial. For example, the Richmond Tour, an organized tour of the city's major historical sites had arisen during the centennial as a guided tour, but after 1965 was replaced with signs and maps that would guide visitors who moved through the city by car or on foot.

As the centennial ended, Geary, the chair of the state commission, made overtures to the state and Richmond governments encouraging both bodies to maintain the centennial center and turn it into a "State History and Travel Center." In a presentation made to the Virginia General Assembly that he sent to James C. Wheat, who at the time was the chair of the Richmond CPC, Geary indicated that visitors to the Centennial Center wanted information on all historic sites in Richmond. Geary envisioned refurbishing the Centennial Center to provide tourists with just this information. At the crossroads of Interstates 95 and 64, "those two great arterial highways of tomorrow," the center, as Geary envisioned it, would draw from and relate to Richmond's location as a crossroads of the Upper South and its proximity to Washington, DC and Williamsburg. Speaking to the General Assembly, Geary encouraged the state legislature to

> picture a family motoring through Virginia at 65 miles an hour on an interstate highway. They are bound somewhere south. But they have heard of this HISTORY AND TRAVEL CENTER through their friends who have told them that it is something they must see; or they have heard of it through the State's national advertising and publicity program. A sign on the interstate highway has refreshed their memory and moreover the "center" is only five minutes out of their way at one of the interchanges.
>
> They enter the travel center and are immediately dazzled by the display before them. Now I don't suggest what form this building should take, but let's imagine something along this line. In front of our visitors is a large information station and behind the counter are attractive, educated, well-informed young ladies ready and willing to answer all their questions about travel in Virginia. … And when the family has finished their tour of the "center" they would be saying to themselves, "Why, I didn't know Virginia had all of this—this variety of vacation opportunities, summer, winter, spring and fall. Where else can the children have so much fun and at the same time learn so much about American history?"[57]

While Geary's image of a happy family motoring along the East Coast and stopping in Richmond to take in all that Virginia had to offer is rather excessive, it points to the perceived markets for and the preferred methods for delivering Richmond's and Virginia's historical tourism industries. The key markets were families that lived and traveled along the East Coast. The historic sites were marketed as tourist sites through well organized, informed materials and employees who could highlight what areas in Virginia were of most educational value for children.

As the center of a proposed network of state- and time-spanning historical sites, Richmond would have been forced to partially move away from its Civil War-focused historical identity. This would have proved a hard cultural shift to make. The legacies of the Lost Cause as well as the tensions inherent in the rest of Virginia's embrace of the colonial era solidified Richmond's attachment to the Civil War as its defining moment. One case makes clear the attachment elite Richmonders had to the architecture of the Civil War era. In 1964 the City Planning Commission (CPC) began hearings on proposals to tear down Broad Street Methodist Church. In a letter to Wheat, Anne Ryland, a resident of Richmond, argued for its preservation as a significant structure and urged the city government to resist moves to overly modernize Richmond's buildings. She urged the Planning Commission "to make sure that our city doesn't become just an area of plate glass and stainless steel and streets like canyons. We need to bring about a compromise with the urgency of commercialism in order to preserve the pleasantness and graciousness here by keeping a continuity with the past."[58] Ryland would continue to agitate for the preservation of the church and other structures. In 1968, after the church had been torn down, she and Wheat engaged in a somewhat testy exchange that centered on the modernization of the city at the expense of its nineteenth-century buildings. Responding to Wheat, Ryland argued that "it is high time that Richmond recognizes and takes pride in the fact that it is a good *19th century* city. And monuments such as Broad Street Methodist Church are, in many ways, more characteristic of the essential nature of the city than some of its older buildings."[59] This theme was echoed in an earlier letter in which she compares visitors' reactions to Richmond with their reactions to Fredericksburg and Williamsburg: "their reaction to Richmond is one of dismay and that only the bravest strangers stay for more than a quick look. Perhaps we have an inferiority complex because we are a 19>th century city and not an 18th century city. But there is nothing wrong with the 19th century, and when we realize what we are missing just in terms of tourist dollars, perhaps we will take better care of our old buildings and neighborhoods."[60] Again, there is an expressed connection to the nineteenth century and the Civil War in Richmond as opposed to a larger, Virginia-wide attachment to the colonial era. In this exchange, Ryland argues for better preservation of nineteenth century sites and a deeper commitment to the memories of the Civil War as a crucial aspect of local identity and tourist revenue.

While the memories and historical identities promoted by Ryland and by the planners of the Richmond Tour did gesture to Geary's desire to locate Richmond at the center of a historically diverse tourism industry, Richmond remained invested in the Civil War. While this narrative maintained the practice of memorializing Virginia's role in the Civil War as a preserver of the nation and avoiding the difficulties of race, the continued attachment to a Civil War historical identity had the advantage of resonating with discussions of race in regards to political change and the ongoing attempts to annex portions of Henrico County and Chesterfield County. Throughout the annexation debates, fears of an African American majority were expressed by the common concern that when they gained political control of the city African Americans would tear down the statues on Monument Avenue.[61] While the prospect of that actually happening was unlikely, there was the palpable feeling of a threat posed to Richmond's dominant historical identity by an African American community assumed to be hostile to those memories and, as was evident in RF's documents on the RCV, "against everything." The common cause business and political leaders had in developing a Civil War historical identity performed cultural and discursive work that underlay anti-integration projects.

MONUMENT AVENUE IN THE 1960s: SALVADOR DALI COMES TO THE OLD DOMINION

The fears invested in the protection of Monument Avenue would become a major concern throughout the late 1960s and would carry meanings that cut across the symbolic and material landscape of Richmond. The connection among Richmond's historical identity, urban planning projects, political annexation, and racial fears is evident not only in a survey of the distinct histories of these aspects of city life but also in the individuals who worked across these areas. Prominent figures in Richmond's local government and RF had close personal ties to those figures who worked on reviving Monument Avenue and continuing the celebration of the Civil War.[62]

Monument Avenue remained a central feature of these projects, not simply because of its racially resonant features but because it was "an uncommon landmark" that set Richmond apart from other cities and which furnished "a pleasant physical environment for the learning process" and was "often used for relaxation and escape from the asphalt jungle."[63] In 1965, the Richmond CPC examined plans to modernize Monument Avenue and centralize the city's Confederate iconography. These plans were laid out in the December 1965 pamphlet, "Design for Monument Avenue."[64] Describing Monument Avenue as a "bridge from past to present," the CPC reasoned that it was "incumbent upon the community today to be aware of this heritage and the artifacts which preserve it, so that our activities reinforce rather than obscure those elements of our heritage which we value." This duty to preserve was understood to extend not only to the protection of the existing statues but the extension of the network of monuments. The CPC "recommended that the theme of featuring prominent Confederate figures on Monument Avenue adopted earlier in this century be continued" because "the impression will be more vivid in the minds of the public than a random assortment of figures, and the impact will have greater appeal to tourists." This proposal makes the explicit expression of Monument Avenue as a key site of public identity, recreation, and tourism. And, while the official language of the CPC did not endorse the racialized fears that assumed the assured destruction of Monument Avenue by an African American majority, the description of the boulevard as a "pleasant physical environment" that offers relief from the "asphalt jungle" speaks to the racialization of space within Richmond's built and memorial landscapes.

Recognizing the major changes in transportation that occurred between 1920 and 1965, the CPC presented a plan to make Monument Avenue safer for and more visible from automobiles. A major aspect of this plan was the proposal to pave over the brick surface of the boulevard with asphalt. An asphalt surface might have made the avenue into a more traffic-friendly corridor and, possibly, contributed to urban renewal projects. However, among some Richmonders, the brick surface was a historically resonant feature that defined Monument Avenue's location at the center of Richmond's historical identity. Out of these fears grew the Monument Avenue Preservation Society (MAPS). MAPS convinced the Richmond CPC to forgo efforts to pave Monument Avenue and encouraged it to go ahead with the development and expansion of the boulevard's historical focus. The planning commission approved plans to move and turn the Stuart and Davis monuments in order to make them more visible from passing cars. Specifically, the Stuart statue would have been moved from its location on a traffic circle at the intersection of Lombardy and Monument to a site on the northwest corner of that intersection. The Davis statue would also be moved from its location abutting the roadway and be moved back to a location on Monument Avenue's central median that was farther from the stream of traffic. The plans also called for the erection of seven new statues of Confederate leaders and figures. The statues were to be placed at intersections between Lombardy and Belmont Street. The short distance between Monument Avenue's eastern terminus and Lombardy streets was filled with statues and the new plan would have filled in the more sparsely monumented western section of the street.[65]

These ideas, supported by the *Richmond News-Leader* but opposed by the *Richmond Times-Dispatch*, never gained significant public support and were never completed. The first of these new statues was actually an already existing statue that simply would have been relocated within Richmond. The CPC, noting that its location caused problems for the smooth flow of traffic, urged the city to move a statue of General A. P. Hill from its location at the intersection of Laburnum Road and Heritage Road on the city's far North Side. Because the statue posed a visual and physical impediment to the flow of traffic and because the construction I- 95 and I-64 cut Richmond's North Side off from the Fan District, the A. P. Hill monument was both a threat to motorists and was spatially at a far remove from Monument Avenue. The CPC proposed moving the statue to a location at the intersection of Monument and Allison Street. All these plans ran into the formidable UDC and the Richmond Civil War Roundtable, a group of amateur and professional scholars, who resisted efforts to alter the location of any Confederate memorials. While the CPC had attempted to streamline and extend the marketable imagery of the Confederacy on Monument Avenue, the UDC and the Roundtable were able to prevent this modernization and keep the statues where they had originally been sited.

Of the other proposed statues, only one was the subject of extensive planning. Although unfruitful, this project bears our notice, in that it provides an insight into the logics and terms that surrounded and supported the nexus of race, politics, memory, and historical identity in 1960s Richmond. In 1966 prominent Richmonders funded plans to erect a statue to Sally Tompkins, a Confederate nurse who had been given the rank of captain in the cavalry by Jefferson Davis. As a captain in the cavalry, Tompkins drew a significant pay and had freedom to organize Richmond's hospitals. She was selected for inclusion on Monument Avenue as a representative of all women of the Confederacy. Headed by Roland Reynolds, an executive of the Eskimo Pie Corporation, a subsidiary of Reynolds Metal Company, the committee included Lieutenant Governor Fred Pollard, Senator Byrd, and General Edwin Conquest. They were joined by Confederate historian Clifford Dowdey, the curator of the Museum of the Confederacy. The committee made overtures to the United Daughters of the Confederacy, who eventually offered financial support and were represented by Alice Whitely Jones and India Thomas, and the Virginia Federation of Women's Clubs, which was represented by E. Parker Brown and Alvah Riggins. Along with these politically and culturally influential men and women, the committee included Virginia Goddin Freeman, the wife of editor and historian Douglas Southall Freeman, and Margaret Freeman Cabell, the wife of novelist James Branch Cabell. Although she was invited to participate, first lady of the United States Lady Bird Johnson did not join the committee.[66,67]

The committee got to work rather quickly after the CPC announced their plans to develop Monument Avenue. Reynolds originally suggested the Tompkins memorial in January 1966, when he appeared before the planning commission to offer 1,000 pounds of Reynolds aluminum castings to be used for the statue.[68] Aluminum is both easily malleable and can be anodized to any color. These qualities would have given the monument a modem, space-age quality that might perpetuate Richmond's historical identity but make a bold break from older styles of public art. This desire to continue a traditional historical identity through more modem art also influenced the committee's decision to commission Salvador Dali to design the Tompkins monument.[69] By the mid-1960s, Dali had moved far from the Surrealist radicalism of his youth, embracing Catholicism and Spanish nationalism and marketing himself and his artwork to the highest bidder. Immediately prior to the Tompkins Monument, Dali had been commissioned by the Italian government to create a statue of Dante and by an anonymous donor to complete a statue of John F. Kennedy that was given as a gift to the French government. The statue of Dante is a three-faced, life-sized head that shows Dante in inferno, purgatory, and paradise. The statue has a laurel crown made of gilt spoons. The slightly larger than life-sized bust of Kennedy is completely classical, except that the hair and facial features are rendered with paper clips.[70]

While Dali may have become passé among the avant-garde, he retained his celebrity and his technical mastery and was an attractive artist for governments seeking less-traditional public art projects and monuments. A Dali statue would have given Monument Avenue and Richmond renown as a site of artistic experimentation. There was hope that his interest in the project would blossom into a union of the existing traditionalism of Monument Avenue and Dali's exuberant commercial surrealism. According to Reynolds, "If Dali were willing to work within the context of what exists on Monument Avenue, then Dali would be the best person in the world to come here now." However, the committee wanted to verify that "the existing monuments [were] compatible with his style."[71]

Unfortunately for those who would relish such a union, Dali's proposal was too shocking for the rather conservative members of Reynolds's planning committee and the Richmond press. Unable to make the presentation himself, Dali sent his assistant, Peter Moore. Moore, who traveled with Dali's pet baby ocelot Babou, was taken on a tour of Richmond and Monument Avenue. Calling the existing statues on Monument Avenue "fine enough for Rome or London," Moore explained that Dali envisioned the statue as a "tribute to America ... a kind of Statue of Liberty, you know." He explained that Dali envisioned Tompkins dressed as a latter-day St. George, fiercely battling a germ/microbe in the form of a dragon; this duel would be placed atop a pedestal composed of a petri dish balanced on a column designed to look like Dali's index finger.[72] Specifically, Moore explained that the "facial likeness would be as near as possible to Captain Sally, but the form of the actual body would depend on whether she were in a uniform or not. ... Probably the dragon will be an enlarged microbe of some kind, not the standard dragon of medieval times."[73] He explained that Dali planned to use Reynolds' 1,000 pounds of aluminum and would have the metal anodized pink. Impressed by the traditionalism of Reynolds's commission and their benefactors, Moore indicated that he would let Dali know that "this idea to honor Capt. Sally Tompkins is an obvious extension of a tradition—not just a crazy hamburger nouveau riche idea."[74] The planning committee asked local artist Walter Ursy to prepare a sketch of Dali's proposal that was distributed to the press.

Despite Moore's overtures to Richmond traditionalism, the plans "did not resonate with Richmond's philanthropic quarters" and were very quickly challenged.[75] The planning committee opened up the project to other artists' proposals, announcing plans for a design competition. Ursy also produced sketches of ideas proposed by members of the committee. One showed Tompkins offering water to a wounded soldier. The two were to be placed atop thirteen vertical columns, each of which would be inscribed with the name of one of the states of the Confederacy and the names of the women from that state who worked for the Confederate Army. The other showed her cradling a dying soldier atop a pedestal with thirteen pleats inscribed in a similar fashion.[76] The committee, recognizing the need for further publicity, opened the competition up to other proposals and announced plans to organize a non-profit organization to raise funds for the memorial.[77]

Commissioning Salvador Dali was, in part, designed to push Richmond forward and outward into the global mainstream while simultaneously maintaining a foothold in Richmond traditionalism. However, Dali's eccentricities proved fatal to the project. The *Richmond Times-Dispatch* and *Richmond News-Leader* closely covered the visit of Moore and fixated intently on his companion, the ocelot Babou. As Dali's proposal was debated, the press and conservative members of the planning committee repeatedly questioned the purpose of the monument, arguing that Dali's statue would be a monument to Dali, not Tompkins. These arguments oftentimes used the near-rhyme of the words Sally and Dali to play up the suspected tensions of what the monument would honor and whether Dali's mode of self-presentation would mesh with Virginia traditionalism. General Conquest asked the committee if they were "erecting a monument to Sally or Dali?" He threatened the dissolution of the project, stating that "if this is what we're going to put up, I won't have anything to do with it."[78]

A *Richmond Times-Dispatch* editorial, "Sally and Dali," stated that if Richmond wanted "some sort of freak monument to the women of the Confederacy" they could keep Dali's designs.[79] The *Times-Dispatch* felt that "the famous Richmond thoroughfare ought to express in dignified fashion the gratitude of Virginia to her famous sons, and daughters. A statue there to the women of the Confederacy, or the women of the South, would seem to be entirely appropriate—provided it harmonize in general with the monuments already on the avenue."[80] Dali was derided not only for the Tompkins proposal but also his Kennedy statue and a little-known painting he completed after spending seven months in Virginia during World War II. Forced to flee the Spanish Civil War and the Nazi occupation of France, Dali spent much of the 1940s in the United States. In 1941 he spent seven months at the Bowling Green, Virginia, home of friends. In his autobiography and in interviews he indicated that he was deeply impressed with the size and agility of the spiders he encountered there. He even used this experience in his painting "Daddy Long Legs of the Evening-Hope!" which features a large spider, a cannon vomiting out an airplane, and victory being bom out of the wings of a plane.[81]

The Richmond press's and Reynolds's committee's ridicule of Dali's eccentricity carried with it an important detail in the future of Monument Avenue. Not only was Dali's proposal out of step with the larger themes of the avenue, his life's work and his relationship to Virginia was outside the deeply entrenched aristocratic traditions of Richmond's and Virginia's white elites. While Dali and Moore might have been earnest in their expressed respect for Virginia and Monument Avenue, their manner and surrealism precluded their engagement with the subtleties of Virginia's and Richmond's historical identities. These identities were rooted in a sense of ageless values of patrician leadership, morals, and dignity. While Moore and Dali said they recognized this tradition, they may well have been ignorant of the racial and gender politics upheld through this historical identity.

This short-lived attempt to revive the projects of memorialization on Monument Avenue reveals the cultural logics of anti-integration politics. The repeated concerns that African Americans would tear down Monument Avenue make clear that Monument Avenue came to embody the fears of white victimhood that lay close to the surface of racial segregation. Although the Richmond civil rights movement was rather moderate, white elites had projected the imagined violence posed by their potential political success. By finally erecting a statue of a woman on Monument Avenue, white elites would have positioned the collective monuments as victims threatened by an African American majority. While the decision to remember the contributions of women occurred during the early years of the women's rights movement, it is probably unlikely that they were informed by second-wave feminism. Rather, the Tompkins monument would have altered the public perception of Monument Avenue; the figure of a female nurse would shift the perception that Monument Avenue was a celebration of masculine, military values and would have repositioned the memorial landscapes of the boulevard as feminized, caring, and compassionate. Subtly, the assumed African American threats to Monument Avenue as a whole could then be read as sexual attacks on white, Southern femininity and thus resonate with a larger culture in which white supremacy was based on myths which painted African American masculinity as a threat to white womanhood.[82] By rearticulating Monument Avenue as feminine, Richmond would have been able to rearticulate larger struggles for political control in terms which would elicit reminders of the "black brutes" so common to American film since *Birth of a Nation*. The Tompkins monument would have articulated values similar to those at the heart of *Birth of a Nation* or the lynching of African American men accused of sexual assault without actually representing sexual violence.

This point is crucial because it is evidence that the shifting nature of Monument Avenue and its memorials have occluded consistent cultural values. Just as the Maury monument worked to reinsert Lost Cause ideologies through claims to national and international values of science and reason, the failed Tompkins monument would have tacitly endorsed cultural values in which whiteness is a threatened ideal embodied as feminine. Importantly, this enshrinement of cultural values would have endorsed these values without employing violent images or acts. While the visible elements of Monument Avenue would have changed by the addition of a woman nurse, it would have reasserted Richmond's and Virginia's self-perception as a polity rooted in aristocratic values of gentility, which presupposes a rigid social hierarchy. The Tompkins monument came at a moment of heightened awareness of women's rights and histories but would have had the effect of reasserting patriarchal gender roles through an appeal toward racial fears and myths. This moment is not only interesting, it is important because Monument Avenue's mercurially consistent values reappear in the Ashe monument.

The furor over Dali's proposal, ultimately, defused the 1965 and 1966 efforts to expand Monument Avenue. While the CPC and the state General Assembly did extend protection over the avenue, ensuring the statues could not be removed by an African American majority, attempts to introduce new statues ground to a halt. Lastly, it is important to note that the mid-1960s plans to expand Monument Avenue had roots in opposition toward plans to pave over the brick roadway. Connected to white victimhood and racialized patrician traditionalism were concerns regarding the effects of urban renewal. Some Richmonders did embrace the wholesale razing of older buildings in favor of new urban complexes similar to those built in postwar Norfolk. However, those residents of Richmond who embraced a sense of traditionalism recognized that wholesale urban renewal would lead to the degradation of the city's defining architectural elements. By marshalling support for the preservation of Monument Avenue, they were able to ensure that their neighborhoods were not obliterated in the same way that Jackson Ward had been when Interstate 95 was built in the 1950s. While fighting the dangerous and destructive tides of renewal, MAPS' investment in designation of their spaces as historically significant is a stern reminder of the localized spatial manifestations of de jure and economic racial segregation.

NOTES

1. Alexander Keyssar, *The Right to Vote: The Contested History of Democracy in the United States*, (New York: Basic Books, 2000), xxi.
2. Andrew Buni, *The Negro in Virginia Politics, 1902–1965*, (Charlottesville, VA: University of Virginia Press, 1967), 145.
3. Ibid.
4. Ibid.
5. Ibid., 157.
6. For more on the influence Howard had on Marshall and Hill see Juan Williams, *Thurgood Marshall: American Revolutionary*, (New York: Times Books. 1998).

7. Jean Harris Ellis. Transcript of Interview with Akida T. Mensah. September 29, 1982, Virginia Black History Archives, Church Hill Oral History Project, Virginia Commonwealth University, accessed June 16, 2008. http://www.library.vcu.edu/jbc/speccoll/vbha/church/harrisj.html.

8. W. Ferguson Reid. Transcript of Interview with Ronald E. Carrington. March 21, 2003, Virginia Black History Archives, Church Hill Oral History Project, accessed June 16, 2008. *Voices of Freedom: Videotaped Oral Histories of Leaders of the Civil Rights Movement in Virginia,* http://dig.library.vcu.edu/u?/voices,8.

9. Douglas L. Wilder. Transcript of Interview with Akida T. Mensah, September 23, 1982, Virginia Black History Archives, Church Hill Oral History Project, Virginia Commonwealth University, accessed June 16, 2008. http://www.library.vcu.edu/jbc/speccoll/vbha/church/wilder.html.

10. Reid, Interview with Ronald E. Carrington.

11. Buni, 156–56

12. Lewis A. Randolph and Gayle T. Tate, *Rights for a Season: The Politics of Race, Class and Gender in Richmond, Virginia,* (Knoxville: University of Tennessee Press, 2003), 127

13. Ibid.

14. Ibid.

15. George Lipsitz, "The Possessive Investment in Whiteness: Racialized Social Democracy and the 'White' Problem in American Studies," *American Quarterly* 47.3: (September 1995), 369–87.

16. Christopher Silver, *The Separate City: Black Communities in the Urban South, 1940–1976,* (Lexington, KY: University Press of Kentucky, 1995), 219–22.

17. Dean Levi, "Civil Rights Leader Urged Blacks to Stop Relying Solely on Courts," *Richmond Times-Dispatch,* June 29,1989, Bl.

18. Quoted in Levi.

19. Randolph and Tate, 131–54.

20. Reid, Interview with Ronald E. Carrington.

21. Ibid.

22. John V. Moeser and Rutledge M. Dennis, *The Politics of Annexation: Oligarchic Power in a Southern City,* (Cambridge, MA: Schenkman Press, 1982), 26.

23. Michelle D. Byng, "A New Face in the Structure of Community: The Black Political Elite of Richmond, Virginia," PhD Diss., University of Virginia, 1994, 30–35

24. Annexation in Virginia involves a long process of legal proceedings and ballot measures. There is not space here to discuss the entirety of this history, but is important to point out that though the proceedings on the surface were issues of development and tax bases, they were driven by and furthered the racial segregation practices of Byrd's Massive Resistance campaign. As stated by John Moeser and Rutledge Dennis, whose study *The Politics of Annexation: Oligarchic Power in a Southern City* provides an insightful survey of these events, "the racial nexus became the unspoken theme and the hidden agenda and white leaders, while refraining from introducing race as a topic for public discussion, understood the important of consolidation for its economic as well as its racial advantages to the white political and business sectors."

25. It is possible to gain insight into this social network and its transformation into a local political action group through the papers of James C. Wheat. A nephew of General Conquest, Wheat was a founding member of RF. An architect, he served on the Richmond City Planning Commission (CPC) throughout most of the 1960s. His papers are held at the Virginia Historical Society. Through them it is possible to trace the origins and inner workings of RF as well as look at the actions of one of its representatives as he worked within the city government.

26. Schwarzschild and Thalhimer play an important role in the lives of Arthur Ashe and his father, and will be mentioned in chapter 5.

27. Papers of James C. Wheat (JCW), Private Correspondence, August 26, 1963, Virginia Historical Society (VHS).

28. Ibid.

29. JCW, Private Correspondence, October 22, 1963

30. JCW, Richmond Forward Newsletter, No Date

31. JCW, RF Platform, April 7, 1964

32. JCW, January 29, 1963

33. Ibid.

34. Ibid.

35. JCW, League of Women Voters Questionnaire, 1964.

36. While a student at Virginia Union University, Charity met an elementary school-aged Arthur Ashe and introduced him to tennis. Charity would play a crucial role in first sparking Ashe's interest in the sport, teaching him the fundamentals of the game and, eventually, finding him the coaches that would drastically improve Ashe's game.

37. A trade and vocational school, RPI eventually became the comprehensive Virginia Commonwealth University.

38. JWC, LWV Questionnaire, 1964.

39. Ibid.

40. See K. Michael Prince, *Rally 'Round the Flag, Boys: South Carolina and the Confederate Flag*, (Columbia, SC: University of South Carolina Press, 2004), 33–49

41. Archives of the Virginia Civil War Centennial Commission (VCWCC)

42. Jon Wiener, "Civil War, Cold War, Civil Rights: The Civil War Centennial in Context, 1960–1965, *The Memory of the Civil War in American Culture*, Alice Fahs and Joan Waugh, eds. (Chapel Hill: University of North Carolina Press, 2004), 237–257.

43. James J Geary, "'When Dedication was Fierce and from the Heart': Planning Virginia's Civil War Centennial," *Virginia Cavalcade*, Spring 2001, 77–87.

44. Ibid., 80.

45. Ibid.

46. Ibid.

47. Quoted in Prince, 37.

48. Prince, 33–49.

49. Archives of the VCWCC.

50. VCWCC, Newsletter, 1959

51. Ibid., 26.

52. Archives of the VCWCC.

53. Gary Robertson, "Amid Pageantry, Pride—A Cloud." *Richmond Times-Dispatch.* July 11, 1996. City Ed. A3.

54. Surprisingly, his platform also included calls for the repeal of all blue laws and the legalization of abortion.

55. Robertson, "Amid Pageantry, Pride—A Cloud.".

56. However, in 1964 Waitt resigned his post after being indicted on charges of statutory rape. He was convicted and served twenty one months in jail. After release he went to work for the *Richmond Afro-American* newspaper.

57. JCW, January 5, 1965.

58. JCW, September 11, 1964.

59. JCW, August 1, 1968, emphasis original

60. JCW, July 30, 1968.

61. Moeser and Dennis, 77; Randolph and Tate, 120; Byng, 64. This important detail is, understandably, treated as a minor footnote by these authors. I have not traced their sources to ascertain the extent of these fears. While thus not fully dependable as a historical fact, this detail appears regularly enough in the relevant literature for us to assume it is accurate.

62. Through the Wheat Papers we can trace some of these relationships and the development of these projects. Wheat had personal relationships with a number of concerned figures, and, as a chair of the CPC, was involved in the governmental decisions on reservation and tourism.

63. JCW, Letter from Wheat, May 17, 1965.

64. Richmond City Planning Commission, "Design for Monument Avenue," JCW

65. John T. Kneebone, "Location, Location, Location," *CRM Online,* No. 9 (1999).

66. Karen Schultz, "Capt. Tompkins as St. George in Artist's View," *Richmond News-Leader,* April 4, 1966; Karen Schultz, "Dali Statue of Nurse Suggested," *Richmond News-Leader,* March 17, 1966, Page 1; Karen Schultz, "Statue Backers Study Dali vs. Capt. Sally," *Richmon News-Leader,* April 17, 1966.

67. Freeman and Cabell are of note because of their own biographies and those of their husbands. Virginia Freeman's husband, Douglas Southall Freeman, had been the longtime editor of the *Richmond News-Leader,* a position which, as J. Douglas Smith shows, he used to further white supremacy through the careful endorsements of cultural and political causes. He is best known for his work as a leader of the Southern Historical Association and his Pulitzer Prize-winning work *Lee's Lieutenants.* That book and his multivolume *R.E. Lee: A Biography* were, as Gary Gallagher notes, crucial to the resurrection and preservation of the Lost Cause and, especially, the heroic status bestowed upon Lee. In this way, Freeman cast a long shadow over writers and historians working within and about Richmond. Margaret Cabell's husband, James Branch Cabell, had been the other most famous writer from Richmond in the first half of the twentieth century. A member of an elite Richmond family, Cabell was a modernist prose writer associated

with Dreiser, O'Neill, Fitzgerald, and other better remembered writers. His most successful book, *Jurgen,* was, like Fitzgerald's early work, a selfconsciously decadent novel about privilege. His wife was also a member of elite Richmond social circles. A graduate of the prestigious St. Catherine's School, she was a member of the UDC and the Colonial Dames and worked to preserve the Confederate Chapel at the Virginia Museum of Fine Arts. However, her public life extended beyond the ordinary circles of Richmond provincialism and, like her husband, she traveled in larger circles. After studying interior design in France, she opened and ran a clothing and design shop in New York City. In the 1920s, she was an editor of the *Reviewer,* an acclaimed Richmond literary journal with which her husband and H.L Mencken were associated. And, during World War II she managed the Stage Door Canteen in Washington, DC. While Margaret Cabell, like Virginia Freeman, was on the committee because of her husband's reputation as an important literary figure within Richmond, she had personal ties to the worlds of art and celebrity that the other members of the committee lacked. See "James Branch Cabell," *Dictionary of Virginia Biography,* (Richmond, VA: Library of Virginia, 2001); "Margaret Cabell," *Dictionary of Virginia Biography,* (Richmond, VA: Library of Virginia, 2001); Gary Gallagher, "Shaping Public Memory of the Civil War: Robert E. Lee, Jubal A. Early, and Douglas Southall Freeman," *The Memory of the Civil War in American Culture,* Alice Fahs and Joan Waugh, eds, (Chapel Hill: University of North Carolina Press, 2004), 39–63.

68. Schultz, March 17, 1966.

69. For a discussion of Dali's plans for the Tompkins monument and Dali's lifelong connections to Virginia see Kevin Concannon, "Dali in Virginia," *SECAC Review,* XV.5 (2010): 598–607.

70. Schultz, April 4, 1966.

71. *Richmond Times-Dispatch,* editorial, "Works by Dali Proposed for Monument Avenue," April 4, 1966.

72. A sketch of Dali's design, held by the Virginia Historical Society, is reproduced in Driggs et al., 240 as well as in Concannon, 599.

73. Schultz, April 27, 1966.

74. Schultz, April 4, 1966

75. Driggs et al., 236–40.

76. Schultz, April 27, 1966.

77. Schultz, April 27, 1966.

78. Ed Grimsley, "Dali's Plan for Statue Given Cool Reception," *Richmond Times-Dispatch,* April 27, 1996.

79. *Richmond Times-Dispatch,* editorial, "Sally and Dali," April 19,1966.

80. Ibid.

81. Ibid.

82. For a discussion of sexual violence in Jim Crow Virginia, see Dorr and Holloway.

Bibliography

Barbee, Matthew Mace. "Civil Rights and Memory, 1948–1970." In *Race and Masculinity in Southern Memory: History of Richmond, Virginia's Monument Avenue, 1948–1996.* 41–71.

Fischer, David Hackett and James C. Kelly. "Problems of Cause and Consequence." In *Bound Away: Virginia and the Westward Movement.* 202–228.

Graham, Sara Hunter. "Woman Suffrage in Virginia: The Equal Suffrage League and Pressure-Group Politics, 1909–1920." *The Virginia Magazine of History and Biography* 101, no. 2 (April 1993). 227–250.

Gudmestad, Robert H. "Baseball, the Lost Cause, and the New South in Richmond, Virginia, 1883–1890." *The Virginia Magazine of History and Biography* 106, no. 3 (Summer 1998). 267–300.

Hatfield, April Lee. "English Atlantic Networks and Religion in Virginia" In *Atlantic Virginia: Intercolonial Relations in the Seventeenth Century.* 110–136.

Heinemann, Ronald L. et al. "Before Virginia." In *Old Dominion, New Commonwealth: A History of Virginia, 1607–2007.* 1–17.

Johnson, Charles W. "V is for Virginia: The Commonwealth Goes to War." *The Virginia Magazine of History and Biography* 100, no.3 (July 1992). 365–398.

Jones, Virgil Carrington. "Libby Prison Break." *Civil War History* 4 no.2 (June 1958). 93–104.

Kaye, Anthony E. "Neighborhoods and Nat Turner: The Making of a Slave Rebel and the Unmaking of a Slave Rebellion." *Journal of the Early Republic* 27, no. 4 (Winter 2007). 705–720.

Maass, John R. "'We Wage War Like Gentlemen': Two Battles and the Path to Yorktown." In *The Road to Yorktown: Jefferson, Lafayette and the British Invasion of Virginia.* 131–147.

McDonough, James L. "John Schofield as Military Director of Reconstruction in Virginia." *Civil War History* 15, no. 3 (Sept. 1969). 237–256.

Tarter, Brent. "For the Glory of God and the Good of the Plantation." In *The Grandees of Government: The Origins and Persistence of Undemocratic Politics in Virginia.* 10–32.